VICTORIAN POETRY

CLOUGH TO KIPLING

VICTORIAN POETRY

CLOUGH TO KIPLING

Second Edition

Selected with an Introduction
and Notes
by

ARTHUR J. CARR

HOLT, RINEHART AND WINSTON, INC.
New York Chicago San Francisco Atlanta Dallas

Acknowledgment is made below for the use of copyright material:

Robert Bridges: "All earthly beauty . . .," "Eros," "My Delight and Thy Delight," "Nightingales," and "Pater Filio" from *The Shorter Poems of Robert Bridges* by permission of Clarendon Press, Oxford.

Arthur Hugh Clough: "Dipsychus," Scene V, the concluding lines of "The Latest Decalogue," and "Les Vaches" from *The Poems of Arthur Hugh Clough*, edited by H. F. Lowry, A. L. P. Norrington and F. L. Mulhauser, 1951. Reprinted by permission of the Clarendon Press, Oxford.

Thomas Hardy: All selections (pp. 245–273) from *Collected Poems* by Thomas Hardy. Copyright 1925, by The Macmillan Company, renewed 1953 by Lloyds Bank, Ltd. Reprinted by permission of The Macmillan Company.

Gerard Manley Hopkins: "As kingfishers catch fire," "At the Wedding March," "Carrion Comfort," "Duns Scotus's Oxford," "Felix Randal," "I wake and feel the fell of dark," "Inversnaid," "Nondum," "No worst there is none," "Pied Beauty," "That Nature Is a Heraclitean Fire," "The Wreck of the Deutschland," and "The Windhover" from *Poems of Gerard Manley Hopkins*, 4th edition, edited by W. H. Gardner and N. H. Mackenzie. Published by and reprinted with the permission of Oxford University Press by arrangement with the Society of Jesus.

A. E. Housman: "Diffugere Nives," "Eight O'Clock," "The chestnut casts his flambeaux," and "Epitaph on an Army of Mercenaries" from *The Collected Poems of A. E. Housman*. Copyright, 1936, by Barclays Bank Limited. Copyright © 1964 by Robert E. Symons. Reprinted by permission of Holt, Rinehart and Winston, Inc. "Loveliest of trees," "Reveille," "March," "When I was one-and-twenty," "To an Athlete Dying Young," "Bredon Hill," "Is my team ploughing," "The Lent Lily," "On Wenlock Edge," "In valleys of springs of rivers," "Far in a western brookland," "With rue my heart is laden," and "Terence, this is stupid stuff" from *A Shropshire Lad* by permission of Holt, Rinehart and Winston, Inc.

Rudyard Kipling: "A Death Bed," "Giffen's Debt," "The Ladies," "Pan in Vermont," "Recessional," and "The White Man's Burden" from *Rudyard Kipling's Verse, Inclusive Edition*. Reprinted by permission of Mrs. George Bambridge and Doubleday & Company, Inc.

Arthur Symons: "By the Pool at the Third Rosses," "Hérodiade," "Javanese Dancers," "Emmy," "Haschisch," "In the Wood of Finvara," and "The Art of Poetry" reprinted by permission of Martin Secker and Warburg Limited, London.

CONTENTS

INTRODUCTION

Victorian Poetry and the Tradition

In all candor, the describing of literary periods is a game of categories which, although partly playful, is not without its uses. The limits of the present anthology—excluding the poetry but not the influence of Tennyson, Browning, and Arnold—can be set forth in different ways. The initial premise is that all the generalizations, although repeatedly qualified, will demand at least one more qualification, which it is the reader's prerogative to imagine for himself.

With reference simply to biography, the present anthology ranges from 1792, the year John Keble was born, to 1945, the year in which Arthur Symons died. But all the poets represented, except Kipling, Lionel Johnson, and Symons, were born before 1860; and all had made their commitment to poetry and put their distinguishable mark upon it before 1901, which is accordingly taken as the major cut-off point, neatly falling at the death of Queen Victoria and the beginning of the twentieth century. (Not to misrepresent Yeats merely by his "Celtic Twilight" poetry, he is left entirely to the "modern" period, which he did so much to fashion and which perhaps rightfully claims him.) In more strictly literary terms, the outside limits of this collection are set by Keble's *The Christian Year* (1827) and by Bridges' edition of Hopkins' *Poems* (1918). So to project the line of the Oxford Movement—from Keble's very well modulated piety to the piercing originality of the Jesuit father—at least underscores the radical change of sensibility and the crises of religious faith and poetic form which shaped the inward meaning of the period, and which continue.

From the perspective of social and political history our period opens at about the time of the Great Exhibition of 1851 and the Crimean War and ends at the outbreak of World War I; thus it reaches from the dedication of the Crystal Palace—shrine of industrial progress and international commerce—to the sinking of the *Titanic* and the eruption of applied scientific knowledge and mass industrialization into submarine action, aerial bombardment, and the prolonged nausea of trench warfare. Or, to think of poetry, the period extends from the hopeful founding of the Pre-Raphaelite *Germ* in 1850 to Hardy's "Convergence of the Twain" and Kipling's "A Death Bed, 1918." In fact, the table of contents shows that the centrally important years are those from 1860 to 1890, marking the "second wave" of the Victorian generations.

Leaving Tennyson, Browning, and Arnold unrepresented has even a clarifying effect in defining the chronological limit of their achievement. It is well defined by the "bench-mark" of 1859, the year in which were published the first four *Idylls of the King*, *The Origin of Species*, the *Rubáiyát*, *The Ordeal of Richard Feverel*, and *Adam Bede*. At Oxford, Walter Pater was attracting the notice of Benjamin Jowett, Swinburne was an undergraduate, and Arnold, as Professor of Poetry, had delivered, two years before, his inaugural lecture on "The Modern Element in Literature." If in 1859 Tennyson, Browning, and Arnold had ceased to write poetry—as Arnold virtually had— valuable works would no doubt have been lost to us: some fine lyrics in Tennyson's later volumes, Arnold's "Thyrsis," and all of Browning's *The Ring and the Book*. Yet just as certainly their distinctive work was "in": Tennyson's *Poems*, *In Memoriam*, and *Maud*; Browning's *Sordello*, the "Bells and Pomegranates" series, *Christmas Eve and Easter Day*, and *Men and Women*; Arnold's *The Strayed Reveller*, *Empedocles on Etna*, the *Poems* (with preface), *Poems, Second Series*, and *Merope*. The continuing presence and prestige of all three poets, and especially the increasing popularity of Tennyson, then Browning, superimpose upon the landscape of later nineteenth-century poetry a mirage that partly obscures the new work and new ideas and lends a preternaturally middle-aged appearance to the lists of poetry published in the seventies and eighties.

Not that the pervasively "Tennysonian" quality of poetry in the second half of the century is pure illusion. And in quantity at least, much of the poetry derives from him, much less from Browning. Nor does one refer only to the impression that half

the vicars and curates of the Church of England practiced
Tennysonian verses as a none too private vice. From "The Lady
of Shalott," "Mariana," "Œnone," and the songs from *The
Princess* comes much of the Pre-Raphaelite verse of D. G.
Rossetti, Swinburne, and Morris. *In Memoriam* ponders issues
that Clough would ponder. And from Tennyson's patriotic
lyrics and Lincolnshire dialect pieces diverse influences reached
Kipling and (by the mediation of William Barnes' Dorsetshire
poems) even Hardy. To be sure, Meredith and Morris openly
scorned what was vague and conventional in Tennyson's senti-
ments. Swinburne would convert the dreamy sensuousness of
"The Lotos-Eaters" and "Tithonus" into the dreamy eroticism
of "Laus Veneris" and would finally exasperate Tennyson into
producing a Swinburnian "Lucretius." But the quarrels were
family quarrels. Tennyson might not be intellectual enough for
Arnold, but Arnold's conception of a line of verse, of a simile,
and even of a little epic subject, as in *Sohrab and Rustum*, does
not essentially conflict with Tennyson's. The explanation is that
the prevailing idea of poetry was his idea—how it should sound
("beautiful"), what it should utter ("wisdom"); in proportion
as truth eluded, more beauty must be added. The Tennysonian
style was dominant not because the genius of Tennyson pre-
vailed but because he was, for all his deficiencies, the "heir of
all the ages," the indubitable scion—perhaps the last—of the
longest and best honored tradition of English poetry, descend-
ing from Spenser and Milton and, through them, from classical
and Christian origins.

II

"Beauty is truth, truth beauty . . ."

Keats's paradox, if read within that tradition, was a platitude.
From its oracular authority, as uttered by the Grecian Urn,
neither the author of the "Fowre Hymns" nor the author of
"Lycidas" would have dissented. The Psalms of David, the
Platonic dialogues and the explicit pronouncement of Aristotle's
Poetics converged: "Poetry is a higher and more philosophical

thing than history." Long before Spenser wrote his *Amoretti*
every philosophical and artistic finding of Christian Europe
agreed that only by accident, sin, or error could such a pair of
ultimate terms be disordered or denied:

> That is true beautie: that doth argue you
>   to be divine and borne of heavenly seed:
>   deriv'd from that fayre Spirit, from whom al true
>   and perfect beauty did at first proceed.
> He onely fayre, and what he fayre hath made,
>   all other fayre lyke flowers untymely fade.
>   (*Amoretti*, lxxix)

So long as "perfect beauty" lay in heavenly truth (the *Logos* or
"onely fayre") no destructive questioning of the priority of
beauty or of truth could succeed. Both were final terms and
were lodged together in philosophy, theology, and the tradition
of classical and Christian art. Questions of course arose as to
the truth of this or that assertion or the beauty of this or that
work. Even these questions, however, could be resolved by rules
"discovered not devised" (the Law of Nature) and by the
authority of tradition properly assessed and applied. This con-
cept of "true and perfect beauty" expressed the acknowledged
rightness, the felt naturalness, of the Christian interpretation of
nature and history.

The forming of this interpretation—and even more, its as-
similation into the fibers of European sensibility—was the
achievement of centuries of intellectual, religious, and artistic
effort, from St. Augustine to Michelangelo. In origin it was the
marriage of Greek philosophical culture and Christian Gospel
in the "mystery" of the Incarnation. What this doctrine asserts
is a paradox and a platitude not alien to that of Keats. It affirms
the union of the human and the divine, the "definition" that
Jesus Christ is "very God and very man," neither an other-
worldly phantom nor a greater Socrates, but "the Word made
flesh." In this mystery lies certainty. Time is not a meaningless
cycle but a drama, unfolding from the Creation to the Last
Judgment. Good and evil are not illusions. In man's reason lies

knowledge; in his will, the exercise of freedom; in his passions, the possibility of error and the reality of sin; and in the proffer of supernatural grace, redemption:

> In a flash, at a trumpet crash
> I am all at once what Christ is, since he was what I am . . .
> (Hopkins, "That Nature Is a Heraclitean Fire . . .")

To dissent radically from this definition of reality was not simply heretical; it was mainly impossible—simply because this view was not one "view" among others, to be described by the historian of ideas or the anthropologist, but the mode under which the self discovered its identity and formed its social and historical relationships. From birth to death, from baptism to marriage, in family affairs and the affairs of state, in science and the arts, the religion of the Incarnation supplied vocabulary and law. It penetrated with the power of both literal fact and extended metaphor into the deepest privacies of personal experience. To challenge this literal and metaphorical truth required the force and daring of genius. Yet slowly, especially in the seventeenth and eighteenth centuries, the challenge was framed, often almost inadvertently and frequently in the face of protestations to the contrary by the challengers themselves: Bacon, Descartes, Pascal, Locke, Newton—to mention only philosophers. Only after such slow preparations would a Voltaire, a Gibbon, a Kant openly assume the initiative and attack.

In spite of the inroads of such thinkers, at the beginning of the nineteenth century as much energy and originality were required to reject the Christian faith as at the end of the century would be required to embrace it. The distance is just that between Keble and Hopkins, with Christina Rossetti linking them in time and in her calm yet ardent sensibility. For Keble the line of poetry and belief from Spenser and Milton, through Herbert and Cowper and Wordsworth, was still intact. He needed only extend it by letting his own sensibility conform to theirs and by modeling his verse on their patterns. For Hopkins, to write poetry of the Christian faith cost hardly less than a crucifixion. For him the line of continuity was broken. Quite

literally the iambic line was rendered useless. This line that had
carried the poetry of beauty-and-truth had become in his day
a vehicle of only that "Beauty" which, Keats had said, must
"overcome every other consideration." In his extremity, Hopkins
invented a new verse, based on "sprung rhythm." He had also
to imprint upon his mind and even upon his body the literal
meaning of the Incarnation if the metaphors of Christian
poetry were to be restored to life.

Earlier, the Romantic poets had agonized over the function
of poetry, and their sharp debate decisively revealed that the
traditional theory of "true and perfect beauty" had broken into
a rivalry between "beauty" and "truth." For Wordsworth, as for
Shelley, the balance finally tipped to the cause of "truth." For
them poetry had to be in some manner *effectual*, and to its
effects beauty was agent not end. The poet's office was a priestly
office. "Poets," said Shelley in his *Defence of Poetry*, "are the
hierophants of an unapprehended inspiration," and "Poetry is
the image of life expressed in its eternal truth." His emphasis
lay on "eternal truth." Yet, in "Adonais" at least, his rising
fear that poetry really could not mediate between "Life" (which
"stains the white radiance of eternity") and the "unappre-
hended inspiration" broke out in a dreadful exclamation:

> Die,
> If thou wouldst be with that which thou dost seek!

The divorce between poetry and truth could not be more com-
plete. But his despairing conclusion had yet to be tried.

For Keats the issues were no less sharply drawn, and it is
from Keats, historically, that the line of major influence most
visibly descends through Tennyson, the Pre-Raphaelites and
Swinburne, to Wilde and "the decadents." It ends, if we must
postulate an end, in the pastoral lyrics of Housman and the
poetry of Bridges. The same Keats who once called for a "Life
of Sensations rather than of Thoughts" firmly distinguished his
own idea of the poet's office from "the Wordsworthian or
egotistical sublime." Nowhere did he more engagingly reject the
"hierophantic" view of the poet's function than in his letter to

Shelley, ironically contrasting the "magnanimous" ideal of the effectual poet with that of the genuine "artist," who "serves Mammon":

I received a copy of the Cenci, as from yourself from Hunt. There is only one part of it I am judge of—the Poetry and dramatic effect, which by many spirits now a days is considered the mammon. A modern work it is said must have a purpose, which may be the God—*an artist* must serve Mammon; he must have "self-concentration"—selfishness, perhaps. You I am sure will forgive me for sincerely remarking that you might curb your magnanimity and be more of an artist, and load every rift of your subject with ore.

(Letter of August 16, 1820)

"Serving Mammon"—loading the rifts with "ore"—was to become the most characteristic home industry of the Victorian poets, though some differences of opinion were to appear as to the merits of refining that ore in the Tennysonian manner or leaving it somewhat ostentatiously "rough," after the practice of Browning. But the metaphor of wealth applies. For Palgrave and his host of readers the anthology of English verse should be a *Golden Treasury*. To Hopkins it was Tennyson's unquestioned merit to be "chryselephantine." And Pater praised the "gemlike flame" which symbolized the concentrated impression of beauty in the work of art and in the artist's imagination. By the example of Keats (especially in "The Eve of St. Agnes") Rossetti and Swinburne sought to combine the opulent colors of stained glass, liturgical symbolism, and almost palpable and often erotic imagery of bodily states. The Pre-Raphaelites—and more broadly the aesthetic movement itself—explicitly furthered this effort without resolving the issues from which it arose.

No program of the Pre-Raphaelites[1] so well characterizes them as the fact that their leader, Rossetti, could almost simultaneously extol the chaotic though richly quotable *Rubáiyát* of FitzGerald and also labor to translate and appreciate the *Vita*

[1] See note on Christina Rossetti's "The P.R.B.," p. 115.

Nuova of Dante and the exacting poets of his circle. The *Rubáiyát*, which Rossetti "discovered," was a more secular version of *In Memoriam*, more sceptical and much less consistent, masking its cynicism in nostalgia and in a verbal elegance that rivaled Tennyson's subdued and studied artifice. Rossetti's own poetry drew from both Dante and from Tennyson, improbable as that mixture must appear, and also sought to approximate the condition of painting, just as his paintings were strongly literary in subject and treatment. His most characteristic and carefully wrought poems are the sonnets of *The House of Life*, in which he displays his virtuosity at the Italian sonnet and turns the refinements of Petrarchan love convention into a high-pitched, attenuated eroticism that animates the whole cycle. Yet *The House of Life* less resembles the well-marked rituals of the *Vita Nuova* than it does the slowly eddying moods of *In Memoriam*.

III

Out of the Pre-Raphaelite poetry of Rossetti, Morris, and Swinburne there gradually emerged a describable theory of poetry, though it is one which perhaps none of them would have directly affirmed, since it reflects only that portion of their work which belongs to the aesthetic movement. The theory itself depends upon interpreting Keats's beauty-truth equation not as a platitude of the classical and Christian tradition but as a bold epigram: "*Beauty* is truth, truth *beauty*." Read in the light of this motto, Keats's poetry would be valued for the sensuous refinement of feeling to a height of suspended ecstasy. Such a reading of Keats discounted what was realistic and humane in his poems and letters. But it eventually allowed Walter Pater to formulate the assumptions of aestheticist theory in the famous conclusion to the first edition of his *Studies in the History of the Renaissance:*

Not the fruit of experience, but experience itself, is the end. A counted number of pulses only is given to us of a variegated, dramatic life. How may we see in them all that is to be seen in them by the finest senses? How shall we pass most swiftly from point to point, and be present always at the focus where the greatest number of vital forces unite in their purest energy?

To burn always with this hard, gemlike flame, to maintain this ecstasy, is success in life . . .

. . . we have an interval, and then our place knows us no more. Some spend this interval in listlessness, some in high passions; the wisest, at least among "the children of this world," in art and song. For our one chance lies in expanding that interval, in getting as many pulsations as possible into the given time.

This theory was exactly polar to Shelley's demand that poetry mediate effectually between "experience" and "the fruit of experience," between the dazzling but empty flux of the phenomenal world and the otherwise unapproachable fixity of "eternal truth." For Pater the poet is not a Prometheus but a connoisseur of "pulsations," and art is the cabinet in which the choicest ones are preserved, among them, indubitably, the "Grecian Urn."

The discovery which lay behind this theory was made by Rossetti in particular. It was exploited by Swinburne and, more briefly, by Morris. A poem, they found, could be shaped by mixing discordant images and moods, in order to raise the emotional charge of the poem through interplay of contrasts. In this blending of discords even ideas would be treated not as discursive statements but as mental shadows cast by emotions, thus converting statement into mood, "truth" into "beauty." The purest poem would be an arc, or a cloudy arch, of feeling or "pulsations," expressed in imagery at once concrete and allusive. Symbols, drawn especially from medieval art and Christian liturgy, would appear not as a means to knowledge through analogy but as auras of connotations from which the particular signification had been emptied out.

In "The Blessed Damozel," pure prototype of the aestheticist kind, Rossetti presents a Beatrice who is literally in "heaven" yet there made sad by the absence of her earthly lover. The gold bar of heaven is palpably warmed by the damsel's breast. And the precise image of the seven stars in her hair evokes religious connotations that fuse piquantly with the erotic mood of the

poem. The portraiture, the imagery, the hints of narrative, all
exist for the sake of an overall effect—a languorous ecstasy. Into
the poems that first won him notoriety Swinburne brought more
obtrusive erotic imagery than Rossetti, and, like Morris, added
touches of physical brutality. Indeed, the common quality of
this kind of poetry is somatic imagery—the rush or recession
of the blood, the pulse beat, the warmth of the skin, the itch or
stagnation of the nerves. Such imagery set in subtly woven
iambics and bathed in mythological, chivalric, and liturgical
allusions would produce poetry in which all other "meaning"
was irrelevant or unreal. In that respect it was far from Keats.

From the implications of his theory Pater himself at once
drew back. Personally he would not have accepted Wilde's
extension of the theory to the conclusion that "emotion for the
sake of emotion is the aim of art." But other consequences were
less drastic and only gradually became manifest. The declara-
tion of the autonomy of the poet and of poetry made "effect"
a more important consideration and encouraged the tendency to
value poems for the effectiveness of "lines" or of short passages
exhibiting the curious felicities of diction that were more and
more sought after as the bond between form and content
weakened. Although Swinburne, like Tennyson, employs a
greater variety of metrical and stanzaic forms than either Spenser
or Milton (or even both together), such virtuosity meant that
formal patterns were becoming external devices to be manipu-
lated like the "tone colors" of nineteenth century orchestration.
There also developed, from similar impulses, several varieties of
what Hopkins aptly called the "Parnassian tongue," which is the
quotidian style of poets writing "poetically," but somewhat
below the level of poetry. It appears in the rather standardized
verse of Morris' *Life and Death of Jason* and also—with more
colloquial flexibility—in Mrs. Browning's *Aurora Leigh*. Es-
sentially narrative, and of course iambic, the Parnassian was
equally adaptable to aureate description and to lively editorializ-
ing. Yet it could sustain those sudden rises in eloquence that
were needed to prove the poem still a poem. Such a style was a
thing—of beauty, no doubt, but a thing—detachable from "con-
tent" and yielding its own rewards.

In its latest extremes, the aestheticist theory was to be applied to the artist's shaping of his personal life. The instances of Bohemian emancipation leading on to the brink of personal disaster multiplied, or seemed to multiply. Neither were they what Pater had meant by the Epicurean ideal, but in fact there appeared disturbing connections. Wilde himself, in "The Critic as Artist," had decried the connection of life and art, though with a certain ambiguity:

Life! Life! Don't let us go to life for our fulfillment or our ex-perience. It is a thing narrowed by circumstances, incoherent in its utterance, and without that fine correspondence of form and spirit which is the only thing that can satisfy the artistic and critical temperament. It makes us pay too high a price for its wares, and we purchase the meanest of its secrets at a cost that is monstrous and infinite.

When Wilde personified the "début of Beauty" in his costumes and manners, he administered an unanswerable rebuke to the dull hordes of bourgeois complacency. But when his affectations were successfully branded with the charge of homosexuality, the authority of the creative artist suffered a setback that had threatened ever since the careers of Byron, Shelley, and Keats but had been restrained and rebuffed chiefly by the immense personal respectability of Tennyson and Browning. With the Wilde-Douglas scandal the artist became, in the eyes of the unconverted and gloating Philistines, not merely suspect but convict.

Yet the aesthetic movement planted one last and decisive result in the very center of the twentieth century rejection of aestheticism: the poetry of Hopkins. Although he was formed in the Oxford of the sixties, Hopkins was of course no exponent of aestheticism and, indeed, burned his undergraduate poetry when he became a Jesuit. Yet, in his poems of 1876 and after, the possibilities of aestheticist method are carried to such a pitch of achievement that they are transformed. The demand for immediacy, the "arc" of emotion, the sustained ecstasy, the highly individualized imagery, the fondness for brilliant phrase, the clashing of colors, moods, and even ideas—his very Catholicism with its inescapably medieval elements—all these are more than analogous to aestheticist practice. One can even imagine Pater's conclusion adapted to Hopkins' use. "Not the fruit of experience, but experience itself," is in fact the subject of his poetry, with the crucial difference that for Hopkins "experience" is already permeated with value, "beauty" with "truth." And the Epicurean "pulsation" that Pater extols is subsumed in Hopkins' theory of "inscape" and "instress," experience so perfectly individualized and imaginatively understood that it becomes a revelation. To concede Hopkins' connection with the Oxford of Pater and Swinburne as well as that of Pusey and Newman detracts nothing from his originality, let alone from his significance for the twentieth century. To stress the connection is important if only because the delayed publication of his poems obscured it.

IV

In fact the aestheticist doctrines had few unqualified exponents. The discernible implications were found narrow or effete, and the ancient tradition of the dignity of poetry and the vocation of the poet only slowly waned. Swinburne himself wrote poems supporting the cause of the Italian *Risorgimento* and was consistently the purveyor of an atheistic humanism that he set forth explicitly and repeatedly in his serious poems: "Hymn to Proserpine," "To Walt Whitman in America," "Genesis," "Hertha," and many others. Rossetti, less explicitly philosophical, uttered direct criticism of contemporary England in "The Burden of Nineveh" and "Jenny." Morris turned abruptly away from the intense colors and the medieval and mythological narratives of his Pre-Raphaelite "phase" in favor of the heroic stoicism of the Norse sagas, and he wrote usable songs for the socialist-labor movement. From Wilde came not only "The Decay of Lying" but also *The Soul of Man under Socialism*. Meredith had his sympathetic associations with Swinburne and Rossetti in their Pre-Raphaelite years; yet, always more stringent and athletic than they, he approached in such poems as "Phoebus with Admetus" and "Winter Heavens" the cadence and imagistic brilliance of Hopkins. Also he advocated—more openly in his verse than in his fiction—a "nature philosophy" that supplies a necessary if unexpected link between Wordsworth and D. H. Lawrence.

Nor were the opponents of aestheticism without their secret sympathies. Tennyson and Browning had of course publicly repudiated the principles of aesthetic withdrawal. Tennyson doubted that he was "much like Keats," yet he was visibly ill at ease and self-stultifying as official laureate. He was, as Auden has insisted, more naturally a poet of melancholy, the evoker of richly troubled moods and weaver of ambiguous images set in iambic lines that he thought of as "jewels five words long." Browning, despite his full-voiced affirmations and his retort to the *Rubáiyát* in "Rabbi Ben Ezra," expressed—in "The Statue and the Bust," "Fra Lippo Lippi," and other sketches of the Italian Renaissance—some of the essential ideas of Pater. Much of his poetry was recondite, filled with quite private miscellaneous allusions, and highly experimental. In such excellent poems as "Old Pictures in Florence," "Popularity," "Andrea del Sarto," and "Cleon," he reveals his fellow feeling for the perplexed and alienated artist. In these several ways the proponents and the opponents of aestheticism are drawn together by their sensitivity to the plight of the artist in an increasingly alien society. The proponents in fact philosophize or become outright polemical. The opponents do not really conceal the division between their official roles as "bards" (to such was Shelley's idea descended) and their "passion of the past," their complex intuition of loss and isolation.

The extent to which the crisis in the Christian tradition of poetry encompasses divergent views is well illustrated by what might almost be termed the "Balliol Movement," a name relating it to the Oxford Movement of the thirties and forties, with a difference. To Balliol College came Arnold, then Clough, later Swinburne and Hopkins. And there for seeming ages sat the Master of Balliol, Benjamin Jowett, mentor to poets and general factotum of the classics, Christianity, and culture. Although in holy orders, he was so modernist and eclectic that it might be and was doubted that he was definably a Christian at all. He was just the one to "discover" Pater, to intimidate Swinburne, to keep urging Mrs. Tennyson to make Alfred produce more poems, and yet to remember, in later years, to help Hopkins obtain the professorship of classics at Dublin. Through the fringe of his vague yet powerful orbit were to pass—partly as a result of their association with Swinburne—Rossetti, Morris, and even Meredith.

Jowett's Oxford was the Oxford of Newman's ghost, almost tangibly revisitant in the publication of his *Apologia* in 1864. But more evidently it was the Oxford of Matthew Arnold and therefore of Clough. One was the son and both were spiritual heirs of Dr. Thomas Arnold of Rugby, the redoubtable embodiment of a vague but muscular "Broad Churchmanship" that stemmed partly from the Cambridge of John Sterling and F. D. Maurice and so from Coleridge and even Wordsworth. Clough was the less rebellious and perhaps the more deeply stricken of the two. For his poetry the tutelage of Dr. Arnold meant "high seriousness." It meant Clough's earnest striving to write with vigor and sincerity, avoiding ornament but not wit in his struggle to believe that "Christ is yet risen" in some purely metaphorical sense that satisfied his respect for history (also a legacy of Dr. Arnold). For Matthew Arnold it meant condemning his own poetry as "morbid" (in the Preface of 1853) and attempting to repress his gift for lyrical utterance and for incisive phrase—talents that chafed the iambic restraints in "The Strayed Reveller," "The Forsaken Merman," "Empedocles on Etna," and "The Buried Life." (The titles of his poems spoke a language very different from his father's.) He would continue to demand that poetry exercise a religious function in the absence of any "creed that is not shaken," yet could find no exemplars of such poetry after Goethe and Wordsworth. To Arnold the critic, Keats's letters are "unmanly" and Shelley's poetry "ineffectual." His judgment of Shelley may have been faulty, but the word was right. It was the horror that pursued Shelley himself.

The "Balliol Movement" would have crowned its ambiguities if Arnold, Pater, Clough, Swinburne, and Hopkins had taken tea together in Jowett's garden. It did not literally happen so, but it almost happens in Mallock's philosophic parody, *The New Republic*, which ought always to stand between Newman's *Apologia* and Arnold's *Culture and Anarchy*.

V

Writing near the end of the century, Frederick Harrison, the positivist, prefaced his *Studies in Early Victorian Literature* with the satisfying pronouncement that literature "is become but an instrument in the vast field of Sociology,—the science of Society." Clearly it was not poetry he meant, though he did not except it. Ominously—whether for the future of poetry or "the science of Society"—poetry had not become such an instrument. "Society," said Wilde, "often forgives the criminal; it never forgives the dreamer." Had poetry then committed the unforgivable crime—of losing its age-long function in a dream of beauty or of merely prostituting that function in vapid compliments to "the March of Mind"? It had done neither. Its much censured alienation from the qualities that Harrison admired ("practical, social, propagandist") was a dissent, deeper and healthier than its superficial aestheticism. Its faults, its many faults, were largely venial so long as it refused to equate bourgeois respectability, democracy, and industrialization with "love, the beloved Republic, that feeds upon freedom and lives." The phrase was Swinburne's, the inspiration Jowett's. Against the almost unresisted evolution of technological super-nations, progressive and fully armed for war, one nineteenth-century poet would cast "The City of Dreadful Night," another the *Bab Ballads*, a third "The Hound of Heaven."

In a century rightly celebrated for its exploration and consequent swift exploitation of the world of positive knowledge, poetry explored, and sometimes exploited, "the world within." There the chief event was not the appearance of *The Origin of Species, Capital*, or Clerk-Maxwell's *Electricity and Magnetism*, despite their power to alter the course of history. It was what Martin Buber, in our time, has called "the eclipse of God." It is explicitly chronicled by Hardy in "The Darkling Thrush" and

"God-Forgotten" and is implicitly present in even "The Ruined Maid" and "Nobody Comes." It is the undercurrent of Housman's pastorals. Whatever might be said for the inward truth of the Christian faith, its cultural tradition was wrecked, and poetry, no less Swinburne's than Clough's, registers this. "The courts of the City of God," Wilde wrote in "The Critic as Artist," "are not open to us now":

Its gates are guarded by ignorance, and to pass them we must surrender all that in our nature is most divine. It is enough that our fathers believed. They have exhausted the faith-faculty of the species. . . . We cannot go back to the saint. There is more to be learned from the sinner. We cannot go back to the philosopher, and the mystic leads us astray. Who, as Mr. Pater suggests somewhere, would exchange the curve of a single rose leaf for that formless, intangible Being which Plato rates so high?

The "faith-faculty" was not exhausted, as Wilde himself discovered, and as the poetry of Christina Rossetti and Hopkins proved. But the poetic tradition descending from Spenser and Milton, through Pope, Gray, Wordsworth, Shelley, Keats, and Tennyson, was. Even that, perhaps, was not absolutely beyond recovery. But its forces were expended, its principles divided and set at odds. It had spent its treasures in the immense and varied effort to tell the truth about what was happening.

What divides "Victorian" from "modern" poetry is not that effort, which continues, but the quality of demand—the kind of attention and informedness required of the reader by the poet. In Eliot, Yeats, Hart Crane, Pound, or Robert Lowell the demand is notoriously high. It is comparatively low, or uninsistent, in the *Rubáiyát, In Memoriam,* and in parts of Swinburne and Morris. It is higher in Meredith and Hardy. By and large the effort of the poets of the tradition is to yield delight and to minimize difficulties. (Even Milton provides so much to admire and to enjoy that his really high demands and difficulties may be and often are passed over by the bemused reader.) Swinburne asks not so much for attention as acquiescence, a willingness to ride with surges of sound, to be hypnotized and even overwhelmed. What Christina Rossetti demands is only seriousness and taste. But Browning and Hopkins, for all their explicit commitment to the central ideas of the tradition, require extraordinary alertness, exact thought, and the lucky combination of acute hearing and a lively palate. They are "modern" in these respects, no matter how timeless or dated their personal views. If the present anthology, with its occasional deviations from the standard pieces and with some interest in the gayeties of the evening, helps mark the continuities between nineteenth century poetry and our own, it will be of use.

Ann Arbor, Michigan   A.J.C.
September 1958

AFTERWORD TO THE
REVISED EDITION

The occasion of a revised edition makes possible greater breadth of annotation and an improved representation of poets already included; notably, Swinburne ("Laus Veneris"), Meredith (the whole of *Modern Love*), Christina Rossetti ("Monna Innominata"), Hopkins ("Nondum" and "Inversnaid"), and Hardy (poems connected with the death of Emma Gifford Hardy, and late lyrics), and some others. Also, I have provided a dating of each poem (in the right margin at the end), normally the date of first publication or of first publication in a book, when that date is not remote from the probable date of composition, as it sometimes would be, as with Hopkins. When the author himself (for example, Hardy) or an authoritative editor has furnished a markedly earlier date of composition, that date appears in the left margin at the end of the poem. However, the imperfect state of Victorian bibliographical studies, especially of the less well-known writers, dictates a measure of caution against accepting the dating as positively verified in every case.

The revised edition also extends the range of selections toward the end-of-century "decadence," with poems of Henry Arthur Dobson, Ernest Dowson, and Arthur Symons, including some of their translations from the French *symbolistes*. The publication in recent years of such works as Barbara Charlesworth's *Dark Passages* and Edward Engelberg's anthology, *The Symbolist Poem*, has no doubt raised our appreciation of the poignancy and interest—if not the absolute literary achievement—of those writers who flourished somewhat nobly and pathetically in the brief glaring illuminations of the middle Nineties.

The Rhymers' Club was emblematic of the era of *The Yellow Book* and its successor, *The Savoy*. It enrolled, as Yeats remarked (himself in regular attendance), "overwrought, unstable men," such as Dowson and Johnson, though their meetings, said Yeats, were "decorous and dull." With the great exception of Yeats and the lesser one of Arthur Symons, they failed to carry the banner of the aesthetic movement into the promised land of "modernism." What they raised was only a rather falsetto cheer. This judgment is not meant disrespectfully. They were victimized, in part by the dogged philistinism of journalists and publicists, in part by the tempest of hollow moral outrage that broke over the trial of Oscar Wilde, in part by the neurasthenia that then lay in wait for those who resorted to occultist magic, experiments with drugs and alcohol, and self-excoriating infractions of sexual taboos—all these in search of anodynes or of psychic elevation, or both.

Whatever the personal conditions that led to dangerous and often fatal addictions, there were also principles at stake, no matter how imperfectly conceived. The effort of these last martyrs to the aestheticist cause was to storm the bastions or to surrender completely to the allurement of what Wilde (in *The Critic as Artist*) called *"l'Amour de l'Impossible*, which falls like a madness on many who think they live securely and out of reach of harm, so that they sicken suddenly with the poison of unlimited desire, and, in the infinite pursuit of what they may not obtain, grow faint and swoon or stumble." The "Impossible" beckoned beyond whatever barriers prevented the discernment of spiritual essences, certainly beyond the boundaries of physical perception. Making works of art that promised a vast refinement of consciousness and the deliverance of poetry from bondage to mere truth and beauty (that is, the enervating clichés into which those ideas had sunk) appeared to justify the audacity of the attempt. Yet their audacity brought mainly fatigue, not rest but sleeplessness, and rarely any spiritual discernment.

The term of contemptuous disparagement was "decadent"; the defiant slogan of honor was *"Décadence!"* Employed by Baudelaire in an honorific sense, the word was never to signify a perfectly clear and distinct meaning, though its power was not lessened thereby. It was to be understood in several ways— though to distinguish them is to diminish the nebulous luminosity of its connotations. Simply, the term *decadent* as a commendation affirmed that beauty lies not only with the bud and bloom but also with the flower and seed, with the completion of the organic cycle not less than with its inception—in the delicate skeletons of winter no less than in the shoots and spirals of spring. Keats says of Autumn, "Thou hast they music too." It was sentimentalization to deny it.

As applied to languages and the arts, *decadent* extended this organicist or holistic concept to justify a preference for the late stages of a style or manner, as Baudelaire favored late-Latin syntax and vocabulary over the classical norms, or as a special charm might be found in the last extravagances of baroque ornamentation, called "decadent" only by a remote analogy with the organic metaphor. More broadly, historical epochs themselves might be pictured on the model of the natural cycle— born, flourishing, and dying. The reality of such epochal cycles is, to be sure, at best speculative, but the model was long-standing and prevalent and was reinforced in the later nineteenth century by applying Darwinian concepts to cultural history. Hence it was tempting to view the "closing decades" of the century as the decadent stages of an epoch, with accompanying elaboration and exhaustion of once-fertile styles and ideas. To affirm this was to salute the *Zeitgeist*. To embrace the laws of the last stages was also to affirm that at a point just over the brink of the descending cataract a moment of impossible poise might be sustained.

One of the fullest and most entertainingly written celebrations of the decadent spirit is J. K. Huysmans' À *rebours* (1884) —sometimes translated as *Against the Grain*—from which Wilde's *The Picture of Dorian Gray* was in part derived. Huysmans' sole character, the aristocratic aesthete, Des Esseintes, expends all his endowments of wealth and mind and body upon evermore ingeniously refined inversions of feeling, until his stomach and his nerves rebel and he is ordered by his physician to go back to a normal existence. It is the equivalent of a death-sentence: "But I do not want to live like other people!" "Other people" are just those who had not embraced the self-sacrificing gospel of *Décadence*.

If in France the *fin de siècle* did not, however, all but sink under fatigue, it did in England. One reason may lie in a quirk of literary history. In France the Symbolist Movement, which had a substantial alliance with the *Décadence,* was not wholly French. That is, it broke rather more decisively with early nineteenth century French romanticism than the Rhymers did from their English predecessors and older contemporaries. In England the infusion eventually drawn from Verlaine, Rimbaud, and Mallarmé was poured into essentially Pre-Raphaelite poetic patterns. In France one of the several strands of poetic theory and practice that wove the *symboliste* tradition was derived from America and from England, chiefly through the mediation of Edgar Allan Poe, translated by Baudelaire. The author of *Tales of the Grotesque and Arabesque* and of *The Poetic Principle* was himself a disciple, consciously and explicitly, of the poetry of Coleridge, Shelley, Keats, and the young Tennyson—in sum, of those styles and sensibilities that in England directly nurtured the Pre-Raphaelites. But what in England eventually became a constricting influence upon diction, cadence, and even subtler components of poetry, became in France, translated, an element in liberating the *symbolistes* from what they saw as the fatal generalities as well as the philosophical and political chauvinism of their own romanticist predecessors. No doubt they were assisted also by the extremely variegated moral and intellectual milieu of Paris, at least as compared with the relative lethargy of literary London.

Between the English and French languages, as also between English and French poetics, lay vast and subtle differences that mattered decisively as between what a Mallarmé would derive from Poe and what a Dowson could derive from Tennyson. Historically considered, it was a decisive advantage for the *symbolistes* that Poe translated by Baudelaire was no longer Poe, as it was an equally decisive misfortune that Verlaine translated by Dowson was not Verlaine but only a lesser Swinburne. And of course there must be an allowance—only quite unanalyzable—for inequalities of temperament and talent.

In England the poets represented by the Rhymers' Club were unable (perhaps destined to be unable) to free themselves from the oppression of a continuingly romanticised aestheticism. Whether they nursed their sensibility on Catholic sacramentalism and a half-erotic devotionalism, or upon a devout demonism

of the senses, their poetry is not liberated from the overshadow-
ing fatigue of Tennysonian stanzas and Swinburnian metres.
Even Arthur Symons, whose understanding of the French move-
ment was profound, is only a partial exception. The advent of
the modernist movement in England awaited a later infusion
from both America and France. It was to come through T. S.
Eliot and Ezra Pound.

Williamstown, Massachusetts   A.J.C.
March 1972

A NOTE ON ANNOTATIONS

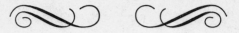

Conscious that explanatory notes sometimes inadvertently mislead, either through brevity or prolixity, and sometimes belabor the obvious, and sometimes intrusively comment, I have provided a note or gloss *only when the point in question seems not to be more or less common knowledge or is not sufficiently and pertinently explained in a standard desk dictionary*. Mythological and Biblical allusions are treated only if specification seems required.

Hence no notes on *Apollo, Muses, Jonah*, nor on *Iago, Bernini*, "the famous Piazza di Spagna," and *rapport*, but notes are supplied for "The Nine," meaning the Muses, for "our Béranger," for *Amor Mundi*, and for "Pride's Lord and Man's," meaning the Devil.

The temptation to provide interpretive aid in hard passages has been resisted, though imperfectly.

A.J.C.

GENERAL BIBLIOGRAPHY

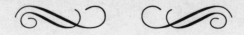

Appleman, Philip; Madden, William; and Wolff, Michael, eds., *1859: Entering an Age of Crisis*, Bloomington, Ind., 1959.

Auden, W. H., ed., *Nineteenth-Century British Minor Poets*, New York, 1966.

Beach, J. W., *The Concept of Nature in Nineteenth-Century English Poetry*, New York, 1936.

Bentley, Nicholas, ed., *The Victorian Scene: A Picture Book of the Period, 1837–1901*, New York, 1968.

Buckley, J. H., *The Triumph of Time*, Cambridge, Mass., 1966.

———, *The Victorian Temper*, Cambridge, Mass., 1951.

Burdett, Osbert, *The Beardsley Period*, London, 1925.

Bush, Douglas, *Mythology and the Romantic Tradition in English Poetry*, Cambridge, Mass., 1937.

———, *Science and English Poetry*, New York, 1950.

Chadwick, Owen, *The Mind of the Oxford Movement*, Stanford, Calif., 1961.

Charlesworth, Barbara, *Dark Passages: The Decadent Consciousness in Victorian Literature*, Madison, Wis., 1965.

Chiari, Joseph, *Symbolisme from Poe to Mallarmé*, New York, 1957.

Colum, Mary, *From These Roots*, New York, 1937.

Daiches, David, *Poetry and the Modern World*, Chicago, 1940.

Davidson, Donald, ed., *British Poetry of the Eighteen-Nineties*, New York, 1937.

Elton, Oliver, *A Survey of English Literature, 1830–1880*, 2 vols., London, 1920.

Engelberg, Edward, ed., *The Symbolist Poem*, New York, 1967.

Evans, B. Ifor, *English Poetry in the Later Nineteenth Century*, London, 1933.

Fairchild, H. N., *Religious Trends in English Poetry*, Vol. 4, (1830–1880), New York, 1957.

Faverty, F. E., ed., *The Victorian Poets, A Guide to Research*, (second edition, revised), New York, 1968.

Fredeman, W. E., *Pre-Raphaelitism, A Bibliocritical Study*, Cambridge, Mass., 1965.

Grierson, H.J.C., *Lyrical Poetry from Blake to Hardy*, New York, 1929.

Heath-Stubbs, J. F. A., *The Darkling Plain: A Study of the Later Fortunes of Romanticism . . .* , London, 1950.

Hough, Graham, *The Last Romantics*, London, 1949.

Houghton, Walter E., *The Victorian Frame of Mind, 1830–1870*, New Haven, 1957.

Hunt, John Dixon, *The Pre-Raphaelite Imagination, 1848–1900*, Lincoln, Neb., 1968.

Johnson, E. D. H., *The Alien Vision of Victorian Poetry*, Princeton, 1952.

Kermode, Frank, *Romantic Image*, London, 1957.

Lang, Cecil Y., ed., *The Pre-Raphaelites and Their Circle*, Boston, 1968.

Langbaum, Robert, *The Poetry of Experience*, New York, 1957.

Parrott, T. M., and Martin, R. B., *A Companion to Victorian Literature*, New York, 1955.

Peckham, Morse, *Beyond the Tragic Vision: The Quest for Identity in the Nineteenth Century*, New York, 1962.

———, *Victorian Revolutionaries*, New York, 1970.

Praz, Mario, *The Romantic Agony*, Oxford, 1933.

Routh, E. V., *Toward the Twentieth Century*, New York, 1937.

Stanford, Derek, ed., *The Poets of the 'Nineties*, London, 1965.

Starkie, Enid, *From Gautier to Eliot: The Influence of France on English Literature, 1851–1939*, London, 1960.

Stevenson, Lionel, *Darwin among the Poets*, New York, 1963.

Tindall, W. Y., *Forces in Modern British Literature, 1885–1946*, New York, 1947.

Willey, Basil, *Nineteenth Century Studies*, London, 1950.

———, *More Nineteenth Century Studies*, London, 1956.

Williams, Charles, *Poetry at Present*, New York, 1930.

Wilson, Edmund, *Axel's Castle*, New York, 1931.

Yeats, W. B., *Autobiographies*, London, 1955.

A CHRONOLOGY, 1832–1901

(Emphasizing the writers represented in this book)

Year	Publications	Events
1832	Tennyson, *Poems* (dated 1833)	First Reform Act
1833	Browning, *Pauline*	Oxford Mvt. begun by
	Carlyle, *Sartor Resartus*	Keble's sermon on "National Apostasy."
1837	Carlyle, *The French Revolution*	William IV, d. (b. 1765)
		Victoria becomes Queen (d. 1901).
		Swinburne, b. (d. 1909)
1840		Hardy, b. (d. 1928)
1841	Browning, *Pippa Passes*	
	Newman, *Tracts for the Times,* XC	
1842	Tennyson, *Poems* (2 vols.)	
1843	Carlyle, *Past and Present*	Wordsworth, Poet
	Ruskin, *Modern Painters,* I	Laureate.
1844		Hopkins, b. (d. 1889)
1846	Anne, Charlotte, Emily Brontë, *Poems by Currer, Ellis, and Acton Bell*	Corn laws repealed.
		Irish "Potato Famine."
	Lear, *A Book of Nonsense*	
	Strauss, *The Life of Jesus Critically Examined* (tr., George Eliot)	
1847	C. Brontë, *Jane Eyre*	
	E. Brontë, *Wuthering Heights*	
	Thackeray, *Vanity Fair*	
1848	Clough, *The Bothie of Toberna-Vuolich*	Revolutions in France, Germany, Austria, Italy.
1848	Milnes (Lord Houghton), *The Life, Letters, and Literary Remains of Keats*	Last eruption of Chartist Mvt.
		Pre-Raphaelite Brotherhood formed.
		Emily Brontë, d. (b. 1818)

Year	Publications	Events
1849	Arnold, *A Strayed Reveller* E. B. Browning, *Sonnets from the Portuguese* Dickens, *David Copperfield*	
1850	Browning, *Christmas Eve and Easter Day* *The Germ* (organ of P.R.B.) Tennyson, *In Memoriam, A.H.H.*	Wordsworth, d. (b. 1770) Tennyson, Poet Laureate. Rom. Cath. hierarchy est. in England ("Papal Aggression").
1851	Meredith, *Poems*	The Great Exhibition.
1852	Arnold, *Empedocles on Etna*	
1853	Arnold, *Poems*, with Preface Dickens, *Bleak House*	
1854	Patmore, *The Angel in the House*	Wilde, b. (d. 1900) Crimean War (to 1856).
1855	Browning, *Men and Women* Tennyson, *Maud*	
1856	E. B. Browning, *Aurora Leigh* *Oxford and Cambridge Magazine* (new organ of P.R.B.)	Shaw, b. (d. 1950)
1857	Trollope, *Barchester Towers*	Arnold, Professor of Poetry, Oxford. Conrad, b. (d. 1924)
1858	Clough, *Amours de Voyage* Morris, *The Defence of Guenevere*	
1859	Darwin, *The Origin of Species* Dickens, *A Tale of Two Cities* Eliot, *Adam Bede* FitzGerald, *The Rubáiyát* Meredith, *The Ordeal of Richard Feverel* Mill, *On Liberty* Tennyson, *The Idylls of the King* (four)	Macaulay, d. (b. 1800) Housman, b. (d. 1936)
1860	Dickens, *Great Expectations* Ruskin, *Unto This Last* Swinburne, *The Queen Mother and Rosamond*	Italian "Risorgimento" (Garibaldi).

Year	Publications	Events
1861	Palgrave, ed., *The Golden Treasury* D. Rossetti, *Early Italian Poets*	Death of Albert, Prince Consort. E. B. Browning, d. (b. 1806) Clough, d. (b. 1819)
1862	Clough, *Dipsychus, Songs in Absence, Mari Magno* Meredith, *Modern Love* C. Rossetti, *Goblin Market*	
1863		Thackeray, d. (b. 1811)
1864	Browning, *Dramatis Personae* Newman, *Apologia Pro Vita Sua*	Landor, d. (b. 1775)
1865	Arnold, *Essays in Criticism*, 1st ser. "Carroll," *Alice in Wonderland* Swinburne, *Atalanta in Calydon*	Yeats, b. (d. 1939) Kipling, b. (d. 1936) Symons, b. (d. 1945)
1866	C. Rossetti, *The Prince's Progress and Other Poems* Swinburne, *Poems and Ballads*, 1st ser.	Atlantic cable opened.
1867	Arnold, *New Poems* Morris, *The Life and Death of Jason*	Marx, *Capital*, I Second Reform Act.
1868	Browning, *The Ring and the Book* Morris, *The Earthly Paradise* (to 1870)	
1869	Arnold, *Culture and Anarchy* Clough, *Poems and Prose Remains* Gilbert, *The Bab Ballads* Tennyson, *The Holy Grail and Other Poems*	Suez Canal opened.
1870	Newman, *The Grammar of Assent* D. Rossetti, *Poems*	Dickens, d. (b. 1812) Education Act. Franco-Prussian War. Italy unified.

Year	Publications	Events
1871	Buchanan, "The Fleshly School of Poetry" "Carroll," *Through the Looking Glass* Darwin, *The Descent of Man* Eliot, *Middlemarch* Hardy, *Desperate Remedies* Swinburne, *Songs before Sunrise* Tylor, *Primitive Culture*	
1872	Butler, *Erewhon* Swinburne, *Under the Microscope*	
1873	Arnold, *Literature and Dogma* Bridges, *Poems* Mill, *Autobiography* Pater, *Studies in the History of the Renaissance* Maxwell, *Electricity and Magnetism*	Mill, d. (b. 1806)
1874	Hardy, *Far from the Madding Crowd* Thomson, *The City of Dreadful Night*	
1875	Gilbert & Sullivan, *Trial by Jury* Trollope, *The Way We Live Now*	Trade Union Act.
1876	Eliot, *Daniel Deronda* Morris, *Sigurd the Volsung*	
1877	Meredith, *The Idea of Comedy* Patmore, *Collected Works* (*Unknown Eros*)	Victoria titled Empress of India.
1878	Gilbert & Sullivan, *H.M.S. Pinafore* Hardy, *The Return of the Native* Swinburne, *Poems and Ballads*, 2nd ser.	Factory Act (consolidating previous regulations).
1879	Meredith, *The Egoist*	

Year	Publications	Events
1881	Gilbert & Sullivan, *Patience* D. Rossetti, *Ballads and Sonnets*	Carlyle, d. (b. 1795)
1882	Swinburne, *Tristram of Lyonesse*	Darwin, d. (b. 1809) D. Rossetti, d. (b. 1828) Trollope, d. (b. 1815) Joyce, b. (d. 1941)
1883	Meredith, *Poems and Lyrics of the Joy of Earth*	
1884		Third Reform Act.
1885	Arnold, *Discourses in America* Gilbert & Sullivan, *The Mikado* Meredith, *Diana of the Crossways* Pater, *Marius the Epicurean* Stevenson, *A Child's Garden of Verses* Swinburne, *Marino Faliero*	D. H. Lawrence, b. (d. 1930) Ezra Pound, b.
1886	Hardy, *The Mayor of Casterbridge* Kipling, *Departmental Ditties*	
1887	Meredith, *Ballads and Poems of Tragic Life*	Victoria's "Golden" Jubilee.
1888	Arnold, *Essays in Criticism,* 2nd ser. Henley, *A Book of Verses* Meredith, *A Reading of Earth* Wilde, *The Happy Prince and Other Tales*	Arnold, d. (b. 1822) T. S. Eliot, b. (d. 1964)
1889	Browning, *Asolando* Pater, *Appreciations* Swinburne, *Poems and Ballads,* 3rd ser. Tennyson, *Demeter and Other Poems* Yeats, *The Wanderings of Oisin*	Browning, d. (b. 1812) Hopkins, d. (b. 1844) London Dock Strike.
1890	Bridges, *Shorter Poems*	Newman, d. (b. 1801)

Year	Publications	Events
	Frazer, *The Golden Bough,* I	Sean O'Casey, b. (d. 1964)
	Morris, *News from Nowhere*	Parnell scandal.
1891	Hardy, *Tess of the D'Urber-villes*	
	Morris, *Poems by the Way*	
	Wilde, *Intentions, The Picture of Dorian Gray*	
1892	Henley, *The Song of the Sword and Other Verses*	Tennyson, d. (b. 1809)
	Kipling, *Barrack-Room Ballads*	Alfred Austin, Poet Laureate.
	Meredith, *Poems*	
	Shaw, *Widower's Houses*	
	Tennyson, *The Death of Œnone and Other Poems*	
	Wilde, *Lady Windemere's Fan*	
1893	C. Rossetti, *Verses*	
	F. Thompson, *Poems*	
	Wilde, *Salomé*	
	Yeats, *The Celtic Twilight*	
1894	Kipling, *The Jungle Book*	C. Rossetti, d. (b. 1830)
	Shaw, *Arms and the Man*	Rhymers' Club founded.
	Swinburne, *Astrophel and Other Poems*	
	The Yellow Book (to 1897)	
1895	Conrad, *Almayer's Folly*	Wilde scandal.
	Hardy, *Jude the Obscure*	
	Johnson, *Poems*	
	Wilde, *The Importance of Being Earnest*	
	Yeats, *Poems*	
1896	Housman, *A Shropshire Lad*	Morris, d. (b. 1834)
	Kipling, *The Seven Seas*	
	C. Rossetti, *New Poems*	
	Swinburne, *The Tale of Balen*	
1897	Conrad, *The Nigger of the Nar-cissus*	Victoria's "Diamond" Jubilee.
	F. Thompson, *New Poems*	Workmen's Compensation Act.

Year	Publications	Events
1898	Hardy, *Wessex Poems* Shaw, *Plays Pleasant and Unpleasant* Wilde, *The Ballad of Reading Gaol*	
1899	Yeats, *The Wind Among the Reeds*	Boer War (to 1902).
1900	Conrad, *Lord Jim*	Wilde, d. (b. 1854)
1901	Meredith, *A Reading of Life* Shaw, *Three Plays for Puritans*	Victoria, d. (b. 1819)

LIST OF POEMS

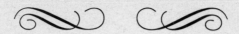

Additional Poems

ARTHUR HUGH CLOUGH

1819–1861

QUA CURSUM VENTUS

As ships, becalmed at eve, that lay
  With canvas drooping, side by side,
Two towers of sail at dawn of day
  Are scarce long leagues apart descried;

When fell the night, upsprung the breeze,
  And all the darkling hours they plied,
Nor dreamt but each the self-same seas
  By each was cleaving, side by side:

E'en so—but why the tale reveal
  Of those, whom, year by year unchanged,   10
Brief absence joined anew, to feel
  Astounded, soul from soul estranged?

At dead of night their sails were filled,
  And onward each rejoicing steered—
Ah, neither blame, for neither willed,
  Or wist, what first with dawn appeared!

To veer, how vain! On, onward strain,
  Brave barks! In light, in darkness too,
Through winds and tides one compass guides—
  To that, and your own selves, be true.   20

But O blithe breeze! and O great seas,
  Though ne'er, that earliest parting past,
On your wide plain they join again,
  Together lead them home at last.

1

One port, methought, alike they sought,
    One purpose hold where'er they fare,—
O bounding breeze, O rushing seas!
    At last, at last, unite them there!

                                        1849

Title: Virgil's *Aeneid*, III, 269, "As the wind, so the ship's course."
l. 12: **estranged** alluding to a falling out, over religious differences,
between Clough and his friend W. G. Ward.

"Is it true, ye gods, who treat us"

Is it true, ye gods, who treat us
As the gambling fool is treated,
O ye, who ever cheat us,
And let us feel we're cheated!
Is it true that poetical power,
The gift of heaven, the dower
Of Apollo and the Nine,
The inborn sense, 'the vision and the faculty divine,'
All we glorify and bless
In our rapturous exaltation,   10
All invention, and creation,
Exuberance of fancy, and sublime imagination,
All a poet's fame is built on,
The fame of Shakespeare, Milton,
Of Wordsworth, Byron, Shelley,
Is in reason's grave precision,
Nothing more, nothing less,
Than a peculiar conformation,
Constitution, and condition
Of the brain and of the belly?   20
Is it true, ye gods who cheat us?
And that's the way ye treat us?

Oh say it, all who think it,
Look straight, and never blink it!

If it is so, let it be so,
And we will all agree so;
But the plot has counterplot,
It may be, and yet be not.

1849

l. 7: **the Nine**   the Muses.   l. 8: **faculty divine**   Wordsworth's phrase
(*Excursion*, I, 79) for the imagination.

NATURA NATURANS

BESIDE me,—in the car,—she sat,
   She spake not, no, nor looked to me:
From her to me, from me to her,
   What passed so subtly stealthily?
As rose to rose that by it blows
   Its interchanged aroma flings;

Or wake to sound of one sweet note
   The virtues of disparted strings.
Beside me, nought but this!—but this,
   That influent as within me dwelt   10
Her life, mine too within her breast,
   Her brain, her every limb she felt:
We sat; while o'er and in us, more
   And more, a power unknown prevailed,
Inhaling, and inhaled,—and still
   'Twas one, inhaling or inhaled.

Beside me, nought but this;—and passed;
   I passed; and know not to this day
If gold or jet her girlish hair,
   If black, or brown, or lucid-grey   20
Her eye's young glance: the fickle chance
   That joined us, yet may join again;
But I no face again could greet
   As hers, whose life was in me then.

As unsuspecting mere a maid
   As, fresh in maidhood's bloomiest bloom,

In casual second-class did e'er
   By casual youth her seat assume;
Or vestal, say, of saintliest clay,
   For once by balmiest airs betrayed   30
Unto emotions too too sweet
   To be unlingeringly gainsaid:

Unowning then, confusing soon
   With dreamier dreams that o'er the glass
Of shyly ripening woman-sense
   Reflected, scarce reflected, pass,
A wife may-be, a mother she
   In Hymen's shrine recalls not now,
She first in hour, ah, not profane,
   With me to Hymen learnt to bow.   40

Ah no!—Yet owned we, fused in one,
   The Power which e'en in stones and earths
By blind elections felt, in forms
   Organic breeds to myriad births;
By lichen small on granite wall
   Approved, its faintest feeblest stir
Slow-spreading, strengthening long, at last
   Vibrated full in me and her.

In me and her—sensation strange!
   The lily grew to pendent head,   50
To vernal airs the mossy bank
   Its sheeny primrose spangles spread,
In roof o'er roof of shade sun-proof
   Did cedar strong itself outclimb,
And altitude of aloe proud
   Aspire in floreal crown sublime;

Flashed flickering forth fantastic flies,
   Big bees their burly bodies swung,
Rooks roused with civic din the elms,
   And lark its wild reveillez rung;   60
In Libyan dell the light gazelle,
   The leopard lithe in Indian glade,
And dolphin, brightening tropic seas,
   In us were living, leapt and played:

Their shells did slow crustacea build,
    Their gilded skins did snakes renew,
While mightier spines for loftier kind
    Their types in amplest limbs outgrew;
Yea, close comprest in human breast,
    What moss, and tree, and livelier thing,   70
What Earth, Sun, Star of force possest,
    Lay budding, burgeoning forth for Spring.

Such sweet preluding sense of old
    Led on in Eden's sinless place
The hour when bodies human first
    Combined the primal prime embrace,
Such genial heat the blissful seat
    In man and woman owned unblamed,
When, naked both, its garden paths
    They walked unconscious, unashamed: 80

Ere, clouded yet in mistiest dawn,
    Above the horizon dusk and dun,
One mountain crest with light had tipped
    That Orb that is the Spirit's Sun;
Ere dreamed young flowers in vernal showers
    Of fruit to rise the flower above,
Or ever yet to young Desire
    Was told the mystic name of Love.

1849

Title: literally, "nurturing nature," *i.e.*, nature as procreative energy as distinguished from a system of fixed laws.   l. 38: **Hymen**   the Greek god of marriage.   l. 77: **blissful seat**   Milton's phrase for the Garden of Eden.

From AMOURS DE VOYAGE

CANTO I

Over the great windy waters, and over the clear-crested summits,
    Unto the sun and the sky, and unto the perfecter earth,
Come, let us go,—to a land wherein gods of the old time
        wandered,

Where every breath even now changes to ether divine.
Come, let us go; though withal a voice whisper, 'The world that
  we live in,
  Whithersoever we turn, still is the same narrow crib;
'Tis but to prove limitation, and measure a cord, that we travel;
  Let who would 'scape and be free go to his chamber and
  think;
'Tis but to change idle fancies for memories wilfully falser;
  'Tis but to go and have been.'—Come, little bark! let us go. 10

I. *Claude to Eustace*

DEAR EUSTATIO, I write that you may write me an answer,
Or at the least to put us again *en rapport* with each other.
Rome disappoints me much,—St. Peter's, perhaps, in especial;
Only the Arch of Titus and view from the Lateran please me:
This, however, perhaps, is the weather, which truly is horrid.
Greece must be better, surely; and yet I am feeling so spiteful,
That I could travel to Athens, to Delphi, and Troy, and Mount
  Sinai,
Though but to see with my eyes that these are vanity also.
  Rome disappoints me much; I hardly as yet understand, but
Rubbishy seems the word that most exactly would suit it. 20
All the foolish destructions, and all the sillier savings,
All the incongruous things of past incompatible ages,
Seem to be treasured up here to make fools of present and future.
Would to Heaven the old Goths had made a cleaner sweep of it!
Would to Heaven some new ones would come and destroy
  these churches!
However, one can live in Rome as also in London.
Rome is better than London, because it is other than London.
It is a blessing, no doubt, to be rid, at least for a time, of
All one's friends and relations,—yourself (forgive me!)
  included,—
All the *assujettissement* of having been what one has been, 30
What one thinks one is, or thinks that others suppose one;
Yet, in despite of all, we turn like fools to the English.
Vernon has been my fate; who is here the same that you knew
  him,—
Making the tour, it seems, with friends of the name of Trevellyn.

II. *Claude to Eustace*

Rome disappoints me still; but I shrink and adapt myself to it.
Somehow a tyrannous sense of a superincumbent oppression
Still, wherever I go, accompanies ever, and makes me
Feel like a tree (shall I say?) buried under a ruin of brickwork.
Rome, believe me, my friend, is like its own Monte Testaceo,
Merely a marvellous mass of broken and castaway wine-pots.   40
Ye gods! what do I want with this rubbish of ages departed,
Things that nature abhors, the experiments that she has failed
    in?
What do I find in the Forum? An archway and two or three
    pillars.
Well, but St. Peter's? Alas, Bernini has filled it with sculpture!
No one can cavil, I grant, at the size of the great Coliseum.
Doubtless the notion of grand and capacious and massive
    amusement,
This the old Romans had; but tell me, is this an idea?
Yet of solidity much, but of splendour little is extant:
'Brickwork I found thee, and marble I left thee!' their
    Emperor vaunted;
'Marble I thought thee, and brickwork I find thee!' the
    Tourist may answer.   50

III. *Georgina Trevellyn to Louisa*

At last, dearest Louisa, I take up my pen to address you.
Here we are, you see, with the seven-and-seventy boxes,
Courier, Papa and Mamma, the children, and Mary and
    Susan:
Here we all are at Rome, and delighted of course with St.
    Peter's,
And very pleasantly lodged in the famous Piazza di Spagna.
Rome is a wonderful place, but Mary shall tell you about it;
Not very gay, however; the English are mostly at Naples;
There are the A.s, we hear, and most of the W. party.
    George, however, is come; did I tell you about his
        mustachios?
Dear, I must really stop, for the carriage, they tell me, is waiting;   60
Mary will finish; and Susan is writing, they say, to Sophia.
Adieu, dearest Louise,—evermore your faithful Georgina.

Who can a Mr. Claude be whom George has taken to be with?
Very stupid, I think, but George says so *very* clever.

IV. *Claude to Eustace*

No, the Christian faith, as at any rate I understood it,
With its humiliations and exaltations combining,
Exaltations sublime, and yet diviner abasements,
Aspirations from something most shameful here upon earth and
In our poor selves to something most perfect above in the
      heavens,—
No, the Christian faith, as I, at least, understand it,   70
Is not here, O Rome, in any of these thy churches;
Is not here, but in Freiburg, or Rheims, or Westminster Abbey.
What in thy Dome I find, in all thy recenter efforts,
Is a something, I think, more *rational* far, more earthly,
Actual, less ideal, devout not in scorn and refusal,
But in a positive, calm, Stoic-Epicurean acceptance.
This I begin to detect in St. Peter's and some of the churches,
Mostly in all that I see of the sixteenth-century masters;
Overlaid of course with infinite gauds and gewgaws,
Innocent, playful follies, the toys and trinkets of childhood,   80
Forced on maturer years, as the serious one thing needful,
By the barbarian will of the rigid and ignorant Spaniard.
    Curious work, meantime, re-entering society: how we
Walk a livelong day, great Heaven, and watch our shadows!
What our shadows seem, forsooth, we will ourselves be.
Do I look like that? you think me that: then I *am* that.

V. *Claude to Eustace*

Luther, they say, was unwise; like a half-taught German, he
    could not
See that old follies were passing most tranquilly out of
    remembrance;
Leo the Tenth was employing all efforts to clear out abuses;
Jupiter, Juno, and Venus, Fine Arts, and Fine Letters, the
    Poets,   90
Scholars, and Sculptors, and Painters, were quietly clearing
    away the
Martyrs, and Virgins, and Saints, or at any rate Thomas Aquinas:

He must forsooth make a fuss and distend his huge Wittenberg
    lungs, and
Bring back Theology once yet again in a flood upon Europe:
Lo you, for forty days from the windows of heaven it fell; the
Waters prevail on the earth yet more for a hundred and fifty;
Are they abating at last? the doves that are sent to explore are
Wearily fain to return, at the best with a leaflet of promise,—
Fain to return, as they went, to the wandering wave-tost
    vessel,—
Fain to re-enter the roof which covers the clean and the
    unclean,—
Luther, they say, was unwise; he didn't see how things were
    going;
Luther was foolish,—but, O great God! what call you Ignatius?   102
O my tolerant soul, be still! but you talk of barbarians,
Alaric, Attila, Genseric;—why, they came, they killed, they
Ravaged, and went on their way; but these vile, tyrannous
    Spaniards,
These are here still,—how long, O ye heavens, in the country
    of Dante?
These, that fanaticized Europe, which now can forget them,
    release not
This, their choicest of prey, this Italy; here you see them,—
Here, with emasculate pupils and gimcrack churches of Gesu,
Pseudo-learning and lies, confessional-boxes and postures,—   110
Here, with metallic beliefs and regimental devotions,—
Here, overcrusting with slime, perverting, defacing, debasing,
Michael Angelo's dome, that had hung the Pantheon in
    heaven,
Raphael's Joys and Graces, and thy clear stars, Galileo!

VI. *Claude to Eustace*

Which of three Misses Trevellyn it is that Vernon shall marry
Is not a thing to be known; for our friend is one of those natures
Which have their perfect delight in the general tender-
    domestic,
So that he trifles with Mary's shawl, ties Susan's bonnet,
Dances with all, but at home is most, they say, with Georgina,
Who is, however, *too* silly in my apprehension for Vernon.   120
I, as before when I wrote, continue to see them a little;

Not that I like them much or care a *bajocco* for Vernon,
But I am slow at Italian, have not many English acquaintance,
And I am asked, in short, and am not good at excuses.
Middle-class people these, bankers very likely, not wholly
Pure of the taint of the shop; will at table d'hôte and restaurant
Have their shilling's worth, their penny's pennyworth even:
Neither man's aristocracy this, nor God's, God knoweth!
Yet they are fairly descended, they give you to know, well
    connected;
Doubtless somewhere in some neighbourhood have, and are
    careful to keep, some   130
Threadbare-genteel relations, who in their turn are enchanted
Grandly among county people to introduce at assemblies
To the unpennied cadets our cousins with excellent fortunes.
Neither man's aristocracy this, nor God's, God knoweth!

VII. *Claude to Eustace*

Ah, what a shame, indeed, to abuse these most worthy people!
Ah, what a sin to have sneered at their innocent rustic
    pretensions!
Is it not laudable really, this reverent worship of station?
Is it not fitting that wealth should tender this homage to
    culture?
Is it not touching to witness these efforts, if little availing,
Painfully made, to perform the old ritual service of manners?   140
Shall not devotion atone for the absence of knowledge? and
    fervour
Palliate, cover, the fault of a superstitious observance?
Dear, dear, what do I say? but, alas, just now, like Iago,
I can be nothing at all, if it is not critical wholly;
So in fantastic height, in coxcomb exaltation,
Here in the Garden I walk, can freely concede to the Maker
That the works of his hand are all very good: his creatures,
Beast of the field and fowl, he brings them before me; I
    name them;
That which I name them, they are,—the bird, the beast, and
    the cattle.
But for Adam,—alas, poor critical coxcomb Adam!   150
But for Adam there is not found an help-meet for him.

VIII. *Claude to Eustace*

No, great Dome of Agrippa, thou art not Christian! canst not,
Strip and replaster and daub and do what they will with thee,
    be so!
Here underneath the great porch of colossal Corinthian
    columns,
Here as I walk, do I dream of the Christian belfries above
    them?
Or on a bench as I sit and abide for long hours, till thy
    whole vast
Round grows dim as in dreams to my eyes, I repeople thy
    niches,
Not with the Martyrs, and Saints, and Confessors, and
    Virgins, and children,
But with the mightier forms of an older, austerer worship;
And I recite to myself, how   160

            Eager for battle here
        Stood Vulcan, here matronal Juno,
            And with the bow to his shoulder faithful
        He who with pure dew laveth of Castaly
        His flowing locks, who holdeth of Lycia
        The oak forest and the wood that bore him,
            Delos' and Patara's own Apollo.

IX. *Claude to Eustace*

Yet it is pleasant, I own it, to be in their company; pleasant,
Whatever else it may be, to abide in the feminine presence.
Pleasant, but wrong, will you say? But this happy, serene
    coexistence   170
Is to some poor soft souls, I fear, a necessity simple,
Meat and drink and life, and music, filling with sweetness,
Thrilling with melody sweet, with harmonies strange
    overhelming,
All the long-silent strings of an awkward, meaningless fabric.
Yet as for that, I could live, I believe, with children; to have
    those
Pure and delicate forms encompassing, moving about you,

This were enough, I could think; and truly with glad
    resignation
Could from the dream of romance, from the fever of flushed
    adolescence,
Look to escape and subside into peaceful avuncular functions.
Nephews and nieces! alas, for as yet I have none! and,
    moreover,   180
Mothers are jealous, I fear me, too often, too rightfully; fathers
Think they have title exclusive to spoiling their own little
    darlings;
And by the law of the land, in despite of Malthusian doctrine,
No sort of proper provision is made for that most patriotic,
Most meritorious subject, the childless and bachelor uncle.

X. *Claude to Eustace*

Ye, too, marvellous Twain, that erect on the Monte Cavallo
Stand by your rearing steeds in the grace of your motionless
    movement,
Stand with your upstretched arms and tranquil regardant faces,
Stand as instinct with life in the might of immutable
    manhood,—
O ye mighty and strange, ye ancient divine ones of Hellas,   190
Are ye Christian too? to convert and redeem and renew you,
Will the brief form have sufficed, that a Pope has set up on
    the apex
Of the Egyptian stone that o'ertops you, the Christian
    symbol?
    And ye, silent, supreme in serene and victorious marble,
Ye that encircle the walls of the stately Vatican chambers,
Juno and Ceres, Minerva, Apollo, the Muses and Bacchus,
Ye unto whom far and near come posting the Christian
    pilgrims,
Ye that are ranged in the halls of the mystic Christian
    Pontiff,
Are ye also baptized? are ye of the kingdom of Heaven?
Utter, O some one, the word that shall reconcile Ancient and
    Modern!   200
Am I to turn me for this unto thee, great Chapel of Sixtus?

XI. *Claude to Eustace*

These are the facts. The uncle, the elder brother, the squire (a
Little embarrased, I fancy), resides in the family place in
Cornwall, of course; 'Papa is in business,' Mary informs me;
He's a good sensible man, whatever his trade is. The mother
Is—shall I call it fine?—herself she would tell you refined, and
Greatly, I fear me, looks down on my bookish and maladroit
    manners;
Somewhat affecteth the blue; would talk to me often of poets;
Quotes, which I hate, Childe Harold; but also appreciates
    Wordsworth;
Sometimes adventures on Schiller; and then to religion
    diverges;   210
Questions me much about Oxford; and yet, in her loftiest
    flights still
Grates the fastidious ear with the slightly mercantile accent.

    Is it contemptible, Eustace—I'm perfectly ready to think
    so,—
Is it,—the horrible pleasure of pleasing inferior people?
I am ashamed my own self; and yet true it is, if disgraceful,
That for the first time in life I am living and moving with
    freedom.
I, who never could talk to the people I meet with my uncle,—
I, who have always failed,—I, trust me, can suit the
    Trevellyns;
I, believe me,—great conquest,—am liked by the country
    bankers.
And I am glad to be liked, and like in return very kindly.   220
So it proceeds; *Laissez faire, laissez aller,*—such is the
    watchword.
Well, I know there are thousands as pretty and hundreds as
    pleasant,
Girls by the dozen as good, and girls in abundance with polish
Higher and manners more perfect than Susan or Mary Trevellyn.
Well, I know, after all, it is only juxtaposition,—
Juxtaposition, in short; and what is juxtaposition?

XII. *Claude to Eustace*

But I am in for it now,—*laissez faire*, of a truth, *laissez aller.*
Yes, I am going,—I feel it, I feel and cannot recall it,—
Fusing with this thing and that, entering into all sorts of
    relations,
Tying I know not what ties, which, whatever they are, I know
    one thing,   230
Will, and must, woe is me, be one day painfully broken,—
Broken with painful remorses, with shrinkings of soul, and
    relentings,
Foolish delays, more foolish evasions, most foolish renewals.
But I have made the step, have quitted the ship of Ulysses;
Quitted the sea and the shore, passed into the magical island;
Yet on my lips is the *moly*, medicinal, offered of Hermes.
I have come into the precinct, the labyrinth closes around me,
Path into path rounding slyly; I pace slowly on, and the fancy,
Struggling awhile to sustain the long sequences, weary,
    bewildered,
Fain must collapse in despair; I yield, I am lost, and know
    nothing;   240
Yet in my bosom unbroken remaineth the clue; I shall use it.
Lo, with the rope on my loins I descend through the fissure;
    I sink, yet
Inly secure in the strength of invisible arms up above me;
Still, wheresoever I swing, wherever to shore, or to shelf, or
Floor of cavern untrodden, shell-sprinkled, enchanting, I
    know I
Yet shall one time feel the strong cord tighten about me,—
Feel it, relentless, upbear me from spots I would rest in; and
    though the
Rope sway wildly, I faint, crags wound me, from crag unto crag re-
Bounding, or, wide in the void, I die ten deaths, ere the end I
Yet shall plant firm foot on the broad lofty spaces I quit, shall   250
Feel underneath me again the great massy strengths of
    abstraction,
Look yet abroad from the height o'er the sea whose salt wave
    I have tasted.

XIII. *Georgina Trevellyn to Louisa*

Dearest Louisa,—Inquire, if you please, about Mr. Claude—.
He has been once at R., and remembers meeting the H.s.
Harriet L., perhaps, may be able to tell you about him.
It is an awkward youth, but still with very good manners;
Not without prospects, we hear; and, George says, highly
    connected.
Georgy declares it absurd, but Mamma is alarmed and insists
    he has
Taken up strange opinions, and may be turning a Papist.
Certainly once he spoke of a daily service he went to.   260
'Where?' we asked, and he laughed and answered, 'At the
    Pantheon.'
This was a temple, you know, and now is a Catholic church;
    and
Though it is said that Mazzini has sold it for Protestant service,
Yet I suppose this change can hardly as yet be effected.
Adieu again,—evermore, my dearest, your loving Georgina.

P.S. by Mary Trevellyn

I am to tell you, you say, what I think of our last new
    acquaintance.
Well, then, I think that George has a very fair right to be
    jealous.
I do not like him much, though I do not dislike being with him.
He is what people call, I suppose, a superior man, and
Certainly seems so to me; but I think he is terribly selfish. 270

Alba, thou findest me still, and, Alba, thou findest me ever,
    Now from the Capitol steps, now over Titus's Arch,
Here from the large grassy spaces that spread from the
    Lateran portal,
    Towering o'er aqueduct lines lost in perspective between,
Or from a Vatican window, or bridge, or the high Coliseum,
    Clear by the garlanded line cut of the Flavian ring.
Beautiful can I not call thee, and yet thou hast power to
    o'ermaster,
    Power of mere beauty; in dreams, Alba, thou hauntest me
    still.

Is it religion? I ask me; or is it a vain superstition?
 Slavery abject and gross? service, too feeble, of truth? 280
Is it an idol I bow to, or is it a god that I worship?
 Do I sink back on the old, or do I soar from the mean?
So through the city I wander and question, unsatified ever,
 Reverent so I accept, doubtful because I revere.

1862

Title: "Love-affairs while travelling." A chronicle in letters of the baffled and eventually stifled romantic attraction between a young English intellectual and a young Englishwoman rather below his rank. The letters contain many of Clough's observations and reflections in Rome in 1849. 1. 30: **assujettissement** imposed burden. 1. 39: **Monte Testaceo** a mound near the Tiber. 1. 49: **Emperor** Caesar Augustus (63 B.C.–14 A.D.). 1. 74: **Dome** of St. Peter's Basilica. 1. 102: **Ignatius** St. Ignatius Loyola (1491–1556), militant anti-Protestant, and founder of the Jesuits. 1. 122: **bajocco** a coin of little value. 1. 133: **cadets** distant relatives. 1. 147: **Garden** See Gen. 2:15–23. 1. 152: **Dome of Agrippa** the Pantheon, once a Roman temple, later a church. 1. 160: **recite** the following lines from Horace, Odes III, 4. 1. 186: **Twain** statues, in the Piazza del Quirinale, of the Greek heroes, the twins Castor and Pollux. 1. 201: **Chapel** the Sistine, named after its builder, Pope Sixtus IV (1471–1484). 1. 208: **the blue** from "blue-stocking," a lady with literary pretentions. 1. 209: **Childe Harold** Byron's very romantic English traveller in *Childe Harold's Pilgrimage,* a work rather below Claude's taste. 1. 235: **island** of Circe in the *Odyssey.* She transformed some of Ulysses' companions into pigs, but Ulysses was protected by the sacred herb, moly. 1. 241: **clue** a thread; such as that which enabled Theseus to find his way back out of the Cretan labyrinth. 1. 263: **Mazzini** Italian patriot then, in 1849, head of the short-lived Roman Republic. (He did not sell the Pantheon.) 1. 271: **Alba** an ancient name for Rome. 1. 271: **findest** stirrest (touch deeply).

From *DIPSYCHUS*

SCENE V

Spirit

What now? the Lido shall it be?
That none may say we didn't see
The ground which Byron used to ride on,
And do I don't know what beside on.

Ho, barca! here! and this light gale
Will let us run it with a sail.

Dipsychus

I dreamt a dream; till morning light
A bell rang in my head all night,
Tinkling and tinkling first, and then
Tolling; and tinkling; tolling again.   10
So brisk and gay, and then so slow!
O joy, and terror! mirth, and woe!
Ting, ting, there is no God; ting, ting—
Dong, there is no God; dong,
There is no God; dong, dong!

Ting, ting, there is no God; ting, ting;
Come dance and play, and merrily sing—
Ting, ting a ding; ting, ting a ding!
O pretty girl who trippest along,
Come to my bed—it isn't wrong.   20
Uncork the bottle, sing the song!
Ting, ting a ding: dong, dong.
Wine has dregs; the song an end;
A silly girl is a poor friend,
And age and weakness who shall mend?
Dong, there is no God; Dong!

Ting, ting a ding! Come dance and sing!
Staid Englishmen, who toil and slave
From your first breeching to your grave,
And seldom spend and always save,   30
And do your duty all your life
By your young family and wife;
Come, be't not said you ne'er had known
What earth can furnish you alone.
The Italian, Frenchman, German even,
Have given up all thoughts of heaven;
And you still linger—oh, you fool!—
Because of what you learnt at school.
You should have gone at least to college,
And got a little ampler knowledge.   40
Ah well, and yet—dong, dong, dong:

Do, if you like, as now you do;
If work's a cheat, so's pleasure too;
And nothing's new and nothing's true;
Dong, there is no God; dong!

O Rosalie, my precious maid,
I think thou thinkest love is true;
And on thy fragrant bosom laid
I almost could believe it too.
O in our nook, unknown, unseen,   50
We'll hold our fancy like a screen,
Us and the dreadful fact between.
And it shall yet be long, aye, long,
The quiet notes of our low song
Shall keep us from that sad dong, dong.
Hark, hark, hark! O voice of fear!
It reaches us here, even here!
Dong, there is no God; dong!

Ring ding, ring ding, tara, tara,   60
To battle, to battle—haste, haste—
To battle, to battle—aha, aha!
On, on, to the conqueror's feast.
From east and west, and south and north,
Ye men of valour and of worth,
Ye mighty men of arms, come forth,
And work your will, for that is just;
And in your impulse put your trust,
Beneath your feet the fools are dust.
Alas, alas! O grief and wrong,
The good are weak, the wicked strong;   70
And O my God, how long, how long?
Dong, there is no God; dong!

Ring, ting; to bow before the strong,
There is a rapture too in this;
Speak, outraged maiden, in thy wrong
Did terror bring no secret bliss?
Were boys' shy lips worth half a song
Compared to the hot soldier's kiss?
Work for thy master, work, thou slave
He is not merciful, but brave.   80

Be't joy to serve, who free and proud
Scorns thee and all the ignoble crowd;
Take that, 'tis all thou art allowed,
Except the snaky hope that they
May some time serve, who rule to-day,
When, by hell-demons, shan't they pay?
O wickedness, O shame and grief,
And heavy load, and no relief!
O God, O God! and which is worst,
To be the curser or the curst,   90
The victim or the murderer? Dong
Dong, there is no God; dong!

Ring ding, ring ding, tara, tara,
Away, and hush that preaching—fagh!
Ye vulgar dreamers about peace,
Who offer noblest hearts, to heal
The tenderest hurts honour can feel,
Paid magistrates and the Police!
O piddling merchant justice, go,
Exacter rules than yours we know;   100
Resentment's rule, and that high law
Of whoso best the sword can draw.
Ah well, and yet—dong, dong, dong.
Go on, my friends, as now you do;
Lawyers are villains, soldiers too;
And nothing's new and nothing's true.
Dong, there is no God; dong!

O Rosalie, my lovely maid,
I think thou thinkest love is true;
And on thy faithful bosom laid   110
I almost could believe it too.
The villainies, the wrongs, the alarms
Forget we in each other's arms.
No justice here, no God above;
But where we are, is there not love?
What? what? thou also go'st? For how
Should dead truth live in lover's vow?
What? what? thou also go'st? For how
Dong, there is no God; dong!

I had a dream, from eve to light   120
A bell went sounding all the night.
Gay mirth, black woe, thin joys, huge pain:
I tried to stop it, but in vain.
It ran right on, and never broke;
Only when day began to stream
Through the white curtains to my bed,
And like an angel at my head
Light stood and touched me—I awoke,
And looked, and said, 'It is a dream.'

Spirit

Ah! not so bad. You've read, I see,   130
Your Béranger, and thought of me.
But really you owe some apology
For harping thus upon theology.
I'm not a judge, I own; in short,
Religion may not be my forte.
The Church of England I belong to,
But think Dissenters not far wrong too;
They're vulgar dogs; but for his *creed*
I hold that no man will be d———d.
My Establishment I much respect,   140
Her ordinances don't neglect;
Attend at Church on Sunday once,
And in the Prayer-book am no dunce;
Baptise my babies; nay, my wife
Would be churched too once in her life.
She's taken, I regret to state,
Rather a Puseyite turn of late.
To set the thing quite right, I went
At Easter to the Sacrament.
'Tis proper once a year or so   150
To do the civil thing and show—
But come and listen in your turn
And you shall hear and mark and learn.

'There is no God,' the wicked saith,
    'And truly it's a blessing,
For what he might have done with us
    It's better only guessing.'

'There is no God,' a youngster thinks,
    'Or really, if there may be,
He surely didn't mean a man   160
    Always to be a baby.'

'There is no God, or if there is,'
    The tradesman thinks, "twere funny
If he should take it ill in me
    To make a little money.'

'Whether there be,' the rich man says,
    'It matters very little,
For I and mine, thank somebody,
    Are not in want of victual.'

Some others, also, to themselves   170
    Who scarce so much as doubt it,
Think there is none, when they are well,
    And do not think about it.

But country folks who live beneath
    The shadow of the steeple;
The parson and the parson's wife,
    And mostly married people;

Youths green and happy in first love,
    So thankful for illusion;
And men caught out in what the world   180
    Calls guilt, in first confusion;

And almost every one when age,
    Disease, or sorrows strike him,
Inclines to think there is a God,
    Or something very like Him.

But *eccoci!* with our *barchetta*,
Here at the Sant' Elisabetta.

Dipsychus

Vineyards and maize, that's pleasant for sore eyes.

Spirit

And on the island's other side,
The place where Murray's faithful Guide   190
Informs us Byron used to ride.

Dipsychus

These trellised vines! enchanting! Sandhills, ho!
The sea, at last the sea—the real broad sea—
Beautiful! and a glorious breeze upon it.

Spirit

Look back; one catches at this station
Lagoon and sea in combination.

Dipsychus

On her still lake the city sits,
Where bark and boat about her flits,
Nor dreams, her soft siesta taking,
Of Adriatic billows breaking.   200
I do; and see and hear them. Come! to the sea!

Spirit

The wind I think is the *sirocco*.
Yonder, I take it, is Malmocco.
Thank you! it never was my passion
To skip o'er sand-hills in that fashion.

Dipsychus

Oh, a grand surge! we'll bathe; quick, quick! undress!
Quick, quick! in, in!
We'll take the crested billows by their backs
And shake them. Quick! in, in!
And I will taste again the old joy   210
I gloried in so when a boy.

Spirit

Well; but it's not so pleasant for the feet;
We should have brought some towels and a sheet.

Dipsychus

In, in! I go. Ye great winds blow,
And break, thou curly waves, upon my breast.

Spirit

Hm! I'm undressing. Doubtless all is well—
I only wish these thistles were at hell.
By heaven, I'll stop before that bad yet worse is,
And take care of our watches—and our purses.

Dipsychus

Aha! come, come—great waters, roll!   220
Accept me, take me, body and soul!—
   Aha!

Spirit

   Come, no more of that stuff,
I'm sure you've stayed in long enough.

Dipsychus

That's done me good. It grieves me though
I never came here long ago.

Spirit

Pleasant perhaps. However, no offence,
Animal spirits are not common sense.
You think perhaps I have outworn them—
Certainly I have learnt to scorn them;
They're good enough as an assistance,   230
But in themselves a poor existence.
But you—with this one bathe, no doubt,
Have solved all questions out and out.
'Tis Easter Day, and on the Lido
Lo, Christ the Lord is risen indeed, O!

1862

Title: The poem is a dialogue between Dipsychus (whose name means "a soul divided") an earnest and idealistic intellectual, and a worldly, satirical Spirit, a kind of Mephistopheles in Victorian dress.   l. 1: **Lido** a promenade and beach on one of the long sandy islands separating the lagoons of Venice from the Adriatic.   l. 3: **Byron used to ride on** Byron lived in Venice much of the time from 1817 to 1819. (See Shelley's "Julian and Maddalo" for a description of such a ride.)   l. 5: **barca** a

large gondola.   l. 46: **Rosalie**   any sweetheart of the moment.   l. 131:
Your Béranger   Pierre Jean de Béranger (1780–1857), poet, author
of "Le Roi d'Yvetot" and other popular songs in a liberal and satiric vein.
l. 139: **d———d**   that is, *damned*, here pronounced "deed."   l. 140:
Establishment   the national church of England.   l. 145: **churched**
"The churching of women" is an ancient rite of thanksgiving after child-
birth.   l. 147: **Puseyite**   "High-Church"; after E. G. Pusey (1800–
1882) one of the founders of the Oxford Movement.   l. 186: **eccoci!**
Here we are!   l. 187: **Sant' Elisabetta**   the landing point on the Lido.
l. 190: **Guide**   *Handbook for Travellers in Northern Italy,* one of a series
of guidebooks published by John Murray, son of Byron's friend and pub-
lisher.   l. 203: **Malmocco**   another island farther down the lagoon.

"Say not the struggle nought availeth"

Say not the struggle nought availeth,
   The labour and the wounds are vain,
The enemy faints not, nor faileth,
   And as things have been, things remain.

If hopes were dupes, fears may be liars;
   It may be, in yon smoke concealed,
Your comrades chase e'en now the fliers,
   And, but for you, possess the field.

For while the tired waves, vainly breaking,
   Seem here no painful inch to gain,   10
Far back through creeks and inlets making
   Came, silent, flooding in, the main,

And not by eastern windows only,
   When daylight comes, comes in the light,
In front the sun climbs slow, how slowly,
   But westward, look, the land is bright.

1862

IN THE GREAT METROPOLIS

Each for himself is still the rule,
We learn it when we go to school—
   The devil take the hindmost, o!

And when the schoolboys grow to men,
In life they learn it o'er again—
   The devil take the hindmost, o!

For in the church, and at the bar,
On 'Change, at court, where'er they are,
   The devil take the hindmost, o!

Husband for husband, wife for wife,   10
Are careful that in married life
   The devil take the hindmost, o!

From youth to age, whate'er the game,
The unvarying practice is the same—
   The devil take the hindmost, o!

And after death, we do not know,
But scarce can doubt, where'er we go,
   The devil takes the hindmost, o!

Tol rol de rol, tol rol de ro,
The devil take the hindmost, o!   20

1862

l. 8: **'Change**   the Exchange, a financial center.

THE LATEST DECALOGUE

Thou shalt have one God only; who
Would be at the expense of two?
No graven images may be
Worshipped, except the currency:
Swear not at all; for for thy curse
Thine enemy is none the worse:
At church on Sunday to attend
Will serve to keep the world thy friend:
Honour thy parents; that is, all
From whom advancement may befall: 10
Thou shalt not kill; but needst not strive
Officiously to keep alive:
Do not adultery commit;
Advantage rarely comes of it:
Thou shalt not steal; an empty feat,
When it's so lucrative to cheat:
Bear not false witness; let the lie

Have time on its own wings to fly:
Thou shalt not covet; but tradition
Approves all forms of competition.   20

The sum of all is, thou shalt love,
If any body, God above;   *a little more agreed?*
At any rate shall never labour   *— the tone here*
More than thyself to love thy neighbour. *does change*

1862

Title: See Exod. 20:1–17.

LES VACHES

The skies have sunk and hid the upper snow,
Home, Rose, and home, Provence and La Palie,
The rainy clouds are filing fast below,
And wet will be the path, and wet shall we.
Home, Rose, and home, Provence and La Palie.

Ah dear, and where is he, a year agone
Who stepped beside and cheered us on and on?
My sweetheart wanders far away from me,
In foreign land or o'er a foreign sea.
Home, Rose, and home, Provence and La Palie.   10

The lightning zigzags shoot across the sky,
(Home, Rose, and home, Provence and La Palie,)
And through the vale the rains go sweeping by,
Ah me, and when in shelter shall we be?
Home, Rose, and home, Provence and La Palie.

Cold, dreary cold, the stormy winds feel they
O'er foreign lands and foreign seas that stray.
(Home, Rose, and home, Provence and La Palie.)
And doth he e'er, I wonder, bring to mind
The pleasant huts and herds he left behind?   20
And doth he sometimes in his slumbering see
The feeding kine, and doth he think of me,
My sweetheart wandering wheresoe'er it be?
Home, Rose, and home, Provence and La Palie.

The thunder bellows far from snow to snow,
(Home, Rose, and home, Provence and La Palie)
And loud and louder roars the flood below.
Heigh ho! but soon in shelter shall we be.
Home, Rose, and home, Provence and La Palie.

Or shall he find before his term be sped,   30
Some comelier maid that he shall wish to wed?
(Home, Rose, and home, Provence and La Palie,)
For weary is work, and weary day by day
To have your comfort miles on miles away.
Home, Rose, and home, Provence and La Palie.
Or may it be 'tis I shall find my mate,
And he returning see himself too late?
For work we must, and what we see, we see,
And God he knows, and what must be, must be,
When sweethearts wander far away from me.   40
Home, Rose, and home, Provence and La Palie.

The sky behind is brightening up anew,
(Home, Rose, and home, Provence and La Palie),
The rain is ending, and our journey too;
Heigh ho! aha! for here at home are we:—
In, Rose, and in, Provence and La Palie.

1862

Title: "The Cows," song of a cowgirl driving home cows named Rose, Provence, and La Palie.

EASTER DAY

NAPLES, 1849

Through the great sinful streets of Naples as I past,
With fiercer heat than flamed above my head
My heart was hot within me; till at last
My brain was lightened, when my tongue had said

    Christ is not risen!

Christ is not risen, no,
He lies and moulders low;
    Christ is not risen.

What though the stone were rolled away, and though
    The grave found empty there!—   10
    If not there, then elsewhere;
If not where Joseph laid Him first, why then
    Where other men
Translaid Him after; in some humbler clay.
    Long ere to-day
Corruption that sad perfect work hath done,
Which here she scarcely, lightly had begun.
    The foul engendered worm
Feeds on the flesh of the life-giving form
Of our most Holy and Anointed One.   20

    He is not risen, no,
    He lies and moulders low;
        Christ is not risen.

    Ashes to ashes, dust to dust;
As of the unjust, also of the just—
        Christ is not risen.

What if the women, ere the dawn was grey,
Saw one or more great angels, as they say,
Angels, or Him himself? Yet neither there, nor then,
Nor afterward, nor elsewhere, nor at all,   30
Hath He appeared to Peter or the Ten,
Nor, save in thunderous terror, to blind Saul;
Save in an after-Gospel and late Creed
    He is not risen indeed,
        Christ is not risen.

Or what if e'en, as runs the tale, the Ten
Saw, heard, and touched, again and yet again?
What if at Emmaüs' inn and by Capernaum's lake
    Came One the bread that brake,
Came One that spake as never mortal spake,   40
And with them ate and drank and stood and walked about?
    Ah! 'some' did well to 'doubt'!
Ah! the true Christ, while these things came to pass,
Nor heard, nor spake, nor walked, nor dreamt, alas!
    He was not risen, no,
    He lay and mouldered low,
        Christ was not risen.

As circulates in some great city crowd
A rumour changeful, vague, importunate, and loud,
From no determined centre, or of fact,   50
    Or authorship exact,
    Which no man can deny
    Nor verify;
    So spread the wondrous fame;
      He all the same
    Lay senseless, mouldering, low.
    He was not risen, no,
      Christ was not risen!

Ashes to ashes, dust to dust;
As of the unjust, also of the just—   60
    Yea, of that Just One too.
This is the one sad Gospel that is true,
    Christ is not risen.

      ———

Is He not risen, and shall we not rise?
    Oh, we unwise!
What did we dream, what wake we to discover?
Ye hills, fall on us, and ye mountains, cover!
    In darkness and great gloom
Come ere we thought it is *our* day of doom,
From the cursed world which is one tomb,   70
    Christ is not risen!

Eat, drink, and die, for we are men deceived,
Of all the creatures under heaven's wide cope
We are most hopeless who had once most hope
We are most wretched that had most believed.
    Christ is not risen.

Eat, drink, and play, and think that this is bliss!
    There is no Heaven but this!
    There is no Hell;—
Save Earth, which serves the purpose doubly well,   80
    Seeing it visits still
With equallest apportionments of ill
Both good and bad alike, and brings to one same dust
    The unjust and the just
    With Christ, who is not risen.

Eat, drink, and die, for we are souls bereaved,
Of all the creatures under this broad sky
We are most hopeless, that had hoped most high,
And most beliefless, that had most believed.
    Ashes to ashes, dust to dust;   90
    As of the unjust, also of the just—
        Yea, of that Just One too.
    It is the one sad Gospel that is true,
        Christ is not risen.

    Weep not beside the Tomb,
    Ye women, unto whom
He was great solace while ye tended Him;
    Ye who with napkin o'er His head
And folds of linen round each wounded limb
    Laid out the Sacred Dead;   100
And thou that bar'st Him in thy Wondering Womb.
Yea, Daughters of Jerusalem, depart,
Bind up as best ye may your own sad bleeding heart;
Go to your homes, your living children tend,
    Your earthly spouses love;
    Set your affections *not* on things above,
Which moth and rust corrupt, which quickliest come to end:
Or pray, if pray ye must, and pray, if pray ye can,
For death; since dead is He whom ye deemed more than man,
    Who is not risen, no,   110
    But lies and moulders low,
        Who is not risen.

    Ye men of Galilee!
Why stand ye looking up to heaven, where Him ye ne'er may
        see,
Neither ascending hence, nor hither returning again?
    Ye ignorant and idle fisherman!
Hence to your huts and boats and inland native shore,
    And catch not men, but fish;
    Whate'er things ye might wish,
Him neither here nor there ye e'er shall meet with more.   120
    Ye poor deluded youths, go home,
    Mend the old nets ye left to roam,

Tie the split oar, patch the torn sail;
It was indeed 'an idle tale',
    He was not risen.

And oh, good men of ages yet to be,
Who shall believe *because* ye did not see,
    Oh, be ye warned! be wise!
    No more with pleading eyes,
    And sobs of strong desire,   130
  Unto the empty vacent void aspire,
Seeking another and impossible birth
That is not of your own and only Mother Earth.
But if there is no other life for you,
Sit down and be content, since this must even do:
    He is not risen.

    One look, and then depart,
    Ye humble and ye holy men of heart!
And ye! ye ministers and stewards of a word
Which ye would preach, because another heard,—   140
    Ye worshippers of that ye do not know,
    Take these things hence and go;
    He is not risen.

    Here on our Easter Day
We rise, we come, and lo! we find Him not;
Gardener nor other on the sacred spot,
Where they have laid Him is there none to say!
No sound, nor in, nor out; no word
Of where to seek the dead or meet the living Lord;
There is no glistering of an angel's wings,   150
There is no voice of heavenly clear behest:
Let us go hence, and think upon these things
In silence, which is best.
    Is He not risen? No—
    But lies and moulders low—
    Christ is not risen.

1849   1865

1. 9: **stone** here and in succeeding stanzas Clough alludes to Christ's
burial, resurrection, and subsequent deeds. See, especially, Luke 24 and
John 20, 21.   1. 32: **blind Saul** St. Paul, who as "Saul" hounded the

early Christians and was suddenly converted and temporarily blinded. See Acts 9:1–9.   l. 42: **'some'** . . . **'doubt'**   See Matthew 28:17.   l. 92: **Just One**   Christ.   l. 118: **not men, but fish**   the reverse of Christ's command. See Mark 1:16–17.   l. 127: **because ye did not see**   See John 20:29.

EASTER DAY

II

*   *   *   *

So in the sinful streets, abstracted and alone,
I with my secret self held communing of mine own.
So in the southern city spake the tongue
   Of one that somewhat overwildly sung;
  But in a later hour I sat and heard
  Another voice that spake, another graver word.
  Weep not, it bade, whatever hath been said,
  Though He be dead, He is not dead.
    In the true Creed
    He is yet risen indeed,   10
      Christ is yet risen.

    Weep not beside His tomb,
    Ye women unto whom
    He was great comfort and yet greater grief;
Nor ye faithful few that went with Him to roam,
Seek sadly what for Him ye left, go hopeless to your home;
Nor ye despair, ye sharers yet to be of their belief;
  Though He be dead, He is not dead,
    Not gone, though fled,
    Not lost, though vanished;   20
    Though He return not, though
    He lies and moulders low;
      In the true Creed
    He is yet risen indeed,
      Christ is yet risen.

  Sit if ye will, sit down upon the ground,
  Yet not to weep and wail, but calmly look around.
    Whate'er befell,
    Earth is not hell;

Now, too, as when it first began,   30
   Life yet is Life and Man is Man.
For all that breathe beneath the heaven's high cope,
   Joy with grief mixes, with despondence hope.
   Hope conquers cowardice, joy grief:
   Or at the least, faith unbelief.
      Though dead, not dead;
      Not gone, though fled;
      Not lost, not vanished.
      In the great Gospel and true Creed,
      He is yet risen indeed;   40
         Christ is yet risen.

1849   1865

l. 39: **great Gospel and true Creed**   That is, even a skeptical modern may
still find figurative truth in the Christian faith.

"To spend uncounted years of pain"

      To spend uncounted years of pain,
      Again, again, and yet again,
      In working out in heart and brain
         The problem of our being here;
      To gather facts from far and near,
      Upon the mind to hold them clear,
      And, knowing more may yet appear,
      Unto one's latest breath to fear
      The premature result to draw—
      Is this the object, end and law,   10
         And purpose of our being here?

                  1869

EPI-STRAUSS-IUM

Matthew and Mark and Luke and holy John
Evanished all and gone!
Yea, he that erst, his dusky curtains quitting,
Through Eastern pictured panes his level beams transmitting,
With gorgeous portraits blent.

Sun (son-christ) & [...]

[handwritten left margin: Casting a sunset light]

On them his glories intercepted spent,
Southwestering now, through windows plainly glassed,
On the inside face his radiance keen hath cast,
And in the lustre lost, invisible and gone,

[handwritten left margin: are you in the academy light]

Are, say you, Matthew, Mark and Luke and holy John?   10
Lost, is it? lost, to be recovered never?
However,
The place of worship the meantime with light
Is, if less richly, more sincerely bright,
And in blue skies the Orb is manifest to sight.

[handwritten right margin: also, the setting of faith on earth.]

[handwritten right margin: why the Sun around?]

[handwritten below line: Sun]

[handwritten: end doesn't fit with his complete loss of faith. Or is he celebrating the truth of the High Critics?]

[handwritten left margin: Does he retain some sort of faith?]

1869

Title: "A Song after having read Strauss," that is, D. F. Strauss's *Life of Jesus Critically Examined* (tr. by George Eliot), 1846, in which the miraculous parts of the Gospels were called fictitious.   l. 1: **Matthew . . . John** The four evangelists as represented in stained glass windows at the eastern end of a church.

GEORGE MEREDITH

1828–1909

MODERN LOVE

1

By this he knew she wept with waking eyes:
That, at his hand's light quiver by her head,
The strange low sobs that shook their common bed
Were called into her with a sharp surprise,
And strangled mute, like little gaping snakes,
Dreadfully venomous to him.   She lay
Stone-still, and the long darkness flowed away
With muffled pulses.   Then, as midnight makes
Her giant heart of Memory and Tears
Drink the pale drug of silence, and so beat   10
Sleep's heavy measure, they from head to feet
Were moveless, looking through their dead black years
By vain regret scrawled over the blank wall.
Like sculptured effigies they might be seen
Upon their marriage-tomb, the sword between;
Each wishing for the sword that severs all.

2

It ended, and the morrow brought the task.
Her eyes were guilty gates, that let him in
By shutting all too zealous for their sin:
Each sucked a secret, and each wore a mask.
But, oh, the bitter taste her beauty had!
He sickened as at breath of poison-flowers:
A languid humour stole among the hours,
And if their smiles encountered, he went mad,
And raged deep inward, till the light was brown
Before his vision, and the world forgot,   10
Looked wicked as some old dull murder-spot.
A star with lurid beams, she seemed to crown

The pit of infamy: and then again
He fainted on his vengefulness, and strove
To ape the magnanimity of love,
And smote himself, a shuddering heap of pain.

3

This was the woman; what now of the man?
But pass him. If he comes beneath a heel,
He shall be crushed until he cannot feel,
Or, being callous, haply till he can.
But he is nothing:—nothing? Only mark
The rich light striking out from her on him!
Ha! what a sense it is when her eyes swim
Across the man she singles, leaving dark
All else! Lord God, who mad'st the thing so fair,
See that I am drawn to her even now!   10
It cannot be such harm on her cool brow
To put a kiss?   Yet if I meet him there!
But she is mine! Ah, no! I know too well
I claim a star whose light is overcast:
I claim a phantom-woman in the Past.
The hour has struck, though I heard not the bell!

4

All other joys of life he strove to warm,
And magnify, and catch them to his lip:
But they had suffered shipwreck with the ship,
And gazed upon him sallow from the storm.
Or if Delusion came, 'twas but to show
The coming minute mock the one that went.
Cold as a mountain in its star-pitched tent,
Stood high Philosophy, less friend than foe:
Whom self-caged Passion, from its prison-bars,
Is always watching with a wondering hate.   10
Not till the fire is dying in the grate,
Look we for any kinship with the stars.
Oh, wisdom never comes when it is gold,
And the great price we pay for it full worth:
We have it only when we are half earth.
Little avails that coinage to the old!

5

A message from her set his brain aflame.
A world of household matters filled her mind,
Wherein he saw hypocrisy designed:
She treated him as something that is tame,
And but at other provocation bites.
Familiar was her shoulder in the glass,
Through that dark rain: yet it may come to pass
That a changed eye finds such familiar sights
More keenly tempting than new loveliness.
The "What has been" a moment seemed his own: 10
The splendours, mysteries, dearer because known,
Nor less divine: Love's inmost sacredness
Called to him, "Come!"—In his restraining start,
Eyes nurtured to be looked at scarce could see
A wave of the great waves of Destiny
Convulsed at a checked impulse of the heart.

6

It chanced his lips did meet her forehead cool.
She had no blush, but slanted down her eye.
Shamed nature, then, confesses love can die:
And most she punishes the tender fool
Who will believe what honours her the most!
Dead! is it dead? She has a pulse, and flow
Of tears, the price of blood-drops, as I know,
For whom the midnight sobs around Love's ghost,
Since then I heard her, and so will sob on.
The love is here; it has but changed its aim.   10
O bitter barren woman! what's the name?
The name, the name, the new name thou hast won?
Behold me striking the world's coward stroke!
That will I not do, though the sting is dire.
—Beneath the surface this, while by the fire
They sat, she laughing at a quiet joke.

7

She issues radiant from her dressing-room,
Like one prepared to scale an upper sphere:

—By stirring up a lower, much I fear!
How deftly that oiled barber lays his bloom!
That long-shanked dapper Cupid with frisked curls
Can make known women torturingly fair;
The gold-eyed serpent dwelling in rich hair
Awakes beneath his magic whisks and twirls.
His art can take the eyes from out my head,
Until I see with eyes of other men;   10
While deeper knowledge crouches in its den,
And sends a spark up:—is it true we are wed?
Yea! filthiness of body is most vile,
But faithlessness of heart I do hold worse.
The former, it were not so great a curse
To read on the steel-mirror of her smile.

8

Yet it was plain she struggled, and that salt
Of righteous feeling made her pitiful.
Poor twisting worm, so queenly beautiful!
Where came the cleft between us? whose the fault?
My tears are on thee, that have rarely dropped
As balm for any bitter wound of mine:
My breast will open for thee at a sign!
But, no: we are two reed-pipes, coarsely stopped:
The God once filled them with his mellow breath;
And they were music till he flung them down,   10
Used! used!   Hear now the discord-loving clown
Puff his gross spirit in them, worse than death!
I do not know myself without thee more:
In this unholy battle I grow base:
If the same soul be under the same face,
Speak, and a taste of that old time restore!

9

He felt the wild beast in him betweenwhiles
So masterfully rude, that he would grieve
To see the helpless delicate thing receive
His guardianship through certain dark defiles.
Had he not teeth to rend, and hunger too?

But still he spared her. Once: "Have you no fear?"
He said: 'twas dusk; she in his grasp; none near.
She laughed: "No, surely; am I not with you?"
And uttering that soft starry "you," she leaned
Her gentle body near him, looking up;   10
And from her eyes, as from a poison-cup,
He drank until the flittering eyelids screened.
Devilish malignant witch! and oh, young beam
Of heaven's circle-glory! Here thy shape
To squeeze like an intoxicating grape—
I might, and yet thou goest safe, supreme.

10

But where began the change; and what's my crime?
The wretch condemned, who has not been arraigned,
Chafes at his sentence. Shall I, unsustained,
Drag on Love's nerveless body through all time?
I must have slept, since now I wake. Prepare,
You lovers, to know Love a thing of moods:
Not, like hard life, of laws. In Love's deep woods,
I dreamt of loyal Life:—the offense is there!
Love's jealous woods about the sun are curled;
At least, the sun far brighter there did beam.—   10
My crime is, that the puppet of a dream,
I plotted to be worthy of the world.
Oh, had I with my darling helped to mince
The facts of life, you still had seen me go
With hindward feather and with forward toe,
Her much-adored delightful Fairy Prince!

11

Out in the yellow meadows, where the bee
Hums by us with the honey of the Spring,
And showers of sweet notes from the larks on wing
Are dropping like a noon-dew, wander we.
Or is it now? or was it then? for now,
As then, the larks from running rings pour showers:
The golden foot of May is on the flowers,
And friendly shadows dance upon her brow.

What's this, when Nature swears there is no change
To challenge eyesight? Now, as then, the grace   10
Of heaven seems holding earth in its embrace.
Nor eyes, nor heart, has she to feel it strange?
Look, woman, in the West. There wilt thou see
An amber cradle near the sun's decline:
Within it, featured even in death divine,
Is lying a dead infant, slain by thee.

12

Not solely that the Future she destroys,
And the fair life which in the distance lies
For all men, beckoning out from dim rich skies:
Nor that the passing hour's supporting joys
Have lost the keen-edged flavour, which begat
Distinction in old times, and still should breed
Sweet Memory, and Hope,—earth's modest seed,
And heaven's high-prompting: not that the world is flat
Since that soft-luring creature I embraced
Among the children of Illusion went: 10
Methinks with all this loss I were content,
If the mad Past, on which my foot is based,
Were firm, or might be blotted: but the whole
Of life is mixed: the mocking Past will stay:
And if I drink oblivion of a day,
So shorten I the stature of my soul.

13

"I play for Seasons; not Eternities!"
Says Nature, laughing on her way. "So must
All those whose stake is nothing more than dust!"
And lo, she wins, and of her harmonies
She is full sure! Upon her dying rose
She drops a look of fondness, and goes by,
Scarce any retrospection in her eye;
For she the laws of growth most deeply knows,
Whose hands bear, here, a seed-bag—there, an urn.
Pledged she herself to aught, 'twould mark her end!   10
This lesson of our only visible friend

Can we not teach our foolish hearts to learn?
Yes! yes!—but, oh, our human rose is fair
Surpassingly! Lose calmly Love's great bliss,
When the renewed forever of a kiss
Whirls life within the shower of loosened hair!

14

What soul would bargain for a cure that brings
Contempt the nobler agony to kill?
Rather let me bear on the bitter ill,
And strike this rusty bosom with new stings!
It seems there is another veering fit,
Since on a gold-haired lady's eyeballs pure
I looked with little prospect of a cure,
The while her mouth's red bow loosed shafts of wit.
Just heaven! can it be true that jealousy
Has decked the woman thus? and does her head   10
Swim somewhat for possessions forfeited?
Madam, you teach me many things that be.
I open an old book, and there I find
That "Women still may love whom they deceive."
Such love I prize not, madam: by your leave,
The game you play at is not to my mind.

15

I think she sleeps: it must be sleep, when low
Hangs that abandoned arm toward the floor;
The face turned with it. Now make fast the door.
Sleep on: it is your husband, not your foe.
The Poet's black stage-lion of wronged love
Frights not our modern dames:—well if he did!
Now will I pour new light upon that lid,
Full-sloping like the breasts beneath. "Sweet dove,
Your sleep is pure. Nay, pardon: I disturb.
I do not? good!" Her waking infant-stare   10
Grows woman to the burden my hands bear:
Her own handwriting to me when no curb
Was left on Passion's tongue. She trembles through;
A woman's tremble—the whole instrument:—

I show another letter lately sent.
The words are very like: the name is new.

16

In our old shipwrecked days there was an hour,
When in the firelight steadily aglow,
Joined slackly, we beheld the red chasm grow
Among the clicking coals.   Our library-bower
That eve was left to us: and hushed we sat
As lovers to whom Time is whispering.
From sudden-opened doors we heard them sing:
The nodding elders mixed good wine with chat.
Well knew we that Life's greatest treasure lay
With us, and of it was our talk.   "Ah, yes!   10
Love dies!" I said: I never thought it less.
She yearned to me that sentence to unsay.
Then when the fire domed blackening, I found
Her cheek was salt against my kiss, and swift
Up the sharp scale of sobs her breast did lift:—
Now am I haunted by that taste! that sound!

17

At dinner, she is hostess, I am host.
Went the feast ever cheerfuller?   She keeps
The Topic over intellectual deeps
In buoyancy afloat.   They see no ghost.
With sparkling surface-eyes we ply the ball:
It is in truth a most contagious game:
Hiding the Skeleton, shall be its name.
Such play as this the devils might appal!
But here's the greater wonder: in that we,
Enamored of an acting naught can tire,   10
Each other, like true hypocrites, admire;
Warm-lighted looks, Love's ephemerioë,
Shoot gayly o'er the dishes and the wine.
We waken envy of our happy lot.
Fast, sweet, and golden, shows the marriage-knot.
Dear guests, you now have seen Love's corpse-light shine.

18

Here Jack and Tom are paired with Moll and Meg.
Curved open to the river-reach is seen
A country merry-making on the green.
Fair space for signal shakings of the leg.
That little screwy fiddler from his booth,
Whence flows one nut-brown stream, commands the
    joints
Of all who caper here at various points.
I have known rustic revels in my youth:
The May-fly pleasures of a mind at ease.
An early goddess was a country lass: 10
A charmed Amphion-oak she tripped the grass.
What life was that I lived?   The life of these?
Heaven keep them happy!   Nature they seem near.
They must, I think, be wiser than I am;
They have the secret of the bull and lamb.
'Tis true that when we trace its source, 'tis beer.

19

No state is enviable.   To the luck alone
Of some few favored men I would put claim.
I bleed, but her who wounds I will not blame.
Have I not felt her heart as 'twere my own
Beat through me? could I hurt her? heaven and hell!
But I could hurt her cruelly!   Can I let
My Love's old time-piece to another set,
Swear it can't stop, and must forever swell?
Sure, that's one way Love drifts into the mart
Where goat-legged buyers throng.   I see not plain:—   10
My meaning is, it must not be again.
Great God! the maddest gambler throws his heart.
If any state be enviable on earth,
'Tis yon born idiot's, who, as days go by,
Still rubs his hands before him, like a fly,
In a queer sort of meditative mirth.

20

I am not of those miserable males
Who sniff at vice and, daring not to snap,

Do therefore hope for heaven. I take the hap
Of all my deeds. The wind that fills my sails
Propels; but I am helmsman. Am I wrecked,
I know the devil has sufficient weight
To bear: I lay it not on him, or fate.
Besides, he's damned. That man I do suspect
A coward, who would burden the poor deuce
With what ensues from his own slipperiness.   10
I have just found a wanton-scented tress
In an old desk, dusty for lack of use.
Of days and nights it is demonstrative,
That, like some agéd star, gleam luridly.
If for those times I must ask charity,
Have I not any charity to give?

21

We three are on the cedar-shadowed lawn;
My friend being third. He who at love once laughed
Is in the weak rib by a fatal shaft
Struck through, and tells his passion's bashful dawn
And radiant culmination, glorious crown,
When "this" she said: went "thus": most wondrous she.
Our eyes grow white, encountering: that we are three,
Forgeful; then together we look down.
But he demands our blessing; is convinced
That words of wedded lovers must bring good.   10
We question; if we dare! or if we should!
And pat him, with light laugh. We have not winced.
Next, she has fallen. Fainting points the sign
To happy things in wedlock. When she wakes,
She looks the star that through the cedar shakes:
Her lost moist hand clings mortally to mine.

22

What may the woman labor to confess?
There is about her mouth a nervous twitch.
'Tis something to be told, or hidden:—which?
I get a glimpse of hell in this mild guess.
She has desires of touch, as if to feel

That all the household things are things she knew.
She stops before the glass. What sight in view?
A face that seems the latest to reveal!
For she turns from it hastily, and tossed
Irresolute steals shadow-like to where   10
I stand; and wavering pale before me there,
Her tears fall still as oak-leaves after frost.
She will not speak. I will not ask. We are
League-sundered by the silent gulf between.
You burly lovers on the village green,
Yours is a lower, and a happier star!

23

'Tis Christmas weather, and a country house
Receives us: rooms are full: we can but get
An attic-crib. Such lovers will not fret
At that, it is half-said. The great carouse
Knocks hard upon the midnight's hollow door,
But when I knock at hers, I see the pit.
Why did I come here in that dullard fit?
I enter, and lie couched upon the floor.
Passing, I caught the coverlet's quick beat:—
Come, Shame, burn to my soul! and Pride, and Pain—   10
Foul demons that have tortured me, enchain!
Out in the freezing darkness the lambs bleat.
The small bird stiffens in the low starlight.
I know not how, but shuddering as I slept,
I dreamed a banished angel to me crept:
My feet were nourished on her breasts all night.

24

The misery is greater, as I live!
To know her flesh so pure, so keen her sense,
That she does penance now for no offense,
Save against Love. The less can I forgive!
The less can I forgive, though I adore
That cruel lovely pallor which surrounds
Her footsteps; and the low vibrating sounds
That come on me, as from a magic shore.

Low are they, but most subtle to find out
The shrinking soul. Madam, 'tis understood   10
When women play upon their womanhood,
It means, a Season gone. And yet I doubt
But I am duped. That nun-like look waylays
My fancy. Oh! I do but wait a sign!
Pluck out the eyes of pride! thy mouth to mine!
Never! though I die thirsting. Go thy ways!

25

You like not that French novel? Tell me why.
You think it quite unnatural. Let us see.
The actors are, it seems, the usual three:
Husband, and wife, and lover. She—but fie!
In England we'll not hear of it. Edmond,
The lover, her devout chagrin doth share;
Blancmange and absinthe are his penitent fare,
Till his pale aspect makes her over-fond:
So, to preclude fresh sin, he tries *rosbif*.
Meantime the husband is no more abused: 10
Auguste forgives her ere the tear is used.
Then hangeth all on one tremendous IF:—
If she will choose between them. She does choose;
And takes her husband, like a proper wife.
Unnatural? My dear, these things are life:
And life, some think, is worthy of the Muse.

26

Love ere he bleeds, an eagle in high skies,
Has earth beneath his wings: from reddened eve
He views the rosy dawn. In vain they weave
The fatal web below while far he flies.
But when the arrow strikes him, there's a change.
He moves but in the track of his spent pain,
Whose red drops are the links of a harsh chain,
Binding him to the ground, with narrow range.
A subtle serpent then has Love become.
I had the eagle in my bosom erst: 10
Henceforward with the serpent I am cursed.
I can interpret where the mouth is dumb.

Speak, and I see the side-lie of a truth.
Perchance my heart may pardon you this deed:
But be no coward:—you that made Love bleed,
You must bear all the venom of his tooth!

27

Distraction is the panacea, Sir!
I hear my oracle of Medicine say.
Doctor! that same specific yesterday
I tried, and the result will not deter
A second trial. Is the devil's line
Of golden hair, or raven black, composed?
And does a cheek, like any sea-shell rosed,
Or clear as widowed sky, seem most divine?
No matter, so I taste forgetfulness.
And if the devil snare me, body and mind,   10
Here gratefully I score:—he seeméd kind,
When not a soul would comfort my distress!
O sweet new world, in which I rise new made!
O Lady, once I gave love: now I take!
Lady, I must be flattered. Shouldst thou wake
The passion of a demon, be not afraid.

28

I must be flattered. The imperious
Desire speaks out. Lady, I am content
To play with you the game of Sentiment,
And with you enter on paths perilous;
But if across your beauty I throw light,
To make it threefold, it must be all mine.
First secret; then avowed. For I must shine
Envied,—I, lessened in my proper sight!
Be watchful of your beauty, Lady dear!
How much hangs on that lamp you cannot tell.   10
Most earnestly I pray you, tend it well:
And men shall see me as a burning sphere;
And men shall mark you eyeing me, and groan
To be the God of such a grand sunflower!
I feel the promptings of Satanic power,
While you do homage unto me alone.

29

Am I failing? For no longer can I cast
A glory round about this head of gold.
Glory she wears, but springing from the mold;
Not like the consecration of the Past!
Is my soul beggared? Something more than earth
I cry for still; I cannot be at peace
In having Love upon a mortal lease.
I cannot take the woman at her worth!
Where is the ancient wealth wherewith I clothed
Our human nakedness, and could endow   10
With spiritual splendour a white brow
That else had grinned at me the fact I loathed?
A kiss is but a kiss now! and no wave
Of a great flood that whirls me to the sea.
But, as you will! we'll sit contentedly,
And eat our pot of honey on the grave.

30

What are we first? First, animals; and next
Intelligences at a leap; on whom
Pale lies the distant shadow of the tomb,
And all that draweth on the tomb for text.
Into which state comes Love, the crowning sun:
Beneath whose light the shadow loses form.
We are the lords of life, and life is warm.
Intelligence and instinct now are one.
But Nature says: "My children most they seem
When they least know me: therefore I decree   10
That they shall suffer." Swift doth young Love flee,
And we stand wakened, shivering from our dream.
Then if we study Nature we are wise.
Thus do the few who live but with the day:
The scientific animals are they.—
Lady, this is my sonnet to your eyes.

31

This golden head has wit in it. I live
Again, and a far higher life, near her.

Some women like a young philosopher;
Perchance because he is diminutive.
For woman's manly god must not exceed
Proportions of the natural nursing size.
Great poets and great sages draw no prize
With women: but the little lap-dog breed,
Who can be hugged, or on a mantel-piece
Perched up for adoration, these obtain   10
Her homage. And of this we men are vain?
Of this! 'Tis ordered for the world's increase!
Small flattery! Yet she has that rare gift
To beauty, Common Sense. I am approved.
It is not half so nice as being loved,
And yet I do prefer it. What's my drift?

32

Full faith I have she holds that rarest gift
To beauty, Common Sense. To see her lie
With her fair visage an inverted sky
Bloom-covered, while the underlids uplift,
Would almost wreck the faith; but when her mouth
(Can it kiss sweetly? sweetly!) would address
The inner me that thirsts for her no less,
And has so long been languishing in drouth,
I feel that I am matched; that I am man!
One restless corner of my heart or head,   10
That holds a dying something never dead,
Still frets, though Nature giveth all she can.
It means, that woman is not, I opine,
Her sex's antidote. Who seeks the asp
For serpents' bites? 'Twould calm me could I clasp
Shrieking Bacchantes with their souls of wine!

33

"In Paris, at the Louvre, there have I seen
The sumptuously-feathered angel pierce
Prone Lucifer, descending. Looked he fierce,
Showing the fight a fair one? Too serene!
The young Pharsalians did not disarray

Less willingly their locks of floating silk:
That suckling mouth of his upon the milk
Of heaven might still be feasting through the fray.
Oh, Raphael! when men the Fiend do fight,
They conquer not upon such easy terms.   10
Half serpent in the struggle grow these worms.
And does he grow half human, all is right."
This to my Lady in a distant spot,
Upon the theme: *While mind is mastering clay,*
Gross clay invades it.   If the spy you play,
My wife, read this!   Strange love-talk, is it not?

34

Madam would speak with me.   So, now it comes:
The Deluge or else Fire!   She's well; she thanks
My husbandship.   Our chain on silence clanks.
Time leers between, above his twiddling thumbs.
Am I quite well?   Most excellent in health!
The journals, too, I diligently peruse.
Vesuvius is expected to give news:
Niagara is no noisier.   By stealth
Our eyes dart scrutinizing snakes.   She's glad
I'm happy, says her quivering under-lip.   10
"And are not you?"   "How can I be?"   "Take ship!
For happiness is somewhere to be had."
"Nowhere for me!"   Her voice is barely heard.
I am not melted, and make no pretense.
With commonplace I freeze her, tongue and sense.
Niagara or Vesuvius is deferred.

35

It is no vulgar nature I have wived.
Secretive, sensitive, she takes a wound
Deep to her soul, as if the sense had swooned,
And not a thought of vengeance had survived.
No confidences has she: but relief
Must come to one whose suffering is acute.
O have a care of natures that are mute!
They punish you in acts: their steps are brief.
What is she doing?   What does she demand

From Providence or me?   She is not one   10
Long to endure this torpidly, and shun
The drugs that crowd about a woman's hand.
At Forfeits during snow we played, and I
Must kiss her.   "Well performed!" I said: then she:
" 'Tis hardly worth the money, you agree?"
Save her?   What for?   To act this wedded lie!

36

My Lady unto Madam makes her bow.
The charm of women is, that even while
You're probed by them for tears, you yet may smile,
Nay, laugh outright, as I have done just now.
The interview was gracious: they anoint
(To me aside) each other with fine praise:
Discriminating compliments they raise,
That hit with wondrous aim on the weak point:
My Lady's nose of Nature might complain.
It is not fashioned aptly to express   10
Her character of large-browed steadfastness.
But Madam says: Thereof she may be vain!
Now, Madam's faulty feature is a glazed
And inaccessible eye, that has soft fires,
Wide gates, at love-time, only.   This admires
My Lady.   At the two I stand amazed.

37

Along the garden terrace, under which
A purple valley (lighted at its edge
By smoky torch-flame on the long cloud-ledge
Whereunder dropped the chariot) glimmers rich,
A quiet company we pace, and wait
The dinner-bell in prae-digestive calm.
So sweet up violet banks the Southern balm
Breathes round, we care not if the bell be late:
Though here and there gray seniors question Time
In irritable coughings.   With slow foot   10
The low rosed moon, the face of Music mute,
Begins among her silent bars to climb.
As in and out, in silvery dusk, we thread,

I hear the laugh of Madam, and discern
My Lady's heel before me at each turn.
Our tragedy, is it alive or dead?

38

Give to imagination some pure light
In human form to fix it, or you shame
The devils with that hideous human game:—
Imagination urging appetite!
Thus fallen have earth's greatest Gogmagogs,
Who dazzle us, whom we cannot revere:
Imagination is the charioteer
That, in default of better, drives the hogs.
So, therefore, my dear Lady, let me love!
My soul is arrowy to the light in you.   10
You know me that I never can renew
The bond that woman broke: what would you have?
'Tis Love, or Vileness! not a choice between,
Save petrifaction!   What does Pity here?
She killed a thing, and now it's dead, 'tis dear.
Oh, when you counsel me, think what you mean!

39

She yields: my Lady in her noblest mood
Has yielded: she, my golden-crownéd rose!
The bride of every sense! more sweet than those
Who breathe the violet breath of maidenhood.
O visage of still music in the sky!
Soft moon! I feel thy song, my fairest friend!
True harmony within can apprehend
Dumb harmony without. And hark! 'tis nigh!
Belief has struck the note of sound: a gleam
Of living silver shows me where she shook   10
Her long white fingers down the shadowy brook,
That sings her song, half waking, half in dream.
What two come here to mar this heavenly tune?
A man is one: the woman bears my name,
And honour. Their hands touch! Am I still tame?
God, what a dancing spectre seems the moon!

40

I bade my Lady think what she might mean.
Know I my meaning, I?   Can I love one,
And yet be jealous of another?   None
Commits such folly.   Terrible Love, I ween,
Has might, even dead, half sighing to upheave
The lightless seas of selfishness amain:
Seas that in a man's heart have no rain
To fall and still them.   Peace can I achieve,
By turning to this fountain-source of woe,
This woman, who's to Love as fire to wood?   10
She breathed the violet breath of maidenhood
Against my kisses once! but I say, No!
The thing is mocked at!   Helplessly afloat,
I know not what I do, whereto I strive.
The dread that my old love may be alive
Has seized my nursling new love by the throat.

41

How many a thing which we cast to the ground,
When others pick it up becomes a gem!
We grasp at all the wealth it is to them;
And by reflected light its worth is found.
Yet for us still 'tis nothing! and that zeal
Of false appreciation quickly fades.
This truth is little known to human shades,
How rare from their own instinct 'tis to feel!
They waste the soul with spurious desire,
That is not the ripe flame upon the bough.   10
We two have taken up a lifeless vow
To rob a living passion: dust for fire!
Madam is grave, and eyes the clock that tells
Approaching midnight.   We have struck despair
Into two hearts.   Oh, look we like a pair
Who for fresh nuptials joyfully yield all else?

42

I am to follow her.   There is much grace
In women when thus bent on martyrdom.

They think that dignity of soul may come,
Perchance, with dignity of body.   Base!
But I was taken by that air of cold
And statuesque sedateness, when she said
"I'm going"; lit a taper, bowed her head,
And went, as with the stride of Pallas bold.
Fleshly indifference horrible!   The hands
Of Time now signal: O, she's safe from me!   10
Within those secret walls what do I see?
Where first she set the taper down she stands:
Not Pallas: Hebe shamed!   Thoughts black as death
Like a stirred pool in sunshine break.   Her wrists
I catch: she faltering, as she half resists,
"You love . . . ? love . . . ? love . . . ?" all on an indrawn
    breath.

43

Mark where the pressing wind shoots javelin-like
Its skeleton shadow on the broad-backed wave!
Here is a fitting spot to dig Love's grave;
Here where the ponderous breakers plunge and strike,
And dart their hissing tongues high up the sand:
In hearing of the ocean, and in sight
Of those ribbed wind-streaks running into white.
If I the death of Love had deeply planned,
I never could have made it half so sure,
As by the unblest kisses which upbraid   10
The full-waked sense; or failing that, degrade!
'Tis morning: but no morning can restore
What we have forfeited.   I see no sin:
The wrong is mixed.   In tragic life, God wot,
No villain need be! Passions spin the plot:
We are betrayed by what is false within.

44

They say, that Pity in Love's service dwells,
A porter at the rosy temple's gate.
I missed him going: but it is my fate
To come upon him now beside his wells;

Whereby I know that I Love's temple leave,
And that the purple doors have closed behind.
Poor soul! if, in those early days unkind,
Thy power to sting had been but power to grieve,
We now might with an equal spirit meet,
And not be matched like innocence and vice.   10
She for the Temple's worship has paid price,
And takes the coin of Pity as a cheat.
She sees through simulation to the bone:
What's best in her impels her to the worst:
Never, she cries, shall Pity soothe Love's thirst,
Or foul hypocrisy for truth atone!

45

It is the season of the sweet wild rose,
My Lady's emblem in the heart of me!
So golden-crownéd shines she gloriously,
And with that softest dream of blood she glows:
Mild as an evening heaven round Hesper bright!
I pluck the flower, and smell it, and revive
The time when in her eyes I stood alive.
I seem to look upon it out of Night.
Here's Madam, stepping hastily.   Her whims
Bid her demand the flower, which I let drop.   10
As I proceed, I feel her sharply stop,
And crush it under heel with trembling limbs.
She joins me in a cat-like way, and talks
Of company, and even condescends
To utter laughing scandal of old friends.
These are the summer days, and these our walks.

46

At last we parley: we so strangely dumb
In such a close communion! It befell
About the sounding of the Matin-bell,
And lo! her place was vacant, and the hum
Of loneliness was round me. Then I rose,
And my disordered brain did guide my foot
To that old wood where our first love-salute

Was interchanged: the source of many throes!
There did I see her, not alone. I moved
Toward her, and made proffer of my arm.   10
She took it simply, with no rude alarm;
And that disturbing shadow passed reproved.
I felt the pained speech coming, and declared
My firm belief in her, ere she could speak.
A ghastly morning came into her cheek,
While with a widening soul on me she stared.

47

We saw the swallows gathering in the sky,
And in the osier-isle we heard them noise.
We had not to look back on summer joys,
Or forward to a summer of bright dye;
But in the largeness of the evening earth
Our spirits grew as we went side by side.
The hour became her husband and my bride.
Love, that had robbed us so, thus blessed our dearth!
The pilgrims of the year waxed very loud
In multitudinous chatterings, as the flood   10
Full brown came from the West, and like pale blood
Expanded to the upper crimson cloud.
Love, that had robbed us of immortal things,
This little moment mercifully gave,
Where I have seen across the twilight wave
The swan sail with her young beneath her wings.

48

Their sense is with their senses all mixed in,
Destroyed by subtleties these women are!
More brain, O Lord, more brain! or we shall mar
Utterly this fair garden we might win.
Behold! I looked for peace, and thought it near.
Our inmost hearts had opened, each to each.
We drank the pure daylight of honest speech.
Alas! that was the fatal draft, I fear.
For when of my lost Lady came the word,

This woman, O this agony of flesh!   10
Jealous devotion bade her break the mesh,
That I might seek that other like a bird.
I do adore the nobleness! despise
The act!   She has gone forth, I know not where.
Will the hard world my sentience of her share?
I feel the truth; so let the world surmise.

49

He found her by the ocean's moaning verge.
Nor any wicked change in her discerned;
And she believed his old love had returned,
Which was her exultation, and her scourge.
She took his hand, and walked with him, and seemed
The wife he sought, though shadow-like and dry.
She had one terror, lest her heart should sigh,
And tell her loudly she no longer dreamed.
She dared not say, "This is my breast: look in."
But there's a strength to help the desperate weak.   10
That night he learned how silence best can speak
The awful things when Pity pleads for Sin.
About the middle of the night her call
Was heard, and he came wondering to the bed.
"Now kiss me, dear! it may be, now!" she said.
Lethe had passed those lips, and he knew all.

50

Thus piteously Love closed what he begat:
The union of this ever-diverse pair!
These two were rapid falcons in a snare,
Condemned to do the flitting of the bat.
Lovers beneath the singing sky of May,
They wandered once; clear as the dew on flowers:
But they fed not on the advancing hours:
Their hearts held cravings for the buried day.
Then each applied to each that fatal knife,
Deep questioning, which probes to endless dole.   10
Ah, what a dusty answer gets the soul

When hot for certainties in this our life!—
In tragic hints here see what evermore
Moves dark as yonder midnight ocean's force,
Thundering like ramping hosts of warrior horse,
To throw that faint thin line upon the shore!

1862

Title: A husband, referred to as both "I" and "He," narrates ironic moments in the course of a dissolving marriage. His wife ("Madam") is drawn to another man and the husband begins an affair with a "Lady." After a separation the wife takes her life. The course of Meredith's first marriage is reflected in the poem.
Sonnet 1: l. 15: **sword** In medieval courtly love a naked sword laid in bed between two lovers symbolized their chastity; but here, their disaffection.
Sonnet 3: l. 1: **man** the "other man."
Sonnet 8: l. 8: **coarsely stopped** with holes, or "stops," not finely made; hence, poorly tuned.
Sonnet 15: l. 5: **stage-lion** probably Shakespeare's Othello, who out of jealousy murdered his wife.
Sonnet 17: l. 12: **ephemerioë** brief-lived things.
Sonnet 18: l. 5: **screwy** half-drunk.   l. 6: **stream** of ale.   l. 11: **Amphion-oak** dancing as trees did to the music of the lyre of Amphion, a son of Zeus.
Sonnet 19: l. 10: **goat-legged** lecherous.
Sonnet 20: l. 2: **sniff at . . . snap** are attracted by, but dare not partake.   l. 9: **deuce** devil.
Sonnet 21: l. 3: **weak rib** a man's fondness for women.
Sonnet 25: l. 9: **rosbif** roast beef, a strengthening diet.   l. 10: **abused** deceived.
Sonnet 33: l. 1: **Louvre** Raphael's painting shows the Archangel Michael in combat with fallen Lucifer.   l. 5: **Pharsalians** the dandified young Roman patricians who helped Julius Caesar defeat Pompey at the Battle of Pharsalus, 48 B.C.
Sonnet 35: l. 13: **Forfeits** "Kiss-in-the-Ring," a traditional holiday game, something like "Drop-the-Handkerchief," in which the winner may claim a kiss.
Sonnet 38: l. 5: **Gogmagogs** grotesque figures formerly carried in the Lord Mayor of London's annual parade; probably representing a pair of fabled British giants.
Sonnet 48: l. 10: **this woman** his wife.
Sonnet 49: l. 1: **He** the husband.

LOVE IN THE VALLEY

Under yonder beech-tree single on the greensward,
　　Couched with her arms behind her golden head,
Knees and tresses folded to slip and ripple idly,
　　Lies my young love sleeping in the shade.
Had I the heart to slide an arm beneath her,
　　Press her parting lips as her waist I gather slow,
Waking in amazement she could not but embrace me;
　　Then would she hold me and never let me go?

　　　　·　　·　　·　　·　　·

Shy as the squirrel and wayward as the swallow,
　　Swift as the swallow along the river's light　　　　　　　10
·Circleting the surface to meet his mirrored winglets,
　　Fleeter she seems in her stay than in her flight.
Shy as the squirrel that leaps among the pine-tops,
　　Wayward as the swallow overhead at set of sun,
She whom I love is hard to catch and conquer,
　　Hard, but O the glory of the winning were she won!

When her mother tends her before the laughing mirror,
　　Tying up her laces, looping up her hair,
Often she thinks, were this wild thing wedded,
　　More love should I have, and much less care.　　　　　20
When her mother tends her before the lighted mirror,
　　Loosening her laces, combing down her curls,
Often she thinks, were this wild thing wedded,
　　I should miss but one for many boys and girls.

　　　　·　　·　　·　　·

Heartless she is as the shadow in the meadows
　　Flying to the hills on a blue and breezy noon.
No, she is athirst and drinking up her wonder;
　　Earth to her is young as the slip of the new moon.
Deals she an unkindness, 'tis but her rapid measure,
　　Even as in a dance; and her smile can heal no less:　　30
Like the swinging May-cloud that pelts the flowers with hail-
　　　　stones
　　Off a sunny border, she was made to bruise and bless.

Lovely are the curves of the white owl sweeping
　　Wavy in the dusk lit by one large star.

Lone on the fir-branch, his rattle-note unvaried,
    Brooding o'er the gloom, spins the brown eve-jar.
Darker grows the valley, more and more forgetting:
    So were it with me if forgetting could be willed.
Tell the grassy hollow that holds the bubbling wellspring
    Tell it to forget the source that keeps it filled.   40

. . . . .

Stepping down the hill with her fair companions,
    Arm in arm, all against the raying West,
Boldly she sings, to the merry tune she marches,
    Brave in her shape, and sweeter unpossessed.
Sweeter, for she is what my heart first awaking
    Whispered the world was; morning light is she.
Love that so desires would fain keep her changeless;
    Fain would fling the net, and fain have her free.

Happy happy time, when the white star hovers
    Low over dim fields fresh with gloomy dew,   50
Near the face of dawn, that draws athwart the darkness,
    Threading it with color, like yewberries the yew.
Thicker crowd the shades as the grave East deepens
    Glowing, and with crimson a long cloud swells.
Maiden still the morn is; and strange she is, and secret;
    Strange her eyes; her cheeks are cold as cold seashells.

. . . . .

Sunrays, leaning on our southern hills and lighting
    Wild cloud-mountains that drag the hills along,
Oft ends the day of your shifting brilliant laughter
    Chill as a dull face frowning on a song.   60
Aye, but shows the Southwest a ripple-feathered bosom
    Blown to silver while the clouds are shaken and ascend,
Scaling the mid-heavens as they stream—there comes a sunset
    Rich, deep like love in beauty without end.

When at dawn she sighs, and like an infant to the window
    Turns grave eyes craving light, released from dreams,
Beautiful she looks, like a white water-lily
    Bursting out of bud in havens of the streams.
When from bed she rises clothed from neck to ankle
    In her long nightgown sweet as boughs of May,   70

Beautiful she looks, like a tall garden lily
    Pure from the night, and splendid for the day.

      .   .   .   .

Mother of the dews, dark eye-lashed twilight,
    Low-lidded twilight, o'er the valley's brim,
Rounding on thy breast sings the dew-delighted skylark,
    Clear as though the dewdrops had their voice in him.
Hidden where the rose-flush drinks the rayless planet,
    Fountain-full he pours the spraying fountain-showers.
Let me hear her laughter, I would have her ever
    Cool as dew in twilight, the lark above the flowers.   80

All the girls are out with their baskets for the primrose;
    Up lanes, woods through, they troop in joyful bands.
My sweet leads; she knows not why, but now she loiters,
    Eyes the bent anemones, and hangs her hands.
Such a look will tell that the violets are peeping,
    Coming the rose; and unaware a cry
Springs in her bosom for odours and for colour,
    Covert and the nightingale—she knows not why.

      .   .   .   .

Kerchiefed head and chin she darts between her tulips,
    Streaming like a willow gray in arrowy rain.   90
Some bend beaten cheek to gravel, and their angel
    She will be; she lifts them, and on she speeds again.
Black the driving raincloud breasts the iron gateway;
    She is forth to cheer a neighbour lacking mirth.
So when sky and grass met rolling dumb for thunder
    Saw I once a white dove, sole light of earth.

Prim little scholars are the flowers of her garden,
    Trained to stand in rows, and asking if they please.
I might love them well but for loving more the wild ones—
    O my wild ones! they tell me more than these.   100
You, my wild one, you tell of honeyed fieldrose,
    Violet, blushing eglantine in life; and even as they,
They by the wayside are earnest of your goodness,
    You are of life's, on the banks that line the way.

      .   .   .   .

Peering at her chamber the white crowns the red rose,
    Jasmine winds the porch with stars two and three.

Parted is the window; she sleeps; the starry jasmine
    Breathes a falling breath that carries thoughts of me.
Sweeter unpossessed, have I said of her my sweetest?
    Not while she sleeps—while she sleeps the jasmine
        breathes,   110
Luring her to love; she sleeps; the starry jasmine
    Bears me to her pillow under white rose-wreaths.

Yellow with birdfoot-trefoil are the grass-glades;
    Yellow with cinquefoil of the dew-gray leaf;
Yellow with stonecrop; the moss-mounds are yellow;
    Blue-necked the wheat sways, yellowing to the sheaf.
Green-yellow bursts from the copse the laughing yaffle;
    Sharp as a sickle is the edge of shade and shine.
Earth in her heart laughs looking at the heavens,
    Thinking of the harvest: I look and think of mine.   120

.   .   .   .   .

This I may know: her dressing and undressing
    Such a change of light shows as when the skies in sport
Shift from cloud to moonlight; or edging over thunder
    Slips a ray of sun; or sweeping into port
White sails furl; or on the ocean borders
    White sails lean along the waves leaping green.
Visions of her shower before me, but from eyesight
    Guarded she would be like the sun were she seen.

Front door and back of the mossed old farmhouse
    Open with the morn; and in a breezy link   130
Freshly sparkles garden to stripe-shadowed orchard,
    Green across a rill where on sand the minnows wink.
Busy in the grass the early sun of summer
    Swarms, and the blackbird's mellow fluting notes
Call my darling up with round and roguish challenge—
    Quaintest, richest carol of all the singing throats!

.   .   .   .   .

Cool was the woodside; cool as her white dairy
    Keeping sweet the cream-pan; and there the boys from school,
Cricketing below, rushed brown and red with sunshine;
    O the dark translucence of the deep-eyed cool!   140
Spying from the farm, herself she fetched a pitcher
    Full of milk, and tilted for each in turn the beak.

Then a little fellow, mouth up and on tiptoe,
    Said, "I will kiss you"; she laughed and leaned her cheek.

Doves of the fir-wood walling high our red roof
    Through the long noon coo, crooning through the coo.
Loose droop the leaves, and down the sleepy roadway
    Sometimes pipes a chaffinch; loose droops the blue.
Cows flap a slow tail knee-deep in the river,
    Breathless, given up to sun and gnat and fly.   150
Nowhere is she seen; and if I see her nowhere,
    Lightning may come, straight rains and tiger sky.

.   .   .   .   .

O the golden sheaf, the rustling treasure-armful!
    O the nutbrown tresses nodding interlaced!
O the treasure-tresses one another over
    Nodding! O the girdle slack about the waist!
Slain are the poppies that shot their random scarlet
    Quick amid the wheatears; wound about the waist,
Gathered, see these brides of Earth one blush of ripeness!
    O the nutbrown tresses nodding interlaced!   160

Large and smoky red the sun's cold disk drops,
    Clipped by naked hills, on violet shaded snow;
Eastward large and still lights up a bower of moonrise,
    Whence at her leisure steps the moon aglow.
Nightlong on black print-branches our beech-tree
    Gazes in this whiteness; nightlong could I.
Here may life on death or death on life be painted.
    Let me clasp her soul to know she cannot die!

.   .   .   .   .

Gossips count her faults; they scour a narrow chamber
    Where there is no window, read not heaven or her.   170
"When she was a tiny," one aged woman quavers,
    Plucks at my heart and leads me by the ear.
Faults she had once as she learned to run and tumbled:
    Faults of feature some see, beauty not complete.
Yet, good gossips, beauty that makes holy
    Earth and air, may have faults from head to feet.

Hither she comes; she comes to me; she lingers,
    Deepens her brown eyebrows, while in new surprise

High rise the lashes in wonder of a stranger;
    Yet am I the light and living of her eyes.   180
Something friends have told her fills her heart to brimming,
    Nets her in her blushes, and wounds her, and tames.—
Sure of her haven, O like a dove alighting,
    Arms up, she dropped; our souls were in our names.

       .   .   .   .   .

Soon will she lie like a white-frost sunrise.
    Yellow oats and brown wheat, barley pale as rye,
Long since your sheaves have yielded to the thresher,
    Felt the girdle loosened, seen the tresses fly.
Soon will she lie like a blood-red sunset.
    Swift with the tomorrow, green-winged Spring!   190
Sing from the Southwest, bring her back the truants,
    Nightingale and swallow, song and dipping wing.

Soft new beech-leaves, up to beamy April
    Spreading bough on bough a primrose mountain, you
Lucid in the moon, raise lilies to the sky fields,
    Youngest green transfused in silver shining through—
Fairer than the lily, than the wild white cherry;
    Fair as in image my seraph love appears
Borne to me by dreams when dawn is at my eyelids;
    Fair as in the flesh she swims to me on tears.   200

       .   .   .   .   .

Could I find a place to be alone with heaven,
    I would speak my heart out; heaven is my need.
Every woodland tree is flushing like the dogwood,
    Flashing like the whitebeam, swaying like the reed—
Flushing like the dogwood crimson in October;
    Streaming like the flag-reed Southwest blown;
Flashing as in gusts the sudden-lighted whitebeam.
    All seem to know what is for heaven alone.

                                       1878

PHOEBUS WITH ADMETUS

I

When by Zeus relenting the mandate was revoked,
    Sentencing to exile the bright Sun-God,
Mindful were the ploughmen of who the steer had yoked,
    Who: and what a track showed the upturned sod!
Mindful were the shepherds as now the noon severe
    Bent a burning eyebrow to brown evetide,
How the rustic flute drew the silver to the sphere,
    Sister of his own, till her rays fell wide.
        God! of whom music
        And song and blood are pure,   10
        The day is never darkened
        That had thee here obscure.

II

Chirping none the scarlet cicalas crouched in ranks:
    Slack the thistle-head piled its down-silk grey:
Scarce the stony lizard sucked hollows in his flanks:
    Thick on spots of umbrage our drowsed flocks lay.
Sudden bowed the chestnuts beneath a wind unheard,
    Lengthened ran the grasses, the sky grew slate:
Then amid a swift flight of winged seed white as curd,
    Clear of limb a Youth smote the master's gate.   20
        God! of whom music
        And song and blood are pure,
        The day is never darkened
        That had thee here obscure.

III

Water, first of singers, o'er rocky mount and mead,
    First of earthly singers, the sun-loved rill,
Sang of him, and flooded the ripples on the reed,
    Seeking whom to waken and what ear fill.
Water, sweetest soother to kiss a wound and cool,
    Sweetest and divinest, the sky-born brook,   30
Chuckled, with a whimper, and made a mirror-pool
    Round the guest we welcomed, the strange hand shook.

God! of whom music
And song and blood are pure,
The day is never darkened
That had thee here obscure.

IV

Many swarms of wild bees descended on our fields;
   Stately stood the wheatstalk with head bent high:
Big of heart we laboured at storing mighty yields,
   Wool and corn, and clusters to make men cry!   40
Hand-like rushed the vintage; we strung the bellied skins
   Plump, and at the sealing the Youth's voice rose:
Maidens clung in circle, on little fists their chins;
   Gentle beasties through pushed a cold long nose.
     God! of whom music
     And song and blood are pure,
     The day is never darkened
     That had thee here obscure.

V

Foot to fire in snowtime we trimmed the slender shaft:
   Often down the pit spied the lean wolf's teeth   50
Grin against his will, trapped by masterstrokes of craft;
   Helpless in his froth-wrath as green logs seethe!
Safe the tender lambs tugged the teats, and winter sped
   Whirled before the crocus, the year's new gold.
Hung the hooky beak up aloft the arrow head
   Reddened through his feathers for our dear fold.
     God! of whom music
     And song and blood are pure,
     The day is never darkened
     That had thee here obscure.   60

VI

Tales we drank of giants at war with Gods above:
   Rocks were they to look on, and earth climbed air!
Tales of search for simples, and those who sought of love
   Ease because the creature was all too fair.
Pleasant ran our thinking that while our work was good,
   Sure as fruits for sweat would the praise come fast.

He that wrestled stoutest and tamed the billow-brood
    Danced in rings with girls, like a sail-flapped mast.
      God! of whom music
      And song and blood are pure,   70
      The day is never darkened
      That had thee here obscure.

VII

Lo, the herb of healing, when once the herb is known,
    Shines in shady woods bright as new-sprung flame.
Ere the string was tightened we heard the mellow tone,
    After he had taught how the sweet sounds came.
Stretched about his feet, labour done, 'twas as you see
    Red pomegranates tumble and burst hard rind.
So began contention to give delight and be
    Excellent in things aimed to make life kind.   80
      God! of whom music
      And song and blood are pure,
      The day is never darkened
      That had thee here obscure.

VIII

You with shelly horns, rams! and promontory goats,
    You whose browsing beards dip in coldest dew!
Bulls, that walk the pastures in kingly-flashing coats!
    Laurel, ivy, vine, wreathed for feasts not few!
You that build the shade-roof, and you that court the rays,
    You that leap besprinkling the rock stream-rent: 90
He has been our fellow, the morning of our days;
    Us he chose for housemates, and this way went.
      God! of whom music
      And song and blood are pure,
      The day is never darkened
      That had thee here obscure.

                                            1880

Title: For having slain the Cyclops, Apollo was sentenced to serve Admetus, King of Thessaly, in the form of a shepherd. The poem is spoken after his departure.

LUCIFER IN STARLIGHT

On a starred night Prince Lucifer uprose.
Tired of his dark dominion, swung the fiend
Above the rolling ball, in cloud part screened,
Where sinners hugged their spectre of repose.
Poor prey to his hot fit of pride were those.
And now upon his western wing he leaned,
Now his huge bulk o'er Afric's sands careened,
Now the black planet shadowed Arctic snows.
Soaring through wider zones that pricked his scars
With memory of the old revolt from Awe,   10
He reached a middle height, and at the stars,
Which are the brain of heaven, he looked, and sank.
Around the ancient track marched, rank on rank,
The army of unalterable law.

                                                    1883

Title: Meredith's sonnet is a sequel to Milton's description of Satan's first approach to the newly created world (*Paradise Lost*, II, 1034–55).

MELAMPUS

With love exceeding a simple love of things
    That glide in grasses and rubble of woody wreck;
Or change their perch on a beat of quivering wings
    From branch to branch, only restful to pipe and peck;
Or, bristled, curl at a touch their snouts in a ball;
    Or cast their web between bramble and thorny hook;
The good physician Melampus, loving them all,
    Among them walked, as a scholar who reads a book.

For him the woods were a home and gave him the key
    Of knowledge, thirst for their treasures in herbs and flowers,   10
The secrets held by the creatures nearer than we
    To earth he sought and the link of their life with ours:
And where alike we are, unlike where, and the veined
    Division, veined parallel, of a blood that flows
In them, in us, from the source by man unattained
    Save marks he well what the mystical woods disclose.

And this he deemed might be boon of love to a breast
    Embracing tenderly each little motive shape,
The prone, the flitting, who seek their food whither best
    Their wits direct, whither best from their foes escape;   20
For closer drawn to our mother's natural milk,
    As babes they learn where her motherly help is great:
They know the juice for the honey, juice for the silk,
    And, need they medical antidotes, find them straight.

Of earth and sun they are wise, they nourish their broods,
    Weave, build, hive, burrow, and battle, take joy and pain
Like swimmers varying billows. Never in woods
    Runs white insanity fleeing itself; all sane
The woods revolve: as the tree its shadowing limns
    To some resemblance in motion, the rooted life   30
Restrains disorder; you hear the primitive hymns
    Of earth in woods issue wild of the web of strife.

Now sleeping once on a day of marvelous fire,
    A brood of snakes he had cherished in grave regret
That death his people had dealt their dam and their sire,
    Through savage dread of them, crept to his neck, and set
Their tongues to lick him. The swift affectionate tongue
    Of each ran licking the slumberer; then his ears
A forked red tongue tickled shrewdly; sudden upsprung,
    He heard a voice piping: Ay, for he has no fears!   40

A bird said that, in the notes of birds, and the speech
    Of men, it seemed; and another renewed: He moves
To learn and not to pursue, he gathers to teach;
    He feeds his young as do we, and as we love loves.
No fears have I of a man who goes with his head
    To earth, chance looking aloft at us, kind of hand.
I feel to him as to earth of whom we are fed;
    I pipe him much for his good could he understand.

Melampus touched at his ears, laid finger on wrist;
    He was not dreaming, he sensibly felt and heard   50
Above, through leaves, where the tree-twigs thick intertwist,
    He spied the birds and the bill of the speaking bird.
His cushion mosses in shades of various green,
    The lumped, the antlered, he pressed, while the sunny snake

Slipped under; drafts he had drunk of clear Hippocrene,
   It seemed, and sat with a gift of the gods awake.

Divinely thrilled was the man, exultingly full,
   As quick well-waters that come of the heart of earth,
Ere yet they dart in a brook are one bubble-pool
   To light and sound, wedding both at the leap of birth.   60
The soul of light vivid shone, a stream within stream;
   The soul of sound from a musical shell outflew;
Where others hear but a hum and see but a beam,
   The tongue and eye of the fountain of life he knew.

He knew the Hours: they were round him, laden with seed
   Of hours bestrewn upon vapour, and one by one
They winged as ripened in fruit the burden decreed
   For each to scatter; they flushed like the buds in sun,
Bequeathing seed to successive similar rings,
   Their sisters, bearers to men of what men have earned.   70
He knew them, talked with the yet unreddened; the stings,
   The sweets, they warmed at their bosoms divined, discerned.

Not unsolicited, sought by diligent feet,
   By riddling fingers expanded, oft watched in growth
With brooding deep as the noon-ray's quickening wheat,
   Ere touched, the pendulous flower of the plants of sloth,
The plants of rigidness, answered question and squeeze,
   Revealing wherefore it bloomed uninviting, bent,
Yet making harmony breathe of life and disease,
   The deeper chord of a wonderful instrument.   80

So passed he luminous-eyed for earth and the fates
   We arm to bruise or caress us; his ears were charged
With tones of love in a whirl of voluble hates,
   With music wrought of distraction his ear enlarged.
Celestial-shining, though mortal, singer, though mute,
   He drew the Master of harmonies, voiced or stilled,
To seek him; heard at the silent medicine-root
   A song, beheld in fulfillment the unfulfilled.

Him Phœbus, lending to darkness colour and form
   Of light's excess, many lessons and counsels gave;   90
Showed Wisdom lord of the human intricate swarm,
   And whence prophetic it looks on the hives that rave,

And how acquired, of the zeal of love to acquire,
    And where it stands, in the center of life a sphere;
And Measure, mood of the lyre, the rapturous lyre,
    He said was Wisdom, and struck him the notes to hear.

Sweet, sweet: 'twas glory of vision, honey, the breeze
    In heat, the run of the river on root and stone,
All senses joined, as the sister Pierides
    Are one, uplifting their chorus, the Nine, his own.   100
In stately order, evolved of sound into sight,
    From sight to sound intershifting, the man descried
The growths of earth, his adored, like day out of night,
    Ascend in song, seeing nature and song allied.

And there vitality, there, there solely in song,
    Resides, where earth and her uses to men, their needs,
Their forceful cravings, the theme are: there is it strong,
    The Master said: and the studious eye that reads
(Yea, even as earth to the crown of gods on the mount),
    In links divine with the lyrical tongue is bound.   110
Pursue thy craft: it is music drawn of a fount
    To spring perennial; well-spring is common ground.

Melampus dwelt among men: physician and sage,
    He served them, loving them, healing them; sick or maimed
Or them that frenzied in some delirious rage
    Outran the measure, his juice of the woods reclaimed.
He played on men, as his master, Phœbus, on strings
    Melodious; as the God did he drive and check,
Through love exceeding a simple love of the things
    That glide in grasses and rubble of woody wreck.   120

1883

Title: A prophet and physician who was endowed with the power to understand the speech of birds and animals as a reward for saving the lives of some magical serpents (ll. 33–40).   l. 65: **Hours** the Horae, goddesses of times and seasons.   l. 86: **Master** Phoebus Apollo.   l. 99: **Pierides** the Muses ("the Nine," l. 100) born at Pieria, near Mt. Olympus.

NATURE AND LIFE

Leave the uproar! At a leap
Thou shalt strike a woodland path,
Enter silence, not of sleep,
Under shadows, not of wrath;
Breath which is the spirit's bath,
In the old Beginnings find,
And endow them with a mind,
Seed for seedling, swathe for swathe.
That gives Nature to us, this
Give we her, and so we kiss.   10

Fruitful is it so—but hear
How within the shell thou art,
Music sounds; nor other near
Can to such a tremor start.
Of the waves our life is part;
They our running harvests bear—
Back to them for manful air,
Laden with the woodland's heart!
That gives Battle to us, this
Give we it, and good the kiss.   20

1888

ll. 11–14: **but hear . . . start**   that is, within our physical being ("shell")
sounds a music to which nothing else around responds.

HARD WEATHER

Bursts from a rending East in flaws
The young green leaflet's harrier, sworn
To strew the garden, strip the shaws,
And show our spring with banner torn.
Was ever such virago morn?
The wind has teeth, the wind has claws.
All the wind's wolves through woods are loose,
The wild wind's falconry aloft.
Shrill underfoot the grassblade shrews,
At gallop, clumped, and down the croft   10
Bestrid by shadows, beaten, tossed;
It seems a scythe, it seems a rod.

The howl is up at the howl's accost;
The shivers greet and the shivers nod.
Is the land ship? we are rolled, we drive
Tritonly, cleaving hiss and hum;
Whirl with the dead, or mount or dive,
Or down in dregs, or on in scum.
And drums the distant, pipes the near,
And vale and hill are gray in gray,   20
As when the surge is crumbling sheer,
And sea-mews wing the haze of spray.
Clouds—are they bony witches?—swarms,
Darting swift on the robber's flight,
Hurry an infant sky in arms:
It peeps, it becks; 'tis day, 'tis night.
Black while over the loop of blue
The swathe is closed, like shroud on corse.
Lo, as if swift the Furies flew,
The Fates at heel at a cry to horse!   30

Interpret me the savage whirr:
And is it Nature scourged, or she,
Her offspring's executioner,
Reducing land to barren sea?
But is there meaning in a day
When this fierce angel of the air,
Intent to throw, and haply slay,
Can, for what breath of life we bear
Exact the wrestle? Call to mind
The many meanings glistening up   40
When Nature to her nurslings kind,
Hands them the fruitage and the cup!
And seek we rich significance
Not otherwhere than with those tides
Of pleasure on the sunned expanse,
Whose flow deludes, whose ebb derides?

Look in the face of men who fare
Lock-mouthed, a match in lungs and thews
For this fierce angel of the air,
To twist with him and take his bruise.   50
That is the face beloved of old
Of Earth, young mother of her brood.
Nor broken for us shows the mold

When muscle is in mind renewed:
Though farther from her nature rude,
Yet nearer to her spirit's hold;
And though of gentler mood serene,
Still forceful of her fountain-jet.
So shall her blows be shrewdly met,
Be luminously read the scene   60
Where Life is at her grindstone set,
That she may give us edging keen,
String us for battle, till as play
The common strokes of fortune shower.
Such meaning in a dagger-day
Our wits may clasp to wax in power—
Yea, feel us warmer at her breast,
By spin of blood in lusty drill,
Than when her honeyed hands caressed,
And Pleasure, sapping, seemed to fill.   70

Behold the life at ease; it drifts.
The sharpened life commands its course.
She winnows, winnows roughly; sifts,
To dip her chosen in her source.
Contention is the vital force,
Whence pluck they brain, her prize of gifts,
Sky of the senses! on which height,
Not disconnected, yet released,
They see how spirit comes to light,
Through conquest of the inner beast,   80
Which Measure tames to movement sane,
In harmony with what is fair.
Never is Earth misread by brain:
That is the welling of her, there
The mirror—with one step beyond,
For likewise is it voice; and more:
Benignest kinship bids respond,
When wail the weak, and then restore
Whom days as fell as this may rive,
While Earth sits ebon in her gloom,   90
Us atomies of life alive
Unheeding, bent on life to come.
Her children of the labouring brain,
These are the champions of the race,

True parents, and the sole humane,
With understanding for their base
Earth yields the milk, but all her mind
Is vowed to thresh for stouter stock.
Her passion for old giantkind,
That scaled the mount, uphurled the rock,   100
Devolves on them who read aright
Her meaning and devoutly serve;
Nor in her starlessness of night
Peruse her with the craven nerve:
But even as she from grass to corn,
To eagle high from grubbing mole,
Prove in strong brain her noblest born,
The station for the flight of soul.

                                      1888

MEDITATION UNDER STARS

What links are ours with orbs that are
    So resolutely far?—
The solitary asks, and they
Give radiance as from a shield:
    Still at the death of day,
    The seen, the unrevealed.
    Implacable they shine
To us who would of Life obtain
An answer for the life we strain,
    To nourish with one sign.   10
Nor can imagination throw
The penetrative shaft: we pass
The breath of thought, who would divine
    If haply they may grow
As Earth; have our desire to know;
If life comes there to grain from grass,
And flowers like ours of toil and pain;
    Has passion to beat bar,
    Win space from cleaving brain;
    The mystic link attain,   20
    Whereby star holds on star.

Those visible immortals beam
    Allurement to the dream:

Ireful at human hungers brook
   No question in the look.
   Forever virgin to our sense,
   Remote they wane to gaze intense:
Prolong it, and in ruthlessness they smite
The beating heart behind the ball of sight:
   Till we conceive their heavens hoar,   30
   Those lights they raise but sparkles frore,
And Earth, our blood-warm Earth, a shuddering prey
To that frigidity of brainless ray.
Yet space is given for breath of thought
Beyond our bounds when musing: more
When to that musing love is brought,
And love is asked of love's wherefore.
'Tis Earth's, her gift; else have we naught:
Her gift, her secret, here our tie.
And not with her and yonder sky?   40
Bethink you: were it Earth alone
Breeds love, would not her region be
   The sole delight and throne
   Of generous Deity?

   To deeper than this ball of sight
Appeal the lustrous people of the night.
Fronting yon shoreless, sown with fiery sails,
   It is our ravenous that quails,
Flesh by its craven thirsts and fears distraught.
     The spirit leaps alight,   50
     Doubts not in them is he,
The binder of his sheaves, the same, the right:
Of magnitude to magnitude is wrought,
To feel it large of the great life they hold:
In them to come, or vaster intervolved,
The issues known in us, our unsolved solved:
That there with toil Life climbs the selfsame Tree,
Whose roots enrichment have from ripeness dropped.
So may we read and little find them cold:
Let it but be the lord of Mind to guide   60
Our eyes; no branch of Reason's growing lopped;
Nor dreaming on a dream; but fortified
By day to penetrate black midnight; see,
Hear, feel, outside the senses; even that we,

The specks of dust upon a mound of mold,
We who reflect those rays, though low our place,
   To them are lastingly allied.

So may we read, and little find them cold:
Not frosty lamps illumining dead space,
Not distant aliens, not senseless Powers.   70
The fire is in them whereof we are born;
The music of their motion may be ours.
Spirit shall deem them beckoning Earth and voiced
Sisterly to her, in her beams rejoiced.
Of love, the grand impulsion, we behold
   The love that lends her grace
   Among the starry fold.
Then at new flood of customary morn,
   Look at her through her showers,
   Her mists, her streaming gold,   80
A wonder edges the familiar face:
She wears no more that robe of printed hours;
Half strange seems Earth, and sweeter than her flowers.

                                    1888

l. 48: **ravenous**   physical being.

WINTER HEAVENS

   Sharp is the night, but stars with frost alive
   Leap off the rim of earth across the dome.
   It is a night to make the heavens our home
   More than the nest whereto apace we strive.
   Lengths down our road each fir-tree seems a hive,
   In swarms outrushing from the golden comb.
   They waken waves of thoughts that burst to foam:
   The living throb in me, the dead revive.
   Yon mantle clothes us: there, past mortal breath,
   Life glistens on the river of the death.   10
   It folds us, flesh and dust; and have we knelt,
   Or never knelt, or eyed as kine the springs
   Of radiance, the radiance enrings:
   And this is the soul's haven to have felt.

                                    1888

DANTE GABRIEL ROSSETTI

1828–1882

THE BLESSÉD DAMOZEL

The blesséd damozel leaned out
    From the gold bar of heaven;
Her eyes were deeper than the depth
    Of waters stilled at even;
She had three lilies in her hand,
    And the stars in her hair were seven.

Her robe, ungirt from clasp to hem,
    No wrought flowers did adorn,
But a white rose of Mary's gift,
    For service meetly worn;   10
Her hair that lay along her back
    Was yellow like ripe corn.

Herseemed she scarce had been a day
    One of God's choristers;
The wonder was not yet quite gone
    From that still look of hers;
Albeit, to them she left, her day
    Had counted as ten years.

(To *one* it is ten years of years.
    . . . Yet now, and in this place,   20
Surely she leaned o'er me—her hair
    Fell all about my face. . . .
Nothing: the autumn fall of leaves.
    The whole year sets apace.)

It was the rampart of God's house
    That she was standing on;

By God built over the sheer depth
   The which is Space begun;
So high, that looking downward thence
   She scarce could see the sun.   30

It lies in heaven, across the flood
   Of ether, as a bridge.
Beneath the tides of day and night
   With flame and darkness ridge
The void, as low as where this earth
   Spins like a fretful midge.

Around her, lovers, newly met
   'Mid deathless love's acclaims,
Spoke evermore among themselves
   Their heart-remembered names;   40
And the souls mounting up to God
   Went by her like thin flames.

And still she bowed herself and stooped
   Out of the circling charm;
Until her bosom must have made
   The bar she leaned on warm,
And the lilies lay as if asleep
   Along her bended arm.

From the fixed place of heaven she saw
   Time like a pulse shake fierce   50
Through all the worlds. Her gaze still strove
   Within the gulf to pierce
Its path; and now she spoke as when
   The stars sang in their spheres.

The sun was gone now; the curled moon
   Was like a little feather
Fluttering far down the gulf; and now
   She spoke through the still weather.
Her voice was like the voice the stars
   Had when they sang together.   60

(Ah, sweet! Even now, in that bird's song,
   Strove not her accents there,

[handwritten margin note: Stairs to heaven, only now supposes the woman is creeping down to him.]

Fain to be harkened? When those bells
    Possessed the mid-day air,
Strove not her steps to reach my side
    Down all the echoing stair?)

"I wish that he were come to me,
    For he will come," she said.
"Have I not prayed in heaven?—on earth,
    Lord, Lord, has he not prayed?   70
Are not two prayers a perfect strength?
    And shall I feel afraid?

"When round his head the aureole clings,
    And he is clothed in white,
I'll take his hand and go with him
    To the deep wells of light;
As unto a stream we will step down,
    And bathe there in God's sight.

"We two will stand beside that shrine,
    Occult, withheld, untrod,   80
Whose lamps are stirred continually
    With prayers sent up to God;
And see our old prayers, granted, melt
    Each like a little cloud.

"We two will lie i' the shadow of
    That living mystic tree
Within whose secret growth the Dove
    Is sometimes felt to be,
While every leaf that His plumes touch
    Saith His Name audibly.   90

"And I myself will teach to him,
    I myself, lying so,
The songs I sing here; which his voice
    Shall pause in, hushed and slow,
And find some knowledge at each pause,
    Or some new thing to know."

(Alas! We two, we two, thou say'st!
    Yea, one wast thou with me
That once of old. But shall God lift
    To endless unity   100

The soul whose likeness with thy soul
    Was but its love for thee?)

"We two," she said, "will seek the groves
    Where the lady Mary is,
With her five handmaidens, whose names
    Are five sweet symphonies,
Cecily, Gertrude, Magdalen,
    Margaret, and Rosalys.

"Circlewise sit they, with bound locks
    And foreheads garlanded;   110
Into the fine cloth white like flame
    Weaving the golden thread,
To fashion the birth-robes for them
    Who are just born, being dead.

"He shall fear, haply, and be dumb;
    Then will I lay my cheek
To his, and tell about our love,
    Not once abashed or weak;
And the dear Mother will approve
    My pride, and let me speak.   120

"Herself shall bring us, hand in hand,
    To Him round whom all souls
Kneel, the clear-ranged unnumbered heads
    Bowed with their aureoles;
And angels meeting us shall sing
    To their citherns and citoles.

"There will I ask of Christ the Lord
    Thus much for him and me—
Only to live as once on earth
    With Love, only to be,   130
And then awhile, forever now,
    Together, I and he."

She gazed and listened and then said,
    Less sad of speech than mild—
"All this is when he comes." She ceased.
    The light thrilled toward her, filled
With angels in strong, level flight.
    Her eyes prayed, and she smiled.

(I saw her smile.) But soon their path
    Was vague in distant spheres;   140
And then she cast her arms along
    The golden barriers,
And laid her face between her hands,
    And wept. (I heard her tears.)

                                    1850–1870

l. 59: **stars** at the creation (Job 38:4–7).   l. 86: **tree** of life (Rev. 22:1–2).   ll. 107–108: **Cecily . . . Rosalys** Saints; here mentioned because of their euphonious names.

MY SISTER'S SLEEP

She fell asleep on Christmas Eve.
    At length the long-ungranted shade
    Of weary eyelids overweighed
The pain naught else might yet relieve.

Our mother, who had leaned all day
    Over the bed from chime to chime,
    Then raised herself for the first time,
And as she sat her down, did pray.

Her little worktable was spread
    With work to finish. For the glare   10
    Made by her candle, she had care
To work some distance from the bed.

Without, there was a cold moon up,
    Of winter radiance sheer and thin;
    The hollow halo it was in
Was like an icy crystal cup.

Through the small room, with subtle sound
    Of flame, by vents the fireshine drove
    And reddened. In its dim alcove
The mirror shed a clearness round.   20

I had been sitting up some nights,
    And my tired mind felt weak and blank;
    Like a sharp strengthening wine it drank
The stillness and the broken lights.

Twelve struck. That sound, by dwindling years
 Heard in each hour, crept off; and then
 The ruffled silence spread again,
Like water that a pebble stirs.

Our mother rose from where she sat;
 Her needles, as she laid them down,   30
 Met lightly, and her silken gown
Settled—no other noise than that.

"Glory unto the Newly Born!"
 So, as said angels, she did say,
 Because we were in Christmas Day,
Though it would still be long till morn.

Just then in the room over us
 There was a pushing back of chairs,
 As some who had sat unawares
So late, now heard the hour, and rose.   40

With anxious softly-stepping haste
 Our mother went where Margaret lay,
 Fearing the sounds o'erhead—should they
Have broken her long watched-for rest!

She stooped an instant, calm, and turned,
 But suddenly turned back again;
 And all her features seemed in pain
With woe, and her eyes gazed and yearned.

For my part, I but hid my face,
 And held my breath, and spoke no word.   50
 There was none spoken; but I heard
 The silence for a little space.

Our mother bowed herself and wept;
 And both my arms fell, and I said,
 "God knows I knew that she was dead."
And there, all white, my sister slept.

Then kneeling, upon Christmas morn
 A little after twelve o'clock,
 We said, ere the first quarter struck,
"Christ's blessing on the newly born!"   60

1850

FOR A VENETIAN PASTORAL

BY GIORGIONE

(In the Louvre)

Water, for anguish of the solstice—nay,
But dip the vessel, slowly—nay, but lean
And hark how at its verge the wave sighs in,
Reluctant. Hush! Beyond all depth away
The heat lies silent at the brink of day;
Now the hand trails upon the viol-string
That sobs, and the brown faces cease to sing,
Sad with the whole of pleasure. Whither stray
Her eyes now, from whose mouth the slim pipes creep
And leave it pouting, while the shadowed grass   10
Is cool against her naked side? Let be—
Say nothing now unto her lest she weep,
Nor name this ever. Be it as it was—
Life touching lips with Immortality.

1850

Title: Rossetti's interpretation of a rather mysterious painting by Giorgione (1478–1511), depicting a garden in which sit two fine gentlemen and a nude woman who is playing a pipe while another woman draws water at a well.

CANTICA

OUR LORD CHRIST: OF ORDER

Set Love in order, thou that lovest Me.
  Never was virtue out of order found;
And though I fill thy heart desirously,
  By thine own virtue I must keep My ground:
When to My love thou dost bring charity,
  Even she must come with order girt and gown'd.
    Look how the trees are bound
    To order, bearing fruit;
    And by one thing compute,
In all things earthly, order's grace or gain.   10

All earthly things I had the making of
    Were numbered and were measured then by Me;
And each was ordered to its end by Love,
    Each kept, through order, clean for ministry.
Charity most of all, when known enough,
    Is of her very nature orderly.
        Lo, now! what heat in thee,
        Soul, can have bred this rout?
        Thou putt'st all order out.
Even this love's heat must be its curb and rein.   20

1861

Title: "A Song"; translation of a segment of a poem attributed to St. Francis of Assisi. The speaker is Christ.

SESTINA

(From Dante)

To the dim light and the large circle of shade
I have clomb, and to the whitening of the hills
There where we see no colour in the grass.
Natheless my longing loses not its green,
It has so taken root in the hard stone
Which talks and hears as though it were a lady.

Utterly frozen is this youthful lady
Even as the snow that lies within the shade:
For she is no more moved than is a stone
By the sweet season which makes warm the hills   10
And alters them afresh from white to green,
Covering their sides again with flowers and grass.

When on her hair she sets a crown of grass
The thought has no more room for other lady;
Because she weaves the yellow with the green
So well that Love sits down there in the shade,—
Love who has shut me in among low hills
Faster than between walls of granite-stone.

She is more bright than is a precious stone;
The wound she gives may not be healed with grass: 20

I therefore have fled far o'er plains and hills
For refuge from so dangerous a lady;
But from her sunshine nothing can give shade,—
Not any hill, nor wall, nor summer-green.

A while ago, I saw her dressed in green,—
So fair, she might have wakened in a stone
This love which I do feel even for her shade;
And therefore, as one woos a graceful lady,
I wooed her in a field that was all grass
Girdled about with very lofty hills.   30

Yet shall the streams turn back and climb the hills
Before Love's flame in this damp wood and green
Burn, as it burns within a youthful lady,
For my sake, who would sleep away in stone
My life, or feed like beasts upon the grass,
Only to see her garments cast a shade.

How dark soe'er the hills throw out their shade,
Under her summer-green the beautiful lady
Covers it, like a stone covered in grass.

                                          1861

THE BURDEN OF NINEVEH

In our Museum galleries
Today I lingered o'er the prize
Dead Greece vouchsafes to living eyes—
Her Art forever in fresh wise
    From hour to hour rejoicing me.
Sighing I turned at last to win
Once more the London dirt and din;
And as I made the swing-door spin
And issued, they were hoisting in
    A wingéd beast from Nineveh.   10

A human face the creature wore,
And hoofs behind and hoofs before,
And flanks with dark runes fretted o'er.
'Twas bull, 'twas mitered Minotaur,

A dead disboweled mystery;
The mummy of a buried faith
Stark from the charnel without scathe,
Its wings stood for the light to bathe—
Such fossil cerements as might swathe
    The very corpse of Nineveh.   20

The print of its first rush-wrapping,
Wound ere it dried, still ribbed the thing.
What song did the brown maidens sing,
From purple mouths alternating,
    When that was woven languidly?
What vows, what rites, what prayers preferred,
What songs has the strange image heard?
In what blind vigil stood interred
For ages, till an English word
    Broke silence first at Nineveh?   30

Oh, when upon each sculptured court,
Where even the wind might not resort—
O'er which Time passed, of like import
With the wild Arab boys at sport—
    A living face looked in to see.—
Oh, seemed it not—the spell once broke—
As though the carven warriors woke,
As though the shaft the string forsook,
The cymbals clashed, the chariots shook,
    And there was life in Nineveh?   40

On London stones our sun anew
The beast's recovered shadow threw.
(No shade that plague of darkness knew,
No light, no shade, while older grew
    By ages the old earth and sea.)
Lo thou! could all thy priests have shown
Such proof to make thy godhead known?
From their dead Past thou liv'st alone;
And still thy shadow is thine own,
    Even as of yore in Nineveh.   50

That day whereof we keep record,
When near thy city-gates the Lord

Sheltered his Jonah with a gourd
This sun (I said), here present, poured
    Even thus this shadow that I see.
This shadow has been shed the same
From sun and moon—from lamps which came
For prayer—from fifteen days of flame,
The last, while smoldered to a name
    Sardanapalus' Nineveh.   60

Within thy shadow, haply, once
Sennacherib has knelt, whose sons
Smote him between the altar-stones;
Or pale Semiramis her zones
    Of gold, her incense brought to thee,
In love for grace, in war for aid . . .
Aye, and who else? . . . till 'neath thy shade
Within his trenches newly made
Last year the Christian knelt and prayed—
    Not to thy strength—in Nineveh.   70

Now, thou poor god, within this hall
Where the blank windows blind the wall
From pedestal to pedestal,
The kind of light shall on thee fall
    Which London takes the day to be;
While school-foundations in the act
Of holiday, three files compact,
Shall learn to view thee as a fact
Connected with that zealous tract:
    "Rome—Babylon and Nineveh."   80

Deemed they of this, those worshipers,
When, in some mythic chain of verse
Which man shall not again rehearse,
The faces of thy ministers
    Yearned pale with bitter ecstasy?
Greece, Egypt, Rome—did any god
Before whose feet men knelt unshod
Deem that in this unblest abode
Another scarce more unknown god
    Should house with him, from Nineveh?   90

Ah! in what quarries lay the stone
From which this pygmy pile has grown,
Unto man's need how long unknown,
Since thy vast temples, court, and cone,
    Rose far in desert history?
Ah! what is here that does not lie
All strange to thine awakened eye?
Ah! what is here can testify
(Save that dumb presence of the sky)
    Unto thy day and Nineveh?   100

Why, of those mummies in the room
Above, there might indeed have come
One out of Egypt to thy home,
An alien. Nay, but were not some
    Of these thine own "antiquity"?
And now—they and their gods and thou
All relics here together—now
Whose profit? whether bull or cow,
Isis or Ibis, who or how,
    Whether of Thebes or Nineveh?   110

The consecrated metals found,
And ivory tablets, underground,
Winged teraphim and creatures crowned
When air and daylight filled the mound,
    Fell into dust immediately.
And even as these, the images
Of awe and worship—even as these—
So, smitten with the sun's increase,
Her glory moldered and did cease
    From immemorial Nineveh.   120

The day her builders made their halt,
Those cities of the lake of salt
Stood firmly 'stablished without fault,
Made proud with pillars of basalt,
    With sardonyx and porphyry.
The day that Jonah bore abroad
To Nineveh the voice of God,
A brackish lake lay in his road,

Where erst Pride fixed her sure abode,
  As then in royal Nineveh.   130

The day when he, Pride's lord and Man's,
Showed all the kingdoms at a glance
To Him before whose countenance
The years recede, the years advance,
  And said, Fall down and worship me—
'Mid all the pomp beneath that look,
Then stirred there, haply, some rebuke,
Where to the wind the salt pools shook,
And in those tracts, of life forsook,
  That knew thee not, O Nineveh!   140

Delicate harlot! On thy throne
Thou with a world beneath thee prone
In state for ages sat'st alone;
And needs were years and lusters flown
  Ere strength of man could vanquish thee,
Whom even thy victor foes must bring,
Still royal, among maids that sing
As with doves' voices, taboring
Upon their breasts, unto the King—
  A kingly conquest, Nineveh!   150

. . . Here woke my thought. The wind's slow sway
Had waxed; and like the human play
Of scorn that smiling spreads away,
The sunshine shivered off the day;
  The callous wind, it seemed to me,
Swept up the shadow from the ground;
And pale as whom the Fates astound,
The god forlorn stood winged and crowned;
Within I knew the cry lay bound
  Of the dumb soul of Nineveh.   160

And as I turned, my sense half shut
Still saw the crowds of curb and rut
Go past as marshaled to the strut
Of ranks in gypsum quaintly cut.
  It seemed in one same pageantry
They followed forms which had been erst;

To pass, till on my sight should burst
That future of the best or worst
When some may question which was first,
    Of London or of Nineveh. 170

For as that Bull-god once did stand
And watched the burial-clouds of sand,
Till these at last without a hand
Rose o'er his eyes, another land,
    And blinded him with destiny—
So may he stand again; till now,
In ships of unknown sail and prow,
Some tribe of the Australian plow
Bear him afar—a relic now
    Of London, not of Nineveh! 180

Or it may chance indeed that when
Man's age is hoary among men—
His centuries threescore and ten—
His furthest childhood shall seem then
    More clear than later times may be;
Who, finding in this desert place
This form, shall hold us for some race
That walked not in Christ's lowly ways,
But bowed its pride and vowed its praise
    Unto the god of Nineveh. 190

The smile rose first—anon drew nigh
The thought: . . . Those heavy wings spread high
So sure of flight, which do not fly;
That set gaze never on the sky;
    Those scriptured flanks it cannot see;
Its crown, a brow-contracting load;
Its planted feet which trust the sod: . . .
(So grew the image as I trod)
O Nineveh, was this thy God—
    Thine also, mighty Nineveh? 200

1870

Title: The song or refrain of Nineveh, an ancient Assyrian capital, destroyed
c. 600 B.C. In the Bible, Nineveh, like Babylon, is an emblem of a godless
city.   l. 9: **they were hoisting in** English archaeologists had unearthed

Assyrian sculpture which Rossetti saw being uncrated at the British Museum.   l. 53: **his Jonah** See Jonah 4.   l. 60: **Sardanapalus** last great king of Assyria.   l. 62: **Sennacherib** Assyrian king who captured and razed Babylon.   l. 63: **smote him** See II Kings 19:37.   l. 64: **Semiramis** Assyrian queen, one of the founders of Nineveh.   l. 76: **school-foundations** school children touring the museum.   l. 109: **Ibis** a bird sacred in ancient Egypt.   l. 110: **Thebes** one of the ancient Egyptian capitals.   l. 122: **Those cities** Sodom and Gomorrah, notoriously wicked (See Gen. 13:10–13; 19:24–29).   l. 131: **day** when Jesus was tempted by Satan ("Pride's lord and Man's"). See Matt. 4:1–11.

TROY TOWN

Heavenborn Helen, Sparta's queen,
        (*O Troy Town!*)
Had two breasts of heavenly sheen,
The sun and moon of the heart's desire;
All Love's lordship lay between.
        (*O Troy's down,*
        Tall Troy's on fire!)

Helen knelt at Venus' shrine,
        (*O Troy Town!*)
Saying, "A little gift is mine,   10
A little gift for a heart's desire.
Hear me speak and make me a sign!
        (*O Troy's down,*
        Tall Troy's on fire!)

"Look, I bring thee a carven cup;
        (*O Troy Town!*)
See it here as I hold it up—
Shaped it is to the heart's desire,
Fit to fill when the gods would sup.
        (*O Troy's down,*   20
        Tall Troy's on fire!)

"It was molded like my breast;
        (*O Troy Town!*)
He that sees it may not rest,
Rest at all for his heart's desire.
O give ear to my heart's behest!
        (*O Troy's down,*
        Tall Troy's on fire!)

"See my breast, how like it is;   30
     (*O Troy Town!*)
See it bare for the air to kiss!
Is the cup to thy heart's desire?
O for the breast, O make it his!
     (*O Troy's down,*
     Tall Troy's on fire!)

"Yea, for my bosom here I sue;
     (*O Troy Town!*)
Thou must give it where 'tis due,
Give it there to the heart's desire.
Whom do I give my bosom to?   40
     (*O Troy's down,*
     Tall Troy's on fire!)

"Each twin breast is an apple sweet!
     (*O Troy Town!*)
Once an apple stirred the beat
Of thy heart with the heart's desire;
Say, who brought it then to thy feet?
     (*O Troy's down,*
     Tall Troy's on fire!)

"They that claimed it then were three;   50
     (*O Troy Town!*)
For thy sake two hearts did he
Make forlorn of the heart's desire.
Do for him as he did for thee!
     (*O Troy's down,*
     Tall Troy's on fire!)

"Mine are apples grown to the south,
     (*O Troy Town!*)
Grown to taste in the days of drouth,
Taste and waste to the heart's desire;   60
Mine are apples meet for his mouth!"
     (*O Troy's down,*
     Tall Troy's on fire!)

Venus looked on Helen's gift,
     (*O Troy Town!*)
Looked and smiled with subtle drift,

Saw the work of her heart's desire—
"There thou kneel'st for Love to lift!"
     (*O Troy's down,*
      Tall Troy's on fire!)   70

Venus looked in Helen's face,
     (*O Troy Town!*)
Knew far off an hour and place,
And fire lit from the heart's desire;
Laughed and said, "Thy gift hath grace!"
     (*O Troy's down,*
      Tall Troy's on fire!)

Cupid looked on Helen's breast,
     (*O Troy Town!*)
Saw the heart within its nest,   80
Saw the flame of the heart's desire—
Marked his arrow's burning crest.
     (*O Troy's down,*
      Tall Troy's on fire!)

Cupid took another dart,
     (*O Troy Town!*)
Fledged it for another heart,
Winged the shaft with the heart's desire,
Drew the string and said, "Depart!"
     (*O Troy's down,*   90
      Tall Troy's on fire!)

Paris turned upon his bed,
     (*O Troy Town!*)
Turned upon his bed and said,
Dead at heart with the heart's desire—
"O to clasp her golden head!"
     (*O Troy's down,*
      Tall Troy's on fire!)

1870

l. 45: **an apple** the apple of Discord which Paris of Troy awarded to Venus in return for her promise to give him the most beautiful of women. His abduction of Helen, wife of Menelaus, led to the Trojan War and to the sacking and burning of Troy.   l. 50: **three** Venus, Athena, and Hera, who contested for the apple.   l. 51: **he** Paris.

THE CARD-DEALER

Could you not drink her gaze like wine?
    Yet though its splendour swoon
Into the silence languidly
    As a tune into a tune,
Those eyes unravel the coiled night
    And know the stars at noon.

The gold that's heaped beside her hand,
    In truth rich prize it were;
And rich the dreams that wreathe her brows
    With magic stillness there;   10
And he were rich who should unwind
    That woven golden hair.

Around her, where she sits, the dance
    Now breathes its eager heat;
And not more lightly or more true
    Fall there the dancers' feet
Than fall her cards on the bright board
    As 'twere an heart that beat.

Her fingers let them softly through,
    Smooth polished silent things;   20
And each one as it falls reflects
    In swift light-shadowings,
Blood-red and purple, green and blue,
    The great eyes of her rings.

Whom plays she with? With thee, who lov'st
    Those gems upon her hand;
With me, who search her secret brows;
    With all men, blessed or banned.
We play together, she and we,
    Within a vain strange land: 30

A land without any order—
    Day even as night (one saith)—
Where who lieth down ariseth not
    Nor the sleeper awakeneth;
A land of darkness as darkness itself
    And of the shadow of death.

What be her cards, you ask? Even these:
    The heart, that doth but crave
More, having fed; the diamond,
    Skilled to make base seem brave;   40
The club, for smiting in the dark;
    The spade, to dig a grave.

And do you ask what game she plays?
    With me 'tis lost or won;
With thee it is playing still; with him
    It is not well begun;
But 'tis a game she plays with all
    Beneath the sway o' the sun.

Thou seest the card that falls, she knows
    The card that followeth;   50
Her game in thy tongue is called Life,
    As ebbs thy daily breath.
When she shall speak, thou'lt learn her tongue
    And knows she calls it Death.

                    1870

Title: The subject of a painting, described in the poem, by Rossetti's contemporary, von Holst.

JENNY

"Vengeance of Jenny's case! Fie on her! Never
name her, child!"—Mrs. Quickly

Lazy laughing languid Jenny,
Fond of a kiss and fond of a guinea,
Whose head upon my knee to-night
Rests for a while, as if grown light
With all our dances and the sound
To which the wild tunes spun you round:
Fair Jenny mine, the thoughtless queen
Of kisses which the blush between
Could hardly make much daintier;
Whose eyes are as blue skies, whose hair   10
Is countless gold incomparable:

Fresh flower, scarce touched with signs that tell
Of Love's exuberant hotbed:—Nay,
Poor flower left torn since yesterday
Until to-morrow leave you bare;
Poor handful of bright spring-water
Flung in the whirlpool's shrieking face;
Poor shameful Jenny, full of grace
Thus with your head upon my knee;—
Whose person or whose purse may be   20
The lodestar of your reverie?

   This room of yours, my Jenny, looks
A change from mine so full of books,
Whose serried ranks hold fast, forsooth,
So many captive hours of youth,—
The hours they thieve from day and night
To make one's cherished work come right,
And leave it wrong for all their theft,
Even as to-night my work was left:
Until I vowed that since my brain   30
And eyes of dancing seemed so fain,
My feet should have some dancing too:—
And thus it was I met with you.
Well, I suppose 'twas hard to part,
For here I am. And now, sweetheart,
You seem too tired to get to bed.

   It was a careless life I led
When rooms like this were scarce so strange
Not long ago. What breeds the change,—
The many aims or the few years?   40
Because to-night it all appears
Something I do not know again.

   The cloud's not danced out of my brain,—
The cloud that made it turn and swim
While hour by hour the books grew dim.
Why, Jenny, as I watch you there,—
For all your wealth of loosened hair,
Your silk ungirdled and unlaced
And warm sweets open to the waist,
All golden in the lamplight's gleam,—   50
You know not what a book you seem,

Half-read by lightning in a dream!
How should you know, my Jenny? Nay,
And I should be ashamed to say:—
Poor beauty, so well worth a kiss!
But while my thought runs on like this
With wasteful whims more than enough,
I wonder what you're thinking of.

    If of myself you think at all,
What is the thought?—conjectural   60
On sorry matters best unsolved?—
Or inly is each grace revolved
To fit me with a lure?—or (sad
To think!) perhaps you're merely glad
That I'm not drunk or ruffianly
And let you rest upon my knee.

    For sometimes, were the truth confessed,
You're thankful for a little rest,—
Glad from the crush to rest within,
From the heart-sickness and the din   70
Where envy's voice at virtue's pitch
Mocks you because your gown is rich;
And from the pale girl's dumb rebuke,
Whose ill-clad grace and toil-worn look
Proclaim the strength that keeps her weak,
And other nights than yours bespeak;
And from the wise unchildish elf,
To schoolmate lesser than himself
Pointing you out, what thing you are:—
Yes, from the daily jeer and jar,   80
From shame and shame's outbraving too,
Is rest not sometimes sweet to you?—
But most from the hatefulness of man
Who spares not to end what he began,
Whose acts are ill and his speech ill,
Who, having used you at his will,
Thrusts you aside, as when I dine
I serve the dishes and the wine.

    Well, handsome Jenny mine, sit up:
I've filled our glasses, let us sup,   90
And do not let me think of you,

Lest shame of yours suffice for two.
What, still so tired? Well, well then, keep
Your head there, so you do not sleep;
But that the weariness may pass
And leave you merry, take this glass.
Ah! lazy lily hand, more blessed
If ne'er in rings it had been dressed
Nor ever by a glove concealed!

Behold the lilies of the field,   100
They toil not neither do they spin;
(So doth the ancient text begin,—
Not of such rest as one of these
Can share.) Another rest and ease.
Along each summer-sated path
From its new lord the garden hath,
Than that whose spring in blessings ran
Which praised the bounteous husbandman,
Ere yet, in days of hankering breath,
The lilies sickened unto death.   110

What, Jenny, are your lilies dead?
Aye, and the snow-white leaves are spread
Like winter on the garden-bed.
But you had roses left in May,—
They were not gone too. Jenny, nay,
But must your roses die, and those
Their purfled buds that should unclose?
Even so; the leaves are curled apart,
Still red as from the broken heart,
And here's the naked stem of thorns.   120

Nay, nay, mere words. Here nothing warns
As yet of winter. Sickness here
Or want alone could waken fear,—
Nothing but passion wrings a tear.
Except when there may rise unsought
Haply at times a passing thought
Of the old days which seem to be
Much older than any history
That is written in any book;
When she would lie in fields and look   130

Along the ground through the blown grass,
And wonder where the city was,
Far out of sight, whose broil and bale
They told her then for a child's tale.

Jenny, you know the city now,
A child can tell the tale there, how
Some things which are not yet enrolled
In market-lists are bought and sold
Even till the early Sunday light,
When Saturday night is market-night   140
Everywhere, be it dry or wet,
And market-night in the Haymarket.
Our learned London children know,
Poor Jenny, all your pride and woe;
Have seen your lifted silken skirt
Advertise dainties through the dirt;
Have seen your coach-wheels splash rebuke
On virtue; and have learned your look
When, wealth and health slipped past, you stare
Along the streets alone, and there,   150
Round the long park, across the bridge,
The cold lamps at the pavement's edge
Wind on together and apart,
A fiery serpent for your heart.

Let the thoughts pass, an empty cloud!
Suppose I were to think aloud,—
What if to her all this were said?
Why, as a volume seldom read
Being opened halfway shuts again,
So might the pages of her brain   160
Be parted at such words, and thence
Close back upon the dusty sense.
For is there hue or shape defined
In Jenny's desecrated mind,
Where all contagious currents meet,
A Lethe of the middle street?
Nay, it reflects not any face,
Nor sound is in its sluggish pace,
But as they coil those eddies clot,
And night and day remember not.   170

[handwritten margin note: Looked down at, she becomes an object to stare at.]

Why, Jenny, you're asleep at last!—
Asleep, poor Jenny, hard and fast,—
So young and soft and tired; so fair,
With chin thus nestled in your hair,
Mouth quiet, eyelids almost blue
As if some sky of dreams shone through!

Just as another woman sleeps!
Enough to throw one's thoughts in heaps
Of doubt and horror,—what to say
Or think,—this awful secret sway,   180
The potter's power over the clay!
Of the same lump (it has been said)
For honour and dishonour made,
Two sister vessels. Here is one.

My cousin Nell is fond of fun,
And fond of dress, and change, and praise,
So mere a woman in her ways:
And if her sweet eyes rich in youth
Are like her lips that tell the truth,
My cousin Nell is fond of love.   190
And she's the girl I'm proudest of.
Who does not prize her, guard her well?
The love of change, in cousin Nell,
Shall find the best and hold it dear:
The unconquered mirth turn quieter
Not through her own, through others' woe:
The conscious pride of beauty glow
Beside another's pride in her,
One little part of all they share.
For Love himself shall ripen these   200
In a kind soil to just increase
Through years of fertilizing peace.

Of the same lump (as it is said)
For honour and dishonour made,
Two sister vessels. Here is one.

It makes a goblin of the sun.

So pure,—so fall'n! How dare to think
Of the first common kindred link?
Yet, Jenny, till the world shall burn

It seems that all things take their turn;   210
And who shall say but this fair tree
May need, in changes that may be,
Your children's children's charity?
Scorned then, no doubt, as you are scorned!
Shall no man hold his pride forewarned,
Till in the end, the Day of Days,
At Judgment, one of his own race,
As frail and lost as you, shall rise,—
His daughter, with his mother's eyes?

men
have children
that could
become prost.

How Jenny's clock ticks on the shelf!   220
Might not the dial scorn itself
That has such hours to register?
Yet as to me, even so to her
Are golden sun and silver moon,
In daily largesse of earth's boon,
Counted for life-coins to one tune.
And if, as blindfold fates are tossed
Through some one man this life be lost,
Shall soul not somehow pay for soul?

Fair shines the gilded aureole   230
In which our highest painters place
Some living woman's simple face.
And the stilled features thus descried
As Jenny's long throat droops aside,—
The shadows where the cheeks are thin,
And pure wide curve from ear to chin,—
With Raffael's or Da Vinci's hand
To show them to men's souls, might stand,
Whole ages long, the whole world through,
For preachings of what God can do.   240
What has man done here? How atone,
Great God, for this which man has done?
And for the body and soul which by
Man's pitiless doom must now comply
With lifelong hell, what lullaby
Of sweet forgetful second birth
Remains? All dark. No sign on earth
What measure of God's rest endows
The many mansions of this house.

If but a woman's heart might see   250
Such erring heart unerringly
For once! But that can never be.

    Like a rose shut in a book
In which pure women may not look,
For its base pages claim control
To crush the flower within the soul;
Where through each dead rose-leaf that clings,
Pale as transparent psyche-wings,
To the vile text, are traced such things
As might make lady's cheek indeed   260
More than a living rose to read;
So nought save foolish foulness may
Watch with hard eyes the sure decay;
And so the life-blood of this rose,
Puddled with shameful knowledge, flows
Through leaves no chaste hand may unclose:
Yet still it keeps such faded show
Of when 'twas gathered long ago,
That the crushed petals' lovely grain,
The sweetness of the sanguine stain,   270
Seen of a woman's eyes, must make
Her pitiful heart, so prone to ache,
Love roses better for its sake:—
Only that this can never be:—
Even so unto her sex is she.

    Yet, Jenny, looking long at you,
The woman almost fades from view.
A cipher of man's changeless sum
Of lust, past, present, and to come,
Is left. A riddle that one shrinks   280
To challenge from the scornful sphinx.

    Like a toad within a stone
Seated while Time crumbles on;
Which sits there since the earth was cursed
For Man's transgression at the first;
Which, living through all centuries,
Not once has seen the sun arise;
Whose life, to its cold circle charmed,
The earth's whole summers have not warmed;   290

Which always—whitherso the stone
Be flung—sits there, deaf, blind, alone;—
Aye, and shall not be driven out
Till that which shuts him round about
Break at the very Master's stroke,
And the dust thereof vanish as smoke,
And the seed of Man vanish as dust:—
Even so within this world is Lust.

Come, come, what use in thoughts like this?
Poor little Jenny, good to kiss,—   300
You'd not believe by what strange roads
Thought travels, when your beauty goads
A man to-night to think of toads!
Jenny, wake up. . . . Why, there's the dawn!

And there's an early waggon drawn
To market, and some sheep that jog
Bleating before a barking dog;
And the old streets come peering through
Another night that London knew;
And all as ghostlike as the lamps.   310

So on the wings of day decamps
My last night's frolic. Glooms begin
To shiver off as lights creep in
Past the gauze curtains half drawn-to,
And the lamp's doubled shade grows blue,—
Your lamp, my Jenny, kept alight,
Like a wise virgin's, all one night!
And in the alcove coolly spread
Glimmers with dawn your empty bed;
And yonder your fair face I see   320
Reflected lying on my knee,
Where teems with first foreshadowings
Your pier-glass scrawled with diamond rings:
And on your bosom all night worn
Yesterday's rose now droops forlorn,
But dies not yet this summer morn.

And now without, as if some word
Had called upon them that they heard,
The London sparrows far and nigh

Clamour together suddenly;   330
And Jenny's cage-bird grown awake
Here in their song his part must take,
Because here too the day doth break.

   And somehow in myself the dawn
Among stirred clouds and veils withdrawn
Strikes greyly on her. Let her sleep.
But will it wake her if I heap
These cushions thus beneath her head
Where my knee was? No,—there's your bed.
My Jenny, while you dream. And there   340
I lay among your golden hair
Perhaps the subject of your dreams,
These golden coins.
                For still one deems
That Jenny's flattering sleep confers
New magic on the magic purse,—
Grim web, how clogged with shrivelled flies!
Between the threads fine fumes arise
And shape their pictures in the brain.
There roll no streets in glare and rain,
Nor flagrant man-swine whets his tusk;   350
But delicately sighs in musk
The homage of the dim boudoir;
Or like a palpitating star
Thrilled into song, the opera-night
Breathes faint in the quick pulse of light;
Or at the carriage-window shine
Rich wares for choice; or, free to dine,
Whirls through its hour of health (divine
For her) the concourse of the Park.
And though in the discounted dark   360
Her functions there and here are one,
Beneath the lamps and in the sun
There reigns at least the acknowledged belle
Apparelled beyond parallel.
Ah Jenny, yes, we know your dreams.

   For even the Paphian Venus seems,
A goddess o'er the realms of love,
When silver-shrined in shadowy grove:

Aye, or let offerings nicely placed
But hide Priapus to the waist,   370
And whoso looks on him shall see
An eligible deity.

    Why, Jenny, waking here alone
May help you to remember one,
Though all the memory's long outworn
Of many a double-pillowed morn.
I think I see you when you wake,
And rub your eyes for me, and shake
My gold, in rising, from your hair,
A Danaë for a moment there.   380

    Jenny, my love rang true! for still
Love at first sight is vague, until
That tinkling makes him audible.

    And must I mock you to the last,
Ashamed of my own shame,—aghast
Because some thoughts not born amiss
Rose at a poor fair face like this?
Well, of such thoughts so much I know:
In my life, as in hers, they show,
By a far gleam which I may near,   390
A dark path I can strive to clear.

    Only one kiss. Good-bye, my dear.

1870

Epigraph: Shakespeare's *The Merry Wives of Windsor*, IV, 64–65. The
rest of Mrs. Quickly's line is, "if she be a whore."   l. 102: **text** Luke
12:27–28.   l. 142: **Haymarket** district where prostitutes solicited.
l. 317: **wise virgin's** whose lamp was provided with oil. See Matt. 25:1–
13.   l. 366: **Paphian Venus** worshipped with erotic rites.   l. 370:
Priapus whose statues were phallic.   l. 380: **Danae** a maiden to
whom Zeus descended in a shower of gold.

THE BALLAD OF DEAD LADIES

FROM FRANÇOIS VILLON

Tell me now in what hidden way is
   Lady Flora the lovely Roman?
Where's Hipparchia, and where is Thais,
   Neither of them the fairer woman?
   Where is Echo, beheld of no man,
Only heard on river and mere—
   She whose beauty was more than human?—
But where are the snows of yester-year?

Where's Héloïse, the learned nun,
   For whose sake Abeillard, I ween,   10
Lost manhood and put priesthood on?
   (From Love he won such dule and teen!)
   And where, I pray you, is the Queen
Who willed that Buridan should steer
   Sewed in a sack's mouth down the Seine?—
But where are the snows of yester-year?

White Queen Blanche, like a queen of lilies,
   With a voice like any mermaiden—
Bertha Broadfoot, Beatrice, Alice,
   And Ermengarde the lady of Maine—   20
   And that good Joan whom Englishmen
At Rouen doomed and burned her there—
   Mother of God, where are they then?—
But where are the snows of yester-year?

Nay, never ask this week, fair lord,
   Where they are gone, nor yet this year,
Except with this for an overword—
   But where are the snows of yester-year?

1870

Title: a translation of a famous *ballade* by Villon (1431–1463?). Not all
the ladies mentioned can be confidently identified.   l. 3: **Hipparchia**
who lived in Thebes, Greece, in the 3rd century B.C.   l. 5: **Echo** a
nymph who pined for love until only her voice remained.   l. 9: **Héloïse**
(1101?–1164), wife of the famous French theologian, Abelard (l. 10).
After he was castrated at the behest of his enemies, he became a monk, his

wife a nun.   l. 13: **Queen**   Marguerite of Burgundy (1290–1315). She
was accused of lewd and riotous conduct.   l. 14: **Buridan**   Jean Buridan
(1295–1366?), French theologian; reputed to be one of the lovers of Mar-
guerite of Burgundy, who had him dumped into the Seine in a sack, from
which he escaped.   l. 19: **Bertha**   (d. 783), the mother of Charle-
magne, greatly celebrated.   l. 21: **Joan**   St. Joan of Arc (1412–1431),
who rallied the French against the English, but was captured and burned
at the stake at Rouen.

From *THE HOUSE OF LIFE*

THE SONNET

A SONNET *is a moment's monument—*
Memorial from the Soul's eternity
To one dead deathless hour. Look that it be,
Whether for lustral rite or dire portent,
Of its own arduous fullness reverent;
Carve it in ivory or in ebony
As Day or Night may rule; and let Time see
Its flowering crest impearled and orient.
A Sonnet is a coin; its face reveals
The soul—its converse, to what Power 'tis due—   10
Whether for tribute to the august appeals
Of Life, or dower in Love's high retinue,
It serve; or, 'mid the dark wharf's cavernous breath,
In Charon's palm it pay the toll to Death.

5. *Heart's Hope*

By what word's power, the key of paths untrod,
Shall I the difficult deeps of Love explore,
Till parted waves of Song yield up the shore
Even as that sea which Israel crossed dryshod?
For lo! in some poor rhythmic period,
Lady, I fain would tell how evermore
Thy soul I know not from thy body, nor
Thee from myself, neither our love from God.
Yea, in God's name, and Love's, and thine, would I
Draw from one loving heart such evidence   10
As to all hearts all things shall signify;

Tender as dawn's first hill-fire, and intense
As instantaneous penetrating sense,
In Spring's birth-hour, of other Springs gone by.

18. Genius in Beauty

Beauty like hers is genius. Not the call
Of Homer's or of Dante's heart sublime—
Not Michael's hand furrowing the zones of time—
Is more with compassed mysteries musical;
Nay, not in Spring's or Summer's sweet footfall
More gathered gifts exuberant Life bequeathes
Than doth this sovereign face, whose love-spell breathes
Even from its shadowed contour on the wall.
As many men are poets in their youth,
But for one sweet-strung soul the wires prolong   10
Even through all change the indomitable song;
So in likewise the envenomed years, whose tooth
Rends shallower grace with ruin void of ruth,
Upon this beauty's power shall wreak no wrong.

19. Silent Noon

Your hands lie open in the long fresh grass—
The finger-points look through like rosy blooms;
Your eyes smile peace. The pasture gleams and glooms
'Neath billowing skies that scatter and amass.
All round our nest, far as the eye can pass,
Are golden kingcup-fields with silver edge
Where the cow-parsley skirts the hawthorn-hedge
'Tis visible silence, still as the hourglass.
Deep in the sun-searched growths the dragonfly,
Hangs like a blue thread loosened from the sky—   10
So this winged hour is dropped to us from above.
Oh! clasp we to our hearts, for deathless dower,
This close-companioned inarticulate hour
When twofold silence was the song of love.

48. Death-in-Love

There came an image in Life's retinue
That had Love's wings and bore his gonfalon;

Fair was the web, and nobly wrought thereon,
O soul-sequestered face, thy form and hue!
Bewildering sounds, such as spring wakens to,
Shook in its folds; and through my heart its power
Sped trackless as the immemorable hour
When birth's dark portal groaned and all was new.
But a veiled woman followed, and she caught
The banner round its staff, to furl and cling—   10
Then plucked a feather from the bearer's wing,
And held it to his lips that stirred it not,
And said to me, "Behold, there is no breath;
I and this Love are one, and I am Death."

49. Willowwood—1

sort of hellish, sweaty

I sat with Love upon a woodside well,
Leaning across the water, I and he;
Nor ever did he speak nor looked at me,
But touched his lute wherein was audible
The certain secret thing he had to tell.
Only our mirrored eyes met silently
In the low wave; and that sound came to be
The passionate voice I knew; and my tears fell.
And at their fall, his eyes beneath grew hers;
And with his foot and with his wing-feathers   10
He swept the spring that watered my heart's drouth.
Then the dark ripples spread to waving hair,
And as I stooped, her own lips rising there
Bubbled with brimming kisses at my mouth.

50. Willowwood—2

And now Love sang; but his was such a song,
So meshed with half-remembrance hard to free,
As souls disused in death's sterility
May sing when the new birthday tarries long.
And I was made aware of a dumb throng
That stood aloof, one form by every tree,
All mournful forms, for each was I or she,
The shades of those our days that had no tongue.
They looked on us, and knew us and were known;
While fast together, alive from the abyss,   10

not people, but days that seem like people.

Clung the soul-wrung implacable close kiss;
And pity of self through all made broken moan
Which said, "For once, for once, for once alone!"
And still Love sang, and what he sang was this:

51. *Willowwood—3*

"O ye, all ye that walk in Willowwood,   ~~dost-like~~
That walk with hollow faces burning white:
What fathom-depth of soul-struck widowhood,
What long, what longer hours, one lifelong night,
Ere ye again, who so in vain have wooed
Your last hope lost, who so in vain invite
Your lips to that their unforgotten food,
Ere ye, ere ye again shall see the light!
Alas! the bitter banks in Willowwood,
With tear-spurge wan, with blood-wort burning red.   10
Alas, if ever such a pillow could
Steep deep the soul in sleep till she were dead—
Better all life forget her than this thing,
That Willowwood should hold her wandering!"

52. *Willowwood—4*

So sang he; and as meeting rose and rose
Together cling through the wind's well-away
Nor change at once, yet near the end of day
The leaves drop loosened where the heart-stain glows—
So when the song died did the kiss unclose;
And her face fell back drowned, and was as gray
As its gray eyes; and if it ever may
Meet mine again I know not if Love knows.
Only I know that I leaned low and drank
A long draft from the water where she sank,   10
Her breath and all her tears and all her soul;
And as I leaned, I know I felt Love's face
Pressed on my neck with moan of pity and grace,
Till both our heads were in his aureole.

53. *Without Her*

What of her glass without her? The blank gray
There where the pool is blind of the moon's face.

Her dress without her? The tossed empty space
Of cloud-rack whence the moon has passed away.
Her paths without her? Day's appointed sway
Usurped by desolate night. Her pillowed place
Without her? Tears, ah me! for love's good grace,
And cold forgetfulness of night or day.
What of the heart without her? Nay, poor heart,
Of thee what word remains ere speech be still?   10
A wayfarer by barren ways and chill,
Steep ways and weary, without her thou art,
Where the long cloud, the long wood's counterpart,
Sheds doubled darkness up the labouring hill.

77. Soul's Beauty

Under the arch of Life, where love and death,
Terror and mystery, guard her shrine, I saw
Beauty enthroned; and though her gaze struck awe,
I drew it in as simply as my breath.
Hers are the eyes which, over and beneath,
The sky and sea bend on thee—which can draw,
By sea or sky or woman, to one law,
The allotted bondman of her palm and wreath.
This is that Lady Beauty, in whose praise
Thy voice and hand shake still;—long known to thee   10
By flying hair and fluttering hem—the beat
Following her daily of thy heart and feet,
How passionately and irretrievably,
In what fond flight, how many ways and days!

78. Body's Beauty

Of Adam's first wife, Lilith, it is told
(The witch he loved before the gift of Eve)
That, ere the snake's, her sweet tongue could deceive,
And her enchanted hair was the first gold.
And still she sits, young while the earth is old,
And, subtly of herself contemplative,
Draws men to watch the bright web she can weave,
Till heart and body and life are in its hold.
The rose and poppy are her flowers; for where

Is he not found, O Lilith, whom shed scent   10
And soft-shed kisses and soft sleep shall snare?
Lo! as that youth's eyes burned at thine, so went
Thy spell through him, and left his straight neck bent
And round his heart one strangling golden hair.

1870, 1881

Title: In astrology the heavens are divided into twelve sectors or "houses,"
the first of which is the House of Life. The sequence of sonnets reflects
Rossetti's relationship with Elizabeth Siddal, whom he met in 1850 and
married in 1860; she died suddenly in 1862.
The Sonnet: l. 13: **wharf** of the Underworld.   l. 14: **toll** a small
coin paid by the souls of the dead to be ferried to Hades.
Sonnet 5: l. 4: **sea** the Red Sea. See Exod. 14:13–27.
Sonnet 18: l. 3: **Michael's** Michelangelo's.
Sonnet 49: **Title:** The meeting-place of Love and Death; the willow sym-
bolizes lasting grief.
Sonnet 77: **Title:** This sonnet interprets Rossetti's painting, *Sibylla Palmi-
fera*, in which a prophetess holding a palm branch presides over symbols
of Love and Death.
Sonnet 78: **Title:** descriptive of Rossetti's painting *Lady Lilith*. In ancient
tradition Lilith was Adam's first wife and the mother of demons. l. 9: **rose
and poppy** symbols of love and of oblivion.

THE ORCHARD-PIT

Piled deep below the screening apple-branch
   They lie with bitter apples in their hands:
And some are only ancient bones that blanch,
And some had ships that last year's wind did launch,
   And some were yesterday the lords of lands.

In the soft dell, among the apple-trees,
   High up above the hidden pit she stands,
And there for ever sings, who gave to these,
That lie below, her magic hour of ease,
   And those her apples holden in their hands.   10

This in my dreams is shown me; and her hair
   Crosses my lips and draws my burning breath;
Her song spreads golden wings upon the air,
Life's eyes are gleaming from her forehead fair,
   And from her breasts the ravishing eyes of Death.

Men say to me that sleep hath many dreams,
    Yet I knew never but this dream alone:
There, from a dried-up channel, once the stream's,
The glen slopes up; even such in sleep it seems
    As to my waking sight the place well known.   20

.   .   .   .   .

My love I call her, and she loves me well:
    But I love her as in the maelstrom's cup
The whirled stone loves the leaf inseparable
That clings to it round all the circling swell,
    And that the same last eddy swallows up.

1888

CHRISTINA GEORGINA ROSSETTI

1830–1894

THE P.R.B.

The two Rossettis (brothers they)
And Holman Hunt and John Millais,
With Stephens chivalrous and bland,
And Woolner in a distant land—
In these six men I awestruck see
Embodied the great P.R.B.
D. G. Rossetti offered two
Good pictures to the public view;
Unnumbered ones great John Millais,
And Holman more than I can say.   10

William Rossetti, calm and solemn,
Cuts up his brethren by the column.

1853

Title: The Pre-Raphaelite Brotherhood, so called because its members
wished to revive what they conceived to be the purer artistic ideals that had
been sacrificed to academicism by the "Raphaelites," the imitators of
Raphael.   ll. 2–4: **Hunt . . . Woolner** The first two were leading
painters of the group. Stephens was Hunt's pupil and later an art critic.
Woolner was a sculptor who emigrated to Australia.   l. 11: **William**
Christina Rossetti's brother.   l. 12: **column** that is, in the pages of
critical journals.

UP-HILL

Does the road wind up-hill all the way?
    Yes, to the very end.
Will the day's journey take the whole long day?
    From morn to night, my friend.

But is there for the night a resting-place?
  A roof for when the slow dark hours begin.
May not the darkness hide it from my face?
  You cannot miss that inn.

Shall I meet other wayfarers at night?
  Those who have gone before.   10
Then must I knock, or call when just in sight?
  They will not keep you standing at that door.

Shall I find comfort, travel-sore and weak?
  Of labour you shall find the sum.
Will there be beds for me and all who seek?
  Yea, beds for all who come.

                                                        1862

REST

O Earth, lie heavily upon her eyes;
  Seal her sweet eyes weary of watching, Earth;
  Lie close around her; leave no room for mirth
With its harsh laughter, nor for sound of sighs.
She hath no questions, she hath no replies,
  Hushed in and curtained with a blesséd dearth
  Of all that irked her from the hour of birth;
With stillness that is almost Paradise.
Darkness more clear than noonday holdeth her,
  Silence more musical than any song;   10
Even her very heart has ceased to stir:
Until the morning of Eternity
Her rest shall not begin nor end, but be;
  And when she wakes she will not think it long.

1849   1862

SONG

When I am dead, my dearest,
  Sing no sad songs for me;
Plant thou no roses at my head,
  Nor shady cypress tree.

Be the green grass above me
    With showers and dewdrops wet;
And if thou wilt, remember,
    And if thou wilt, forget.

I shall not see the shadows,
    I shall not feel the rain;   10
I shall not hear the nightingale
    Sing on as if in pain.
And dreaming through the twilight
    That doth not rise nor set,
Haply I may remember,
    And haply may forget.

1848   1862

A BIRTHDAY

My heart is like a singing bird
    Whose nest is in a watered shoot;
My heart is like an apple-tree
Whose boughs are bent with thick-set fruit;
My heart is like a rainbow shell
    That paddles in a halcyon sea;
My heart is gladder than all these
    Because my love is come to me.

Raise me a dais of silk and down;
    Hang it with vair and purple dyes;   10
Carve it in doves, and pomegranates,
    And peacocks with a hundred eyes;
Work it in gold and silver grapes,
    In leaves, and silver fleurs-de-lys;
Because the birthday of my life
    Is come, my love is come to me.

1862

GOOD FRIDAY

Am I a stone, and not a sheep,
    That I can stand, O Christ, beneath Thy cross,
    To number drop by drop Thy Blood's slow loss,
And yet not weep?

Not so those women loved
    Who with exceeding grief lamented Thee;
    Not so fallen Peter weeping bitterly;
Not so the thief was moved;

Not so the Sun and Moon
    Which hid their faces in a starless sky,   10
    A horror of great darkness at broad noon—
I, only I.

Yet give not o'er,
    But seek Thy sheep, true Shepherd of the flock;
    Greater than Moses, turn and look once more
And smite a rock.

                                                        1862

l. 16: **smite a rock** as Moses did to produce water in the desert. See
Exod. 17:4–6.

GOBLIN MARKET

Morning and evening
Maids heard the goblins cry:
"Come buy our orchard fruits,
Come buy, come buy:
Apples and quinces,
Lemons and oranges,
Plump unpecked cherries,
Melons and raspberries,
Bloom-down-cheeked peaches,
Swart-headed mulberries,   10
Wild free-born cranberries,
Crab-apples, dewberries,
Pine-apples, blackberries,
Apricots, strawberries;—

All ripe together
In summer weather,—
Morns that pass by,
Fair eves that fly;
Come buy, come buy:
Our grapes fresh from the vine,   20
Pomegranates full and fine,
Dates and sharp bullaces,
Rare pears and greengages,
Damsons and bilberries,
Taste them and try:
Currants and gooseberries,
Bright-fire-like barberries,
Figs to fill your mouth,
Citrons from the South,
Sweet to tongue and sound to eye;   30
Come buy, come buy."

Evening by evening
Among the brookside rushes,
Laura bowed her head to hear,
Lizzie veiled her blushes:
Crouching close together
In the cooling weather,
With clasping arms and cautioning lips,
With tingling cheeks and finger tips.
"Lie close," Laura said,   40
Pricking up her golden head:
"We must not look at goblin men,
We must not buy their fruits:
Who knows upon what soil they fed
Their hungry thirsty roots?"
"Come buy," call the goblins
Hobbling down the glen.
"Oh," cried Lizzie, "Laura, Laura,
You should not peep at goblin men."
Lizzie covered up her eyes,   50
Covered close lest they should look;
Laura reared her glossy head,
And whispered like the restless brook:
"Look, Lizzie, look, Lizzie,

Down the glen tramp little men.
One hauls a basket,
One bears a plate,
One lugs a golden dish
Of many pounds' weight.
How fair the vine must grow　　　　　　　　　　60
Whose grapes are so luscious;
How warm the wind must blow
Through those fruit bushes."
"No," said Lizzie: "No, no, no;
Their offers should not charm us,
Their evil gifts would harm us."
She thrust a dimpled finger
In each ear, shut eyes and ran:
Curious Laura chose to linger
Wondering at each merchant man.　　　　　　　70
One had a cat's face,
One whisked a tail,
One tramped at a rat's pace,
One crawled like a snail,
One like a wombat prowled obtuse and furry,
One like a ratel tumbled hurry skurry.
She heard a voice like voice of doves
Cooing all together:
They sounded kind and full of loves
In the pleasant weather.　　　　　　　　　　80

Laura stretched her gleaming neck
Like a rush-imbedded swan,
Like a lily from the beck,
Like a moonlit poplar branch,
Like a vessel at the launch
When its last restraint is gone.

Backward up the mossy glen
Turned and trooped the goblin men,
With their shrill repeated cry,
"Come buy, come buy."　　　　　　　　　　　90
When they reached where Laura was
They stood stock still upon the moss,
Leering at each other,
Brother with queer brother;

Signaling each other,
Brother with sly brother.
One set his basket down,
One reared his plate;
One began to weave a crown
Of tendrils, leaves and rough nuts brown   100
(Men sell not such in any town);
One heaved the golden weight
Of dish and fruit to offer her:
"Come buy, come buy," was still their cry.
Laura stared but did not stir,
Longed but had no money:
The whisk-tailed merchant bade her taste
In tones as smooth as honey,
The cat-faced purred,
The rat-paced spoke a word   110
Of welcome, and the snail-paced even was heard;
One parrot-voiced and jolly
Cried, "Pretty Goblin" still for "Pretty Polly";—
One whistled like a bird.

But sweet-tooth Laura spoke in haste:
"Good folk, I have no coin;
To take were to purloin:
I have no copper in my purse,
I have no silver either,
And all my gold is on the furze   120
That shakes in windy weather
Above the rusty heather."
"You have much gold upon your head,"
They answered all together:
"Buy from us with a golden curl."
She clipped a precious golden lock,
She dropped a tear more rare than pearl,
Then sucked their fruit globes fair or red:
Sweeter than honey from the rock,
Stronger than man-rejoicing wine,   130
Clearer than water flowed that juice;
She never tasted such before,
How should it cloy with length of use?
She sucked and sucked and sucked the more

Fruits which that unknown orchard bore;
She sucked until her lips were sore;
Then flung the emptied rinds away
But gathered up one kernel-stone,
And knew not was it night or day
As she turned home alone.   140

Lizzie met her at the gate,
Full of wise upbraidings:
"Dear, you should not stay so late,
Twilight is not good for maidens;
Should not loiter in the glen
In the haunts of goblin men.
Do you not remember Jeanie,
How she met them in the moonlight,
Took their gifts both choice and many,
Ate their fruits and wore their flowers   150
Plucked from bowers
Where summer ripens at all hours?
But ever in the moonlight
She pined and pined away;
Sought them by night and day,
Found them no more but dwindled and grew grey;
Then fell with the first snow,
While to this day no grass will grow
Where she lies low:
I planted daisies there a year ago   160
That never blow.
You should not loiter so."
"Nay, hush," said Laura:
"Nay, hush, my sister:
I ate and ate my fill,
Yet my mouth waters still;
Tomorrow night I will
Buy more": and kissed her:
"Have done with sorrow;
I'll bring you plums tomorrow   170
Fresh on their mother twigs,
Cherries worth getting;
You cannot think what figs
My teeth have met in,

What melons icy-cold
Piled on a dish of gold
Too huge for me to hold,
What peaches with a velvet nap,
Pellucid grapes without one seed:
Odorous indeed must be the mead   180
Whereon they grow, and pure the wave they drink
With lilies at the brink,
And sugar-sweet their sap."

Golden head by golden head,
Like two pigeons in one nest
Folded in each other's wings,
They lay down in their curtained bed:
Like two blossoms on one stem,
Like two flakes of new-fall'n snow,
Like two wands of ivory   190
Tipped with gold for awful kings.
Moon and stars gazed in at them,
Wind sang to them lullaby,
Lumbering owls forebore to fly,
Not a bat flapped to and fro
Round their nest:
Cheek to cheek and breast to breast
Locked together in one nest.

Early in the morning
When the first cock crowed his warning,   200
Neat like bees, as sweet and busy,
Laura rose with Lizzie:
Fetched in honey, milked the cows,
Aired and set to rights the house,
Kneaded cakes of whitest wheat,
Cakes for dainty mouths to eat,
Next churned butter, whipped up cream,
Fed their poultry, sat and sewed;
Talked as modest maidens should:
Lizzie with an open heart,   210
Laura in an absent dream,
One content, one sick in part;
One warbling for the mere bright day's delight,
One longing for the night.

At length slow evening came:
They went with pitchers to the reedy brook;
Lizzie most placid in her look,
Laura most like a leaping flame.
They drew the gurgling water from its deep;
Lizzie plucked purple and rich golden flags,   220
Then turning homeward said: "The sunset flushes
Those furthest loftiest crags;
Come, Laura, not another maiden lags,
No willful squirrel wags,
The beasts and birds are fast sleep."

But Laura loitered still among the rushes
And said the bank was steep.
And said the hour was early still,
The dew not fall'n, the wind not chill:
Listening ever, but not catching   230
The customary cry,
"Come buy, come buy,"
With its iterated jingle
Of sugar-baited words:
Not for all her watching
Once discerning even one goblin
Racing, whisking, tumbling, hobbling;
Let alone the herds
That used to tramp along the glen,
In groups or single,   240
Of brisk fruit-merchant men.
Till Lizzie urged, "O Laura, come;
I hear the fruit-call but I dare not look:
You should not loiter longer at this brook:
Come with me home.
The stars rise, the moon bends her arc,
Each glowworm winks her spark,
Let us get home before the night grows dark:
For clouds may gather
Though this is summer weather,   250
Put out the lights and drench us through;
Then if we lost our way what should we do?"

Laura turned cold as stone
To find her sister heard that cry alone,

That goblin cry,
"Come buy our fruits, come buy."
Must she then buy no more such dainty fruit?
Must she no more such succous pasture find,
Gone deaf and blind?
Her tree of life drooped from the root: 260
She said not one word in her heart's sore ache;
But peering through the dimness, naught discerning,
Trudged home, her pitcher dripping all the way;
So crept to bed, and lay
Silent till Lizzie slept;
Then sat up in a passionate yearning,
And gnashed her teeth for balked desire, and wept
As if her heart would break.

Day after day, night after night,
Laura kept watch in vain   270
In sullen silence of exceeding pain.
She never caught again the goblin cry:
"Come buy, come buy";—
She never spied the goblin men
Hawking their fruits along the glen:
But when the noon waxed bright
Her hair grew thin and gray;
She dwindled, as the fair full moon doth turn
To swift decay and burn
Her fire away.   280

One day remembering her kernel-stone
She set it by a wall that faced the south;
Dewed it with tears, hoped for a root,
Watched for a waxing shoot,
But there came none;
It never saw the sun,
It never felt the trickling moisture run:
While with sunk eyes and faded mouth
She dreamed of melons, as a traveler sees
False waves in desert drouth   290
With shade of leaf-crowned trees,
And burns the thirstier in the sandful breeze.

She no more swept the house,
Tended the fowls or cows,

Fetched honey, kneaded cakes of wheat,
Brought water from the brook:
But sat down listless in the chimney-nook
And would not eat.

Tender Lizzie could not bear
To watch her sister's cankerous care   300
Yet not to share.
She night and morning
Caught the goblins' cry:
"Come buy our orchard fruits,
Come buy, come buy":—
Beside the brook, along the glen,
She heard the tramp of goblin men,
The voice and stir
Poor Laura could not hear;
Longed to buy fruit to comfort her,   310
But feared to pay too dear.
She thought of Jeanie in her grave,
Who should have been a bride;
But who for joys brides hope to have
Fell sick and died
In her gay prime,
In earliest Winter time,
With the first glazing rime,
With the first snow-fall of crisp Winter time.

Till Laura dwindling   320
Seemed knocking at Death's door:
Then Lizzie weighed no more
Better and worse;
But put a silver penny in her purse,
Kissed Laura, crossed the heath with clumps of furze
At twilight, halted by the brook:
And for the first time in her life
Began to listen and look.

Laughed every goblin
When they spied her peeping: 330
Came toward her hobbling,
Flying, running, leaping,
Puffing and blowing,

Chuckling, clapping, crowing,
Clucking and gobbling,
Mopping and mowing,
Full of airs and graces,
Pulling wry faces,
Demure grimaces,
Cat-like and rat-like,   340
Ratel- and wombat-like,
Snail-paced in a hurry,
Parrot-voiced and whistler,
Helter skelter, hurry skurry,
Chattering like magpies,
Fluttering like pigeons,
Gliding like fishes,—
Hugged her and kissed her,
Squeezed and caressed her:
Stretched up their dishes,   350
Panniers, and plates:
"Look at our apples
Russet and dun,
Bob at our cherries,
Bite at our peaches,
Citrons and dates,
Grapes for the asking,
Pears red with basking
Out in the sun,
Plums on their twigs;   360
Pluck them and suck them,
Pomegranates, figs."—

"Good folk," said Lizzie,
Mindful of Jeanie:
"Give me much and many":—
Held out her apron,
Tossed them her penny.
"Nay, take a seat with us,
Honour and eat with us,"
They answered grinning: 370
"Our feast is but beginning.
Night yet is early,
Warm and dew-pearly,

Wakeful and starry:
Such fruits as these
No man can carry;
Half their bloom would fly,
Half their dew would dry,
Half their flavour would pass by.
Sit down and feast with us,   380
Be welcome guest with us,
Cheer you and rest with us."—
"Thank you," said Lizzie: "But one waits
At home alone for me:
So without further parleying,
If you will not sell me any
Of your fruits though much and many,
Give me back my silver penny
I tossed you for a fee."—
They began to scratch their pates,   390
No longer wagging, purring,
But visibly demurring,
Grunting and snarling.
One called her proud,
Cross-grained, uncivil;
Their tones waxed loud,
Their looks were evil.
Lashing their tails,
They trod and hustled her,
Elbowed and jostled her,   400
Clawed with their nails,
Barking, mewing, hissing, mocking,
Tore her gown and soiled her stocking,
Twitched her hair out by the roots,
Stamped upon her tender feet,
Held her hands and squeezed their fruits
Against her mouth to make her eat.

White and golden Lizzie stood,
Like a lily in a flood,—
Like a rock of blue-veined stone   410
Lashed by tides obstreperously,—
Like a beacon left alone
In a hoary roaring sea,

Sending up a golden fire,—
Like a fruit-crowned orange-tree
White with blossoms honey-sweet
Sore beset by wasp and bee,—
Like a royal virgin town
Topped with gilded dome and spire
Close beleaguered by a fleet   420
Mad to tug her standard down.
One may lead a horse to water,
Twenty cannot make him drink.
Though the goblins cuffed and caught her,
Coaxed and fought her,
Bullied and besought her,
Scratched her, pinched her black as ink,
Kicked and knocked her,
Mauled and mocked her,
Lizzie uttered not a word;   430
Would not open lip from lip
Lest they should cram a mouthful in:
But laughed in heart to feel the drip
Of juice that syruped all her face,
And lodged in dimples of her chin,
And streaked her neck which quaked like curd.
At last the evil people,
Worn out by her resistance,
Flung back her penny, kicked their fruit
Along whichever road they took,   440
Not leaving root or stone or shoot;
Some writhed into the ground,
Some dived into the brook
With ring and ripple,
Some scudded on the gale without a sound,
Some vanished in the distance.

In a smart, ache, tingle,
Lizzie went her way;
Knew not was it night or day;
Sprang up the bank, tore through the furze,   450
Threaded copse and dingle,
And heard her penny jingle
Bouncing in her purse,—

Its bounce was music to her ear.
She ran and ran
As if she feared some goblin man
Dogged her with gibe or curse
Or something worse:
But not one goblin skurried after,
Nor was she pricked by fear;   460
The kind heart made her windy-paced
That urged her home quite out of breath with haste
And inward laughter.

She cried "Laura," up the garden,
"Did you miss me?
Come and kiss me.
Never mind my bruises,
Hug me, kiss me, suck my juices
Squeezed from goblin fruits for you,
Goblin pulp and goblin dew.   470
Eat me, drink me, love me;
Laura, make much of me:
For your sake I have braved the glen
And had to do with goblin merchant men."

Laura started from her chair,
Flung her arms up in the air,
Clutched her hair:
"Lizzie, Lizzie, have you tasted
For my sake the fruit forbidden?
Must your light like mine be hidden,   480
Your young life like mine be wasted,
Undone in mine undoing
And ruined in my ruin,
Thirsty, cankered, goblin-ridden?"—
She clung about her sister,
Kissed and kissed and kissed her:
Tears once again
Refreshed her shrunken eyes,
Dropping like rain
After long sultry drouth;   490
Shaking with aguish fear, and pain,
She kissed and kissed her with a hungry mouth.

Her lips began to scorch,
That juice was wormwood to her tongue,
She loathed the feast.
Writhing as one possessed she leaped and sung,
Rent all her robe, and wrung
Her hands in lamentable haste,
And beat her breast.
Her locks streamed like the torch   500
Borne by a racer at full speed,
Or like the mane of horses in their flight,
Or like an eagle when she stems the light
Straight toward the sun,
Or like a caged thing freed,
Or like a flying flag when armies run.

Swift fire spread through her veins, knocked at her heart,
Met the fire smoldering there
And overbore its lesser flame;
She gorged on bitterness without a name: 510
Ah! fool, to choose such part
Of soul-consuming care!
Sense failed in the mortal strife:
Like the watch-tower of a town
Which an earthquake shatters down,
Like a lightning-stricken mast,
Like a wind-uprooted tree
Spun about,
Like a foam-topped waterspout
Cast down headlong in the sea,   520
She fell at last;
Pleasure past and anguish past,
Is it death or is it life?

Life out of death.
That night long Lizzie watched by her,
Counted her pulse's flagging stir,
Felt for her breath,
Held water to her lips, and cooled her face
With tears and fanning leaves:
But when the first birds chirped about their eaves,   530
And early reapers plodded to the place

Of golden sheaves,
And dew-wet grass
Bowed in the morning winds so brisk to pass,
And new buds with new day
Opened of cup-like lilies on the stream,
Laura awoke as from a dream,
Laughed in the innocent old way,
Hugged Lizzie but not twice or thrice;
Her gleaming locks showed not one thread of gray,   540
Her breath was sweet as May
And light danced in her eyes.

Days, weeks, months, years,
Afterwards, when both were wives
With children of their own;
Their mother-hearts beset with fears,
Their lives bound up in tender lives;
Laura would call the little ones
And tell them of her early prime,
Those pleasant days long gone   550
Of not-returning time:
Would talk about the haunted glen,
The wicked, quaint fruit-merchant men,
Their fruits like honey to the throat
But poison in the blood;
(Men sell not such in any town):
Would tell them how her sister stood
In deadly peril to do her good,
And win the fiery antidote:
Then joining hands to little hands   560
Would bid them cling together,
"For there is no friend like a sister
In calm or stormy weather;
To cheer one on the tedious way,
To fetch one if one goes astray,
To lift one if one totters down,
To strengthen whilst one stands."

1862

l. 258: **succous** juicy.   l. 336: **mopping and mowing** making gro-
tesque faces.

From OLD AND NEW YEAR DITTIES

Passing away, saith the World, passing away

Passing away, saith the World, passing away:
Chances, beauty, and youth, sapped day by day:
Thy life never continueth in one stay.
Is the eye waxen dim, is the dark hair changing to gray
That hath won neither laurel nor bay?
I shall clothe myself in Spring and bud in May:
Thou, root-stricken, shalt not rebild thy decay
On my bosom for aye.
Then I answered: Yea.

Passing away, saith my Soul, passing away: 10
With its burden of fear and hope, of labour and play,
Hearken what the past doth witness and say:
Rust in thy gold, a moth is in thine array,
A canker is in thy bud, thy leaf must decay.
At midnight, at cockcrow, at morning one certain day,
Lo the Bridegroom shall come and shall not delay:
Watch thou and pray.
Then I answered: Yea.

Passing away, saith my God, passing away:
Winter passeth after the long delay: 20
New grapes on the vine, new figs on the tender spray,
Turtle calleth turtle in Heaven's May.
Though I tarry, wait for Me, trust Me, watch and pray:
Arise, come away, night is past, and lo, it is day,
My love, My sister, My spouse, thou shalt hear Me say—
Then I answered: Yea.

1862

l. 16: **Bridegroom** Christ. See Matt. 25:1–14.   l. 22: **turtle** turtle-
dove. See Song of Solomon 2:10–12.

AMOR MUNDI

"Oh, where are you going with your lovelocks flowing,
    On the west wind blowing along this valley track?"
"The downhill path is easy, come with me an it please ye,
    We shall escape the uphill by never turning back."

So they two went together in glowing August weather,
  The honey-breathing heather lay to their left and right;
And dear she was to dote on, her swift feet seemed to float on
  The air like soft twin pigeons too sportive to alight.

"Oh, what is that in heaven where gray cloud-flakes are seven,
  Where blackest clouds hang riven just at the rainy skirt?"   10
"Oh, that's a meteor sent us, a message dumb, portentous,
  An undeciphered solemn signal of help or hurt."

"Oh, what is that glides quickly where velvet flowers grow
      thickly,
  Their scent comes rich and sickly?" "A scaled and hooded
      worm."
"Oh, what's that in the hollow, so pale I quake to follow?"
  "Oh, that's a thin dead body which waits the eternal term."

"Turn again, O my sweetest—turn again, false and fleetest;
  This beaten way thou beatest, I fear, is hell's own track."
"Nay, too steep for hill mounting; nay, too late for cost
      counting;
  This downhill path is easy, but there's no turning back."   20

                                                        1875

Title: the love of the World, that is, of worldly pleasure.

MONNA INNOMINATA

A SONNET OF SONNETS

1

> Lo dì che han detto a' dolci amici addio.
>   DANTE.
> Amor, con quanto sforzo oggi mi vinci!
>   PETRARCA.

COME back to me, who wait and watch for you:—
  Or come not yet, for it is over then,
  And long it is before you come again,
So far between my pleasures are and few.
While, when you come not, what I do I do

Thinking "Now when he comes," my sweetest "when":
    For one man is my world of all the men
This wide world holds; O love, my world is you.
Howbeit, to meet you grows almost a pang
    Because the pang of parting comes so soon;   10
My hope hangs waning, waxing, like a moon
    Between the heavenly days on which we meet:
Ah me, but where are now the songs I sang
    When life was sweet because you called them sweet?

2

> Era già l'ora che volge il desio.
>   DANTE.
> Riccorro al tempo ch' io vi vidi prima.
>   PETRARCA.

I wish I could remember that first day,
    First hour, first moment of your meeting me,
    If bright or dim the season, it might be
Summer or Winter for aught I can say;
So unrecorded did it slip away,
    So blind was I to see and to foresee,
    So dull to mark the budding of my tree
That would not blossom yet for many a May.
If only I could recollect it, such
    A day of days! I let it come and go   10
    As traceless as a thaw of bygone snow;
It seemed to mean so little, meant so much;
If only now I could recall that touch,
    First touch of hand in hand—Did one but know!

3

> O ombre vane, fuor che ne l'aspetto!
>   DANTE.
> Immaginata guida la conduce.
>   PETRARCA.

I dream of you, to wake: would that I might
    Dream of you and not wake but slumber on;
    Nor find with dreams the dear companion gone,
As, Summer ended, Summer birds take flight.
In happy dreams I hold you full in sight,

I blush again who waking look so wan;
 Brighter than sunniest day that ever shone,
In happy dreams your smile makes day of night.
 Thus only in a dream we are at one,
  Thus only in a dream we give and take   10
   ' The faith that maketh rich who take or give;
 If thus to sleep is sweeter than to wake,
  To die were surely sweeter than to live,
Though there be nothing new beneath the sun.

4

   Poca favilla gran fiamma seconda.
       Dante.
   Ogni altra cosa, ogni pensier va fore,
   E sol ivi con voi rimansi amore.
       Petrarca.

I loved you first: but afterwards your love,
 Outsoaring mine, sang such a loftier song
As drowned the friendly cooings of my dove.
 Which owes the other most? My love was long,
 And yours one moment seemed to wax more strong;
I loved and guessed at you, you construed me
And loved me for what might or might not be—
 Nay, weights and measures do us both a wrong.
For verily love knows not "mine" or "thine";
 With separate "I" and "thou" free love has done, 10
  For one is both and both are one in love:
Rich love knows nought of "thine that is not mine;"
 Both have the strength and both the length thereof,
Both of us, of the love which makes us one.

5

   Amor che a nullo amato amar perdona.
       Dante.
   Amor m'addusse in sì gioiosa spene.
       Petrarca.

O my heart's heart, and you who are to me
 More than myself myself, God be with you,
 Keep you in strong obedience leal and true
To Him whose noble service setteth free;

Give you all good we see or can foresee,
  Make your joys many and your sorrows few,
  Bless you in what you bear and what you do,
Yea, perfect you as He would have you be.
So much for you; but what for me, dear friend?
  To love you without stint and all I can,   10
To-day, to-morrow, world without an end;
To love you much and yet to love you more,
As Jordan at his flood sweeps either shore;
  Since woman is the helpmeet made for man.

6

Or puoi la quantitate
Comprender de l'amor che a te mi scalda.
                                    DANTE.
Non vo' che da tal nodo amor mi scioglia.
                                    PETRARCA.

Trust me, I have not earned your dear rebuke,—
  I love, as you would have me, God the most;
  Would lose not Him, but you, must one be lost,
Nor with Lot's wife cast back a faithless look,
Unready to forego what I forsook;
  This say I, having counted up the cost,
  This, though I be the feeblest of God's host,
The sorriest sheep Christ shepherds with His crook.
Yet while I love my God the most, I deem
  That I can never love you overmuch;   10
  I love Him more, so let me love you too;
Yea, as I apprehend it, love is such
I cannot love you if I love not Him,
  I cannot love Him if I love not you.

7

Qui primavera sempre ed ogni frutto.
                                    DANTE.
Ragionando con meco ed io con lui.
                                    PETRARCA.

"Love me, for I love you"—and answer me,
  "Love me, for I love you": so shall we stand
  As happy equals in the flowering land

Of love, that knows not a dividing sea.
Love builds the house on rock and not on sand,
   Love laughs what while the winds rave desperately;
And who hath found love's citadel unmanned?
   And who hath held in bonds love's liberty?—
My heart's a coward though my words are brave—
   We meet so seldom, yet we surely part   10
   So often; there's a problem for your art!
Still I find comfort in his Book who saith,
Though jealousy be cruel as the grave,
   And death be strong, yet love is strong as death.

8

Come dicesse a Dio, D'altro non calme.
DANTE.
Spero trovar pietà non che perdono.
PETRARCA.

"I, if I perish, perish"—Esther spake;
   And bride of life or death she made her fair
   In all the lustre of her perfumed hair
And smiles that kindle longing but to slake.
She put on pomp of loveliness, to take
   Her husband through his eyes at unaware;
   She spread abroad her beauty for a snare,
Harmless as doves and subtle as a snake.
She trapped him with one mesh of silken hair,
   She vanquished him by wisdom of her wit,   10
      And built her people's house that it should stand:—
   If I might take my life so in my hand,
And for my love to Love put up my prayer,
   And for love's sake by Love be granted it!

9

O dignitosa coscienza e netta!
DANTE.
Spirto più acceso di virtuti ardenti.
PETRARCA.

Thinking of you, and all that was, and all
   That might have been and now can never be,
   I feel your honoured excellence, and see

Myself unworthy of the happier call:
For woe is me who walk so apt to fall,
　　So apt to shrink afraid, so apt to flee,
　　Apt to lie down and die (ah woe is me!)
Faithless and hopeless turning to the wall.
And yet not hopeless quite nor faithless quite,
Because not loveless; love may toil all night,   10
But take at morning; wrestle till the break
　　Of day, but then wield power with God and man:—
　　So take I heart of grace as best I can,
Ready to spend and be spent for your sake.

10

　　Con miglior corso e con migliore stella.
　　　　　　　　　　DANTE.
　　La vita fugge e non s'arresta un' ora.
　　　　　　　　　　PETRARCA.

Time flies, hope flags, life plies a wearied wing;
　　Death following hard on life gains ground apace;
　　Faith runs with each and rears an eager face,
Outruns the rest, makes light of everything,
Spurns earth, and still finds breath to pray and sing;
　　While love ahead of all uplifts his praise,
　　Still asks for grace and still gives thanks for grace,
Content with all day brings and night will bring.
Life wanes; and when love folds his wings above
　　Tired hope, and less we feel his conscious pulse,   10
　　　Let us go fall asleep, dear friend, in peace:
　　　A little while, and age and sorrow cease;
　　A little while, and life reborn annuls
Loss and decay and death, and all is love.

11

　　Vien dietro a me e lascia dir le genti.
　　　　　　　　　　DANTE.
　　Contando i casi della vita nostra.
　　　　　　　　　　PETRARCA.

Many in aftertimes will say of you
　　"He loved her"—while of me what will they say?
　　Not that I loved you more than just in play,

For fashion's sake as idle women do.
Even let them prate; who know not what we knew
    Of love and parting in exceeding pain,
    Of parting hopeless here to meet again,
Hopeless on earth, and heaven is out of view.
But by my heart of love laid bare to you,
    My love that you can make not void nor vain,   10
Love that foregoes you but to claim anew
Beyond this passage of the gate of death,
    I charge you at the Judgment make it plain
My love of you was life and not a breath.

12

    Amor che ne la mente mi ragiona.
                DANTE.
    Amor vien nel bel viso di costei.
                PETRARCA.

If there be any one can take my place
    And make you happy whom I grieve to grieve,
    Think not that I can grudge it, but believe
I do commend you to that nobler grace,
That readier wit than mine, that sweeter face;
    Yea, since your riches make me rich, conceive
    I too am crowned, while bridal crowns I weave,
And thread the bridal dance with jocund pace.
For if I did not love you, it might be
    That I should grudge you some one dear delight;   10
    But since the heart is yours that was mine own,
Your pleasure is my pleasure, right my right,
Your honourable freedom makes me free,
    And you companioned I am not alone.

13

    E drizzeremo gli occhi al Primo Amore.
                DANTE.
    Ma trovo peso non da le mie braccia.
                PETRARCA.

If I could trust mine own self with your fate,
    Shall I not rather trust it in God's hand?
    Without Whose Will one lily doth not stand,

Nor sparrow fall at his appointed date;
   Who numbereth the innumerable sand,
Who weighs the wind and water with a weight,
To Whom the world is neither small nor great,
   Whose knowledge foreknew every plan we planned.
Searching my heart for all that touches you,
   I find there only love and love's goodwill   10
Helpless to help and impotent to do,
Of understanding dull, of sight most dim;
And therefore I commend you back to Him
   Whose love your love's capacity can fill.

14

    E la Sua Volontade è nostra pace.
          DANTE.
    Sol con questi pensier, con altre chiome.
          PETRARCA.

Youth gone, and beauty gone if ever there
   Dwelt beauty in so poor a face as this;
   Youth gone and beauty, what remains of bliss?
I will not bind fresh roses in my hair,
To shame a cheek at best but little fair,—
   Leave youth his roses, who can bear a thorn,—
I will not seek for blossoms anywhere,
   Except such common flowers as blow with corn.
Youth gone and beauty gone, what doth remain?
   The longing of a heart pent up forlorn,   10
    A silent heart whose silence loves and longs;
    The silence of a heart which sang its songs
   While youth and beauty made a summer morn,
Silence of love that cannot sing again.

                  1881

Title: A Lady Unnamed. Christina Rossetti explained that whereas Beatrice
was "immortalized" by Dante and Laura by Petrarch there were other ladies
unnamed who inspired lesser poets. In these fourteen sonnets (one for each
line of a sonnet, hence the subtitle) such a lady, herself a poet, portrays
the stages of a "mutual love incompatible with mutual honour." The
poems may be autobiographical, but the facts are uncertain.
Sonnet 1: Epigraphs: all translations supplied by W. M. Rossetti.
Dante: "The day that they have said adieu to their sweet friends."
Petrarch: "Love with how great a stress dost thou vanquish me to-day!"
Sonnet 2: Epigraphs:

Dante: "It was already the hour which turns back the desire."
Petrarch: "I recur to the time when I first saw thee."
Sonnet 3: Epigraphs:
Dante: "Oh shades, empty save in semblance!"
Petrarch: "An imaginary guide conducts her."
Sonnet 4: Epigraphs:
Dante: "A small spark fosters a great flame."
Petrarch: "Every other thing, every thought, goes off, and love alone remains there with you."
l. 10: **free** spontaneous and blameless (See V, 1.4).   **done** done away.
Sonnet 5: Epigraphs:
Dante: "Love, who exempts no loved one from loving."
Petrarch: "Love led me into such joyous hope."
Sonnet 6: Epigraphs:
Dante: "Now canst thou comprehend the quantity of the love which glows in towards thee."
Petrarch: "I do not choose that Love should release me from such a tie."
l. 4: **Lot's wife** who, when fleeing from the destruction of Sodom and Gommorah, broke the Lord's command and looked back and was turned into a pillar of salt. See Gen. 19:24–26.
Sonnet 7: Epigraphs:
Dante: "Here always Spring and every fruit."
Petrarch: "Conversing with me, and I with him."
l. 11: **problem** the kind of paradox ("We meet seldom yet part often") that the Italian poets were fond of.   l. 12: **Book** Song of Solomon 8:6.
Sonnet 8: Epigraphs:
Dante: "As if he were to say to God, 'I care for nought else.' "
Petrarch: "I hope to find pity, and not only pardon."
l. 1: **Esther** the Jewish queen of the Persian king, Ahasuerus, from whom she obtained her people's freedom at the risk of her life. See Esther 4:16.
Sonnet 9: Epigraphs:
Dante: "O dignified and pure conscience!"
Petrarch: "Spirit more lit with burning virtues."
l. 11: **wrestle** as Jacob did with an angel, who gave him God's blessing. See Gen. 32:24–28.
Sonnet 10: Epigraphs:
Dante: "With better course and with better star."
Petrarch: "Life flees, and stays not an hour."
Sonnet 11: Epigraphs:
Dante: "Come after me, and leave folk to talk."
Petrarch: "Relating the casualties of our life."
Sonnet 12: Epigraphs:
Dante: "Love, who speaks within my mind."
Petrarch: "Love comes in the beautiful face of this lady."
Sonnet 13: Epigraphs:
Dante: "And we will direct our eyes to the Primal Love."
Petrarch: "But I find a burden to which my arms suffice not."
Sonnet 14: Epigraphs:
Dante: "And His will is our peace."
Petrarch: "Only with these thoughts, with different locks."

"*All heaven is blazing yet*"

All heaven is blazing yet
   With the meridian sun:
Make haste, unshadowing sun, make haste to set;
   O lifeless life, have done.
I choose what once I chose;
   What once I willed, I will:
Only the heart its own bereavement knows;
   O clamorous heart, lie still.

That which I chose, I choose;
   That which I willed, I will;   10
That which I once refused, I still refuse:
   O hope deferred, be still.
That which I chose and choose
   And will is Jesus' Will:
He hath not lost his life who seems to lose:
   O hope deferred, hope still.

Before 1886   1904

From *CHRIST OUR ALL IN ALL*

Lord, I am here.—But, child, I look for thee
         Elsewhere and nearer Me.—
Lord, that way moans a wide insatiate sea:
         How can I come to Thee?—
Set foot upon the water, test and see
         If thou canst come to Me.—
Couldst Thou not send a boat to carry me,
         Or dolphin swimming free?—
Nay, boat nor fish if thy will faileth thee:
         For My Will too is free.—   10
O Lord, I am afraid.—Take hold on Me:
         I am stronger than the sea.—
Save, Lord, I perish.—I have hold of thee,
         I made and rule the sea,
I bring thee to the haven where thou wouldst be.

Before 1893   1904

WILLIAM MORRIS

1834–1896

IN PRISON

Wearily, drearily,
Half the day long,
Flap the great banners
High over the stone;
Strangely and eerily
Sounds the wind's song,
Bending the banner-poles.

While, all alone,
Watching the loophole's spark,
Lie I, with life all dark,   10
Feet tethered, hands fettered
Fast to the stone,
The grim wall, square lettered
With prisoned men's groan.

Still strain the banner-poles
Through the wind's song,
Westward the banner rolls
Over my wrong.

THE DEFENCE OF GUENEVERE

But, knowing now that they would have her speak,
She threw her wet hair backward from her brow.
Her hand close to her mouth touching her cheek,

As though she had had there a shameful blow,
And feeling it shameful to feel aught but shame
All through her heart, yet felt her cheek burned so,

She must a little touch it; like one lame
She walked away from Gauwaine, with her head
Still lifted up; and on her cheek of flame

The tears dried quick; she stopped at last and said: 10
"O knights and lords, it seems but little skill
To talk of well-known things past now and dead.

"God wot I ought to say, I have done ill,
And pray you all forgiveness heartily!
Because you must be right, such great lords; still

"Listen—suppose your time were come to die,
And you were quite alone and very weak;
Yea, laid a-dying, while very mightily

"The wind was ruffling up the narrow streak
Of river through your broad lands running well;   20
Suppose a hush should come, then someone speak:

" 'One of these cloths is heaven, and one is hell;
Now choose one cloth forever—which they be,
I will not tell you; you must somehow tell

" 'Of your own strength and mightiness; here, see!'
Yea, yea, my lord, and you to ope your eyes,
At foot of your familiar bed to see

"A great God's angel standing, with such dyes
Not known on earth, on his great wings, and hands,
Held out two ways, light from the inner skies   30

"Showing him well, and making his commands
Seem to be God's commands, moreover, too,
Holding within his hands the cloths on wands;

"And one of these strange choosing cloths was blue,
Wavy and long and one cut short and red;
No man could tell the better of the two.

"After a shivering half-hour you said:
'God help! heaven's colour, the blue'; and he said, 'hell.'
Perhaps you would then roll upon your bed,

"And cry to all good men that loved you well,   40
'Ah, Christ! if only I had known, known, known';
Launcelot went away, then I could tell,

"Like wisest man how all things would be, moan,
And roll and hurt myself, and long to die,
And yet fear much to die for what was sown.

"Nevertheless, you, O Sir Gauwaine, lie;
Whatever may have happened through these years,
God knows I speak truth, saying that you lie."

Her voice was low at first, being full of tears,
But as it cleared, it grew full loud and shrill,   50
Growing a windy shriek in all men's ears,

A ringing in their startled brains, until
She said that Gauwaine lied, then her voice sunk,
And her great eyes began again to fill,

Though still she stood right up, and never shrunk,
But spoke on bravely, glorious lady fair!
Whatever tears her full lips may have drunk,

She stood, and seemed to think, and wrung her hair,
Spoke out at last with no more trace of shame,
With passionate twisting of her body there: 60

"It chanced upon a day that Launcelot came
To dwell at Arthur's court—at Christmastime
This happened; when the heralds sung his name,

"Son of King Ban of Benwick, seemed to chime
Along with all the bells that rang that day,
O'er the white roofs, with little change of rime.

"Christmas and whitened winter passed away,
And over me the April sunshine came,
Made very awful with black hail-clouds; yea,

"And in the summer I grew white with flame,   70
And bowed my head down; autumn, and the sick
Sure knowledge things would never be the same,

"However often spring might be most thick
Of blossoms and buds, smote on me, and I grew
Careless of most things, let the clock tick, tick,

"To my unhappy pulse, that beat right through
My eager body; while I laughed out loud,
And let my lips curl up at false or true,

"Seemed cold and shallow without any cloud.
Behold, my judges, then the cloths were brought;   80
While I was dizzied thus, old thoughts would crowd,

"Belonging to the time ere I was bought
By Arthur's great name and his little love;
Must I give up forever then, I thought,

"That which I deemed would ever round me move
Glorifying all things; for a little word,
Scarce ever meant at all, must I now prove

"Stone-cold forever? Pray you, does the Lord
Will that all folks should be quite happy and good?
I love God now a little, if this cord   90

"Were broken, once for all what striving could
Make me love anything in earth or heaven?
So day by day it grew, as if one should

"Slip slowly down some path worn smooth and even,
Down to a cool sea on a summer day;
Yet still in slipping there was some small leaven

"Of stretched hands catching small stones by the way
Until one surely reached the sea at last,
And felt strange new joy as the worn head lay

"Back, with the hair like sea-weed; yea, all past   100
Sweat of the forehead, dryness of the lips,
Washed utterly out by the dear waves o'ercast,

"In the lone sea, far off from any ships!
Do I not know now of a day in spring?
No minute of that wild day ever slips

"From out my memory; I hear thrushes sing,
And wheresoever I may be, straightway
Thoughts of it all come up with most fresh sting.

"I was half mad with beauty on that day,
And went, without my ladies, all alone,   110
In a quiet garden walled round every way;

"I was right joyful of that wall of stone,
That shut the flowers and trees up with the sky,
And trebled all the beauty; to the bone—

"Yea, right through to my heart, grown very shy
With wary thoughts—it pierced, and made me glad,
Exceedingly glad, and I knew verily,

"A little thing just then had made me mad;
I dared not think, as I was wont to do,
Sometimes, upon my beauty; if I had   120

"Held out my long hand up against the blue,
And, looking on the tenderly darkened fingers,
Thoughts that by rights one ought to see quite through,

"There, see you, where the soft still light yet lingers,
Round by the edges; what should I have done,
If this had joined with yellow spotted singers,

"And startling green drawn upward by the sun?
But shouting, loosed out, see now! all my hair,
And trancedly stood watching the west wind run

"With faintest half-heard breathing sound—why there   130
I lose my head e'en now in doing this.
But shortly listen: In that garden fair

"Came Launcelot walking; this is true, the kiss
Wherewith we kissed in meeting that spring day,
I scarce dare talk of the remembered bliss,

"When both our mouths went wandering in one way,
And aching sorely, met among the leaves;
Our hands, being left behind, strained far away.

"Never within a yard of my bright sleeves
Had Launcelot come before—and now so nigh!   140
After that day why is it Guenevere grieves?

"Nevertheless, you, O Sir Gauwaine, lie,
Whatever happened on through all those years—
God knows I speak truth, saying that you lie.

"Being such a lady, could I weep these tears
If this were true? A great queen such as I,
Having sinned this way, straight her conscience sears;

"And afterwards she liveth hatefully,
Slaying and poisoning—certes never weeps;
Gauwaine, be friends now, speak me lovingly.   150

"Do I not see how God's dear pity creeps
All through your frame, and trembles in your mouth?
Remember in what grave your mother sleeps,

"Buried in some place far down in the south,
Men are forgetting as I speak to you;
By her head, severed in that awful drouth

"Of pity that drew Agravaine's fell blow,
I pray your pity! let me not scream out
Forever after, when the shrill winds blow

"Through half your castle-locks! let me not shout   160
Forever after in the winter night
When you ride out alone! in battle-rout

"Let not my rusting tears make your sword light!
Ah! God of mercy, how he turns away!
So, ever must I dress me to the fight,

"So—let God's justice work! Gauwaine, I say,
See me hew down your proofs; yea, all men know,
Even as you said, how Mellyagraunce one day,

"One bitter day in *la Fausse Garde*, for so
All good knights held it after, saw—   170
Yea, sirs, by cursed unknightly outrage, though

"You, Gauwaine, held his word without a flaw,
This Mellyagraunce saw blood upon my bed—
Whose blood then pray you? is there any law

"To make a queen say why some spots of red
Lie on her coverlet? or will you say,
'Your hands are white, lady, as when you wed,

" 'Where did you bleed?' and must I stammer out—'Nay,
I blush indeed, fair lord, only to rend
My sleeve up to my shoulder, where there lay   180

" 'A knife-point last night': so must I defend
The honour of the Lady Guenevere?
Not so, fair lords, even if the world should end

"This very day, and you were judges here
Instead of God. Did you see Mellyagraunce
When Launcelot stood by him?—what white fear

"Curdled his blood, and how his teeth did dance,
His side sink in? as my knight cried and said:
'Slayer of unarmed men, here is a chance!

" 'Setter of traps, I pray you guard your head;   190
By God, I am so glad to fight with you,
Stripper of ladies, that my hand feels lead

" 'For driving weight; hurrah now! draw and do,
For all my wounds are moving in my breast,
And I am getting mad with waiting so.'

"He struck his hands together o'er the beast,
Who fell down flat, and groveled at his feet,
And groaned at being slain so young. 'At least,'

"My knight said, 'Rise you, sir, who are so fleet
At catching ladies; half-armed will I fight,   200
My left side all uncovered!' Then, I weet,

"Up sprang Sir Mellyagraunce with great delight
Upon his knave's face; not until just then
Did I quite hate him, as I saw my knight

"Along the lists look to my stake and pen
With such a joyous smile, it made me sigh
From agony beneath my waist-chain, when

"The fight began, and to me they drew nigh;
Ever Sir Launcelot kept him on the right,
And traversed warily, and ever high   210

"And fast leapt caitiff's sword, until my knight
Sudden threw up his sword to his left hand,
Caught it, and swung it; that was all the fight,

"Except a spout of blood on the hot land;
For it was hottest summer; and I know
I wondered how the fire, while I should stand,

"And burn, against the heat, would quiver so,
Yards above my head; thus these matters went;
Which things were only warnings of the woe

"That fell on me. Yet Mellyagraunce was shent,   220
For Mellyagraunce had fought against the Lord;
Therefore, my lords, take heed lest you be blent

"With all his wickedness—say no rash word
Against me, being so beautiful; my eyes,
Wept all away to gray, may bring some sword

"To drown you in your blood; see my breast rise,
Like waves of purple sea, as here I stand;
And how my arms are moved in wonderful wise;

"Yea, also at my full heart's strong command,
See through my long throat how the words go up   230
In ripples to my mouth; how in my hand

"The shadow lies like wine within a cup
Of marvelously coloured gold; yea, now
This little wind is rising, look you up,

"And wonder how the light is falling so
Within my moving tresses. Will you dare
When you have looked a little on my brow,

"To say this thing is vile? or will you care
For any plausible lies of cunning woof,
When you can see my face with no lie there   240

"Forever? Am I not a gracious proof?—
'But in your chamber Launcelot was found'—
Is there a good knight then would stand aloof,

"When a queen says with gentle queenly sound,
'O true as steel, come now and talk with me;
I love to see your step upon the ground

" 'Unwavering; also well I love to see
That gracious smile light up your face, and hear
Your wonderful words, that all mean verily

" 'The thing they seem to mean. Good friend, so dear   250
To me in everything, come here tonight,
Or else the hours will pass most dull and drear.

" 'If you come not, I fear this time I might
Get thinking overmuch of times gone by,
When I was young, and green hope was in sight;

" 'For no man cares now to know why I sigh;
And no man comes to sing me pleasant songs
Nor any brings me the sweet flowers that lie

" 'So thick in the gardens; therefore one so longs
To see you, Launcelot, that we may be   260
Like children once again, free from all wrongs

" 'Just for one night.' Did he not come to me?
What thing could keep true Launcelot away
If I said, 'Come'? There was one less than three

"In my quiet room that night, and we were gay;
Till sudden I rose up, weak, pale, and sick,
Because a bawling broke our dream up; yea,

"I looked at Launcelot's face and could not speak,
For he looked helpless, too, for a little while;
Then I remember how I tried to shriek,   270

"And could not, but fell down; from tile to tile
The stones they threw up rattled o'er my head
And made me dizzier; till within a while

"My maids were all about me, and my head
On Launcelot's breast was being soothed away
From its white chattering, until Launcelot said . . .

"By God! I will not tell you more today—
Judge any way you will; what matters it?
You know quite well the story of that fray,

"How Launcelot stilled their bawling, the mad fit   280
That caught up Gauwaine, all, all, verily,
But just that which would save me; these things flit.

"Nevertheless, you, O Sir Gauwaine, lie;
Whatever may have happened these long years,
God knows I speak truth, saying that you lie!

"All I have said is truth, by Christ's dear tears."
She would not speak another word, but stood
Turned sideways, listening, like a man who hears

His brother's trumpet sounding through the wood
Of his foes' lances. She leaned eagerly,   290
And gave a slight spring sometimes, as she could

At last hear something really; joyfully
Her cheek grew crimson, as the headlong speed
Of the roan charger drew all men to see,
The knight who came was Launcelot at good need.

1858

Title: The circumstances are mainly from Malory's *Morte d'Arthur*, Bks. XIX–XX, but the speech of Guenevere is Morris's. Guenevere is accused by Sir Gauwaine of adultery with Sir Launcelot, which would entail treason to her husband, King Arthur. While trying to gain time for Launcelot to rescue her, she pleads her case on the ground that her marriage was an empty formality and that her love for Launcelot was sincere and hence not shameful adultery.   l. 80: **cloths**   described in ll. 19–39.   l. 153: **Your Mother**   Gauwaine's, murdered by his brother Agravaine (l. 157) because she had committed adultery.   l. 168: **Mellyagraunce**   He had imprisoned Guenevere in his castle, *la Fausse Garde* ("prison of broken faith") and, finding blood on her bedclothes, accused her of adultery with a young knight. Then Launcelot had come to her rescue and, wearing only half his armour (l. 200), killed Mellyagraunce and freed Guenevere. l. 207: **waist-chain**   fettering her to the stake.   l. 220: **shent**   shamed. l. 222: **blent**   blinded.

SHAMEFUL DEATH

There were four of us about that bed:
    The mass-priest knelt at the side,
I and his mother stood at the head,
    Over his feet lay the bride;
We were quite sure that he was dead,
    Though his eyes were open wide.

He did not die in the night,
    He did not die in the day,
But in the morning twilight
    His spirit passed away,   10
When neither sun nor moon was bright,
    And the trees were merely gray.

He was not slain with the sword,
    Knight's ax, or the knightly spear,
Yet spoke he never a word
    After he came in here;
I cut away the cord
    From the neck of my brother dear.

He did not strike one blow,
   For the recreants came behind,   20
In a place where the hornbeams grow,
   A path right hard to find,
For the hornbeam boughs swing so
   That the twilight makes it blind.

They lighted a great torch then,
   When his arms were pinioned fast,
Sir John the knight of the Fen,
   Sir Guy of the Dolorous Blast,
With knights threescore and ten,
   Hung brave Lord Hugh at last.   30

I am threescore and ten,
   And my hair is all turned gray,
But I met Sir John of the Fen,
   Long ago on a summer day,
And am glad to think of the moment when
   I took his life away.

I am threescore and ten,
   And my strength is mostly passed,
But long ago I and my men,
   When the sky was overcast,   40
And the smoke rolled over the reeds of the fen,
   Slew Guy of the Dolorous Blast.

And now, knights all of you,
   I pray you pray for Sir Hugh,
A good knight and a true,
   And for Alice, his wife, pray too.

                           1858

TWO RED ROSES ACROSS THE MOON

There was a lady lived in a hall,
Large of her eyes and slim and tall;
And ever she sung from noon to noon,
Two red roses across the moon.

There was a knight came riding by
In early spring, when the roads were dry;
And he heard that lady sing at the noon,
Two red roses across the moon.

Yet none the more he stopped at all,
But he rode a-gallop past the hall;   10
And left that lady singing at noon,
Two red roses across the moon.

Because, forsooth, the battle was set,
And the scarlet and blue had got to be met,
He rode on the spur till the next warm noon;
Two red roses across the moon.

But the battle was scattered from hill to hill,
From the windmill to the watermill;
And he said to himself, as it neared the noon,
Two red roses across the moon.   20

You scarce could see for the scarlet and blue,
A golden helm or a golden shoe;
So he cried, as the fight grew thick at the noon,
Two red roses across the moon!

Verily then the gold bore through
The huddled spears of the scarlet and blue;
And they cried, as they cut them down at the noon,
Two red roses across the moon!

I trow he stopped when he rode again
By the hall, though draggled sore with the rain;   30
And his lips were pinched to kiss at the noon
Two red roses across the moon.

Under the may she stooped to the crown;
All was gold, there was nothing of brown,
And the horns blew up in the hall at noon,
Two red roses across the moon.

1858

THE HAYSTACK IN THE FLOODS

Had she come all the way for this,
To part at last without a kiss?
Yea, had she borne the dirt and rain
That her own eyes might see him slain
Beside the haystack in the floods?

Along the dripping leafless woods,
The stirrup touching either shoe,
She rode astride as troopers do;
With kirtle kilted to her knee,
To which the mud splashed wretchedly;   10
And the wet dripped from every tree
Upon her head and heavy hair,
And on her eyelids broad and fair;
The tears and rain ran down her face.

By fits and starts they rode apace,
And very often was his place
Far off from her; he had to ride
Ahead, to see what might betide
When the roads crossed; and sometimes, when
There rose a murmuring from his men,   20
Had to turn back with promises.
Ah me! she had but little ease;
And often for pure doubt and dread
She sobbed, made giddy in the head
By the swift riding; while, for cold,
Her slender fingers scarce could hold
The wet reins; yea, and scarcely, too,
She felt the foot within her shoe
Against the stirrup: all for this,
To part at last without a kiss   30
Beside the haystack in the floods.

For when they neared that old soaked hay,
They saw across the only way
That Judas, Godmar, and the three
Red running lions dismally
Grinned from his pennon, under which
In one straight line along the ditch,
They counted thirty heads.

So then
While Robert turned round to his men,
She saw at once the wretched end,   40
And, stooping down, tried hard to rend
Her coif the wrong way from her head,
And hid her eyes; while Robert said:
"Nay, love, 'tis scarcely two to one;
At Poictiers where we made them run
So fast—why, sweet my love, good cheer,
The Gascon frontier is so near,
Nought after us."

         But: "O!" she said,
"My God! my God! I have to tread
The long way back without you; then   50
The court at Paris; those six men;
The gratings of the Chatelet;
The swift Seine on some rainy day
Like this, and people standing by,
And laughing, while my weak hands try
To recollect how strong men swim.
All this, or else a life with him,
For which I should be damned at last,
Would God that this next hour were past!"

He answered not, but cried his cry,   60
"St. George for Marny!" cheerily;
And laid his hand upon her rein.
Alas! no man of all his train
Gave back that cheery cry again;
And, while for rage his thumb beat fast
Upon his sword-hilt, someone cast
About his neck a kerchief long,
And bound him.

         Then they went along
To Godmar; who said: "Now, Jehane,
Your lover's life is on the wane   70
So fast, that, if this very hour
You yield not as my paramour,
He will not see the rain leave off:
Nay, keep your tongue from gibe and scoff,
Sir Robert, or I slay you now."

She laid her hand upon her brow,
Then gazed upon the palm, as though
She thought her forehead bled, and: "No!"
She said, and turned her head away,
As there was nothing else to say,   80
And everything was settled: red
Grew Godmar's face from chin to head:
"Jehane, on yonder hill there stands
My castle, guarding well my lands;
What hinders me from taking you,
And doing that I list to do
To your fair willful body, while
Your knight lies dead?"
               A wicked smile
Wrinkled her face, her lips grew thin,
A long way out she thrust her chin: 90
"You know that I should strangle you
While you were sleeping; or bite through
Your throat, by God's help: ah!" she said,
"Lord Jesus, pity your poor maid!
For in such wise they hem me in,
I cannot choose but sin and sin,
Whatever happens: yet I think
They could not make me eat or drink,
And so should I just reach my rest."

"Nay, if you do not my behest,   100
O Jehane! though I love you well,"
Said Godmar, "would I fail to tell
All that I know?" "Foul lies," she said.
"Eh? lies, my Jehane? by God's head,
At Paris folks would deem them true!
Do you know, Jehane, they cry for you:
'Jehane the brown! Jehane the brown!
Give us Jehane to burn or drown!'
Eh!—gag me Robert!—sweet my friend,
This were indeed a piteous end   110
For those long fingers, and long feet,
And long neck, and smooth shoulders sweet;
An end that few men would forget
That saw it. So, an hour yet:
Consider, Jehane, which to take

Of life or death!"
               So, scarce awake,
Dismounting, did she leave that place,
And totter some yards: with her face
Turned upward to the sky she lay,
Her head on a wet heap of hay,   120
And fell asleep: and while she slept,
And did not dream, the minutes crept
Round to the twelve again; but she,
Being waked at last, sighed quietly,
And strangely childlike came, and said:
"I will not." Straightway Godmar's head,
As though it hung on strong wires, turned
Most sharply round, and his face burned.

For Robert, both his eyes were dry,
He could not weep, but gloomily   130
He seemed to watch the rain; yea, too,
His lips were firm; he tried once more
To touch her lips; she reached out, sore
And vain desire so tortured them,
The poor gray lips, and now the hem
Of his sleeve brushed them.
                    With a start
Up Godmar rose, thrust them apart;
From Robert's throat he loosed the bands
Of silk and mail; with empty hands
Held out, she stood and gazed, and saw,   140
The long bright blade without a flaw
Glide out from Godmar's sheath, his hand
In Robert's hair; she saw him bend
Back Robert's head; she saw him send
The thin steel down; the blow told well,
Right backward the knight Robert fell,
And moaned as dogs do, being half dead,
Unwitting, as I deem: so then
Godmar turned grinning to his men,
Who ran, some five or six, and beat   150
His head to pieces at their feet.

Then Godmar turned again and said:
"So, Jehane, the first fitte is read!
Take note, my lady, that your way

Lies backward to the Chatelet!"
She shook her head and gazed awhile
At her cold hands with a rueful smile,
As though this thing had made her mad.

This was the parting that they had
Beside the haystack in the floods.   160

1858

Title: In France, shortly after the Battle of Poitiers (1356), Sir Robert de Marny and his mistress, Jehane, are trying to reach the safety of English-held Gascony when they are captured by Godmar and his men.   ll. 51–53: **court . . . day** She will be taken to Paris and imprisoned in the infamous Chatelet prison. Her six judges will sentence her to be cast into the river Seine, to drown if she is innocent, to swim if she is guilty, and if guilty to be burned as a witch.   l. 61: **St. George** patron saint of the English.   l. 109: **gag me** gag him for me.   l. 153: **fitte** episode of a narrative.

From THE EARTHLY PARADISE

AN APOLOGY

Of Heaven or Hell I have no power to sing,
I cannot ease the burden of your fears,
Or make quick-coming death a little thing,
Or bring again the pleasure of past years,
Nor for my words shall ye forget your tears,
Or hope again for aught that I can say,
The idle singer of an empty day.

But rather, when, aweary of your mirth,
From full hearts still unsatisfied ye sigh,
And, feeling kindly unto all the earth,   10
Grudge every minute as it passes by,
Made the more mindful that the sweet days die—
Remember me a little then, I pray,
The idle singer of an empty day.

The heavy trouble, the bewildering care
That weighs us down who live and earn our bread,
These idle verses have no power to bear;
So let me sing of names rememberèd,

Because they, living not, can ne'er be dead,
Or long time take their memory quite away   20
From us poor singers of an empty day.

   Dreamer of dreams, born out of my due time,
Why should I strive to set the crooked straight?
Let it suffice me that my murmuring rhyme
Beats with light wing against the ivory gate,
Telling a tale not too importunate
To those who in the sleepy region stay,
Lulled by the singer of an empty day.

   Folk say, a wizard to a northern king
At Christmas-tide such wondrous things did show,   30
That through one window men beheld the spring,
And through another saw the summer glow,
And through a third the fruited vines a-row,
While still, unheard, but in its wonted way,
Piped the drear wind of that December day.

   So with this Earthly Paradise it is,
If we will read aright, and pardon me,
Who strive to build a shadowy isle of bliss
Midmost the beating of the steely sea,
Where tossed about all hearts of men must be;   40
Whose ravening monsters mighty men shall slay,
Not the poor singer of an empty day.

                          1868

Subtitle: An explanation; on an idyllic island descendents of Norse and of Greek heroes exchange their traditional stories, twenty-four in all, at a series of banquets held through one year.   l. 25: **ivory gate** From the cave of Morpheus, god of sleep, fictitious dreams pass out through an ivory gate, truly prophetic ones through a gate of horn.

L'ENVOI

   Here are we for the last time face to face,
Thou and I, Book, before I bid thee speed
Upon thy perilous journey to that place
For which I have done on thee pilgrim's weed
Striving to get thee all things for thy need—

I love thee, whatso time or men may say
Of the poor singer of an empty day.

Good reason why I love thee, e'en if thou
Be mocked or clean forgot as time wears on;
For ever as thy fashioning did grow,
Kind word and praise because of thee I won
From those without whom were my world all gone,
My hope fallen dead, my singing cast away,
And I set soothly in an empty day.

I love thee; yet this last time must it be
That thou must hold thy peace and I must speak,
Lest if thou babble I begin to see
Thy gear too thin, thy limbs and heart too weak,
To find the land thou goest forth to seek—
Though what harm if thou die upon the way,
Thou idle singer of an empty day?

But though this land desired thou never reach,
Yet folk who know it mayst thou meet, or death;
Therefore a word unto thee would I teach
To answer these, who, noting thy weak breath,
Thy wandering eyes, thy heart of little faith,
May make thy fond desire a sport and play
Mocking the singer of an empty day.

That land's name, say'st thou? and the road thereto?
Nay, Book, thou mockest, saying thou know'st it not;
Surely no book of verse I ever knew
But ever was the heart within him hot
To gain the Land of Matters Unforgot—
There, now we both laugh—as the whole world may,
At us poor singers of an empty day.

Nay, let it pass, and harken! Hast thou heard
That therein I believe I have a friend,
Of whom for love I may not be afeared?
It is to him indeed I bid thee wend;
Yea, he perchance may meet thee ere thou end,
Dying so far off from the hedge of bay,
Thou idle singer of an empty day!

10

20

30

40

Well, think of him, I bid thee, on the road,
And if it hap that midst of thy defeat,
Fainting beneath thy follies' heavy load,
My Master, GEOFFREY CHAUCER, thou do meet,
Then shalt thou win a space of rest full sweet;
Then be thou bold, and speak the words I say,
The idle singer of an empty day!

"O Master, O thou great of heart and tongue,   50
Thou well mayst ask me why I wander here,
In raiment rent of stories oft besung!
But of thy gentleness draw thou anear,
And then the heart of one who held thee dear
Mayst thou behold! So near as that I lay
Unto the singer of an empty day.

"For this he ever said, who sent me forth
To seek a place amid thy company:
That howsoever little was my worth,
Yet was he worth e'en just so much as I;   60
He said that rhyme hath little skill to lie;
Nor feigned to cast his worser part away;
In idle singing for an empty day.

"I have beheld him tremble oft enough
At things he could not choose but trust to me,
Although he knew the world was wise and rough;
And never did he fail to let me see
His love,—his folly and faithlessness, maybe;
And still in turn I gave him voice to pray
Such prayers as cling about an empty day.   70

"Thou, keen-eyed, reading me, mayst read him through,
For surely little is there left behind;
No power great deeds unnameable to do;
No knowledge for which words he may not find,
No love of things as vague as autumn wind—
Earth of the earth lies hidden by my clay,
The idle singer of an empty day!

"Children we twain are, saith he, late made wise
In love, but in all else most childish still,
And seeking still the pleasure of our eyes,   80

And what our ears with sweetest sounds may fill;
Not fearing Love, lest these things he should kill;
Howe'er his pain by pleasure doth he lay,
Making a strange tale of an empty day.

"Death have we hated, knowing not what it meant;
Life have we loved, through green leaf and through sere,
Though still the less we knew of its intent;
The Earth and Heaven through countless year on year,
Slow changing, were to us but curtains fair,
Hung around about a little room, where play   90
Weeping and laughter of man's empty day.

"O Master, if thine heart could love us yet,
Spite of things left undone, and wrongly done,
Some place in loving hearts then should we get,
For thou, sweet-souled, didst never stand alone,
But knew'st the joy and woe of many an one—
By lovers dead, who live through thee, we pray,
Help thou us singers of an empty day!"

Fearest thou, Book, what answer thou mayst gain
Lest he should scorn thee, and thereof thou die?   100
Nay, it shall not be.—Thou mayst toil in vain,
And never draw the House of Fame anigh;
Yet he and his shall know whereof we cry,
Shall call it not ill done to strive to lay
The ghosts that crowd about life's empty day.

Then let the other go! and if indeed
In some old garden thou and I have wrought,
And made fresh flowers spring up from hoarded seed,
And fragrance of old days and deeds have brought
Back to folk weary; all was not for nought,   110
—No little part it was for me to play—
The idle singer of an empty day.

1870

Title: Afterword (to *The Earthly Paradise*; see preceding poem).   l. 4:
pilgrim's weed   dress for a journey; that is, for publication.   l. 46:
Chaucer   whose example as a story-teller Morris has tried to follow.
l. 102: **House of Fame**   a punning allusion to one of Chaucer's poems.
l. 106: **the other**   hope of fame.

From *CHANTS FOR SOCIALISTS*

THE MARCH OF THE WORKERS

What is this, the sound and rumour? What is this that all men
    hear,
Like the wind in hollow valleys when the storm is drawing near,
Like the rolling on of ocean in the eventide of fear?
               'Tis the people marching on.

Whither go they, and whence come they? What are these of
    whom ye tell?
In what country are they dwelling 'twixt the gates of heaven and
    hell?
Are they mine or thine for money? Will they serve a master
    well?
               Still the rumour's marching on.

       Hark the rolling of the thunder!
       Lo the sun! and lo thereunder   10
       Riseth wrath, and hope, and wonder,
           And the host comes marching on.

Forth they come from grief and torment; on they wend toward
    health and mirth,
All the wide world is their dwelling, every corner of the earth.
Buy them, sell them for thy service! Try the bargain what 'tis
    worth,
               For the days are marching on.

These are thy who build thy houses, weave thy raiment, win
    thy wheat,
Smooth the rugged, fill the barren, turn the bitter into sweet,
All for thee this day—and ever. What reward for them is meet
            Till the host comes marching on?   20

       Hark the rolling of the thunder!
       Lo the sun! and lo thereunder
       Riseth wrath, and hope, and wonder,
           And the host comes marching on.

Many a hundred years passed over have they laboured deaf and
    blind;

Never tidings reached their sorrow, never hope their toil might
  find.
Now at last they've heard and hear it, and the cry comes down
  the wind,
                  And their feet are marching on.

O ye rich men hear and tremble; for with words the sound is
  rife;
"Once for you and death we laboured; changed henceforward
  is the strife.   30
We are men, and we shall battle for the world of men and life;
                  And our host is marching on."

              Hark the rolling of the thunder!
              Lo the sun! and lo thereunder
              Riseth wrath, and hope, and wonder,
                  And the host comes marching on.

"Is it war, then? Will ye perish as the dry wood in the fire?
Is it peace? Then be ye of us, let your hope be our desire.
Come and live! for life awaketh, and the world shall never tire;
                  And hope is marching on.   40

"On we march then, we the workers, and the rumour that ye
  hear
Is the blended sound of battle and deliv'rance drawing near;
For the hope of every creature is the banner that we bear,
                  And the world is marching on."

              Hark the rolling of the thunder!
              Lo the sun! and lo thereunder
              Riseth wrath, and hope, and wonder,
                  And the host comes marching on.

                                                    1884

Title: written in imitation of Julia Ward Howe's "Battle Hymn of the
Republic."

TO THE MUSE OF THE NORTH

O muse that swayest the sad Northern Song,
Thy right hand full of smiting and of wrong,
Thy left hand holding pity, and thy breast
Heaving with hope of that so certain rest;
Thou, with the gray eyes kind and unafraid,
The soft lips trembling not, though they have said
The doom of the World and those that dwell therein,
The lips that smile not though thy children win
The fated Love that draws the fated Death—
O, borne adown the fresh stream of thy breath,   10
Let some word reach my ears and touch my heart,
That, if it may be, I may have a part
In that great sorrow of thy children dead
That vexed the brow, and bowed adown the head,
Whitened the hair, made life a wondrous dream,
And death the murmur of a restful stream,
But left no stain upon those souls of thine
Whose greatness through the tangled world doth shine.
O Mother, and Love and Sister all in one,
Come thou; for sure I am enough alone   20
That thou thine arms about my heart shouldst throw,
And wrap me in the grief of long ago.

                                        1891

Title: an invocation to the spirit of the Scandinavian sagas.

ICELAND FIRST SEEN

Lo, from our loitering ship
a new land at last to be seen;
Toothed rocks down the side of the firth
on the east guard a weary wide lea,
And black slope the hillsides above,
striped adown with their desolate green:
And a peak rises up on the west
from the meeting of cloud and of sea,
Foursquare from base unto point
like the building of Gods that have been,   10

The last of that waste of the mountains
all cloud-wreathed and snow-flecked and gray,
And bright with the dawn that began
just now at the ending of day.

Ah! what came we forth for to see
that our hearts are so hot with desire?
Is it enough for our rest,
the sight of this desolate strand,
And the mountain-waste voiceless as death
but for winds that may sleep not nor tire?   20
Why do we long to wend forth
through the length and breadth of a land,
Dreadful with grinding of ice,
and record of scarce hidden fire,
But that there 'mid the gray grassy dales
sore scarred by the ruining streams
Lives the tale of the Northland of old
and the undying glory of dreams?
O land, as some cave by the sea
where the treasures of old have been laid,   30
The sword it may be of a king
whose name was the turning of fight:
Or the staff of some wise of the world
that many things made and unmade.
Or the ring of a woman maybe
whose woe is grown wealth and delight.
No wheat and no wine grows above it,
no orchard for blossom and shade;
The few ships that sail by its blackness
but deem it the mouth of a grave;   40
Yet sure when the world shall awaken,
this too shall be mighty to save.
Or rather, O land, if a marvel
it seemeth that men ever sought
Thy wastes for a field and a garden
fulfilled of all wonder and doubt,
And feasted amidst of the winter
when the fight of the year had been fought,
Whose plunder all gathered together
was little to babble about;   50

Cry aloud from thy waste, O thou land,
"Not for this nor for that was I wrought
Amid waning of realms and of riches
and death of things worshipped and sure,
I abide here the spouse of a God,
and I made and I make and endure."

O Queen of the grief without knowledge,
of the courage that may not avail,
Of the longing that may not attain,
of the love that shall never forget,   60
More joy than the gladness of laughter
thy voice hath amidst of its wail:
More hope than of pleasure fulfilled
amidst of thy blindness is set;
More glorious than gaining of all
thine unfaltering hand that shall fail:
For what is the mark on thy brow
but the brand that thy Brynhild doth bear?
Lone once, and loved and undone
by a love that no ages outwear.   70
Ah! when thy Balder comes back,
and bears from the heart of the Sun
Peace and the healing of pain,
and the wisdom that waiteth no more;
And the lilies are laid on thy brow
'mid the crown of the deeds thou hast done;
And the roses spring up by thy feet
that the rocks of the wilderness wore.
Ah! when thy Balder comes back
and we gather the gains he hath won,   80
Shall we not linger a little
to talk of thy sweetness of old,
Yea, turn back awhile to thy travail
whence the Gods stood aloof to behold?

1891

l. 68: **Brynhild** in the saga of the Niblungs, a Valkyrie, one of the
daughters of Wotan. She was the bride of Sigurd (or Siegfried) who was
forced by magic to forget her.   l. 71: **Balder** Norse god of sunlight
and spring. Slain by treachery, he was annually mourned and his resurrec-
tion was expected.

THUNDER IN THE GARDEN

When the boughs of the garden hang heavy with rain
And the blackbird reneweth his song,
And the thunder departing yet rolleth again,
I remember the ending of wrong.

When the day that was dusk while his death was aloof
Is ending wide-gleaming and strange
For the clearness of all things beneath the world's roof,
I call back the wild chance and the change.

For once we twain sat through the hot afternoon
While the rain held aloof for a while,   10
Till she, the soft-clad, for the glory of June
Changed all with the change of her smile.

For her smile was of longing, no longer of glee,
And her fingers, entwined with mine own,
With caresses unquiet sought kindness of me
For the gift that I never had known.

Then down rushed the rain, and the voice of the thunder
Smote dumb all the sound of the street,
And I to myself was grown nought but a wonder,
As she leaned down my kisses to meet.   20

That she craved for my lips that had craved her so often,
And the hand that had trembled to touch,
That the tears filled her eyes I had hoped not to soften
In this world was a marvel too much.

It was dusk 'mid the thunder, dusk e'en as the night,
When first brake out our love like the storm,
But no night-hour was it, and back came the light
While our hands with each other were warm.

And her smile killed with kisses, came back as at first
As she rose up and led me along,   30
And out to the garden, where nought was athirst,
And the blackbird renewing his song.

Earth's fragrance went with her, as in the wet grass
Her feet little hidden were set;

170

She bent down her head, 'neath the roses to pass,
And her arm with the lily was wet.

In the garden we wandered while day waned apace
And the thunder was dying aloof;
Till the moon o'er the minster-wall lifted his face,
And grey gleamed out the lead of the roof.   40

Then we turned from the blossoms, and cold were they grown
In the trees the wind westering moved;
Till over the threshold back fluttered her gown,
And in the dark house was I loved.

                                                    1891

FOR THE BED AT KELMSCOTT

The wind's on the wold
And the night is a-cold,
And Thames runs chill
'Twixt mead and hill;
But kind and dear
Is the old house here,
And my heart is warm
'Midst winter's harm.

Rest, then, and rest,
And think of the best   10
'Twixt summer and spring,
When all birds sing
In the town of the tree,
And ye lie in me
And scarce dare move,
Lest the earth and its love
Should fade away
Ere the full of the day.

I am old and have seen
Many things that have been—   20
Both grief and peace
And wane and increase.
No tale I tell

Of ill or well,
But this I say,
Night treadeth on day.
And for worst and best
Right good is rest.

1893

Title: Kelmscott Manor was Morris's home in his later years.

ALGERNON CHARLES SWINBURNE

1837–1909

From ATALANTA IN CALYDON

CHORUS

When the hounds of spring are on winter's traces,
    The mother of months in meadow or plain
Fills the shadows and windy places
    With lisp of leaves and ripple of rain;
And the brown bright nightingale amorous
Is half assuaged for Itylus,
For the Thracian ships and the foreign faces,
    The tongueless vigil and all the pain.

Come with bows bent and with emptying of quivers,
    Maiden most perfect, lady of light,   10
With a noise of winds and many rivers,
    With a clamour of waters, and with might;
Bind on thy sandals, O thou most fleet,
Over the splendour and speed of thy feet;
For the faint east quickens, the wan west shivers,
    Round the feet of the day and the feet of the night.

Where shall we find her, how shall we sing to her,
    Fold our hands round her knees, and cling?
O that man's heart were as fire and could spring to her,
    Fire, or the strength of the streams that spring!   20
For the stars and the winds are unto her
As raiment, as songs of the harp-player;
For the risen stars and the fallen cling to her,
    And the southwest-wind and the west-wind sing.

For winter's rains and ruins are over,
    And all the season of snows and sins;
The days dividing lover and lover,
    The light that loses, the night that wins;
And time remembered is grief forgotten,
And frosts are slain and flowers begotten,   30
And in green underwood and cover
    Blossom by blossom the spring begins.

The full streams feed on flower of rushes,
    Ripe grasses trammel a traveling foot,
The faint fresh flame of the young years flushes
    From leaf to flower and flower to fruit;
And fruit and leaf are as gold and fire,
And the oat is heard above the lyre,
And the hoofed heel of a satyr crushes
    The chestnut-husk at the chestnut-root.   40

And Pan by noon and Bacchus by night,
    Fleeter of foot than the fleet-foot kid,
Follows with dancing and fills with delight
    The Mænad and the Bassarid;
And soft as lips that laugh and hide,
The laughing leaves of the trees divide,
And screen from seeing and leave in sight
    The god pursuing, the maiden hid.

The ivy falls with the Bacchanal's hair
    Over her eyebrows hiding her eyes;   50
The wild vine slipping down leaves bare
    Her bright breast shortening into sighs;
The wild vine slips with the weight of its leaves,
But the berried ivy catches and cleaves
To the limbs that glitter, the feet that scare
    The wolf that follows, the fawn that flies.

l. 2: **Mother of months** Artemis, goddess of the moon and the lunar
cycles.   ll. 5–8: **nightingale . . . pain** In legend, Tereus of Thrace,
husband of Procne, seduced her sister, Philomel, and cut out her tongue.
In revenge Procne killed her son, Itylus, and tricked Tereus into eating his
son's flesh. Procne and Philomel fled, Tereus in pursuit. The gods trans-
formed them into birds: Procne into a nightingale, Philomel into a
swallow, Tereus into a hawk. (Some versions make Philomel the nightin-
gale.)   l. 38: **oat** shepherd's pipe.   l. 44: **Maenad . . . Bassarid**
Female devotees of Bacchus. Their rites were reputedly bloody and lewd.

CHORUS

a sort of theorising
about the beginning.

His tone is
not too
serious.

Before the beginning of years
  There came to the making of man
Time, with a gift of tears;
  Grief, with a glass that ran;
Pleasure, with pain for leaven;
  Summer, with flowers that fell;
Remembrance fallen from heaven,
  And madness risen from hell;
Strength without hands to smite;
  Love that endures for a breath;   10
Night, the shadow of light,
  And life, the shadow of death.

And the high gods took in hand
  Fire, and the falling of tears,
And a measure of sliding sand
  From under the feet of the years;
And froth and drift of the sea;
  And dust of the labouring earth;
And bodies of things to be
  In the houses of death and of birth;   20
And wrought with weeping and laughter,
  And fashioned with loathing and love,

The making of
man yet

With life before and after
  And death beneath and above,
For a day and a night and a morrow,
  That his strength might endure for a span
With travail and heavy sorrow,
  The holy spirit of man.

From the winds of the north and the south
  They gathered as unto strife;   30
They breathed upon his mouth,
  They filled his body with life;
Eyesight and speech they wrought
  For the veils of the soul therein,
A time for labour and thought,
  A time to serve and to sin;

might have been
shocking.

They gave him light in his ways,
  And love, and a space for delight,

And beauty and length of days,
　　And night, and sleep in the night.   40
His speech is a burning fire;
　　With his lips he travaileth;
In his heart is a blind desire,
　　In his eyes foreknowledge of death;
He weaves, and is clothed with derision;
　　Sows, and he shall not reap;
His life is a watch or a vision
　　Between a sleep and a sleep.

man

*Ambiguos
characteristics
of man.*

1865

THE SUNDEW

A little marsh-plant, yellow green,
And pricked at lip with tender red.
Tread close, and either way you tread
Some faint black water jets between
Lest you should bruise the curious head.

A live thing may be; who shall know?
The summer knows and suffers it;
For the cool moss is thick and sweet
Each side, and saves the blossom so
That it lives out the long June heat.   10

The deep scent of the heather burns
About it; breathless though it be,
Bow down and worship; more than we,
Is the least flower whose life returns,
Least weed renascent in the sea.

We are vexed and cumbered in earth's sight
With wants, with many memories;
These see their mother what she is,
Glad-growing, till August leave more bright
The apple-coloured cranberries.   20

Wind blows and bleaches the strong grass,
Blown all one way to shelter it
From trample of strayed kine, with feet

Felt heavier than the moorhen was,
Strayed up past patches of wild wheat.

You call it sundew: how it grows,
If with its colour it have breath,
If life taste sweet to it, if death
Pain its soft petal, no man knows:
Man has no sight or sense that saith.   30

My sundew, grown of gentle days,
In these green miles the spring begun
Thy growth ere April had half done
With the soft secret of her ways
Or June made ready for the sun.

O red-lipped mouth of marsh-flower,
I have a secret halved with thee.
The name that is love's name to me
Thou knowest, and the face of her
Who is my festival to see.   40

The hard sun, as thy petal knew,
Coloured the heavy moss-water:
Thou wert not worth green midsummer
Nor fit to live to August blue,
O sundew, not remembering her.

1866

HYMN TO PROSERPINE

(AFTER THE PROCLAMATION IN ROME OF THE CHRISTIAN FAITH)

Vicisti, Galilæe

I have lived long enough, having seen one thing, that love hath
    an end;
Goddess and maiden and queen, be near me now and befriend.
Thou art more than the day or the morrow, the seasons that
    laugh or that weep;

For these give joy and sorrow; but thou, Proserpina, sleep.
Sweet is the treading of wine, and sweet the feet of the dove;
But a goodlier gift is thine than foam of the grapes or love.
Yea, is not even Apollo, with hair and harpstring of gold,
A bitter god to follow, a beautiful god to behold?
I am sick of singing; the bays burn deep and chafe. I am fain
To rest a little from praise and grievous pleasure and pain.   10
For the gods we know not of, who give us our daily breath,
We know they are cruel as love or life, and lovely as death.

O gods dethroned and deceased, cast forth, wiped out in a day!
From your wrath is the world released, redeemed from your
    chains, men say.
New gods are crowned in the city; their flowers have broken
    your rods;
They are merciful, clothed with pity, the young compassionate
    gods.
But for me their new device is barren, the days are bare;
Things long past over suffice, and men forgotten that were.
Time and the gods are at strife; ye dwell in the midst thereof,
Draining a little life from the barren breasts of love.   20
I say to you, cease, take rest; yea, I say to you all, be at peace,
Till the bitter milk of her breast and the barren bosom shall
    cease.

Wilt thou yet take all, Galilean? But these thou shalt not
    take—
The laurel, the palms, and the pæan, the breasts of the nymphs
    in the brake,
Breasts more soft than a dove's, that tremble with tenderer
    breath;
And all the wings of the Loves, and all the joy before death;
All the feet of the hours that sound as a single lyre,
Dropped and deep in the flowers, with strings that flicker like
    fire.
More than these wilt thou give, things fairer than all these
    things?
Nay, for a little we live, and life hath mutable wings.   30
A little while and we die; shall life not thrive as it may?
For no man under the sky lives twice, outliving his day.
And grief is a grievous thing, and a man hath enough of his tears;
Why should he labour, and bring fresh grief to blacken his years?

Thou hast conquered, O pale Galilean; the world has grown
    gray from thy breath;
We have drunken of things Lethean, and fed on the fullness of
    death.
Laurel is green for a season, and love is sweet for a day;
But love grows bitter with treason, and laurel outlives not
    May.
Sleep, shall we sleep after all? for the world is not sweet in the
    end;
For the old faiths loosen and fall, the new years ruin and rend.   40
Fate is a sea without shore, and the soul is a rock that abides;
But her ears are vexed with the roar and her face with the foam
    of the tides.
O lips that the live blood faints in, the leavings of racks and
    rods!
O ghastly glories of saints, dead limbs of gibbeted gods!
Though all men abase them before you in spirit, and all knees
    bend,
I kneel not, neither adore you, but standing look to the end.

All delicate days and pleasant, all spirits and sorrows are cast
Far out with the foam of the present that sweeps to the surf of
    the past;
Where beyond the extreme sea-wall, and between the remote
    sea-gates,
Waste water washes, and tall ships founder, and deep death
    waits;   50
Where, mighty with deepening sides, clad about with the seas
    as with wings,
And impelled of invisible tides, and fulfilled of unspeakable
    things,
White-eyed and poisonous-finned, shark-toothed and serpen-
    tine-curled,
Rolls, under the whitening wind of the future, the wave of the
    world.
The depths stand naked in sunder behind it, the storms flee
    away;
In the hollow before it the thunder is taken and snared as a
    prey;
In its sides is the north-wind bound; and its salt is of all men's
    tears,

With light of ruin, and sound of changes, and pulse of years;
With travail of day after day, and with trouble of hour upon
    hour.
And bitter as blood is the spray; and the crests are as fangs that
    devour;   60
And its vapour and storm of its steam as the sighing of spirits
    to be;
And its noise as the noise in a dream; and its depths as the roots
    of the sea;
And the height of its heads as the height of the utmost stars of
    the air;
And the ends of the earth at the might thereof tremble, and
    time is made bare.
Will ye bridle the deep sea with reins, will ye chasten the high
    sea with rods?
Will ye take her to chain her with chains, who is older than all
    ye gods?
All ye as a wind shall go by, as a fire shall ye pass and be past;
Ye are gods, and behold, ye shall die, and the waves be upon
    you at last.
In the darkness of time, in the deeps of the years, in the changes
    of things,
Ye shall sleep as a slain man sleeps, and the world shall forget
    you for kings.   70
Though the feet of thine high priests tread where thy lords and
    our forefathers trod,
Though these that were gods are dead, and thou being dead
    art a god,
Though before thee the throned Cytherean be fallen, and
    hidden her head,
Yet thy kingdom shall pass, Galilean, thy dead shall go down to
    thee dead.

Of the maiden thy mother men sing as a goddess with grace
    clad around:
Thou art throned where another was king; where another was
    queen she is crowned.
Yea, once we had sight of another; but now she is queen, say
    these.
Not as thine, not as thine was our mother, a blossom of
    flowering seas,

Clothed round with the world's desire as with raiment, and fair
    as the foam,
And fleeter than kindled fire, and a goddess, and mother of
    Rome.   80
For thine came pale and a maiden, and sister to sorrow; but
    ours,
Her deep hair heavily laden with odour and colour of flowers,
White rose of the rose-white water, a silver splendour, a flame,
Bent down unto us that besought her, and earth grew sweet
    with her name.
For thine came weeping, a slave among slaves, and rejected;
    but she
Came flushed from the full-flushed wave, and imperial, her foot
    on the sea.
And the wonderful waters knew her, the winds and the viewless
    ways,
And the roses grew rosier, and bluer the sea-blue stream of the
    bays.

Ye are fallen, our lords, by what token? we wist that ye should
    not fall.
Ye were all so fair that are broken; and one more fair than ye
    all.   90
But I turn to her still, having seen she shall surely abide in the
    end;
Goddess and maiden and queen, be near me now and befriend.
O daughter of earth, of my mother, her crown and blossom of
    birth,
I am also, I also, thy brother; I go as I came unto earth.
In the night where thine eyes are as moons are in heaven, the
    night where thou art,
Where the silence is more than all tunes, where sleep overflows
    from the heart,
Where the poppies are sweet as the rose in our world, and the
    red rose is white,
And the wind falls faint as it blows with the fume of the flowers
    of the night,
And the murmur of spirits that sleep in the shadow of gods
    from afar
Grows dim in thine ears and deep as the deep dim soul of a
    star,   100

In the sweet low light of thy face, under heavens untrod by the
sun,
Let my soul with their souls find place, and forget what is done
and undone.
Thou art more than the gods who number the days of our
temporal breath;
For these give labour and slumber; but thou, Proserpina, death.
Therefore now at thy feet I abide for a season in silence. I know
I shall die as my fathers died, and sleep as they sleep; even so.
For the glass of the years is brittle wherein we gaze for a span.
A little soul for a little bears up this corpse which is man.
So long I endure, no longer; and laugh not again, neither weep.
For there is no god found stronger than death; and death is a
sleep.   110

1866

Title: a lament by a pagan still loyal to the gods dethroned by the official
recognition of Christianity.   *Vicisti, Galilæe* a saying ascribed to the
Emperor Julian (A.D. 333–363) who tried to restore the old religions but
confessed on his death-bed, "Thou hast conquered, Galilean" (that is,
Christ).   l. 24: **laurel, palm** sacred to the gods and worn as wreaths
by their devotees.   l. 73: **Cytherean** Venus.   l. 76: **king . . . queen**
Jupiter, Venus.   l. 80: **Mother of Rome** Venus, as the mother of
Aeneas, founder of Rome.   l. 92: **queen** that is, Proserpine.   l. 108:
A little soul . . . quoted from Epictetus, Roman philosopher of the
first century.

LAUS VENERIS

Asleep or waking is it? for her neck,
Kissed over close, wears yet a purple speck
    Wherein the pained blood falters and goes out;
Soft, and stung softly—fairer for a fleck.

But though my lips shut sucking on the place,
There is no vein at work upon her face;
    Her eyelids are so peaceable, no doubt
Deep sleep has warmed her blood through all its ways.

Lo, this is she that was the world's delight;
The old gray years were parcels of her might;   10
    The strewings of the ways wherein she trod
Were the twain seasons of the day and night.

Lo, she was thus when her clear limbs enticed
All lips that now grow sad with kissing Christ,
    Stained with blood fallen from the feet of God,
The feet and hands whereat our souls were priced.

Alas, Lord, surely thou art great and fair.
But, lo, her wonderfully woven hair!
    And thou didst heal us with thy piteous kiss;
But see now, Lord, her mouth is lovelier.   20

She is right fair; what hath she done to thee?
Nay, fair Lord Christ, lift up thine eyes and see;
    Had now thy mother such a lip—like this?
Thou knowest how sweet a thing it is to me.

Inside the Horsel here the air is hot;
Right little peace one hath for it, God wot;
    The scented dusty daylight burns the air,
And my heart chokes me till I hear it not.

Behold, my Venus, my soul's body, lies
With my love laid upon her garment-wise,   30
    Feeling my love in all her limbs and hair
And shed between her eyelids through her eyes.

She holds my heart in her sweet open hands
Hanging asleep; hard by her head there stands,
    Crowned with gilt thorns and clothed with flesh like fire,
Love, wan as foam blown up the salt burnt sands—

Hot as the brackish waifs of yellow spume
That shift and steam—loose clots of arid fume
    From the sea's panting mouth of dry desire;
There stands he, like one labouring at a loom.   40

The warp holds fast across; and every thread
That makes the woof up has dry specks of red;
    Always the shuttle cleaves clean through, and he
Weaves with the hair of many a ruined head.

Love is not glad nor sorry, as I deem;
Labouring he dreams, and labours in the dream,
    Till when the spool is finished, lo, I see
His web, reeled off, curls and goes out like steam.

Night falls like fire; the heavy lights run low,
And as they drop, my blood and body so   50
    Shake as the flame shakes, full of days and hours
That sleep not neither weep they as they go.

Ah, yet would God, this flesh of mine might be
Where air might wash and long leaves cover me,
    Where tides of grass break into foam of flowers,
Or where the wind's feet shine along the sea.

Ah, yet would God, that stems and roots were bred
Out of my weary body and my head,
    That sleep were sealed upon me with a seal
And I were as the least of all his dead.   60

Would God my blood were dew to feed the grass,
Mine ears made deaf and mine eyes blind as glass,
    My body broken as a turning wheel,
And my mouth stricken ere it saith Alas!

Ah, God, that love were as a flower or flame,
That life were as the naming of a name,
    That death were not more pitiful than desire,
That these things were not one thing and the same!

Behold now, surely somewhere there is death;
For each man hath some space of years, he saith,   70
    A little space of time ere time expire,
A little day, a little way of breath.

And, lo, between the sundawn and the sun,
His day's work and his night's work are undone;
    And, lo, between the nightfall and the light,
He is not, and none knoweth of such an one.

Ah, God, that I were as all souls that be,
As any herb or leaf of any tree,
    As men that toil through hours of labouring night,
As bones of men under the deep sharp sea.   80

Outside it must be winter among men;
For at the gold bars of the gates again
    I heard all night and all the hours of it
The wind's wet wings and fingers drip with rain.

Knights gather, riding sharp for cold; I know
The ways and woods are strangled with the snow;
    And with short song the maidens spin and sit
Until Christ's birthnight, lily-like, arow.

The scent and shadow shed about me make
The very soul in all my senses ache;   90
    The hot hard night is fed upon my breath,
And sleep beholds me from afar awake.

Alas, but surely where the hills grow deep,
Or where the wild ways of the sea are steep,
    Or in strange places somewhere there is death,
And on death's face the scattered hair of sleep.

There lover-like with lips and limbs that meet
They lie, they pluck sweet fruit of life and eat;
    But me the hot and hungry days devour,
And in my mouth no fruit of theirs is sweet.   100

No fruit of theirs, but fruit of my desire,
For her love's sake whose lips through mine respire;
    Her eyelids on her eyes like flower on flower,
Mine eyelids on mine eyes like fire on fire.

So lie we, not as sleep that lies by death,
With heavy kisses and with happy breath;
    Not as man lies by woman, when the bride
Laughs low for love's sake and the words he saith.

For she lies, laughing low with love; she lies
And turns his kisses on her lips to sighs,   110
    To sighing sound of lips unsatisfied,
And the sweet tears are tender with her eyes.

Ah, not as they, but as the souls that were
Slain in the old time, having found her fair;
    Who, sleeping with her lips upon their eyes,
Heard sudden serpents hiss across her hair.

Their blood runs round the roots of time like rain;
She casts them forth and gathers them again;
    With nerve and bone she weaves and multiplies
Exceeding pleasure out of extreme pain.   120

Her little chambers drip with flower-like red,
Her girdles, and the chaplets of her head,
    Her armlets and her anklets; with her feet
She tramples all that wine-press of the dead.

Her gateways smoke with fume of flowers and fires,
With loves burnt out and unassuaged desires;
    Between her lips the steam of them is sweet,
The languor in her ears of many lyres.

Her beds are full of perfume and sad sound,
Her doors are made with music, and barred round   130
    With sighing and with laughter and with tears,
With tears whereby strong souls of men are bound.

There is the knight Adonis that was slain;
With flesh and blood she chains him for a chain;
    The body and the spirit in her ears
Cry, for her lips divide him vein by vein.

Yea, all she slayeth; yea, every man save me;
Me, love, thy lover that must cleave to thee
    Till the ending of the days and ways of earth,
The shaking of the sources of the sea.   140

Me, most forsaken of all souls that fell;
Me, satiated with things insatiable;
    Me, for whose sake the extreme hell makes mirth,
Yea, laughter kindles at the heart of hell.

Alas thy beauty! for thy mouth's sweet sake
My soul is bitter to me, my limbs quake
    As water, as the flesh of men that weep,
As their heart's vein whose heart goes nigh to break.

Ah, God, that sleep with flower-sweet fingertips
Would crush the fruit of death upon my lips;   150
Ah, God, that death would tread the grapes of sleep
And wring their juice upon me as it drips.

There is no change of cheer for many days,
But change of chimes high up in the air, that sways
    Rung by the running fingers of the wind;
And singing sorrows heard on hidden ways.

Day smiteth day in twain, night sundereth night,
And on mine eyes the dark sits as the light;
    Yea, Lord, thou knowest I know not, having sinned,
If heaven be clean or unclean in thy sight. 160

Yea, as if earth were sprinkled over me,
Such chafed harsh earth as chokes a sandy sea,
    Each pore doth yearn, and the dried blood thereof
Gasps by sick fits; my heart swims heavily;

There is a feverish famine in my veins;
Below her bosom, where a crushed grape stains
    The white and blue, there my lips caught and clove
An hour since, and what mark of me remains?

I dare not always touch her, lest the kiss
Leave my lips charred. Yea, Lord, a little bliss, 170
    Brief bitter bliss, one hath for a great sin;
Nathless thou knowest how sweet a thing it is.

Sin, is it sin whereby men's souls are thrust
Into the pit? yet had I a good trust
    To save my soul before it slipped therein,
Trod under by the fire-shod feet of lust.

For if mine eyes fail and my soul takes breath,
I look between the iron sides of death
    Into sad hell, where all sweet love hath end—
All but the pain that never finisheth. 180

There are the naked faces of great kings,
The singing folk with all their lute-playings;
    There when one cometh he shall have to friend
The grave that covets and the worm that clings.

There sit the knights that were so great of hand,
The ladies that were queens of fair green land,
    Grown gray and black now, brought unto the dust,
Soiled, without raiment, clad about with sand.

There is one end for all of them; they sit
Naked and sad, they drink the dregs of it, 190
    Trodden as grapes in the wine-press of lust,
Trampled and trodden by the fiery feet.

I see the marvelous mouth whereby there fell
Cities and people whom the gods loved well,
 Yet for her sake on them the fire gat hold,
And for their sakes on her the fire of hell.

And softer than the Egyptian lote-leaf is,
The queen whose face was worth the world to kiss,
 Wearing at breast a suckling snake of gold;
And large pale lips of strong Semiramis,   200

Curled like a tiger's that curl back to feed;
Red only where the last kiss made them bleed;
 Her hair most thick with many a carven gem,
Deep in the mane, great-chested, like a steed.

Yea, with red sin the faces of them shine;
But in all these there was no sin like mine;
 No, not in all the strange great sins of them
That made the wine-press froth and foam with wine.

For I was of Christ's choosing, I God's knight,
No blinkard heathen stumbling for scant light;   210
 I can well see, for all the dusty days
Gone past, the clean great time of goodly fight.

I smell the breathing battle sharp with blows,
With shriek of shafts and snapping short of bows;
 The fair pure sword smites out in subtle ways,
Sounds and long lights are shed between the rows

Of beautiful mailed men; the edged light slips,
Most like a snake that takes short breath and dips
 Sharp from the beautifully bending head,
With all its gracious body lithe as lips   220

That curl in touching you; right in this wise
My sword doth, seeming fire in mine own eyes,
 Leaving all colours in them brown and red
And flecked with death; then the keen breaths like sighs,

The caught-up choked dry laughters following them,
When all the fighting face is grown a flame
 For pleasure, and the pulse that stuns the ears,
And the heart's gladness of the goodly game.

Let me think yet a little; I do know
These things were sweet, but sweet such years ago,   230
   Their savour is all turned now into tears;
Yea, ten years since, where the blue ripples blow,

The blue curled eddies of the blowing Rhine,
I felt the sharp wind shaking grass and vine
   Touch my blood, too, and sting me with delight
Through all this waste and weary body of mine

That never feels clear air; right gladly then
I rode alone, a great way off my men,
   And heard the chiming bridle smite and smite,
And gave each rime thereof some rime again,   240

Till my song shifted to that iron one;
Seeing there rode up between me and the sun
   Some certain of my foe's men, for his three
White wolves across their painted coats did run.

The first red-bearded, with square cheeks—alack,
I made my knave's blood turn his beard to black;
   The slaying of him was a joy to see.
Perchance, too, when at night he came not back,

Some woman fell a-weeping, whom this thief
Would beat when he had drunken; yet small grief   250
   Hath any for the ridding of such knaves;
Yea, if one wept, I doubt her teen was brief.

This bitter love is sorrow in all lands,
Draining of eyelids, wringing of drenched hands,
   Sighing of hearts and filling up of graves;
A sign across the head of the world he stands,

As one that hath a plague-mark on his brows;
Dust and spilt blood do track him to his house
   Down under earth; sweet smells of lip and cheek,
Like a sweet snake's breath made more poisonous   260

With chewing of some perfumed deadly grass,
Are shed all round his passage if he pass,
   And their quenched savour leaves the whole soul weak,
Sick with keen guessing whence the perfume was.

As one who hidden in deep sedge and reeds
Smells the rare scent made where a panther feeds,
   And tracking ever slotwise the warm smell
Is snapped upon by the sweet mouth and bleeds,

His head far down the hot sweet throat of her—
So one tracks love, whose breath is deadlier,   270
   And, lo, one springe and you are fast in hell,
Fast as the gin's grip of a wayfarer.

I think now, as the heavy hours decease
One after one, and bitter thoughts increase
   One upon one, of all sweet finished things:
The breaking of the battle; the long peace

Wherein we sat clothed softly, each man's hair
Crowned with green leaves beneath white hoods of vair;
   The sounds of sharp spears at great tourneyings,
And noise of singing in the late sweet air.   280

I sang of love too, knowing naught thereof;
"Sweeter," I said, "the little laugh of love
   Than tears out of the eyes of Magdalen,
Or any fallen feather of the Dove.

"The broken little laugh that spoils a kiss,
The ache of purple pulses, and the bliss
   Of blinded eyelids that expand again—
Love draws them open with those lips of his,

"Lips that cling hard till the kissed face has grown
Of one same fire and colour with their own;   290
   Then ere one sleep, appeased with sacrifice,
Where his lips wounded, there his lips atone."

I sang these things long since and knew them not:
"Lo, here is love, or there is love, God wot,
   This man and that finds favour in his eyes,"
I said, "but I, what guerdon have I got?

"The dust of praise that is blown everywhere
In all men's faces with the common air;
   The bay-leaf that wants chafing to be sweet
Before they wind it in a singer's hair."   300

So that one dawn I rode forth sorrowing;
I had no hope but of some evil thing,
    And so rode slowly past the windy wheat
And past the vineyard and the water-spring,

Up to the Horsel.   A great elder-tree
Held back its heaps of flowers to let me see
    The ripe tall grass, and one that walked therein,
Naked, with hair shed over to the knee.

She walked between the blossom and the grass;
I knew the beauty of her, what she was,   310
    The beauty of her body and her sin,
And in my flesh the sin of hers, alas!

Alas! for sorrow is all the end of this.
O sad kissed mouth, how sorrowful it is!
    O breast whereat some suckling sorrow clings,
Red with the bitter blossom of a kiss!

Ah, with blind lips I felt for you, and found
About my neck your hands and hair enwound,
    The hands that stifle and the hair that stings,
I felt them fasten sharply without sound.   320

Yea, for my sin I had great store of bliss;
Rise up, make answer for me, let thy kiss
    Seal my lips hard from speaking of my sin,
Lest one go mad to hear how sweet it is.

Yet I waxed faint with fume of barren bowers,
And murmuring of the heavy-headed hours;
    And let the dove's beak fret and peck within
My lips in vain, and Love shed fruitless flowers.

So that God looked upon me when your hands
Were hot about me; yea, God brake my bands   330
    To save my soul alive, and I came forth
Like a man blind and naked in strange lands

That hears men laugh and weep, and knows not whence
Nor wherefore, but is broken in his sense;
    Howbeit I met folk riding from the north
Toward Rome, to purge them of their souls' offense.

And rode with them, and spake to none; the day
Stunned me like lights upon some wizard way,
 And ate like fire mine eyes and mine eyesight;
So rode I, hearing all these chant and pray,   340

And marveled; till before us rose and fell
White curséd hills, like outer skirts of hell
 Seen where men's eyes look through the day to night,
Like a jagged shell's lips, harsh, untunable,

Blown in between by devils' wrangling breath;
Nathless we won well past that hell and death,
 Down to the sweet land where all airs are good,
Even unto Rome where God's grace tarrieth.

Then came each man and worshiped at his knees
Who in the Lord God's likeness bears the keys   350
 To bind or loose, and called on Christ's shed blood,
And so the sweet-souled father gave him ease.

But when I came I fell down at his feet,
Saying, "Father, though the Lord's blood be right sweet,
 The spot it takes not off the panther's skin,
Nor shall an Ethiop's stain be bleached with it.

"Lo, I have sinned and have spat out at God,
Wherefore his hand is heavier and his rod
 More sharp because of mine exceeding sin,
And all his raiment redder than bright blood   360

"Before mine eyes; yea, for my sake I wot
The heat of hell is waxen seven times hot
 Through my great sin." Then spake he some sweet word,
Giving me cheer; which thing availed me not;

Yea, scarce I wist if such indeed were said;
For when I ceased—lo, as one newly dead
 Who hears a great cry out of hell, I heard
The crying of his voice across my head.

"Until this dry shred staff, that hath no whit
Of leaf nor bark, bear blossom and smell sweet,   370
 Seek thou not any mercy in God's sight,
For so long shalt thou be cast out from it."

Yea, what if dried-up stems wax red and green,
Shall that thing be which is not nor has been?
    Yea, what if sapless bark wax green and white,
Shall any good fruit grow upon my sin?

Nay, though sweet fruit were plucked of a dry tree,
And though men drew sweet waters of the sea,
    There should not grow sweet leaves on this dead stem,
This waste wan body and shaken soul of me.   380

Yea, though God search it warily enough,
There is not one sound thing in all thereof;
    Though he search all my veins through, searching them
He shall find nothing whole therein but love.

For I came home right heavy, with small cheer,
And, lo, my love, mine own soul's heart, more dear
    Than mine own soul, more beautiful than God,
Who hath my being between the hands of her—

Fair still, but fair for no man saving me,
As when she came out of the naked sea   390
    Making the foam as fire whereon she trod,
And as the inner flower of fire was she.

Yea, she laid hold upon me, and her mouth
Clove unto mine as soul to body doth,
    And, laughing, made her lips luxurious;
Her hair had smells of all the sunburnt south,

Strange spice and flower, strange savour of crushed fruit,
And perfume the swart kings tread underfoot
    For pleasure when their minds wax amorous,
Charred frankincense and grated sandal-root.   400

And I forgot fear and all weary things,
All ended prayers and perished thanksgivings,
    Feeling her face with all her eager hair
Cleave to me, clinging as a fire that clings

To the body and to the raiment, burning them;
As after death I know that such-like flame
    Shall cleave to me forever; yea, what care,
Albeit I burn then, having felt the same?

Ah, love, there is no better life than this;
To have known love, how bitter a thing it is,   410
   And afterward be cast out of God's sight;
Yea, these that know not, shall they have such bliss

High up in barren heaven before his face
As we twain in the heavy-hearted place,
   Remembering love and all the dead delight,
And all that time was sweet with for a space?

For till the thunder in the trumpet be,
Soul may divide from body, but not we
   One from another; I hold thee with my hand,
I let mine eyes have all their will of thee,   420

I seal myself upon thee with my might,
Abiding alway out of all men's sight
   Until God loosen over sea and land
The thunder of the trumpets of the night.

                               1866

Title: Praise of Venus. Tannhäuser, a legendary medieval knight, lived
with Venus in her palace-cavern under the Hörselberg in central Germany.
Repenting, he sought absolution from the Pope but was denied; where-
upon he returned to Venus and speaks in this soliloquy, "believing in
Christ," Swinburne explained, "and bound to Venus—desirous of pene-
tential pain, and damned to joyous pleasure."   l. 10: **parcels** portions.
l. 36: **Love** Eros, Venus' son.   l. 88: **arow** in a row.   l. 133:
knight Adonis not a knight in the usual sense but a young Greek hunter
who rejected Venus' advances and was killed, in retribution, by a boar.
l. 197: **lote-leaf** lotus leaf.   l. 198: **queen** Cleopatra.   l. 200:
Semiramis legendary Queen of Assyria.   l. 210: **blinkard** dull of sight.
l. 267: **slotwise** in the manner of following the trail ("slot") of a quarry.
l. 270: **springe** trap.   l. 271: **gin** snare.   l. 283: **Magdalen** Mary
Magdalene, converted from sensual sin by Jesus. See Luke 7:37–47.
l. 284: **Dove** one of the forms of the Holy Spirit.   l. 299: **bay-leaf**
emblem of victory.   l. 342: **hills** the Alps, crossed on the pilgrimage to
Rome.   l. 350: **likeness** the Pope, who, being "Vicar of Christ," has
the "keys" to Heaven and Hell, that is, the power of absolving sin.
l. 355: **the spot** Tannhäuser doubts that even Christ can save him. See
Jeremiah 13:23.   l. 369: **staff** the Pope's pastoral staff; in some ver-
sions it miraculously blossoms as a sign of divine forgiveness.   l. 385:
home to Venus.   l. 389: **saving** except.   l. 390: **sea** Venus is
supposed to have been born from the sea-foam.   l. 417: **trumpet** sig-
nalling the Last Judgment.

IN MEMORY OF WALTER SAVAGE LANDOR

Back to the flower-town, side by side,
    The bright months bring,
New-born, the bridegroom and the bride,
    Freedom and spring.

The sweet land laughs from sea to sea,
    Filled full of sun;
All things come back to her, being free;
    All things but one.

In many a tender wheaten plot
    Flowers that were dead   10
Live, and old suns revive; but not
    That holier head.

By this white wandering waste of sea,
    Far north, I hear
One face shall never turn to me
    As once this year;

Shall never smile and turn and rest
    On mine as there,
Nor one most sacred hand be pressed
    Upon my hair.   20

I came as one whose thoughts half linger,
    Half run before;
The youngest to the oldest singer
    That England bore.

I found him whom I shall not find
    Till all grief end,
In holiest age our mightiest mind,
    Father and friend.

But thou, if anything endure,
    If hope there be   30
O spirit that man's life left pure,
    Man's death set free,

Not with disdain of days that were
    Look earthward now;
Let dreams revive the reverend hair,
    The imperial brow;

Come back in sleep, for in the life
    Where thou art not
We find none like thee. Time and strife
    And the world's lot   40

Move thee no more; but love at least
    And reverent heart
May move thee, royal and released,
    Soul, as thou art.

And thou, his Florence, to thy trust
    Receive and keep,
Keep safe his dedicated dust,
    His sacred sleep.

So shall thy lovers, come from far,
    Mix with thy name   50
As morning star with evening star
    His faultless fame.

1866

Title: Landor (1775–1864), poet, Hellenist, critic, friend of Southey and Shelley, later of Browning. Swinburne idolized him.   l. 1: **flower-town** Florence, Italy, where Landor died.   l. 1: **her** Italy, recently liberated and unified, with Florence as capital.   l. 51: **star . . . star** The planet Venus is both morning star and evening star.

THE GARDEN OF PROSERPINE

[handwritten marginal note: does deal with immortality doesn't seem to be an afterlife: a calm oblivion]

Here, where the world is quiet;
    Here, where all trouble seems
Dead winds' and spent waves' riot
    In doubtful dreams of dreams;
I watch the green field growing
For reaping folk and sowing
For harvest-time and mowing,
    A sleepy world of streams.

I am tired of tears and laughter,
    And men that laugh and weep;   10
Of what may come hereafter
    For men that sow to reap;

I am weary of days and hours,
Blown buds of barren flowers,
Desires and dreams and powers
   And everything but sleep.   *best condition?*

Here life has death for neighbour,   *to have rest.*
   And far from eye or ear
Wan waves and wet winds labour,
   Weak ships and spirits steer;   20
They drive adrift, and whither
They wot not who make thither;
But no such winds blow hither,
   And no such things grow here.

No growth of moor or coppice,
   No heather-flower or vine,
But bloomless buds of poppies,
   Green grapes of Proserpine,
Pale beds of blowing rushes,
Where no leaf blooms or blushes   30
Save this whereout she crushes
   For dead men deadly wine.

Pale, without name or number,
   In fruitless fields of corn,
They bow themselves and slumber
   All night till light is born;
And like a soul belated,
In hell and heaven unmated,
By cloud and mist abated
   Comes out of darkness morn.   40

Though one were strong as seven,
   He too with death shall dwell,
Nor wake with wings in heaven,
   Nor weep for pains in hell;
Though one were fair as roses,
His beauty clouds and closes;
And well though love reposes,
   In the end it is not well.

Pale, beyond porch and portal,
   Crowned with calm leaves, she stands   50

Who gathers all things mortal
　　With cold immortal hands;
Her languid lips are sweeter
Than love's who fears to greet her
To men that mix and meet her
　　From many times and lands.

Better to sleep,
even than to Love

She waits for each and other,
　　She waits for all men born;
Forgets the earth her mother,
　　The life of fruits and corn;
And spring and seed and swallow
Take wing for her and follow
Where summer song rings hollow
　　And flowers are put to scorn.

Queen of
Death
Demeter

no evidence
that she spends
time on earth

60

There go the loves that wither,
　　The old loves with wearier wings;
And all dead years draw thither,
　　And all disastrous things;
Dead dreams of days forsaken,
Blind buds that snows have shaken,
Wild leaves that winds have taken,
　　Red strays of ruined springs.

All
things pass
and come
to her.

70

We are not sure of sorrow,
　　And joy was never sure;
Today will die tomorrow;
　　Time stoops to no man's lure;
And love, grown faint and fretful,
With lips but half regretful
Sighs, and with eyes forgetful
　　Weeps that no loves endure.

Things are
generally sad
for man, Joy
is never sure,
and we are not
even sure of
sorrow, there
is even little
hope for love.

80

From too much love of living,
　　From hope and fear set free,
We thank with brief thanksgiving
　　Whatever gods may be
That no life lives forever;
That dead men rise up never;
That even the weariest river
　　Winds somewhere safe to sea.

probably
none

Then star nor sun shall waken,
   Nor any change of light: 90
Nor sound of waters shaken,
   Nor any sound or sight:
Nor wintry leaves nor vernal,
   Nor days nor things diurnal;
<u>Only the sleep eternal</u>
   <u>In an eternal night.</u>

The ideal according to the poem.

1866

l. 27: **poppies**   sacred to Proserpine because opium, emblem of oblivion, is extracted from them.   l. 28: **grapes**   the bulbous calyxes of poppies.

SAPPHICS

All the night sleep came not upon my eyelids,
   Shed not dew, nor shook nor unclosed a feather,
Yet with lips shut close and with eyes of iron
   Stood and beheld me.

Then to me so lying awake a vision
Came without sleep over the seas and touched me,
Softly touched mine eyelids and lips; and I, too,
   Full of the vision

Saw the white implacable Aphrodite,
Saw the hair unbound and the feet unsandaled   10
Shine as fire of sunset on western waters;
   Saw the reluctant

Feet, the straining plumes of the doves that drew her,
Looking always, looking with necks reverted,
Back to Lesbos, back to the hills whereunder
   Shone Mitylene;

Heard the flying feet of the Loves behind her
Make a sudden thunder upon the waters,
As the thunder flung from the strong unclosing
   Wings of a great wind.   20

So the goddess fled from her place, with awful
Sound of feet and thunder of wings around her;

While behind a clamour of singing women
  Severed the twilight.

Ah, the singing, ah, the delight, the passion!
All the Loves wept, listening; sick with anguish,
Stood the crowned nine Muses about Apollo;
  Fear was upon them,

While the tenth sang wonderful things they knew not.
Ah, the tenth, the Lesbian! the nine were silent,   30
None endured the sound of her song for weeping;
  Laurel by laurel,

Faded all their crowns; but about her forehead,
Round her woven tresses and ashen temples
White as dead snow, paler than grass in summer,
  Ravaged with kisses,

Shone a light of fire as a crown forever.
Yea, almost the implacable Aphrodite
Paused, and almost wept; such a song was that song.
  Yea, by her name, too,   40

Called her, saying, "Turn to me, O my Sappho";
Yet she turned her face from the Loves, she saw not
Tears for laughter darken immortal eyelids,
  Heard not about her

Fearful fitful wings of the doves departing,
Saw not how the bosom of Aphrodite
Shook with weeping, saw not her shaken raiment,
  Saw not her hands wrung;

Saw the Lesbians kissing across their smitten
Lutes with lips more sweet than the sound of lute-strings, 50
Mouth to mouth and hand upon hand, her chosen,
  Fairer than all men;

Only saw the beautiful lips and fingers,
Full of songs and kisses and little whispers,
Full of music; only beheld among them
  Soar, as a bird soars

Newly fledged, her visible song, a marvel,
Made of perfect sound and exceeding passion,

Sweetly shapen, terrible, full of thunders,
    Clothed with the wind's wings.   60

Then rejoiced she, laughing with love, and scattered
Roses, awful roses of holy blossom;
Then the Loves thronged sadly with hidden faces
    Round Aphrodite,

Then the Muses, stricken at heart, were silent;
Yea, the gods waxed pale; such a song was that song.
All reluctant, all with a fresh repulsion,
    Fled from before her.

All withdrew long since, and the land was barren,
Full of fruitless women and music only.   70
Now perchance, when winds are assuaged at sunset,
    Lulled at the dewfall,

By the gray seaside, unassuaged, unheard of,
Unbeloved, unseen in the ebb of twilight,
Ghosts of outcast women return lamenting,
    Purged not in Lethe,

Clothed about with flame and with tears, and singing
Songs that move the heart of the shaken heaven,
Songs that break the heart of the earth with pity,
    Hearing, to hear them.   80

1866

Title: a metrical stanza named for Sappho of Lesbos, the seventh century B.C. poetess. In quantitative rather than accentual verse, the stanza has three lines thus: — ᴗ | — — — | — ‖ ᴗ ᴗ | — ᴗ | — ᴗ̆ ; and a fourth: — ᴗ ᴗ | — ᴗ̆ .

l. 16: **Mitylene** town on the coast of the island of Lesbos.   l. 30: **tenth** Sappho herself; as if she were the tenth Muse.   l. 42: **Loves** Venus' attendants; "Cupids."   l. 49: **Lesbians** here, with the implication that Sappho and the women around her were homosexual.   l. 75: **outcast** refused admission to the realm of the dead because of their offense against Venus in preferring to love women and not men.

AFTER DEATH

The four boards of the coffin lid
Heard all the dead man did.

The first curse was in his mouth,
Made of grave's mould and deadly drouth.

The next curse was in his head,
Made of God's work discomfited.

The next curse was in his hands,
Made out of two grave-bands.

The next curse was in his feet,
Made out of a grave-sheet.   10

"I had fair coins red and white,
And my name was as great light;

I had fair clothes green and red,
And strong gold bound round my head.

But no meat comes in my mouth,
Now I fare as the worm doth;

And no gold binds in my hair,
Now I fare as the blind fare.

My live thews were of great strength,
Now I am waxen a span's length;   20

My live sides were full of lust,
Now are they dried with dust."

The first board spake and saith:
"Is it best eating flesh or bread?"

The second answered it:
"Is wine or honey the more sweet?"

The third board spake and said,
"Is red gold worth a girl's gold head?"

The fourth made answer thus:
"All these things are as one with us."   30

The dead man asked of them:
"Is the green land stained brown with flame?

Have they hewn my son for beasts to eat,
And my wife's body for beasts' meat?

Have they boiled my maid in a brass pan,
And built a gallows to hang my man?"

The boards said to him:
"This is a lewd thing that ye deem.

Your wife has gotten a golden bed,
All the sheets are sewn with red.   40

Your son has gotten a coat of silk,
The sleeves are soft as curded milk.

Your maid has gotten a kirtle new,
All the skirt has braids of blue.

Your man has gotten both ring and glove,
Wrought well for eyes to love."

The dead man answered thus:
"What good gift shall God give us?"

The boards answered him anon:
"Flesh to feed hell's worm upon."   50

                              1866

AVE ATQUE VALE

IN MEMORY OF CHARLES BAUDELAIRE

Nous devrions pourtant lui porter quelques fleurs;
Les morts, les pauvres morts, ont de grandes douleurs,
Et quand Octobre souffle, émondeur des vieux arbres,
Son vent mélancolique à l'entour de leur marbres,
Certe, ils doivent trouver les vivants bien ingrats.
                              —Les Fleurs du mal

I

Shall I strew on thee rose or rue or laurel,
    Brother, on this that was the veil of thee?
    Or quiet sea-flower molded by the sea,
Or simplest growth of meadow-sweet or sorrel,
    Such as the summer-sleepy Dryads weave,
    Waked up by snow-soft sudden rains at eve?

Or wilt thou rather, as on earth before,
    Half-faded fiery blossoms, pale with heat
    And full of bitter summer, but more sweet
To thee than gleanings of a northern shore   10
    Trod by no tropic feet?

II

For always thee the fervid languid glories
    Allured of heavier suns in mightier skies;
    Thine ears knew all the wandering watery sighs
Where the sea sobs round Lesbian promontories,
    The barren kiss of piteous wave to wave
    That knows not where is that Leucadian grave
Which hides too deep the supreme head of song.
    Ah, salt and sterile as her kisses were,
    The wild sea winds her and the green gulfs bear   20
Hither and thither, and vex and work her wrong,
    Blind gods that cannot spare.

III

Thou sawest, in thine old singing season, brother,
    Secrets and sorrows unbeheld of us;
    Fierce loves, and lovely leaf-buds poisonous,
Bare to thy subtler eye, but for none other
    Blowing by night in some unbreathed-in clime;
    The hidden harvest of luxurious time,
Sin without shape, and pleasure without speech;
    And where strange dreams in a tumultuous sleep   30
    Make the shut eyes of stricken spirits weep;
And with each face thou sawest the shadow on each,
    Seeing as men sow men reap.

IV

O sleepless heart and sombre soul unsleeping,
    That were athirst for sleep and no more life
    And no more love, for peace and no more strife!
Now the dim gods of death have in their keeping
    Spirit and body and all the springs of song,
    Is it well now where love can do no wrong,

Where stingless pleasure has no foam or fang   40
    Behind the unopening closure of her lips?
    Is it not well where soul from body slips
And flesh from bone divides without a pang
    As dew from flower-bell drips?

V

It is enough; the end and the beginning
    Are one thing to thee, who art past the end.
    O hand unclasped of unbeholden friend,
For thee no fruits to pluck, no palms for winning,
    No triumphs and no labour and no lust,
    Only dead yew-leaves and a little dust.   50
O quiet eyes wherein the light saith naught,
    Whereto the day is dumb, nor any night
    With obscure finger silences your sight,
Nor in your speech the sudden soul speaks thought,
    Sleep, and have sleep for light.

VI

Now all strange hours and all strange loves are over,
    Dreams and desires and sombre songs and sweet,
    Hast thou found place at the great knees and feet
Of some pale Titan-woman like a lover,
    Such as thy vision here solicited,   60
    Under the shadow of her fair vast head,
The deep division of prodigious breasts,
    The solemn slope of mighty limbs asleep,
    The weight of awful tresses that still keep
The savour and shade of old-world pine-forests
    Where the wet hill-winds weep?

VII

Hast thou found any likeness for thy vision?
    O gardener of strange flowers, what bud, what bloom,
    Hast thou found sown, what gathered in the gloom?
What of despair, of rapture, of derision,   70
    What of life is there, what of ill or good?
    Are the fruits gray like dust or bright like blood?

Does the dim ground grow any seed of ours,
    The faint fields quicken any terrene root,
    In low lands where the sun and moon are mute
And all the stars keep silence? Are there flowers
    At all, or any fruit?

VIII

Alas, but though my flying song flies after,
    O sweet strange elder singer, thy more fleet
    Singing, and footprints of thy fleeter feet,   80
Some dim derision of mysterious laughter
    From the blind tongueless warders of the dead,
    Some gainless glimpse of Proserpine's veiled head,
Some little sound of unregarded tears
    Wept by effaced unprofitable eyes,
    And from pale mouths some cadence of dead sighs—
These only, these the hearkening spirit hears,
    Sees only such things rise.

IX

Thou art far too far for wings of words to follow,
    Far too far off for thought or any prayer.   90
    What ails us with thee, who art wind and air?
What ails us gazing where all seen is hollow?
    Yet with some fancy, yet with some desire,
    Dreams pursue death as winds a flying fire,
Our dreams pursue our dead and do not find.
    Still, and more swift than they, the thin flame flies,
    The low light fails us in elusive skies,
Still the foiled earnest ear is deaf, and blind
    Are still the eluded eyes.

X

Not thee, O never thee, in all time's changes,   100
    Not thee, but this the sound of thy sad soul,
    The shadow of thy swift spirit, this shut scroll
I lay my hand on, and not death estranges
    My spirit from communion of thy song—
    These memories and these melodies that throng

Veiled porches of a Muse funereal—
    These I salute, these touch, these clasp and fold
    As though a hand were in my hand to hold,
Or through mine ears a mourning musical
    Of many mourners rolled.   110

XI

I among these, I also, in such station
    As when the pyre was charred, and piled the sods,
    And offering to the dead made, and their gods,
The old mourners had, standing to make libation,
    I stand, and to the gods and to the dead
    Do reverence without prayer or praise and shed
Offering to these unknown, the gods of gloom,
    And what of honey and spice my seedlands bear,
    And what I may of fruits in this chilled air,
And lay, Orestes-like, across the tomb   120
    A curl of severed hair.

XII

But by no hand nor any treason stricken,
    Not like the low-lying head of Him, the King,
    The flame that made of Troy a ruinous thing,
Thou liest, and on this dust no tears could quicken
    There fall no tears like theirs that all men hear
    Fall tear by sweet imperishable tear
Down the opening leaves of holy poet's pages.
    Thee not Orestes, not Electra mourns;
    But bending us-ward with memorial urns   130
The most high Muses that fulfill all ages
    Weep, and our god's heart yearns.

XIII

For, sparing of his sacred strength, not often
    Among us darkling here the lord of light
    Makes manifest his music and his might
In hearts that open and in lips that soften
    With the soft flame and heat of songs that shine.
    Thy lips indeed he touched with bitter wine,

And nourished them indeed with bitter bread;
  Yet surely from his hand thy soul's food came,   140
  The fire that scarred thy spirit at his flame
Was lighted, and thine hungering heart he fed
  Who feeds our hearts with fame.

XIV

Therefore he too now at thy soul's sunsetting,
  God of all suns and songs, he too bends down
  To mix his laurel with thy cypress crown,
And save thy dust from blame and from forgetting.
  Therefore he too, seeing all thou wert and art,
  Compassionate, with sad and sacred heart,
Mourns thee of many his children the last dead,   150
  And hallows with strange tears and alien sighs
  Thine unmelodious mouth and sunless eyes,
And over thine irrevocable head
  Sheds light from the under skies.

XV

And one weeps with him in the ways Lethean,
  And stains with tears her changing bosom chill—
  That obscure Venus of the hollow hill,
That thing transformed which was the Cytherean,
  With lips that lost their Grecian laugh divine
  Long since, and face no more called Erycine;   160
A ghost, a bitter and luxurious god.
  Thee also with fair flesh and singing spell
  Did she, a sad and second prey, compel
Into the footless places once more trod,
  And shadows hot from hell.

XVI

And now no sacred staff shall break in blossom,
  No choral salutation lure to light
  A spirit sick with perfume and sweet night
And love's tired eyes and hands and barren bosom.
  There is no help for these things; none to mend   170
  And none to mar; not all our songs, O friend,

Will make death clear or make life durable.
  Howbeit with rose and ivy and wild vine
  And with wild notes about this dust of thine
At least I fill the place where white dreams dwell
  And wreathe an unseen shrine.

XVII

Sleep; and if life was bitter to thee, pardon,
  If sweet, give thanks; thou hast no more to live;
  And to give thanks is good, and to forgive.
Out of the mystic and the mournful garden   180
  Where all day through thine hands in barren braid
  Wove the sick flowers of secrecy and shade,
Green buds of sorrow and sin, and remnants gray,
  Sweet-smelling, pale with poison, sanguine-hearted,
  Passions that sprang from sleep and thoughts that started,
Shall death not bring us all as thee one day
  Among the days departed?

XVIII

For thee, O now a silent soul, my brother,
  Take at my hands this garland, and farewell.
  Thin is the leaf, and chill the wintry smell,   190
And chill the solemn earth, a fatal mother,
  With sadder than the Niobean womb,
  And in the hollow of her breasts a tomb.
Content thee, howso'er, whose days are done;
  There lies not any troublous thing before,
  Nor sight nor sound to war against thee more,
For whom all winds are quiet as the sun,
  All waters as the shore.

1868

Title: "Hail and Farewell," a phrase from Catullus' lament for his brother
(*Carmen*, ci). Baudelaire (1820–1867) was one of the founders of modern
French poetry, author of *Les Fleurs du mal* (The Flowers of Evil), 1857.
Epigraph: "Yet we ought to bring him some flowers. The dead, the un-
happy dead, sorrow greatly, and when October, pruner of the old trees,
blows his melancholy breath around their tombs, surely they must find
the living most ungrateful."   l. 17: **grave** of Sappho (see note to pre-

ceding poem) who died by leaping into the sea off the Ionian isle of Leucas.
l. 60: **thy vision** Baudelaire's poem, "The Giantess," paraphrased in
ll. 58–66.   l. 120: **Orestes-like** Orestes and Electra (l. 129) were the
children of Agamemnon ("The King," l. 123), who conquered Troy and
on his homecoming was murdered by his wife, Clytemnestra. Orestes laid
a lock of his hair on his father's tomb as a pledge of the revenge that he
and his sister would take.   l. 132: **our god's** Apollo's, as god of
poetry.   l. 134: **lord** Apollo.   l. 157: **obscure Venus** In Greek
legend she was called both the Cytherean (l. 158), a vernal goddess, and
the Erycine (l. 160), a goddess of love and beauty, but in the Middle Ages
she became "the witch of love" living in a cavern ("the hollow hill").
l. 163: **second prey** Tannhäuser was the first. (See note on title of "Laus
Veneris," p. 194.)   l. 192: **Niobean** Niobe's many children were all
killed.

Prelude to SONGS BEFORE SUNRISE

Between the green bud and the red
Youth sat and sang by Time, and shed
    From eyes and tresses flowers and tears,
    From heart and spirit hopes and fears,
Upon the hollow stream whose bed
    Is channeled by the foamless years;
And with the white the gold-haired head
    Mixed running locks, and in Time's ears
Youth's dreams hung singing, and Time's truth
Was half not harsh in the ears of Youth.   10

Between the bud and the blown flower
Youth talked with joy and grief an hour,
    With footless joy and wingless grief
    And twin-born faith and disbelief
Who share the seasons to devour;
    And long ere these made up their sheaf
Felt the winds round him shake and shower
    The rose-red and the blood-red leaf,
Delight whose germ grew never grain,
And passion dyed in its own pain.   20

Then he stood up, and trod to dust
Fear and desire, mistrust and trust,
    And dreams of bitter sleep and sweet,
    And bound for sandals on his feet
Knowledge and patience of what must
    And what things may be, in the heat

And cold of years that rot and rust
   And alter; and his spirit's meat
Was freedom, and his staff was wrought
Of strength, and his cloak woven of thought.   30

For what has he whose will sees clear
To do with doubt and faith and fear,
   Swift hopes and slow despondencies?
   His heart is equal with the sea's
And with the sea-wind's, and his ear
   Is level to the speech of these,
And his soul communes and takes cheer
   With the actual earth's equalities,
Air, light, and night, hills, winds, and streams,
And seeks not strength from strengthless dreams.   40

His soul is even with the sun
Whose spirit and whose eye are one,
   Who seeks not stars by day, nor light
   And heavy heat of day by night.
Him can no god cast down, whom none
   Can lift in hope beyond the height
Of fate and nature and things done
   By the calm rule of might and right
That bids men be and bear and do,
And die beneath blind skies or blue.   50

To him the lights of even and morn
Speak no vain things of love or scorn,
   Fancies and passions miscreate
   By man in things dispassionate.
Nor holds he fellowship forlorn
   With souls that pray and hope and hate,
And doubt they had better not been born,
   And fain would lure or scare off fate
And charm their doomsman from their doom
And make fear dig its own false tomb.   60

He builds not half of doubts and half
Of dreams his own soul's cenotaph,
   Whence hopes and fears with helpless eyes,
   Wrapped loose in cast-off cerecloths, rise

And dance and wring their hands and laugh,
    And weep thin tears and sigh light sighs,
And without living lips would quaff
    The living spring in man that lies,
And drain his soul of faith and strength
It might have lived on a life's length.   70

He hath given himself and hath not sold
To God for heaven or man for gold,
    Or grief for comfort that it gives,
    Or joy for grief's restoratives.
He hath given himself to time, whose fold
    Shuts in the mortal flock that lives
On its plain pasture's heat and cold
    And the equal year's alternatives.
Earth, heaven, and time, death, life, and he,
Endure while they shall be to be.   80

"Yet between death and life are hours
To flush with love and hide in flowers;
    What profit save in these?" men cry.
    "Ah, see, between soft earth and sky,
What only good things here are ours!"
    They say, "what better wouldst thou try,
What sweeter sing of? or what powers
    Serve, that will give thee ere thou die
More joy to sing and be less sad,
More heart to play and grow more glad?"   90

Play then and sing; we too have played,
We likewise, in that subtle shade.
    We too have twisted through our hair
    Such tendrils as the wild Loves wear,
And heard what mirth the Mænads made,
    Till the wind blew our garlands bare
And left their roses disarrayed,
    And smote the summer with strange air,
And disengirdled and discrowned
The limbs and locks that vine-wreaths bound.   100

We too have tracked by star-proof trees
The tempest of the Thyiades

Scare the loud night on hills that hid
The blood-feasts of the Bassarid,
Heard their song's iron cadences
     Fright the wolf hungering from the kid,
Outroar the lion-throated seas,
     Outchide the north-wind if it chid,
And hush the torrent-tongued ravines
With thunders of their tambourines.   110

But the fierce flute whose notes acclaim
Dim goddesses of fiery fame,
     Cymbal and clamorous kettledrum,
     Timbrels and tabrets, all are dumb
That turned the high chill air to flame;
     The singing tongues of fire are numb
That called on Cotys by her name
     Edonian, till they felt her come
And maddened, and her mystic face
Lightened along the streams of Thrace.   120

For Pleasure slumberless and pale,
And Passion with rejected veil,
     Pass, and the tempest-footed throng
     Of hours that follow them with song
Till their feet flag and voices fail,
     And lips that were so loud so long
Learn silence, or a wearier wail;
     So keen is change, and time so strong,
To weave the robes of life and rend
And weave again till life have end.   130

But weak is change, but strengthless time,
To take the light from heaven, or climb
     The hills of heaven with wasting feet.
     Songs they can stop that earth found meet,
But the stars keep their ageless rime;
     Flowers they can slay that spring thought sweet,
But the stars keep their spring sublime;
     Passions and pleasures can defeat,
Actions and agonies control,
And life and death, but not the soul.   140

Because man's soul is man's God still,
What wind soever waft his will
    Across the waves of day and night
    To port or shipwreck, left or right,
By shores and shoals of good and ill;
    And still its flame at mainmast height
Through the rent air that foam-flakes fill
    Sustains the indomitable light
Whence only man hath strength to steer
Or helm to handle without fear.   150

Save his own soul's light overhead,
None leads him, and none ever led,
    Across birth's hidden harbour-bar,
    Past youth where shoreward shallows are,
Through age that drives on toward the red
    Vast void of sunset hailed from far,
To the equal waters of the dead;
    Save his own soul he hath no star,
And sinks, except his own soul guide,
Helmless in middle turn of tide.   160

No blast of air or fire of sun
Puts out the light whereby we run
    With girded loins our lamplit race.
    And each from each takes heart of grace
And spirit till his turn be done,
    And light of face from each man's face
In whom the light of trust is one;
    Since only souls that keep their place
By their own light, and watch things roll,
And stand, have light for any soul.   170

A little time we gain from time
To set our seasons in some chime,
    For harsh or sweet or loud or low,
    With seasons played out long ago
And souls that in their time and prime
    Took part with summer or with snow,
Lived abject lives out or sublime,
    And had their chance of seed to sow
For service or disservice done
To those days dead and this their son.   180

A little time that we may fill
Or with such good works or such ill
   As loose the bonds or make them strong
   Wherein all manhood suffers wrong.
By rose-hung river and light-foot rill
   There are who rest not; who think long
Till they discern as from a hill
   At the sun's hour of morning song,
Known of souls only, and those souls free,
The sacred spaces of the sea.   190

1871

Title: The "sunrise" is the expected liberation of Italy from Austrian rule.
ll. 102–04: **Thyiades . . . Bassarid** female worshippers of Dionysus.
l. 117: **Cotys** a goddess whose rites were orgiastic.   l. 118: **Edonian**
from Mt. Edon in Thrace; a synonym for *bloodthirsty, barbarous.*   l.
163: **lamplit race** a night race, with torches carried in relay.

HERTHA

I am that which began;
   Out of me the years roll;
Out of me God and man;
   I am equal and whole:
God changes, and man, and the form of them bodily; I am
  the soul.

   Before ever land was,
     Before ever the sea,
   Or soft hair of the grass,
     Or fair limbs of the tree,
Or the flesh-coloured fruit of my branches, I was, and thy
  soul was in me.   10

   First life on my sources
     First drifted and swam;
   Out of me are the forces
     That save it or damn;
Out of me man and woman, and wild-beast and bird; before
  God was, I am.
     Beside or above me
       Naught is there to go;

Love or unlove me,
Unknow me or know,
I am that which unloves me and loves; I am stricken, and
I am the blow.   20

I the mark that is missed
And the arrows that miss,
I the mouth that is kissed
And the breath in the kiss,
The search, and the sought, and the seeker, the soul and the
body that is.

I am that thing which blesses
My spirit elate;
That which caresses
With hands uncreate
My limbs unbegotten that measure the length of the measure
of fate.   30

But what thing dost thou now,
Looking Godward, to cry,
"I am I, thou art thou,
I am low, thou art high"?
I am thou, whom thou seekest to find him; find thou but
thyself, thou art I.

I the grain and the furrow,
The plow-cloven clod
And the plowshare drawn thorough,
The germ and the sod,
The deed and the doer, the seed and the sower, the dust
which is God.   40

Hast thou known how I fashioned thee,
Child, underground?
Fire that impassioned thee,
Iron that bound,
Dim changes of water, what thing of all these hast thou
known of or found?

Canst thou say in thine heart
Thou hast seen with thine eyes
With what cunning of art
Thou wast wrought in what wise,

By what force of what stuff thou wast shapen, and shown
   on my breast to the skies?   50

        Who hath given, who hath sold it thee,
           Knowledge of me?
        Hath the wilderness told it thee?
           Hast thou learnt of the sea?
Hast thou communed in spirit with night? Have the winds
   taken counsel with thee?

        Have I set such a star
           To show light on thy brow
        That thou sawest from afar
           What I show to thee now?
Have ye spoken as brethren together, the sun and the
   mountains and thou?   60

        What is here, dost thou know it?
           What was, hast thou known?
        Prophet nor poet
           Nor tripod nor throne
Nor spirit nor flesh can make answer, but only thy mother
   alone.

        Mother, not maker,
           Born, and not made;
        Though her children forsake her,
           Allured or afraid,
Praying prayers to the God of their fashion, she stirs not
   for all that have prayed.   70

        A creed is a rod,
           And a crown is of night;
        But this thing is God,
           To be man with thy might,
To grow straight in the strength of thy spirit, and live out
   thy life as the light.

        I am in thee to save thee,
           As my soul in thee saith;
        Give thou as I gave thee,
           Thy life-blood and breath,
Green leaves of thy labour, white flowers of thy thought,
   and red fruit of thy death.   80

Be the ways of thy giving
 As mine were to thee;
The free life of thy living,
 Be the gift of it free;
Not as servant to lord, nor as master to slave shalt thou
 give thee to me.

O children of banishment,
 Souls overcast,
Were the lights ye see vanish meant
 Alway to last,
Ye would know not the sun overshining the shadows and
 stars overpast.   90

I that saw where ye trod
 The dim paths of the night
Set the shadow called God
 In your skies to give light;
But the morning of manhood is risen, and the shadowless
 soul is in sight.

The tree many-rooted
 That swells to the sky
With frondage red-fruited,
 The life-tree am I;
In the buds of your lives is the sap of my leaves; ye shall
 live and not die.   100

But the gods of your fashion
 That take and that give,
In their pity and passion
 That scourge and forgive,
They are worms that are bred in the bark that falls off;
 they shall die and not live.

My own blood is what stanches
 The wounds in my bark;
Stars caught in my branches
 Make day of the dark,
And are worshiped as suns till the sunrise shall tread out
 their fires as a spark.   110

Where dead ages hide under
 The live roots of the tree,

In my darkness the thunder
    Makes utterance of me;
In the clash of my boughs with each other ye hear the
waves sound of the sea.

That noise is of Time,
    As his feathers are spread
And his feet set to climb
    Through the boughs overhead,
And my foliage rings round him and rustles, and branches
are bent with his tread.   120

The storm-winds of ages
    Blow through me and cease,
The war-wind that rages,
    The spring-wind of peace,
Ere the breath of them roughen my tresses, ere one of my
blossoms increase.

All sounds of all changes,
    All shadows and lights
On the world's mountain-ranges
    And stream-riven heights,
Whose tongue is the wind's tongue and language of storm-
clouds on earth-shaking nights;   130

All forms of all faces,
    All works of all hands
In unsearchable places
    Of time-stricken lands,
All death and all life, and all reigns and all ruins, drop
through me as sands.

Though sore be my burden
    And more than ye know,
And my growth have no guerdon
    But only to grow,
Yet I fail not of growing for lightnings above me or death-
worms below.   140

These too have their part in me,
    As I too in these;
Such fire is at heart in me,
    Such sap is this tree's,

Which hath in it all sounds and all secrets of infinite lands
and of seas.

> In the spring-coloured hours
> When my mind was as May's,
> There brake forth of me flowers
> By centuries of days,

Strong blossoms with perfume of manhood shot out from
my spirit as rays.   150

> And the sound of them springing
> And smell of their shoots
> Were as warmth and sweet singing
> And strength to my roots;

And the lives of my children made perfect with freedom
of soul were my fruits.

> I bid you but be;
> I have need not of prayer;
> I have need of you free
> As your mouths of mine air;

That my heart may be greater within me, beholding the
fruits of me fair.   160

> More fair than strange fruit is
> Of faiths ye espouse;
> In me only the root is
> That blooms in your boughs;

Behold now your God that ye made you, to feed him with
faith of your vows.

> In the darkening and whitening
> Abysses adored,
> With dayspring and lightning
> For lamp and for sword,

God thunders in heaven, and his angels are red with the
wrath of the Lord.   170

> O my sons, O too dutiful
> Toward gods not of me,
> Was not I enough beautiful?
> Was it hard to be free?

For behold, I am with you, am in you and of you; look
forth now and see.

Lo, winged with world's wonders,
    With miracles shod,
With the fires of his thunders
    For raiment and rod,
God trembles in heaven, and his angels are white with the
terror of God.   180

For his twilight is come on him,
    His anguish is here;
And his spirits gaze dumb on him,
    Grown gray from his fear;
And his hour taketh hold on him stricken, the last of his
infinite year.

Thought made him and breaks him,
    Truth slays and forgives;
But to you, as time takes him,
    This new thing it gives,
Even love, the beloved Republic, that feeds upon freedom
and lives.   190

For truth only is living,
    Truth only is whole,
And the love of his giving
    Man's polestar and pole;
Man, pulse of my center, and fruit of my body, and seed
of my soul;

One birth of my bosom;
    One beam of mine eye;
One topmost blossom
    That scales the sky;
Man, equal and one with me, man that is made of me,
man that is I.   200

1871

Title: the name (Erda, or Earth) of a Norse goddess of fruitfulness, here given a cosmic significance.   l. 15: **I am** an inversion of God's name as revealed to Moses (Exod. 3:14) and also of Christ's claim to have been from the beginning (John 8:58).   l. 64: **tripod** signifying religious oracles.   l. 96: **tree** Yggdrasil, the tree that, in Norse mythology, upholds all worlds.   l. 181: **twilight** from the old Norse belief that the gods themselves will be "darkened" and that they will be succeeded by some greater power.

GENESIS

In the outer world that was before this earth,
    That was before all shape or space was born,
Before the blind first hour of time had birth,
    Before night knew the moonlight or the morn;

Yea, before any world had any light,
    Or anything called God or man drew breath,
Slowly the strong sides of the heaving night
    Moved, and brought forth the strength of life and death.

And the sad shapeless horror increate
    That was all things and one thing, without fruit,   10
Limit, or law; where love was none, nor hate,
    Where no leaf came to blossom from no root;

The very darkness that time knew not of,
    Nor God laid hand on, nor was man found there,
Ceased, and was cloven in several shapes; above
    Light, and night under, and fire, earth, water, and air.

Sunbeans and starbeams, and all coloured things,
    All forms and all similitudes began;
And death, the shadow cast by life's wide wings,
    And God, the shade cast by the soul of man.   20

Then between shadow and substance, night and light,
    Then between birth and death, and deeds and days,
The illimitable embrace and the amorous fight
    That of itself begets, bears, rears, and slays,

The immortal war of mortal things, that is
    Labour and life and growth and good and ill,
The mild antiphonies that melt and kiss,
    The violent symphonies that meet and kill,

All nature of all things began to be.
    But chiefliest in the spirit (beast or man,   30
Planet of heaven or blossom of earth or sea)
    The divine contraries of life began.

For the great labour of growth, being many, is one;
    One thing the white death and the ruddy birth;
The invisible air and the all-beholden sun,
    And barren water and many-childed earth.

And these things are made manifest in men
 From the beginning forth unto this day:
Time writes and life records them, and again
 Death seals them lest the record pass away.   40

For if death were not, then should growth not be,
 Change, nor the life of good nor evil things;
Nor were there night at all nor light to see,
 Nor water of sweet nor water of bitter springs.

For in each man and each year that is born
 Are sown the twin seeds of the strong twin powers;
The white seed of the fruitful helpful morn,
 The black seed of the barren hurtful hours.

And he that of the black seed eateth fruit,
 To him the savour as honey shall be sweet;   50
And he in whom the white seed hath struck root,
 He shall have sorrow and trouble and tears for meat.

And him whose lips the sweet fruit hath made red
 In the end men loathe and make his name a rod;
And him whose mouth on the unsweet fruit hath fed
 In the end men follow and know for very God.

And of these twain, the black seed and the white,
 All things come forth endured of men and done;
And still the day is great with child of night,
 And still the black night labours with the sun.   60

And each man and each year that lives on earth
 Turns hither or thither, and hence or thence is fed;
And as a man before was from his birth,
 So shall a man be after among the dead.

           1871

TO WALT WHITMAN IN AMERICA

  Send but a song oversea for us,
   Heart of their hearts who are free,
  Heart of their singer, to be for us
   More than our singing can be;
  Ours, in the tempest at error,

With no light but the twilight of terror;
    Send us a song oversea!

Sweet-smelling of pine-leaves and grasses,
    And blown as a tree through and through
With the winds of the keen mountain-passes,   10
    And tender as sun-smitten dew;
Sharp-tongued as the winter that shakes
The wastes of your limitless lakes,
    Wide-eyed as the sea-line's blue.

O strong-winged soul with prophetic
    Lips hot with the bloodbeats of song,
With tremor of heartstrings magnetic,
    With thoughts as thunders in throng,
With consonant ardours of chords
That pierce men's souls as with swords   20
    And hale them hearing along,

Make us too music, to be with us
    As a word from a world's heart warm,
To sail the dark as a sea with us,
    Full-sailed, outsinging the storm,
A song to put fire in our ears
Whose burning shall burn up tears,
    Whose sign bid battle re-form;

A note in the ranks of a clarion,
    A word in the wind of cheer,   30
To consume as with lightning the carrion
    That makes time foul for us here;
In the air that our dead things infest
A blast of the breath of the west,
    Till east way as west way is clear.

Out of the sun beyond sunset,
    From the evening whence morning shall be,
With the rollers in measureless onset,
    With the van of the storming sea,
With the world-wide wind, with the breath   40
That breaks ships driven upon death,
    With the passion of all things free,

With the sea-steeds footless and frantic—
    White myriads for death to bestride
In the charge of the ruining Atlantic,
    Where deaths by regiments ride—
With clouds and clamours of waters,
With a long note shriller than slaughter's
    On the furrowless fields world-wide;

With terror, with ardour and wonder—   50
    With the soul of the season that wakes
When the weight of a whole year's thunder
    In the tidestream of autumn breaks—
Let the flight of the wide-winged word
Come over, come in and be heard,
    Take form and fire for our sakes.

For a continent bloodless with travail
    Here toils and brawls as it can;
And the web of it who shall unravel
    Of all that peer on the plan—   60
Would fain grow men, but they grow not,
And fain be free, but they know not
    One name for freedom and man?

One name, not twain for division;
    One thing, not twain, from the birth;
Spirit and substance and vision,
    Worth more than worship is worth;
Unbeheld, unadored, undivined,
The cause, the centre, the mind,
    The secret and sense of the earth.   70

Here as a weakling in irons,
    Here as a weanling in bands,
As a prey that the stake-net environs,
    Our life that we looked for stands;
And the man-child naked and dear,
Democracy, turns on us here
    Eyes trembling, with tremulous hands.

It sees not what season shall bring to it
    Sweet fruit of its bitter desire;

Few voices it hears yet sing to it,   80
  Few pulses of hearts reaspire;
Foresees not time, nor forehears
The noises of imminent years—
  Earthquake, and thunder, and fire;

When crowned and weaponed and curbless
  It shall walk, without helm or shield,
The bare burned furrows and herbless
  Of war's last flame-stricken field—
Till godlike, equal with time,
It stand in the sun sublime,   90
  In the godhead of man revealed.

Round your people and over them
  Light like raiment is drawn,
Close as a garment to cover them,
  Wrought not of mail nor of lawn;
Here, with hope hardly to wear,
Naked nations and bare
  Swim, sink, strike out for the dawn.

Chains are here, and a prison,
  Kings, and subjects, and shame;   100
If the God upon you be arisen,
  How should our songs be the same?
How, in confusion of change,
How shall we sing, in a strange
  Land, songs praising his name?

God is buried and dead to us,
  Even the spirit of earth,
Freedom; so have they said to us,
  Some with mocking and mirth,
Some with heartbreak and tears;   110
And a God without eyes, without ears—
  Who shall sing of him, dead in the birth?

The earth-god Freedom, the lonely
  Face lightening, the footprint unshod—
Not as one man crucified only,
  Nor scourged with but one life's rod;
The soul that is substance of nations,
Reincarnate with fresh generations—
  The great god Man, which is God.

But in weariest of years and obscurest,   120
   Doth it live not at heart of all things—
The one God and one spirit, a purest
   Life, fed from unstanchable springs?
Within love, within hatred it is,
And its seed in the stripe as the kiss,
   And in slaves is the germ, and in kings.

Freedom we call it, for holier
   Name of the soul's there is none;
Surely it labours, if slowlier,
   Than the metres of star or of sun;   130
Slowlier than life into breath,
Surelier than time into death,
   It moves till its labour be done;

Till the motion be done and the measure
   Circling through season and clime—
Slumber and sorrow and pleasure,
   Vision of virtue and crime;
Till consummate with conquering eyes,
A soul disembodied, it rise
   From the body transfigured of time;   140

Till it rise and remain and take station
   With the stars of the world that rejoice;
Till the voice of its heart's exultation
   Be as theirs an invariable voice—
By no discord of evil estranged,
By no pause, by no breach in it changed,
   By no clash in the chord of its choice.

It is one with the world's generations,
   With the spirit, the star, and the sod;
With the kingless and king-stricken nations,   150
   With the cross, and the chain, and the rod;
The most high, the most secret, most lonely,
The earth-soul Freedom, that only
   Lives, and that only is God.

1871

l. 73: **stake-net** a net set like a fence to take fish.   l. 95: **mail** armor,
symbolizing the State.   **lawn** fine linen, symbolizing the Church.
l. 125: **stripe** wound from a whiplash.   l. 126: **germ** seed.

From *TRISTRAM OF LYONESSE*

Love, that is first and last of all things made,
The light that has the living world for shade,
The spirit that for temporal veil has on
The souls of all men woven in unison,
One fiery raiment with all lives inwrought
And lights of sunny and starry deed and thought,
And always through new act and passion new
Shines the divine same body and beauty through,
The body spiritual of fire and light
That is to worldly noon as noon to night;   10
Love, that is flesh upon the spirit of man
And spirit within the flesh whence breath began;
Love, that keeps all the choir of lives in chime;
Love, that is blood within the veins of time;
That wrought the whole world without stroke of hand,
Shaping the breadth of sea, the length of land,
And with the pulse and motion of his breath
Through the great heart of the earth strikes life and death,
The sweet twain chords that make the sweet tune live
Through day and night of things alternative,   20
Through silence and through sound of stress and strife,
And ebb and flow of dying death and life;
Love, that sounds loud or light in all men's ears,
Whence all men's eyes take fire from sparks of tears,
That binds on all men's feet or chains or wings;
Love, that is root and fruit of terrene things;
Love, that the whole world's waters shall not drown,
The whole world's fiery forces not burn down;
Love, that what time his own hands guard his head
The whole world's wrath and strength shall not strike dead;   30
Love, that if once his own hands make his grave
The whole world's pity and sorrow shall not save;
Love, that for very life shall not be sold,
Nor bought nor bound with iron nor with gold;
So strong that heaven, could love bid heaven farewell,
Would turn to fruitless and unflowering hell;
So sweet that hell, to hell could love be given,

Would turn to splendid and sonorous heaven;
Love that is fire within thee and light above,
And lives by grace of nothing but of love;   40
Through many and lovely thoughts and much desire
Led these twain to the life of tears and fire;
Through many and lovely days and much delight
Led these twain to the lifeless life of night.
    Yea, but what then? albeit all this were thus,
And soul smote soul and left it ruinous,
And love led love as eyeless men lead men,
Through chance by chance to deathward—ah, what then?
Hath love not likewise led them further yet,
Out through the years where memories rise and set,   50
Some large as suns, some moon-like warm and pale,
Some starry-sighted, some through clouds that sail
Seen as red flame through spectral float of fume,
Each with the blush of its own special bloom
On the fair face of its own coloured light,
Distinguishable in all the host of night,
Divisible from all the radiant rest
And separable in splendour? Hath the best
Light of love's all, of all that burn and move,
A better heaven than heaven is? Hath not love   60
Made for all these their sweet particular air
To shine in, their own beams and names to bear,
Their ways to wander and their wards to keep,
Till story and song and glory and all things sleep?
Hath he not plucked from death of lovers dead
Their musical soft memories, and kept red
The rose of their remembrance in men's eyes,
The sunsets of their stories in his skies,
The blush of their dead blood in lips that speak
Of their dead lives, and in the listener's cheek   70
That trembles with the kindling pity lit
In gracious hearts for some sweet fever-fit,
A fiery pity enkindled of pure thought
By tales that make their honey out of naught,
The faithless faith that lives without belief
Its light life through, the griefless ghost of grief?
Yea, as warm night refashions the sear blood
In storm-struck petal or in sun-struck bud,

With tender hours and tempering dew to cure
The hunger and thirst of day's distemperature   80
And ravin of the dry discolouring hours,
Hath he not bid relume their flameless flowers
With summer fire and heat of lamping song,
And bid the short-lived things, long dead, live long,
And thought remake their wan funereal fames,
And the sweet shining signs of women's names
That mark the months out and the weeks anew
He moves in changeless change of seasons through
To fill the days up of his dateless year
Flame from Queen Helen to Queen Guenevere?   90
For first of all the sphery signs whereby
Love severs light from darkness, and most high,
In the white front of January there glows
The rose-red sign of Helen like a rose;
And gold-eyed as the short-flower shelterless
Whereon the sharp-breathed sea blows bitterness,
A storm-star that the seafarers of love
Strain their wind-wearied eyes for glimpses of,
Shoots keen through February's gray frost and damp
The lamplike star of Hero for a lamp;   100
The star that Marlowe sang into our skies
With mouth of gold, and morning in his eyes;
And in clear March across the rough blue sea
The signal sapphire of Alcyone
Makes bright the blown brows of the wind-foot year;
And shining like a sunbeam-smitten tear
Full ere it fall, the fair next sign in sight
Burns opal-wise with April-coloured light
When air is quick with song and rain and flame,
My birth-month star that in love's heaven hath name   110
Iseult, a light of blossom and beam and shower,
My singing sign that makes the song-tree flower;
Next like a pale and burning pearl beyond
The rose-white sphere of flower-named Rosamond
Signs the sweet head of Maytime; and for June
Flares like an angered and storm-reddening moon
Her signal sphere, whose Carthaginian pyre
Shadowed her traitor's flying sail with fire;
Next, glittering as the wine-bright jacinth-stone,

A star south-risen that first to music shone,   120
The keen girl-star of golden Juliet bears
Light northward to the month whose forehead wears
Her name for flower upon it, and his trees
Mix their deep English song with Veronese;
And like an awful sovereign chrysolite
Burning, the supreme fire that blinds the night,
The hot gold head of Venus kissed by Mars,
A sun-flower among small spherèd flowers of stars,
The light of Cleopatra fills and burns
The hollow of heaven whence ardent August yearns;   130
And fixed and shining as the sister-shed
Sweet tears for Phaëthon disorbed and dead,
The pale bright autumn's amber-coloured sphere,
That through September sees the saddening year
As love sees change through sorrow, hath to name
Francesca's; and the star that watches flame
The embers of the harvest overgone
Is Thisbe's, slain of love in Babylon,
Set in the golden girdle of sweet signs
A blood-bright ruby; last save one light shines   140
An eastern wonder of sphery chrysopras,
The star that made men mad, Angelica's;
And latest named and lordliest, with a sound
Of swords and harps in heaven that ring it round,
Last love-light and last love-song of the year's
Gleams like a glorious emerald Guenevere's.
These are the signs wherethrough the year sees move,
Full of the sun, the sun-god which is love,
A fiery body blood-red from the heart
Outward, with fire-white wings made wide apart,   150
That close not and unclose not, but upright
Steered without wind by their own light and might
Sweep through the flameless fire of air that rings
From heaven to heaven with thunder of wheels and wings
And antiphones of motion-molded rime
Through spaces out of space and timeless time.
    So shine above dead chance and conquered change
The spherèd signs, and leave without their range
Doubt and desire, and hope with fear for wife,
Pale pains, and pleasures long worn out of life.   160

Yea, even the shadows of them spiritless,
Through the dim door of sleep that seem to press,
Forms without form, a piteous people and blind,
Men and no men, whose lamentable kind
The shadow of death and shadow of life compel
Through semblances of heaven and false-faced hell,
Through dreams of light and dreams of darkness tost
On waves innavigable, are these so lost?
Shapes that wax pale and shift in swift strange wise,
Void faces with unspeculative eyes,   170
Dim things that gaze and glare, dead mouths that move,
Featureless heads discrowned of hate and love,
Mockeries and masks of motion and mute breath,
Leavings of life, the superflux of death—
If these things and no more than these things be
Left when man ends or changes, who can see?
Or who can say with what more subtle sense
Their subtler natures taste in air less dense
A life less thick and palpable than ours,
Warmed with faint fires and sweetened with dead flowers   180
And measured by low music? how time fares
In that wan time-forgotten world of theirs,
Their pale poor world too deep for sun or star
To live in, where the eyes of Helen are,
And hers who made as God's own eyes to shine
The eyes that met them of the Florentine,
Wherein the godhead thence transfigured lit
All time for all men with the shadow of it?
Ah, and these, too, felt on them as God's grace
The pity and glory of this man's breathing face;   190
For these, too, these my lovers, these my twain,
Saw Dante, saw God visible by pain,
With lips that thundered and with feet that trod
Before men's eyes incognizable God;
Saw love and wrath and light and night and fire
Live with one life and at one mouth respire,
And in one golden sound their whole soul heard
Sounding, one sweet immitigable word.
    They have the night, who had like us the day;
We, whom day binds, shall have the night as they.   200
We, from the fetters of the light unbound,
Healed of our wound of living, shall sleep sound.

All gifts but one the jealous God may keep
From our soul's longing, one he cannot—sleep.
This, though he grudge all other grace to prayer,
This grace his closed hand cannot choose but spare.
This, though his ear be sealed to all that live,
Be it lightly given or loathly, God must give.
We, as the men whose name on earth is none,
We too shall surely pass out of the sun;   210
Out of the sound and eyeless light of things,
Wide as the stretch of life's time-wandering wings,
Wide as the naked world and shadowless,
And long-lived as the world's own weariness.
Us too, when all the fires of time are cold,
The heights shall hide us and the depths shall hold.
Us too, when all the tears of time are dry,
The night shall lighten from her tearless eye.
Blind is the day and eyeless all its light,
But the large unbewildered eye of night   220
Hath sense and speculation; and the sheer
Limitless length of lifeless life and clear,
The timeless space wherein the brief worlds move
Clothed with light life and fruitful with light love,
With hopes that threaten, and with fears that cease,
Past fear and hope, hath in it only peace.
   Yet of these lives inlaid with hopes and fears,
Spun fine as fire and jeweled thick with tears,
These lives made out of loves that long since were,
Lives wrought as ours of earth and burning air,   230
Fugitive flame, and water of secret springs,
And clothed with joys and sorrows as with wings,
Some yet are good, if aught be good, to save
Some while from washing wreck and wrecking wave.
Was such not theirs, the twain I take, and give
Out of my life to make their dead life live
Some days of mine, and blow my living breath
Between dead lips forgotten even of death?
So many and many of old have given my twain
Love and live song and honey-hearted pain,   240
Whose root is sweetness and whose fruit is sweet,
So many and with such joy have tracked their feet,
What should I do to follow? Yet I too,
I have the heart to follow, many or few

Be the feet gone before me; for the way,
Rose-red with remnant roses of the day
Westward, and eastward white with stars that break,
Between the green and foam is fair to take
For any sail the sea-wind steers for me
From morning into morning, sea to sea.   250

1871

l. 25: **or . . . or** either, or.   l. 42: **twain** Tristram and Iseult.
ll. 91–147: **sphery signs** Swinburne conceives a zodiac of love in which a
different star, named for a tragic beauty, reigns each month: in January,
Helen of Troy; in February, Hero of Lesbos, whom Leander swam the
Hellespont to meet; in March, Alcyone (Halcyon), who drowned herself
in grief at her husband's death by shipwreck; in April (the month of
Swinburne's birth) Iseult of Ireland, wedded to King Mark but loved by
Tristram; in May, Rosamond, reputedly killed by order of the jealous wife
of Henry II of England; in June, Dido, Queen of Carthage, whose funeral
pyre lighted the departing ships of Aeneas, "her traitor"; in July, Juliet,
the bride of Romeo; in August, Cleopatra, whose love affair with Antony
is likened to that of Venus with Mars; in September, Francesca da Rimini,
whom, with her lover Paolo, Dante met in Hell (*Inferno*, V, ll. 73–142);
in October, Thisbe of Babylon, whose death, and that of her lover,
Pyramus, resembled the fate of Romeo and Juliet; in November, Angelica,
whose coldness drove Roland (Orlando) mad; in December, Guenevere,
the wife of King Arthur.   l. 101: **Marlowe** Christopher Marlowe,
author of *Hero and Leander*, 1598.   l. 124: **Veronese** the dialect of
Verona, Italy, the city of Romeo and Juliet, whose names are also mingled
with Shakespearean, hence English, associations.   l. 132: **tears** shed by
Phaëton's sisters, the Heliades, after he perished while attempting to drive
the sun-chariot of his father Apollo.   l. 185: **her's** Beatrice's. In the
Divine Comedy Beatrice guides Dante ("the Florentine," l. 186) to Para-
dise.   l. 192: **Saw Dante** In Hell, Dante sees Tristram (*Inferno* V,
l. 67) and, Swinburne implies, Iseult also.   l. 239: **many of old** past
writers such as Chaucer and Malory.

*A very macabre
situation, about
a wake and a
song to sing.*

A LYKE-WAKE SONG

Fair of face, full of pride,
Sit ye down by a dead man's side.

*Not a very
comforting song
for a wake.*

Ye sang songs a' the day;
Sit down at night in the red worm's way.

Proud ye were a' day long;
Ye'll be but lean at evensong.

Ye had gowd kells on your hair;
Nae man kens what ye were.

Ye set scorn by the silken stuff;
Now the grave is clean enough.

*offers little
hope beyond
decay and
deep.*

Ye set scorn by the rubis ring;
Now the worm is a saft sweet thing.

Fine gold and blithe fair face,
Ye are come to a grimly place.

Gold hair and glad grey een,
Nae man kens if ye have been.

1877

Title: *Lyke* (corpse); *Wake* (watch).   1. 7: **gowd kells** gold nets.
1. 8: **Nae** no.   1. 11: **rubis** ruby.   1. 15: **een** eyes.

A BALLAD OF FRANÇOIS VILLON

*Swinburne
likened him-
self to him.*

PRINCE OF ALL BALLAD-MAKERS

*A trubador
singer.*

Bird of the bitter bright gray golden morn
    Scarce risen upon the dusk of dolorous years,
First of us all and sweetest singer born

*Few
share this
opinion*

    Whose far shrill note the world of new men hears
    Cleave the cold shuddering shade as twilight clears;
When song newborn put off the old world's attire
And felt its tune on her changed lips expire,
    Writ foremost on the roll of them that came
Fresh girt for service of the latter lyre,
    Villon, our sad bad glad mad brother's name!

*A figure
outside of
society*

Like a chorus   10

Alas the joy, the sorrow, and the scorn,
    That clothed thy life with hopes and sins and fears,
And gave thee stones for bread and tares for corn
    And plume-plucked jailbirds for thy starveling peers
    Till death clipped close their flight with shameful shears;
Till shifts came short and loves were hard to hire,
When lilt of song nor twitch of twangling wire
    Could buy thee bread or kisses; when light fame
Spurned like a ball and haled through brake and brier,
    Villon, our sad bad glad mad brother's name!   20

Poor splendid wings so frayed and soiled and torn!
 Poor kind wild eyes so dashed with light quick tears!
Poor perfect voice, most blithe when most forlorn,
 That rings athwart the sea whence no man steers
 Like joy-bells crossed with death-bells in our ears!
What far delight has cooled the fierce desire
That like some ravenous bird was strong to tire
 On that frail flesh and soul consumed with flame,
But left more sweet than roses to respire,
 Villon, our sad bad glad mad brother's name?   30

This is the French form, S. is a master of form

Envoi

Prince of sweet songs made out of tears and fire,
A harlot was thy nurse, a God thy sire;   *Contradiction*
 Shame soiled thy song, and song assoiled thy shame.
But from thy feet now death has washed the mire,
Love reads out first at head of all our choir,
 Villon, our sad bad glad mad brother's name.

Not too deep.

            1878

Title: a French *ballade*, a form in which Villon (1431–1463?) excelled.
l. 1: **morn** the dawn, in France, of the literary Renaissance. l. 13:
tares for corn weeds instead of grain. l. 16: **shifts** desperate means
of livelihood. l. 33: **assoiled** absolved.

THE BALLAD OF VILLON AND FAT MADGE

Purpose? Is this serious?
No, there seems to be no real purpose, he just shocks his audience.
The metrics are beautiful.

 'Tis no sin for a man to labour in his vocation.—Falstaff.
  The night cometh, when no man can work.

What though the beauty I love and serve be cheap,
 Ought you to take me for a beast or fool?
All things a man could wish are in her keep;
 For her I turn swashbuckler in love's school.
 When folk drop in, I take my pot and stool
And fall to drinking with no more ado.
I fetch them bread, fruit, cheese, and water, too;
 I say all's right so long as I'm well paid;
"Look in again when your flesh troubles you,
 Inside this brothel where we drive our trade."   10
But soon the devil's among us flesh and fell,
 When penniless to bed comes Madge my whore;

I loathe the very sight of her like hell.
　I snatch gown, girdle, surcoat, all she wore,
　And tell her, these shall stand against her score.
She grips her hips with both hands, cursing God,
Swearing by Jesus' body, bones, and blood,
　That they shall not. Then I, no whit dismayed,
Cross her cracked nose with some stray shiver of wood
　Inside this brothel where we drive our trade.　　20

When all's made up she drops me a windy word,
　Bloat like a beetle puffed and poisonous:
Grins, thumps my pate, and calls me dickey-bird,
　And cuffs me with a fist that's ponderous.
We sleep like logs, being drunken both of us;
Then when we wake her womb begins to stir;
To save her seed she gets me under her
　Wheezing and whining, flat as planks are laid:
And thus she spoils me for a whoremonger
　Inside this brothel where we drive our trade.　　30

Blow, hail or freeze, I've bread here baked rent-free!
Whoring's my trade, and my whore pleases me;
　Bad cat, bad rat; we're just the same if weighed.
We that love filth, filth follows us, you see;
Honour flees from us, as from her we flee
　Inside this brothel where we drive our trade.

(1878?)　　　　　　　　　　　　　　　　　　1910

Title: a translation of one of Villon's *ballades*.　**Epigraphs:** " 'Tis no sin . . ." (*Henry IV, Part I*, I, ii. 114.)　"The night cometh . . ." (John 9:4.)　l. 15: **score** unpaid bill.

A FORSAKEN GARDEN

In a coign of the cliff between lowland and highland,
　At the sea-down's edge between windward and lee,
Walled round with rocks as an inland island,
　The ghost of a garden fronts the sea.
A girdle of brushwood and thorn encloses
　The steep square slope of the blossomless bed
Where the weeds that grew green from the graves of its roses
　Now lie dead.

The fields fall southward, abrupt and broken,
    To the low last edge of the long lone land.   10
If a step should sound or a word be spoken,
    Would a ghost not rise at the strange guest's hand?
So long have the gray bare walks lain guestless,
    Through branches and briars if a man make way,
He shall find no life, but the sea-wind's restless
    Night and day.

The dense hard passage is blind and stifled
    That crawls by a track none turn to climb
To the strait waste place that the years have rifled
    Of all but the thorns that are touched not of time.   20
The thorns he spares when the rose is taken;
    The rocks are left when he wastes the plain.
The wind that wanders, the weeds wind-shaken,
    These remain.

Not a flower to be pressed of the foot that falls not;
    As the heart of a dead man the seed-plots are dry;
From the thicket of thorns whence the nightingale calls not,
    Could she call, there were never a rose to reply.
Over the meadows that blossom and wither
    Wings but the note of a sea-bird's song;   30
Only the sun and the rain come hither
    All year long.

The sun burns sear and the rain dishevels
    One gaunt bleak blossom of scentless breath.
Only the wind here hovers and revels
    In a round where life seems barren as death.
Here there was laughing of old, there was weeping,
    Haply, of lovers none ever will know,
Whose eyes went seaward a hundred sleeping
    Years ago.   40

Heart handfast in heart as they stood, "Look thither,"
    Did he whisper? "look forth from the flowers to the sea;
For the foam-flowers endure when the rose-blossoms wither,
    And men that love lightly may die—but we?"
And the same wind sang and the same waves whitened,
    And or ever the garden's last petals were shed,

In the lips that had whispered, the eyes that had lightened,
    Love was dead.

Or they loved their life through, and then went whither?
    And were one to the end—but what end who knows?   50
Love deep as the sea as a rose must wither,
    As the rose-red seaweed that mocks the rose.
Shall the dead take thought for the dead to love them?
    What love was ever as deep as a grave?
They are loveless now as the grass above them
    Or the wave.

All are at one now, roses and lovers,
    Not known of the cliffs and the fields and the sea.
Not a breath of the time that has been hovers
    In the air now soft with a summer to be.   60
Not a breath shall there sweeten the seasons hereafter
    Of the flowers or the lovers that laugh now or weep,
When as they that are free now of weeping and laughter
    We shall sleep.

Here death may deal not again forever;
    Here change may come not till all change end.
From the graves they have made they shall rise up never,
    Who have left naught living to ravage and rend.
Earth, stones, and thorns of the wild ground growing,
    While the sun and the rain live, these shall be: 70
Till a last wind's breath upon all these blowing
    Roll the sea.

Till the slow sea rise and the sheer cliff crumble,
    Till terrace and meadow the deep gulfs drink,
Till the strength of the waves of the high tides humble
    The fields that lessen, the rocks that shrink,
Here now in his triumph where all things falter,
    Stretched out on the spoils that his own hand spread,
As a god self-slain on his own strange altar,
    Death lies dead.   80

1878

THE HIGHER PANTHEISM IN A NUTSHELL

One, who is not, we see; but one, whom we see not, is;
Surely this is not that; but that is assuredly this.

What, and wherefore, and whence? for under is over and
    under;
If thunder could be without lightning, lightning could be
    without thunder.

Doubt is faith in the main; but faith, on the whole, is doubt;
We cannot believe by proof; but could we believe without?

Why, and whither, and how? for barley and rye are not clover;
Neither are straight lines curves; yet over is under and over.

Two and two may be four; but four and four are not eight;   10
Fate and God may be twain; but God is the same thing as fate.

Ask a man what he thinks, and get from a man what he feels;
God, once caught in the fact, shows you a fair pair of heels.

Body and spirit are twins; God only knows which is which;
The soul squats down in the flesh, like a tinker drunk in a
    ditch.

More is the whole than a part; but half is more than the
    whole;
Clearly, the soul is the body; but is not the body the soul?

One and two are not one; but one and nothing is two;
Truth can hardly be false, if falsehood cannot be true.

Once the mastodon was; pterodactyls were common as cocks;
Then the mammoth was God; now is He a prize ox.   20

Parallels all things are; yet many of these are askew;
You are certainly I; but certainly I am not you.

Springs the rock from the plain, shoots the stream from the
    rock;
Cocks exist for the hen; but hens exist for the cock.

God, whom we see not, is; and God, who is not, we see;
Fiddle, we know, is diddle; and diddle, we take it, is dee.

1880

Title: a parody of Tennyson's "The Higher Pantheism."   l. 20: **ox**
that is, on public exhibition.

a joke on Swinburne's
part, play games with
sounds, A parody
of himself

NEPHELIDIA — little clouds

From the depth of the dreamy decline of the dawn through a
    notable nimbus of nebulous noonshine,
  Pallid and pink as the palm of the flag-flower that flickers
    with fear of the flies as they float,
Are the looks of our lovers that lustrously lean from a marvel
    of mystic miraculous moonshine,
  These that we feel in the blood of our blushes that thicken
    and threaten with throbs through the throat?
Thicken and thrill as a theatre thronged at appeal of an
    actor's appalled agitation,
  Fainter with fear of the fires of the future than pale with
    the promise of pride in the past;
Flushed with the famishing fullness of fever that reddens with
    radiance of rathe recreation,
  Gaunt as the ghastliest of glimpses that gleam through the
    gloom of the gloaming when ghosts go aghast?
Nay, for the nick of the tick of the time is a tremulous touch
    on the temples of terror,
  Strained as the sinews yet strenuous with strife of the dead
    who is dumb as the dust-heaps of death;   10
Surely no soul is it, sweet as the spasm of erotic emotional
    exquisite error,
  Bathed in the balms of beatified bliss, beatific itself by
    beatitude's breath.
Surely no spirit or sense of a soul that was soft to the spirit and
    soul of our senses
  Sweetens the stress of suspiring suspicion that sobs in the
    semblance and sound of a sigh;
Only this oracle opens Olympian, in mystical moods and tri-
    angular tenses—
  "Life is the lust of a lamp for the light that is dark till the
    dawn of the day when we die."
Mild is the mirk and monotonous music of memory, melodi-
    ously mute as it may be,
  While the hope in the heart of a hero is bruised by the
    breach of men's rapiers, resigned to the rod;
Made meek as a mother whose bosom-beats bound with the
    bliss-bringing bulk of a balm-breathing baby,
  As they grope through the graveyard of creeds, under skies
    growing green at a groan for the grimness of God.   20

241

Blank is the book of his bounty beholden of old, and its bind-
  ing is blacker than bluer;
Out of blue into black is the scheme of the skies, and their
  dews are the wine of the bloodshed of things;
Till the darkling desire of delight shall be free as a fawn that is
  freed from the fangs that pursue her,
Till the heartbeats of hell shall be hushed by a hymn from
  the hunt that has harried the kennel of kings.

1880

Title: "Little Clouds," Swinburne's self-parody.

THE TYNESIDE WIDOW

There's mony a man loves land and life,
  Loves life and land and fee;
And mony a man loves fair women,
  But never a man loves me, my love,
  But never a man loves me.

O weel and weel for a' lovers,
  I wot weel may they be;
And weel and weel for a' fair maidens,
  But aye mair woe for me, my love,
  But aye mair woe for me.   10

O weel be wi' you, ye sma' flowers,
  Ye flowers and every tree;
And weel be wi' you, a' birdies,
  But teen and tears wi' me, my love,
  But teen and tears wi' me.

O weel be yours, my three brethren,
  And ever weel be ye,
Wi' deeds for doing and loves for wooing;
  But never a love for me, my love,
  But never a love for me.   20

And weel be yours, my seven sisters,
  And good love-days to see,
And long life-days and true lovers;

But never a day for me, my love,
But never a day for me.

Good times wi' you, ye bauld riders,
　By the hieland and the lee;
And by the leeland and by the hieland
　It's weary times wi' me, my love,
　It's weary times wi' me.　　　　　　　　　　　30

Good days wi' you, ye good sailors,
　Sail in and out the sea;
And by the beaches and by the reaches
　It's heavy days wi' me, my love,
　It's heavy days wi' me.

I had his kiss upon my mouth,
　His bairn upon my knee;
I would my soul and body were twain,
　And the bairn and the kiss wi' me, my love,
　And the bairn and the kiss wi' me.　　　　　40

The bairn down in the mools, my dear,
　O saft and saft lies she;
I would the mools were ower my head,
　And the young bairn fast wi' me, my love,
　And the young bairn fast wi' me.

The father under the faem, my dear,
　O sound and sound sleeps he;
I would the faem were ower my face,
　And the father lay by me, my love,
　And the father lay by me.　　　　　　　　　50

I would the faem were ower my face,
　Or the mools on my ee-bree;
And waking-time with a' lovers,
　But sleeping-time wi' me, my love,
　But sleeping-time wi' me.

I would the mools were meat in my mouth,
　The saut faem in my ee;
And the land-worm and the water-worm
　To feed fu' sweet on me, my love,
　To feed fu' sweet on me.　　　　　　　　　60

My life is sealed with a seal of love,
    And locked with love for a key;
And I lie wrang and I wake lang,
      But ye tak nae thought for me, my love,
      But ye tak' nae thought for me.

We were weel fain of love, my dear,
    O fain and fain were we;
It was weel with a' the weary world,
      But O, sae weel wi' me, my love,
      But O, sae weel wi' me.   70

We were nane ower mony to sleep, my dear,
    I wot we were but three;
And never a bed in the weary world
      For my bairn and my dear and me, my love,
      For my bairn and my dear and me.

                   1889

Title: The Tyne, a river in the English-Scotch borderlands, for centuries an arena of feuds and forays.   1. 41: **mools** earth.   1. 46: **faem** foam.   1. 52: **ee-bree** eyebrow.   1. 59: **fu'** full.

THOMAS HARDY

1844–1928

IN A WOOD

Pale beech and pine so blue,
  Set in one clay,
Bough to bough cannot you
  Live out your day?
When the rains skim and skip,
Why mar sweet comradeship,
Blighting with poison-drip
  Neighbourly spray?

Heart-halt and spirit-lame,
  City-opprest,   10
Unto this wood I came
  As to a nest;
Dreaming that sylvan peace
Offered the harrowed ease—
Nature a soft release
  From men's unrest.

But, having entered in,
  Great growths and small
Show them to men akin—
  Combatants all!   20
Sycamore shoulders oak,
Bines the limp sapling yoke,
Ivy-spun halters choke
  Elms stout and tall.

Touches from ash, O wych,
  Sting you like scorn!
You, too, brave hollies, twitch
  Sidelong from thorn.

Even the rank poplars bear
Lothly a rival's air,
Cankering in black despair
    If overborne.

30

Since, then, no grace I find
    Taught me of trees,
Turn I back to my kind,
    Worthy as these.
There at least smiles abound,
There discourse trills around,
There, now and then, are found
    Life-loyalties.

40

1898

l. 25: **wych** a variety of elm.

FRIENDS BEYOND

William Dewy, Tranter Reuben, Farmer Ledlow late at
    plough,
    Robert's kin, and John's, and Ned's,
And the Squire, and Lady Susan, lie in Mellstock church-
    yard now!

"Gone," I call them, gone for good, that group of local hearts
    and heads;
    Yet at mothy curfew-tide,
And at midnight when the noon-heat breathes it back from
    walls and leads,

They've a way of whispering to me—fellow-wight who yet
    abide—
    In the muted, measured note
Of a ripple under archways, or a lone cave's stillicide:

"We have triumphed; this achievement turns the bane to
    antidote,
    Unsuccesses to success,
Many thought-worn eves and morrows to a morrow free of
    thought.

10

"No more need we corn and clothing, feel of old terrestrial
    stress;
    Chill detraction stirs no sigh;

Fear of death has even bygone us—death gave all that we
  possess."

W. D.—"Ye mid burn the old bass-viol that I set such value
  by."
  Squire.—"You may hold the manse in fee,
You may wed my spouse, may let my children's memory of
  me die."

Lady S.—"You may have my rich brocades, my laces; take each
  household key;
  Ransack coffer, desk, bureau;   20
Quiz the few poor treasures hid there, con the letters kept by
  me."

Far.—"Ye mid zell my favorite heifer, ye mid let the charlock
  grow,
  Foul the grinterns, give up thrift."
Far. Wife.—"If ye break my best blue china, children, I shan't
  care or ho."

All.—"We've no wish to hear the tidings, how the people's
  fortunes shift;
  What your daily doings are;
Who are wedded, born, divided; if your lives beat slow or
  swift.

"Curious not the least are we if our intents you make or mar,
  If you quire to our old tune,
If the City stage still passes, if the weirs still roar afar."   30

—Thus, with very gods' composure, freed those crosses late
  and soon
  Which in life, the Trine allow
(Why, none witteth), and ignoring all that haps beneath the
  moon,

William Dewy, Tranter Reuben, Farmer Ledlow late at
  plough,
  Robert's kin, and John's, and Ned's,
And the Squire, and Lady Susan, murmur mildly to me now.

                                          1898

l. 7: **leads** roof.   l. 9: **stillicide** dripping water.   l. 15: **mid** dial.,
may.   l. 25: **grinterns** storage bins in a granary.   l. 29: **quire** sing
in a choir.   l. 30: **stage** stagecoach.   l. 32: **Trine** the Holy
Trinity; more generally, fate or fortune.

HEIRESS AND ARCHITECT

FOR A. W. BLOMFIELD

A Study in immortality (handwritten)

She sought the Studios, beckoning to her side
An arch-designer, for she planned to build.
He was of wise contrivance, deeply skilled
In every intervolve of high and wide—
    Well fit to be her guide.

who is this arch.? (handwritten)

    "Whatever it be,"
    Responded he,
With cold, clear voice, and cold, clear view,
"In true accord with prudent fashionings
For such vicissitudes as living brings,   10
And thwarting not the law of stable things,
    That will I do."

"Shape me," she said, "high halls with tracery
And open ogive-work, that scent and hue
Of buds, and traveling bees, may come in through,
The note of birds, and singing of the sea,
    For these are much to me."

A place to view nature (handwritten)

    "An idle whim!"
    Broke forth from him,
Whom naught could warm to gallantries;   20
"Cede all these buds and birds, the zephyr's call,
And scents, and hues, and things that falter all,
And choose as best the close and surly wall,
    For winters freeze."

Arch. continually berates her. (handwritten)

"Then frame," she cried, "wide fronts of crystal glass,
That I may show my laughter and my light—
Light like the sun's by day, the stars' by night—
Till rival heart-queens, envying, wail, 'Alas,
    Her glory!' as they pass."

To Highlight her beauty (handwritten)

    "O maid misled!"   30
    He sternly said
Whose facile foresight pierced her dire;
"Where shall abide the soul when, sick of glee,
It shrinks, and hides, and prays no eye may see?
Those house them best who house for secrecy,
    For you will tire."

Put down again. (handwritten)

248

"A little chamber, then, with swan and dove

[handwritten: A bower of Love.]

Ranged thickly, and engrailed with rare device
Of reds and purples, for a Paradise
Wherein my Love may greet me, I my Love,   40
   When he shall know thereof?"

    "This, too, is ill,"

[handwritten: He seems to have sort of power]

    He answered still,
The man who swayed her like a shade.

[handwritten: Forgotten after death]

"An hour will come when sight of such sweet nook
Would bring a bitterness too sharp to brook,
When brighter eyes have won away his look,
    For you will fade."

Then said she faintly: "Oh, contrive some way—

[handwritten: A little place to cry?]

Some narrow winding turret, quite mine own,
To reach a loft where I may grieve alone!
It is a slight thing; hence do not, I pray,

[handwritten: She becomes deluded / she is desperate]

   This last dear fancy slay!"

    "Such winding ways
    Fit not your days,"

[handwritten: He will not even grant this.]

Said he, the man of measuring eye;
"I must even fashion as the rule declares,
To wit: Give space (since life ends unawares)
To hale a coffined corpse adown the stairs;

[handwritten: Even though one plans for life, death is always near.]

   For you will die."   60

    1898

Dedication: an architect under whom Hardy studied in London.   l. 38:
engrailed bordered.

NATURE'S QUESTIONING

[handwritten: what might a god be.]

When I look forth at dawning, pool,
   Field, flock, and lonely tree,
   All seem to gaze at me
Like chastened children sitting silent in a school;

Their faces dulled, constrained, and worn,
   As though the master's ways
   Through the long teaching days
Had cowed them till their early zest was overborne.

Upon them stirs in lippings mere
   (As if once clear in call,
   But now scarce breathed at all)—
"We wonder, ever wonder, why we find us here!   10

"Has some Vast Imbecility
   Mighty to build and blend,   *God?*
   But impotent to tend,
Framed us in jest, and left us now to hazardry?

"Or come we of an Automaton
   Unconscious of our pains? . . .
   Or are we live remains
Of Godhead dying downwards, brain and eye now gone?   20

"Or is it that some high Plan betides,
   As yet not understood,
   Of Evil stormed by Good,
We the Forlorn Hope over which Achievement strides?"

Thus things around. No answerer I . . .
   Meanwhile the winds, and rains,
   And Earth's old glooms and pains
Are still the same, and Death and Life are neighbours nigh.

[Handwritten annotations:]
questing the why and how of existence and the quality of the creator
The Immonent will? Has mind
Here, he questions whether it even has a mind.
Does it even know what it shapes?
Life and nature continue indifferently

                            1898

DRUMMER HODGE

They throw in Drummer Hodge, to rest
   Uncoffined—just as found:
His landmark is a kopje-crest
   That breaks the veldt around;
And foreign constellations west
   Each night above his mound.

Young Hodge the Drummer never knew—
   Fresh from his Wessex home—
The meaning of the broad Karoo,
   The Bush, the dusty loam,   10
And why uprose to nightly view
   Strange stars amid the gloam.

Yet portion of that unknown plain
   Will Hodge forever be;
His homely Northern breast and brain
   Grow to some Southern tree,
And strange-eyed constellations reign
   His stars eternally.

1901

Title: Any of the English farm boys serving with British troops in South Africa during the Boer War, 1899–1902. l. 3: **kopje** small hill. l. 4: **veldt** prairie. l. 9: **Karoo** a South African plateau. l. 10: **Bush** sparsely-settled back country. l. 12: **gloam** dusk. l. 15: **homely** kindly, home-loving.

Another picture of God – differs from the immanent Will.

GOD-FORGOTTEN

God Speaking

Again the integrity of the creator

I towered far, and lo! I stood within
   The presence of the Lord Most High,
Sent thither by the sons of Earth, to win
   Some answer to their cry.

Seems ignorant

—"The Earth, sayest thou? The Human race?
   By Me created? Sad its lot?
Nay: I have no remembrance of such place—
   Such world I fashioned not."—

—"O Lord, forgive me when I say
   Thou spakest the word and made it all."—   10
"The Earth of men—let me bethink me. . . . Yea!
   I dimly do recall

"Some tiny sphere I built long back
   (Mid millions of such shapes of mine)
So named . . . It perished, surely—not a wrack
   Remaining, or a sign?

"It lost my interest from the first,
   My aims therefor succeeding ill;
Haply it died of doing as it durst?"—
   "Lord, it existeth still."—   20

"Dark, then, its life! For not a cry
   Of aught it bears do I now hear;

Of its own act the threads were snapt whereby
    Its plaints had reached mine ear.

"It used to ask for gifts of good,
    Till came its severance, self-entailed,
When sudden silence on that side ensued,
    And has till now prevailed,

"All other orbs have kept in touch;
    Their voicings reach me speedily: 30
Thy people took upon them overmuch
    In sundering them from me!

"And it is strange—though sad enough—
    Earth's race should think that one whose call   *ignored*
Frames, daily, shining spheres of flawless stuff
    Must heed their tainted ball! . . .

"But sayest it is by pangs distraught,
    And strife, and silent suffering?—   *does pity*
Sore grieved am I that injury should be wrought
    Even on so poor a thing!   40

"Thou shouldst have learned that *Not to Mend*
    For Me could mean but *Not to Know:*
to be / going to / put an / end to / the / suffering / on the world? Hence, Messengers! and straightway put an end
    To what men undergo." . . .

Homing at dawn, I thought to see
    One of the Messengers standing by.
—Oh, childish thought! . . . Yet often it comes to me
    When trouble hovers nigh.
                                1901

TO LIZBIE BROWNE

I

Dear Lizbie Browne,
  Where are you now?
In sun, in rain?—
  Or is your brow
Past joy, past pain,
  Dear Lizbie Browne?

II

Sweet Lizbie Browne,
How you could smile,
How you could sing!—
How archly wile
In glance-giving,
Sweet Lizbie Browne!

10

III

And, Lizbie Browne,
Who else had hair
Bay-red as yours,
Or flesh so fair
Bred out of doors,
Sweet Lizbie Browne?

IV

When, Lizbie Browne,
You had just begun
To be endeared
By stealth to one,
You disappeared,
My Lizbie Browne!

20

V

Ay, Lizbie Browne,
So swift your life,
And mine so slow,
You were a wife
Ere I could show
Love, Lizbie Browne.

30

VI

Still, Lizbie Browne,
You won, they said,
The best of men
When you were wed.
Where went you then,
O Lizbie Browne?

VII

Dear Lizbie Browne,
I should have thought,
"Girls ripen fast,"
And coaxed and caught   40
You ere you passed,
Dear Lizbie Browne!

VIII

But, Lizbie Browne,
I let you slip;
Shaped not a sign;
Touched never your lip
With lip of mine,
Lost Lizbie Browne!

IX

So, Lizbie Browne,
When on a day   50
Men speak of me
As not, you'll say,
"And who was he?"—
Yes, Lizbie Browne!

                                    1901

AT A HASTY WEDDING

(TRIOLET)

If hours be years the twain are blest,
For now they solace swift desire
By bonds of every bond the best,
If hours be years. The twain are blest
Do eastern stars slope never west,
Nor pallid ashes follow fire:
If hours be years the twain are blest,
For now they solace swift desire.

                                    1901

l. 5: **Do**   if it be that.

THE LAST CHRYSANTHEMUM

Why should this flower delay so long
       To show its tremulous plumes?
Now is the time of plaintive robin-song,
       When flowers are in their tombs.

Through the slow summer, when the sun
       Called to each frond and whorl
That all he could for flowers was being done,
       Why did it not uncurl?

It must have felt that fervid call
       Although it took no heed,   10
Waking but now, when leaves like corpses fall,
       And saps all retrocede.

Too late its beauty, lonely thing,
       The season's shine is spent,
Nothing remains for it but shivering
       In tempests turbulent.

Had it a reason for delay,
       Dreaming in witlessness
That for a bloom so delicately gay
       Winter would stay its stress?   20

—I talk as if the thing were born
       With sense to work its mind;
Yet it is but one mask of many worn
       By the Great Face behind.

                                                    1901

l. 3: **robin-song** English robins are heard in autumn.   l. 18: **witlessness**
ignorance.

THE RUINED MAID

"O 'melia, my dear, this does everything crown!
Who could have supposed I should meet you in Town?
And whence such fair garments, such prosperi-ty?"—
"O didn't you know I'd been ruined?" said she.

—"You left us in tatters, without shoes or socks,
Tired of digging potatoes, and spudding up docks;

255

And now you've gay bracelets and bright feathers three!"—
"Yes: that's how we dress when we're ruined," said she.

—"At home in the barton you said 'thee' and 'thou,'
And 'thik oon,' and 'theä oon,' and 't'other'; but now   10
Your talking quite fits 'ee for high compa-ny!"—
"Some polish is gained with one's ruin," said she.

—"Your hands were like paws then, your face blue and bleak
But now I'm bewitched by your delicate cheek,
And your little gloves fit as on any la-dy!"—
"We never do work when we're ruined," said she.

—"You used to call home-life a hag-ridden dream.
And you'd sigh, and you'd sock; but at present you seem
To know not of megrims or melancho-ly!"—
"True. One's pretty lively when ruined," said she.   20

—"I wish I had feathers, a fine sweeping gown,
And a delicate face, and could strut about Town!"—
"My dear—a raw country girl, such as you be,   *Loss of innocence*
Cannot quite expect that. You ain't ruined," said she.   *for the better*

Pride   *life?*
and   1901
arrogance

Title: a genteel term for prostitute.   1. 9: **barton** farmstead.   1. 10:
'**thik oon,**' '**theäs oon**'   that one, this one.   1. 18: **sock**   sigh heavily.

THE RESPECTABLE BURGHER

ON "THE HIGHER CRITICISM"

Since Reverend Doctors now declare
That clerks and people must prepare
To doubt if Adam ever were;
To hold the flood a local scare;
To argue, though the stolid stare,
That everything had happened ere
The prophets to its happening sware;
That David was no giant-slayer,
No one to call a God-obeyer
In certain details we could spare,   10

But rather was a debonair
Shrewd bandit, skilled as banjo-player:
That Solomon sang the fleshly Fair,
And gave the Church no thought whate'er,
That Esther with her royal wear,
And Mordecai, the son of Jair,
And Joshua's triumphs, Job's despair,
And Balaam's ass's bitter blare;
Nebuchadnezzar's furnace-flare,
And Daniel and the den affair,   20
And other stories rich and rare,

tales

Were writ to make old doctrine wear
Something of a romantic air:
That the Nain widow's only heir,
And Lazarus with cadaverous glare
(As done in oils by Piombo's care)
Did not return from Sheol's lair:
That Jael set a fiendish snare,
That Pontius Pilate acted square,   30
That never a sword cut Malchus' ear;
And (but for shame I must forbear)
That —— —— did not reappear! . . .
—Since thus they hint, nor turn a hair,
All churchgoing will I forswear,
And sit on Sundays in my chair,
And read that moderate man Voltaire.

1901

Subtitle: The "Higher Criticism" of the Bible, as distinguished from the "lower" study of language and texts, reassessed the scriptures in the light of recent and sometimes hastily embraced scientific evidence.   l. 2: **clerks** clergy.   l. 13: **Fair** The Song of Solomon, which employs erotic imagery, was traditionally interpreted as a spiritual allegory and not as a poem of carnal love.   l. 16: **Mordecai** (See Esther 2:5–7.)   l. 18: **Balaam's ass** (See Num. 22:20–37.)   l. 19: **furnace-flare** (See Dan. 3:10–28.)   l. 24: **Nain widow** (See Luke 7:11–15.)   l. 25: **Lazarus** (See John 11:1–44.)   l. 26: **Piombo** Sebastiano del Piombo, Venetian painter (1485–1547), whose *Raising of Lazarus* is in the National Gallery, London.   l. 29: **Jael** (See Judg. 4:17–22.)   l. 31: **Malchus** (See John 18:10.)   l. 37: **Voltaire** (1694–1778), fierce and witty opponent of religious superstition.

THE COMET AT YELL'HAM

I

It bends far over Yell'ham Plain,
 And we, from Yell'ham Height,
Stand and regard its fiery train,
 So soon to swim from sight.

II

It will return long years hence, when
 As now its strange swift shine
Will fall on Yell'ham; but not then
 On that sweet form of thine.

1901

IN TENEBRIS

I

"Percussus sum sicut foenum, et aruit cor meum."—Ps. ci.

Wintertime nighs;
But my bereavement-pain
It cannot bring again:
 Twice no one dies.

Flower-petals flee;
But, since it once hath been,
No more that severing scene
 Can harrow me.

Birds faint in dread:
I shall not lose old strength   10
In the lone frost's black length:
 Strength long since fled!

Leaves freeze to dun;
But friends can not turn cold
This season as of old
 For him with none.

Tempests may scath;
But love can not make smart
Again this year his heart
Who no heart hath.   20

Black is night's cope;
But death will not appal
One who, past doubtings all,
Waits in unhope.

1901

Title: In Darkness.   **Epigraph:** "I am smitten as grass, and my heart is withered." (Psalm 101 in the Latin Vulgate is Psalm 102 in the King James Bible.)

Hardly to Not alway utterly hopeless

THE DARKLING THRUSH

I leaned upon a coppice gate
    When Frost was spectre-gray,
And Winter's dregs made desolate
    The weakening eye of day.
The tangled bine-stems scored the sky
    Like strings from broken lyres,
And all mankind that haunted nigh
    Had sought their household fires.

Is this a lyric, Yes, Hardy is speaking

Nature goes on its own way, perhaps better than man.

The land's sharp features seemed to be
    The Century's corpse outleant,   10
His crypt the cloudy canopy,
    The wind his death-lament.
The ancient pulse of germ and birth
    Was shrunken hard and dry,
And every spirit upon earth
    Seemed fervourless as I.

At once a voice arose among
    The bleak twigs overhead
In a full-hearted evensong
    Of joy illimited;   20
An aged thrush, frail, gaunt, and small,
    In blast-beruffled plume,

Had chosen thus to fling his soul
Upon the growing gloom.

So little cause for carolings
Of such ecstatic sound
Was written on terrestrial things
Afar or nigh around,
That I could think there trembled through
His happy good-night air   30
Some blessed Hope, whereof he knew
And I was unaware.

December 31, 1900   1901

Does the Thrush know something Hardy doesn't. The bird doesn't seem to see the gloom.

l. 10: **outleant** Hardy's coinage; stretched out at length.   l. 20:
illimited unbounded.

NEW YEAR'S EVE

"I have finished another year," said God,
    "In gray, green, white, and brown;
I have strewn the leaf upon the sod,
Sealed up the worm within the clod,
    And let the last sun down."

"And what's the good of it?" I said,
    "What reasons made you call
From formless void this earth we tread,
When nine-and-ninety can be read
    Why nought should be at all?   10

"Yea, Sire; why shaped you us, 'who in
    This tabernacle groan'—
If ever a joy be found herein,
Such joy no man had wished to win
    If he had never known!"

Then he: "My labours—logicless—
    You may explain; not I:
Sense-sealed I have wrought, without a guess
That I evolved a Consciousness
    To ask for reasons why.   20

"Strange that ephemeral creatures who
    By my own ordering are,
Should see the shortness of my view,
Use ethic tests I never knew,
    Or made provision for!"

He sank to raptness as of yore,
    And opening New Year's Day
Wove it by rote as theretofore,
And went on working evermore
    In his unweeting way.   30

1909

l. 30: **unweeting**   oblivious.

ONE RALPH BLOSSOM SOLILOQUIZES

("It being deposed that vij women who were mayds before he knew them
have been brought upon the towne [rates?] by the fornicacions of one Ralph
Blossom, Mr. Maior inquired why he should not contribute xiv pence weekly
toward their mayntenance. But it being shewn that the sayd R. B. was
dying of a purple feaver, no order was made."—*Budmouth Borough
Minutes*: 16—.)

When I am in hell or some such place,
A-groaning over my sorry case,
What will those seven women say to me
Who, when I coaxed them, answered "Aye" to me?

"I did not understand your sign!"
Will be the words of Caroline;
While Jane will cry, "If I'd had proof of you,
I should have learnt to hold aloof of you!"

"I won't reproach: it was to be!"
Will dryly murmur Cicely;   10
And Rosa: "I feel no hostility,
For I must own I lent facility."

Lizzy says: "Sharp was my regret,
And sometimes it is now! But yet
I joy that, though it brought notoriousness,
I knew Love once and all its gloriousness!"

Says Patience: "Why are we apart?
Small harm did you, my poor Sweet Heart!
A manchild born, now tall and beautiful,
Was worth the ache of days undutiful."   20

And Anne cries: "O the time was fair,
So wherefore should you burn down there?
There is a deed under the sun, my Love,
And that was ours.   What's done is done, my Love.
These trumpets here in Heaven are dumb to me
With you away.   Dear, come, O come to me!"

1909

GOD'S FUNERAL

I

I saw a slowly-stepping train—
Lined on the brows, scoop-eyed and bent and hoar—
Following in files across a twilit plain
A strange and mystic form the foremost bore.

II

And by contagious throbs of thought
Or latent knowledge that within me lay
And had already stirred me, I was wrought
To consciousness of sorrow even as they.

III

The fore-borne shape, to my blurred eyes,
At first seemed man-like, and anon to change   10
To an amorphous cloud of marvellous size,
At times endowed with wings of glorious range.

IV

And this phantasmal variousness
Ever possessed it as they drew along:
Yet throughout all its symboled none the less
Potency vast and loving-kindness strong.

V

Almost before I knew I bent
Towards the moving columns without a word;
They, growing in bulk and numbers as they went,
Struck out sick thoughts that could be overheard:— 20

VI

"O man-projected Figure, of late
Imaged as we, thy knell who shall survive?
Whence came it we were tempted to create
One whom we can no longer keep alive?

VII

"Framing him jealous, fierce, at first,
We gave him justice as the ages rolled,
Will to bless those by circumstance accurst,
And longsuffering, and mercies manifold.

VIII

"And, tricked by our own early dream
And need of solace, we grew self-deceived, 30
Our making soon our maker did we deem,
And what we had imagined we believed.

IX

"Till, in Time's stayless stealthy swing,
Uncompromising rude reality
Mangled the Monarch of our fashioning,
Who quavered, sank; and now has ceased to be.

X

"So, toward our myth's oblivion,
Darkling, and languid-lipped, we creep and grope
Sadlier than those who wept in Babylon,
Whose Zion was a still abiding hope. 40

XI

"How sweet it was in years far hied
To start the wheels of day with trustful prayer,
To lie down liegely at the eventide
And feel a blest assurance he was there!

XII

"And who or what shall fill his place?
Whither will wanderers turn distracted eyes
For some fixed star to stimulate their pace
Towards the goal of their enterprise?" . . .

XIII

Some in the background then I saw,
Sweet women, youths, men, all incredulous,   50
Who chimed: "This is a counterfeit of straw,
This requiem mockery! Still he lives to us!"

XIV

I could not buoy their faith: and yet
Many I had known: with all I sympathized;
And though struck speechless, I did not forget
That what was mourned for, I, too, long had prized.

XV

Still, how to bear such loss I deemed
The insistent question for each animate mind,
And gazing, to my growing sight there seemed
A pale yet positive gleam low down behind,   60

XVI

Whereof, to lift the general night,
A certain few who stood aloof had said,
"See you upon the horizon that small light—
Swelling somewhat?" Each mourner shook his head.

XVII

And they composed a crowd of whom
Some were right good, and many nigh the best. . . .
Thus dazed and puzzled 'twixt the gleam and gloom
Mechanically I followed with the rest.

1908–1910   1914

Title: When first published, it was subtitled, "An Allegorical Conception of the present state of Theology." (J. O. Bailey, *The Poetry of Thomas Hardy, a Handbook and Commentary.*)   l. 39: **Babylon**   where many Israelites were carried into captivity and from which they longed to return to Jerusalem (Zion). See Psalm 137.   l. 41: **hied** gone.   l. 60: **gleam** the dim possibility of a nobly ethical but not supernatural religion.

THE CONVERGENCE OF THE TWAIN

(LINES ON THE LOSS OF THE *Titanic*)

I

In a solitude of the sea
Deep from human vanity,
And the Pride of Life that planned her, stilly couches she.

II

Steel chambers, late the pyres
Of her salamandrine fires,
Cold currents thrid, and turn to rhythmic tidal lyres.

III

Over the mirrors meant
To glass the opulent
The sea-worm crawls—grotesque, slimed, dumb, indifferent.

IV

Jewels in joy designed   10
To ravish the sensuous mind
Lie lightless, all their sparkles bleared and black and blind.

V

Dim moon-eyed fishes near
Gaze at the gilded gear
And query: "What does this vaingloriousness down here?"

VI

Well: while was fashioning
This creature of cleaving wing,
The Immanent Will that stirs and urges everything

VII

Prepared a sinister mate
For her—so gaily great—
A Shape of Ice, for the time far and dissociate.

[handwritten: Seems to be so unlikely that[20] these two should meet.]

VIII

And as the smart ship grew
In stature, grace, and hue,
In shadowy silent distance grew the Iceberg too.

IX

Alien they seemed to be!
No mortal eye could see
The intimate welding of their later history,

X

Or sign that they were bent
By paths coincident
On being anon twin halves of one august event,   30

XI

[handwritten: Fate]
Till the Spinner of the Years
Said "Now!" And each one hears
And consummation comes, and jars two hemispheres.

[handwritten: man and nature, two distinct would come together]

[handwritten: sexual imagry]

                                                        1912

Title: In April 1912 the reputedly "unsinkable" luxury-liner *Titanic*, on
her maiden cruise, struck an iceberg and sank, with the loss of 1,500 lives.
l. 18: Immanent Will Hardy's term for some vast presiding power that
dictates the course of events.

CHANNEL FIRING

[handwritten: WWI, a very great poem.]

That night your great guns, unawares,
Shook all our coffins as we lay, *[handwritten: speaker in grave]*
And broke the chancel window-squares,
We thought it was the Judgment-day

And sat upright. While drearisome
Arose the howl of wakened hounds:
The mouse let fall the altar-crumb,
The worms drew back into the mounds,

The glebe cow drooled. Till God called, "No;
Its gunnery practice out at sea   10
Just as before you went below;
The world is as it used to be: *[handwritten: Always a bad world.]*

"All nations striving strong to make
Red war yet redder. Mad as hatters
They do no more for Christés sake
Than you who are helpless in such matters.

"That this is not the judgment-hour
For some of them's a blessed thing,
For if it were they'd have to scour
Hell's floor for so much threatening. . . .   20

"Ha, ha. It will be warmer when
I blow the trumpet (if indeed
I ever do; for you are men, *[handwritten: men are such poor creatures.]*
And rest eternal sorely need)."

So down we lay again. "I wonder,
Will the world ever saner be,"
Said one, "than when He sent us under
In our indifferent century!"

And many a skeleton shook his head.
"Instead of preaching forty year,"   30
My neighbour Parson Thirdly said, *[handwritten: world is so rotten, no point]*
"I wish I had stuck to pipes and beer."

Again the guns disturbed the hour,
Roaring their readiness to avenge,
As far inland as <u>Stourton Tower,</u>
And <u>Camelot,</u> and starlit Stonehenge.

1914

[handwritten margin notes: what do these leave in common / all civilization / that are gen... great battles / were ... Eugh / here / Human / Sacri... / Blood... / and peace / civilizat...]

Title: with reference to British fleet exercises in the English Channel a
few months before the outbreak of World War I.   l. 9: **glebe cow** on
the "glebe" or pasture belonging to the parish church.   l. 31: **Parson
Thirdly** So named from a parson's custom of marking the points in his
sermon, "Firstly . . . Secondly . . . Thirdly."   l. 35: **Stourton Tower**
in western Wiltshire, a monument to Alfred the Great, King of Wessex
(877–890).   l. 36: **Camelot** King Arthur's legendary city; probably
with reference to Cadbury Castle rather than to Camelford, Cornwall,
though both places have been thought to be Camelot.   **Stonehenge**
the neolithic monument on Salisbury Plain. (All three places are in ancient
Wessex.)

THE VOICE

Woman much missed, how you call to me, call to me,
Saying that now you are not as you were
When you had changed from the one who was all to me
But as at first, when our day was fair.

Can it be you that I hear?   Let me view you, then,
Standing as when I drew near to the town
Where you would wait for me: yes, as I knew you then,
Even to the original air-blue gown!

Or is it only the breeze, in its listlessness
Travelling across the wet mead to me here,   10
You being ever dissolved to wan wistlessness,
Heard no more again far or near?

    Thus I; faltering forward,
    Leaves around me falling,
Wind oozing thin through the thorn from norward,
    And the woman calling.

December 1912   1914

l. 1: **Woman** Emma Gifford Hardy, the poet's first wife, who died sud-
denly, Nov. 27, 1912.   l. 4: **at first** during their courtship, which
began in 1870. (Later their relationship was strained.)

BEENY CLIFF

MARCH 1870—MARCH 1913

I

O the opal and the sapphire of that wandering western sea,
And the woman riding high above with bright hair flapping
free—
The woman whom I loved so, and who loyally loved me.

II

The pale mews plained below us, and the waves seemed far
away
In a nether sky, engrossed in saying their ceaseless babbling
say,
As we laughed light-heartedly aloft on that clear-sunned March
day.

III

A little cloud then cloaked us, and there flew an irised rain,
And the Atlantic dyed its levels with a dull misfeatured stain,
And then the sun burst out again, and purples prinked the
main.

IV

—Still in all its chasmal beauty bulks old Beeny to the sky,   10
And shall she and I not go there once again now March is
nigh,
And the sweet things said in that March say anew there by
and by?

V

What if still in chasmal beauty looms that wild weird western
shore,
The woman now is—elsewhere—whom the ambling pony
bore,
And nor knows nor cares for Beeny, and will laugh there
nevermore.

1914

Title: an ocean cliff near Boscastle, Cornwall, where Hardy first met Emma
Gifford in 1870. She died unexpectedly in 1912. Hardy revisited Cornwall
the following March.   l. 9: **prinked** spangled.

THE SHADOW ON THE STONE

I went by the Druid stone
That broods in the garden white and lone,
And I stopped and looked at the shifting shadows
That at some moments fall thereon
From the tree hard by with a rhythmic swing,
And they shaped in my imagining
To the shade that a well-known head and shoulders
Threw there when she was gardening.

I thought her behind my back,
Yea, her I long had learned to lack,   10
And I said: "I am sure you are standing behind me,
Though how do you get into this old track?"
And there was no sound but the fall of a leaf
As a sad response; and to keep down grief
I would not turn my head to discover
That there was nothing in my belief.

Yet I wanted to look and see
That nobody stood at the back of me;
But I thought once more: "Nay, I'll not unvision
A shape which, somehow, there may be."   20
So I went on softly from the glade,
And left her behind me throwing her shade,
As she were indeed an apparition—
My head unturned lest my dream should fade.

Begun 1913; finished 1916   1917

l. 1: **Druid stone** According to J. O. Bailey (*The Poetry of Thomas Hardy, a Handbook and Commentary*) an ancient hewn stone that Hardy believed was connected with pre-Christian Celtic religion.   l. 9: **her** his first wife, who died in Nov. 1912.   l. 10: **lack** long before her death she and Hardy were on distant terms.

IN TIME OF "THE BREAKING OF NATIONS"

[*Jeremiah* 51 : 20]

a glimmer
of optimism

I

Only a man harrowing clods
In a slow silent walk
With an old horse that stumbles and nods
Half asleep as they stalk.

II

Only thin smoke without flame
  From the heaps of couch-grass;
Yet this will go onward the same
  Though Dynasties pass.

Common, good country life will continue,

III

Yonder a maid and her wight
  Come whispering by:
War's annals will fade into night
  Ere their story die.

10

1916

HEREDITY

I am the family face;
Flesh perishes, I live on,
Projecting trait and trace
Through time to times anon,
And leaping from place to place
Over oblivion.

The years-heired feature that can
In curve and voice and eye
Despise the human span
Of durance—that is I;
The eternal thing in man,
That heeds no call to die.

1917

SNOW IN THE SUBURBS

Every branch big with it,
  Bent every twig with it;
Every fork like a white web-foot;
Every street and pavement mute:
Some flakes have lost their way, and grope back upward, when

Meeting those meandering down they turn and descend again.
  The palings are glued together like a wall,
  And there is no waft of wind with the fleecy fall.

   A sparrow enters the tree,
   Whereon immediately   10
  A snow-lump thrice his own slight size
  Descends on him and showers his head and eyes,
    And overturns him,
    And near inurns him,
  And lights on a nether twig, when its brush
Starts off a volley of other lodging lumps with a rush.

   The steps are a blanched slope,
   Up which, with feeble hope,
  A black cat comes, wide-eyed and thin;
    And we take him in.   20

            1925

NO BUYERS

A STREET SCENE

 A load of brushes and baskets and cradles and chairs
  Labours along the street in the rain:
With it a man, a woman, a pony with whiteybrown hairs.—
  The man foots in front of the horse with a shambling sway
   At a slower tread than a funeral train,
  While to a dirge-like tune he chants his wares,
  Swinging a Turk's-head brush (in a drum-major's way
   When the bandsmen march and play).

A yard from the back of the man is the whiteybrown pony's
        nose:
He mirrors his master in every item of pace and pose: 10
   He stops when the man stops, without being told,
  And seems to be eased by a pause; too plainly he's old,
    Indeed, not strength enough shows
   To steer the disjointed waggon straight,
  Which wriggles left and right in a rambling line,
  Deflected thus by its own warp and weight,
  And pushing the pony with it in each incline.

The woman walks on the pavement verge,
    Parallel to the man:
She wears an apron white and wide in span,   20
And carries a like Turk's-head, but more in nursing-wise:
    Now and then she joins in his dirge,
    But as if her thoughts were on distant things.
    The rain clams her apron till it clings.—
So, step by step, they move with their merchandize,
    And nobody buys.

                                     1925

NOBODY COMES

    Tree-leaves labour up and down,
        And through them the fainting light
        Succumbs to the crawl of night.
    Outside in the road the telegraph wire
        To the town from the darkening land
Intones to travellers like a spectral lyre
        Swept by a spectral hand.

    A car comes up, with lamps full-glare,
        That flash upon a tree:
        It has nothing to do with me,
    And whangs along in a world of its own,
        Leaving a blacker air;
And mute by the gate I stand again alone,
        And nobody pulls up there.

October 9, 1924   1925

GERARD MANLEY HOPKINS

1844–1889

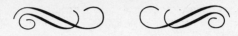

WINTER WITH THE GULF STREAM

The boughs, the boughs are bare enough
But earth has never felt the snow.
Frost-furred our ivies are and rough

With bills of rime the brambles show.
The hoarse leaves crawl on hissing ground
Because the sighing wind is low.

But if the rain-blasts be unbound
And from dank feathers wring the drops
The clogged brook runs with choking sound

Kneading the mounded mire that stops   10
His channel under clammy coats
Of foliage fallen in the copse.

A simple passage of weak notes
Is all the winter bird dare try.
The bugle moon by daylight floats

So glassy white about the sky,
So like a berg of hyaline,
And pencilled blue so daintily,

I never saw her so divine.
But through black branches, rarely drest   20
In scarves of silky shot and shine,

The webbed and the watery west
Where yonder crimson fireball sets
Look laid for feasting and for rest.

I see long reefs of violets
In beryl-covered fens so dim,
A gold-water Pactolus frets

Its brindled wharves and yellow brim,
The waxen colours weep and run,
And slendering to his burning rim   30

Into the flat blue mist the sun
Drops out and all our day is done.

1863

l. 15: **bugle** crescent; that is, curved like the horn of an ox (Latin, *buculus*).   l. 21: **shot** iridescence.

HEAVEN-HAVEN

A NUN TAKES THE VEIL

I have desired to go
    Where springs not fail,
To fields where flies no sharp and sided hail
    And a few lilies blow.

And I have asked to be
    Where no storms come,
Where the green swell is in the havens dumb,
    And out of the swing of the sea.

1864

NONDUM

'*Verily Thou art a God that hidest Thyself.*'
                        ISAIAH xlv. 15.

God, though to Thee our psalm we raise
No answering voice comes from the skies;
To Thee the trembling sinner prays
But no forgiving voice replies;
Our prayer seems lost in desert ways,
Our hymn in the vast silence dies.

We see the glories of the earth
But not the hand that wrought them all:
Night to a myriad worlds gives birth,
Yet like a lighted empty hall   10
Where stands no host at door or hearth
Vacant creation's lamps appal.

We guess; we clothe Thee, unseen King,
With attributes we deem are meet;
Each in his own imagining
Sets up a shadow in Thy seat;
Yet know not how our gifts to bring,
Where seek Thee with unsandalled feet.

And still th'unbroken silence broods
While ages and while aeons run,   20
As erst upon chaotic floods
The Spirit hovered ere the sun
Had called the seasons' changeful moods
And life's first germs from death had won.

And still th'abysses infinite
Surround the peak from which we gaze.
Deep calls to deep, and blackest night
Giddies the soul with blinding daze
That dares to cast its searching sight
On being's dread and vacant maze.   30

And Thou art silent, whilst Thy world
Contends about its many creeds
And hosts confront with flags unfurled
And zeal is flushed and pity bleeds
And truth is heard, with tears impearled,
A moaning voice among the reeds.

My hand upon my lips I lay;
The breast's desponding sob I quell;
I move along life's tomb-decked way
And listen to the passing bell   40
Summoning men from speechless day
To death's more silent, darker spell.

Oh! till Thou givest that sense beyond,
To show Thee that Thou art, and near,
Let patience with her chastening wand

Dispel the doubt and dry the tear;
And lead me child-like by the hand
If still in darkness not in fear.

Speak! whisper to my watching heart   50
One word—as when a mother speaks
Soft, when she sees her infant start,
Till dimpled joy steals o'er its cheeks.
Then, to behold Thee as Thou art,
I'll wait till morn eternal breaks.

1866

Title: "Not as Yet."   l. 18: **unsandalled**   reverent. (See Exod. 3:2–5.)
l. 22: **Spirit**   the Holy Spirit, at the creation. (See Gen. 1:1.)   l. 24:
germs   seeds.   l. 40: **passing bell**   tolled for the dead.

THE HABIT OF PERFECTION

Elected Silence, sing to me
And beat upon my whorlèd ear,
Pipe me to pastures still and be
The music that I care to hear.

Shape nothing, lips; be lovely-dumb:
It is the shut, the curfew sent
From there where all surrenders come
Which only makes you eloquent.

Be shellèd, eyes, with double dark
And find the uncreated light: 10
This ruck and reel which you remark
Coils, keeps, and teases simple sight.

Palate, the hutch of tasty lust,
Desire not to be rinsed with wine:
The can must be so sweet, the crust
So fresh that come in fasts divine!

Nostrils, your careless breath that spend
Upon the stir and keep of pride,
What relish shall the censers send
Along the sanctuary side!   20

O feel-of-primrose hands, O feet
That want the yield of plushy sward,
But you shall walk the golden street
And you unhouse and house the Lord.

And, Poverty, be thou the bride
And now the marriage feast begun,
And lily-coloured clothes provide
Your spouse not laboured-at nor spun.

1866

Title: Habit, meaning both *a customary observance* and *clothes*; the poem is a meditation on spiritual self-discipline and also a priestly preparation for celebrating Mass.   l. 11: **ruck and reel** jumble and tangle. N.B. Hopkins often uses plain and old words with a keen under-sense of their etymologies and past usages. (Recourse to a dictionary with generous etymologies can unlock a range of available meanings.)   l. 15: **can . . . crust** cup . . . bread, with allusion to the chalice and wafer of Holy Communion.   l. 24: **unhouse** with reference to a priest's removing from the tabernacle on the altar the wafer or "host" which presents the "Body of Christ" in the Mass; and with an under-sense of *housel*, which in Old English means *sacrifice*, specifically the Mass.   l. 27: **clothes** (See Matt. 6:28–30.)   l. 28: **spouse** Christ is often compared to a bridegroom, the Church being his bride. (See Matt. 25:1–14.)

THE WRECK OF THE DEUTSCHLAND

To the
happy memory of five Franciscan Nuns
exiles by the Falck Laws
drowned between midnight and morning of
Dec. 7th, 1875

PART THE FIRST

1

Thou mastering me
God! giver of breath and bread;
World's strand, sway of the sea;
Lord of living and dead;
Thou hast bound bones and veins in me, fastened me
flesh,
And after it almost unmade, what with dread,
Thy doing: and dost thou touch me afresh?
Over again I feel thy finger and find thee.

2

I did say yes
O at lightning and lashed rod;   10
Thou heardst me truer than tongue confess
Thy terror, O Christ, O God;
Thou knowest the walls, altar and hour and night:
The swoon of a heart that the sweep and the hurl of
thee trod
Hard down with a horror of height:
And the midriff astrain with leaning of, laced with fire of stress.

3

The frown of his face
Before me, the hurtle of hell
Behind, where, where was a, where was a place?
I whirled out wings that spell   20
And fled with a fling of the heart to the heart of the Host.
My heart, but you were dovewinged, I can tell,
Carrier-witted, I am bold to boast,
To flash from the flame to the flame then, tower from the
grace to the grace.

4

I am soft sift
In an hourglass—at the wall
Fast, but mined with a motion, a drift,
And it crowds and it combs to the fall;
I steady as a water in a well, to a poise, to a pane,
But roped with, always, all the way down from the tall   30
Fells or flanks of the voel, a vein
Of the gospel proffer, a pressure, a principle, Christ's gift.

5

I kiss my hand
To the stars, lovely-asunder
Starlight, wafting him out of it; and
Glow, glory in thunder;
Kiss my hand to the dappled-with-damson west:

Since, tho' he is under the world's splendour and wonder,
        His mystery must be instressed, stressed;
For I greet him the days I meet him, and bless when I under-
    stand.   40

6

            Not out of his bliss
            Springs the stress felt
        Nor first from heaven (and few know this)
            Swings the stroke dealt—
    Stroke and a stress that stars and storms deliver,
    That guilt is hushed by, hearts are flushed by and melt—
        But it rides time like riding a river
(And here the faithful waver, the faithless fable and miss).

7

            It dates from day
            Of his going in Galilee;   50
        Warm-laid grave of a womb-life grey;
            Manger, maiden's knee;
    The dense and the driven Passion, and frightful sweat;
    Thence the discharge of it, there its swelling to be,
        Though felt before, though in high flood yet—
What none would have known of it, only the heart, being
    hard at bay,

8

            Is out with it! Oh,
            We lash with the best or worst
        Word last! How a lush-kept plush-capped sloe
            Will, mouthed to flesh-burst,   60
    Gush!—flush the man, the being with it, sour or sweet
    Brim, in a flash, full!—Hither then, last or first,
        The hero of Calvary, Christ's feet—
Never ask if meaning it, wanting it, warned of it—men go.

9

            Be adored among men,
            God, three-numberèd form;

Wring thy rebel, dogged in den,
      Man's malice, with wrecking and storm.
Beyond saying sweet, past telling of tongue,
Thou art lightning and love, I found it, a winter and
    warm;   70
      Father and fondler of heart thou hast wrung:
Hast thy dark descending and most art merciful then.

10

      With an anvil-ding
    And with fire in him forge thy will
Or rather, rather then, stealing as Spring
      Through him, melt him but master him still:
Whether at once, as once at a crash Paul,
Or as Austin, a lingering-out swéet skíll,
      Make mercy in all of us, out of us all
Mastery, but be adored, but be adored King.   80

PART THE SECOND

11

      'Some find me a sword; some
    The flange and the rail; flame,
Fang, or flood' goes Death on drum,
      And storms bugle his fame.
But wé dream we are rooted in earth—Dust!
Flesh falls within sight of us, we, though our flower the
    same,
      Wave with the meadow, forget that there must
The sour scythe cringe, and the blear share come.

12

      On Saturday sailed from Bremen,
    American-outward-bound,   90
    Take settler and seamen, tell men with women,
      Two hundred souls in the round—
O Father, not under thy feathers nor ever as guessing
The goal was a shoal, of a fourth the doom to be
    drowned;

    Yet did the dark side of the bay of thy blessing
Not vault them, the million of rounds of thy mercy not
   reeve even them in?

13

      Into the snows she sweeps,
      Hurling the haven behind,
   The Deutschland, on Sunday; and so the sky keeps,
     For the infinite air is unkind,   100
And the sea flint-flake, black-backed in the regular blow,
Sitting Eastnortheast, in cursed quarter, the wind;
   Wiry and white-fiery and whirlwind-swivellèd snow
Spins to the widow-making unchilding unfathering deeps.

14

     She drove in the dark to leeward,
     She struck—not a reef or a rock
  But the combs of a smother of sand: night drew her
    Dead to the Kentish Knock;
And she beat the bank down with her bows and the
   ride of her keel:
The breakers rolled on her beam with ruinous shock;   110
    And canvas and compass, the whorl and the wheel
Idle for ever to waft her or wind her with, these she endured.

15

     Hope had grown grey hairs,
     Hope had mourning on,
  Trenched with tears, carved with cares,
    Hope was twelve hours gone;
And frightful a nightfall folded rueful a day
Nor rescue, only rocket and lightship, shone,
    And lives at last were washing away:
To the shrouds they took,—they shook in the hurling and
   horrible airs.   120

16

    One stirred from the rigging to save
    The wild woman-kind below,

With a rope's end round the man, handy and
    brave—
        He was pitched to his death at a blow,
For all his dreadnought breast and braids of thew:
They could tell him for hours, dandled the to and fro
        Through the cobbled foam-fleece. What could he do
With the burl of the fountains of air, buck and the flood of
  the wave?

17

        They fought with God's cold—
        And they could not and fell to the deck   130
   (Crushed them) or water (and drowned them) or
   rolled
        With the sea-romp over the wreck.
Night roared, with the heart-break hearing a heart-broke
  rabble,
The woman's wailing, the crying of child without check—
    Till a lioness arose breasting the babble,
A prophetess towered in the tumult, a virginal tongue told.

18

        Ah, touched in your bower of bone
        Are you! turned for an exquisite smart,
   Have you! make words break from me here all
   alone,
        Do you!—mother of being in me, heart.   140
O unteachably after evil, but uttering truth,
    Why, tears! is it? tears; such a melting, a madrigal start!
    Never-eldering revel and river of youth,
What can it be, this glee? the good you have there of your
  own?

19

        Sister, a sister calling
        A master, her master and mine!—
   And the inboard seas run swirling and hawling;
        The rash smart sloggering brine
Blinds her; but she that weather sees one thing, one;

Has one fetch in her: she rears herself to divine   150
          Ears, and the call of the tall nun
To the men in the tops and the tackle rode over the storm's
    brawling.

20

          She was first of a five and came
              Of a coifèd sisterhood.
          (O Deutschland, double a desperate name!
              O world wide of its good!
    But Gertrude, lily, and Luther, are two of a town,
          Christ's lily and beast of the waste wood:
              From life's dawn it is drawn down,
Abel is Cain's brother and breasts they have sucked the same.)   160

21

          Loathed for a love men knew in them,
              Banned by the land of their birth,
          Rhine refused them, Thames would ruin them;
              Surf, snow, river and earth
    Gnashed: but thou art above, thou Orion of light;
          Thy unchancelling poising palms were weighing the
              worth,
              Thou martyr-master: in thy sight
Storm flakes were scroll-leaved flowers, lily showers—sweet
    heaven was astrew in them.

22

          Five! the finding and sake
              And cipher of suffering Christ.   170
          Mark, the mark is of man's make
              And the word of it Sacrificed.
    But he scores it in scarlet himself on his own bespoken,
          Before-time-taken, dearest prizèd and priced—
              Stigma, signal, cinquefoil token
For lettering of the lamb's fleece, ruddying of the rose-flake.

23

Joy fall to thee, father Francis,
Drawn to the Life that died;
With the gnarls of the nails in thee, niche of the
lance, his
Lovescape crucified   180
And seal of his seraph-arrival! and these thy daughters
And five-livèd and leavèd favour and pride,
Are sisterly sealed in wild waters,
To bathe in his fall-gold mercies, to breathe in his all-fire
glances.

24

Away in the loveable west,
On a pastoral forehead of Wales,
I was under a roof here, I was at rest,
And they the prey of the gales;
She to the black-about air, to the breaker, the thickly
Falling flakes, to the throng that catches and quails   190
Was calling 'O Christ, Christ, come quickly':
The cross to her she calls Christ to her, christens her wild-
worst Best.

25

The majesty! what did she mean?
Breathe, arch and original Breath.
Is it love in her of the being as her lover had been?
Breathe, body of lovely Death.
They were else-minded then, altogether, the men
Woke thee with a *we are perishing* in the weather of
Gennesareth.
Or is it that she cried for the crown then,
The keener to come at the comfort for feeling the combating
keen?   200

26

For how to the heart's cheering
The down-dugged ground-hugged grey

Hovers off, the jay-blue heavens appearing
     Of pied and peeled May!
Blue-beating and hoary-glow height; or night, still higher,
With belled fire and the moth-soft Milky Way,
     What by your measure is the heaven of desire,
The treasure never eyesight got, nor was ever guessed what for
   the hearing?

27

No, but it was not these.
     The jading and jar of the cart,   210
  Time's tasking, it is fathers that asking for ease
     Of the sodden-with-its-sorrowing heart,
Not danger, electrical horror; then further it finds
The appealing of the Passion is tenderer in prayer apart:
     Other, I gather, in measure her mind's
Burden, in wind's burly and beat of endragonèd seas.

28

But how shall I . . . make me room there:
     Reach me a . . . Fancy, come faster—
  Strike you the sight of it? look at it loom there,
     Thing that she . . . there then! the Master,   220
Ipse, the only one, Christ, King, Head:
He was to cure the extremity where he had cast her;
     Do, deal, lord it with living and dead;
Let him ride, her pride, in his triumph, despatch and have
   done with his doom there.

29

Ah! there was a heart right!
     There was single eye!
  Read the unshapeable shock night
     And knew the who and the why;
Wording it how but by him that present and past,
Heaven and earth are word of, worded by?—   230
     The Simon Peter of a soul! to the blast
Tarpeian-fast, but a blown beacon of light.

30

Jesu, heart's light,
Jesu, maid's son,
What was the feast followed the night
Thou hadst glory of this nun?—
Feast of the one woman without stain.
For so conceivèd, so to conceive thee is done;
But here was heart-throe, birth of a brain,
Word, that heard and kept thee and uttered thee outright.   240

31

Well, she has thee for the pain, for the
Patience; but pity of the rest of them!
Heart, go and bleed at a bitterer vein for the
Comfortless unconfessed of them—
No not uncomforted: lovely-felicitous Providence
Finger of a tender of, O of a feathery delicacy, the breast
of the
Maiden could obey so, be a bell to, ring of it, and
Startle the poor sheep back! is the shipwrack then a harvest,
does tempest carry the grain for thee?

32

I admire thee, master of the tides,
Of the Yore-flood, of the year's fall;   250
The recurb and the recovery of the gulf's sides,
The girth of it and the wharf of it and the
wall;
Stanching, quenching ocean of a motionable mind;
Ground of being, and granite of it: past all
Grasp God, throned behind
Death with a sovereignty that heeds but hides, bodes but
abides;

33

With a mercy that outrides
The all of water, an ark
For the listener; for the lingerer with a love glides

Lower than death and the dark;   260
A vein for the visiting of the past-prayer, pent in prison,
The-last-breath penitent spirits—the uttermost mark
     Our passion-plungèd giant risen,
The Christ of the Father compassionate, fetched in the storm
of his strides.

34

Now burn, new born to the world,
     Double-naturèd name,
The heaven-flung, heart-fleshed, maiden-furled
     Miracle-in-Mary-of-flame,
Mid-numberèd he in three of the thunder-throne!
Not a dooms-day dazzle in his coming nor dark as he
     came;   270
     Kind, but royally reclaiming his own;
A released shower, let flash to the shire, not a lightning of fire
hard-hurled.

35

Dame, at our door
     Drowned, and among our shoals,
Remember us in the roads, the heaven-haven of
     the Reward:
     Our King back, oh, upon English souls!
Let him easter in us, be a dayspring to the dimness of us,
     be a crimson-cresseted east,
More brightening her, rare-dear Britain, as his reign rolls,
     Pride, rose, prince, hero of us, high-priest,   280
Our hearts' charity's hearth's fire, our thoughts' chivalry's
throng's Lord.

1876

Title: On Dec. 6, 1875, the steamer *Deutschland*, carrying five nuns
expelled from Germany by the Falck Laws (which suppressed the monas-
teries) ran aground on the Kentish Knock, a sand-bar near the mouth of
the Thames, and was gradually battered to pieces by a winter gale, with
the loss of 157 lives. Hopkins, then in Wales, was stirred by the news-
paper account of the disaster and, upon an encouraging hint from his
Jesuit superior, composed the poem.   l. 31: **voel**   bare hill.   l. 39:

instressed   apprehended with a keenly imagined response.   l. 47: **rides**
bestrides and is borne forward on.   l. 50: **his going**   the beginning of
Christ's ministry, in Galilee, near his home at Nazareth (Matt. 4:12–17).
l. 77: **Paul**   St. Paul, suddenly converted on the road to Damascus (Acts
9:1–9).   l. 78: **Austin**   St. Augustine (354–430), whose conversion,
recorded in his *Confessions*, was gradual.   l. 91: **tell**   count.   l. 95:
bay   here, an alcove or recess, well-buttressed or framed, as in a Gothic
church.   l. 111: **whorl**   propeller.   l. 150: **fetch**   resource.   l.
157: **Gertrude, Luther**   The one a saint (1256?–1302), the other the
leader of the German Reformation; both born in Eisleben, Germany.
l. 165: **Orion**   in Greek legend, a mighty hunter; also a winter constella-
tion associated with storms; here, perhaps signifying Christ, who drove the
nuns forth from safety ("unchancelling" them) so that they might win the
crown of martyrs.   l. 170: **cipher**   the five wounds, in the hands, feet
and side, of Christ; imprinted as stigmata upon St. Francis of Assisi (ll.
177–178).   l. 198: **Woke thee**   Christ, who made the storm be still
(Mark 4:35–41).   l. 215: **Other**   that is, the nun did not plead for
rescue but accepted her sufferings with ecstasy, as being like Christ's.
l. 221: **Ipse**   He, himself.   l. 230: **word of**   an allusion to Christ as the
Word or Logos, "without whom was not anything made" (John 1:1–3).
l. 231: **Simon Peter**   who recognized Jesus as the Christ, and whom Jesus
called a "Rock" (Matt. 16:13–20).   l. 232: **Tarpeian**   referring to a
rock, on the Capitoline hill in ancient Rome, where condemned persons
were put to death.   l. 235: **the feast**   of the Immaculate Conception
(Dec. 8), in which Roman Catholics celebrate the miracle that the Virgin
Mary was herself conceived without stain of sin.   l. 238: **For so con-
ceivèd**   for, being so conceived (without stain), Mary could conceive thee
(Christ).   l. 239: **here**   in the nun's brain and heart.   l. 250: **Yore-
flood**   "Noah's" Flood (Gen. 7:11–24).   l. 260: **Lower than death**
alluding to Christ's death, his descent into Hell, and his resurrection
("Our passion-plungéd giant risen"; see also l. 165), offering a hope of
mercy even for those ("past-prayer") for whom no human hope seems
possible.   l. 266: **Double-naturèd name**   Jesus Christ, truly God and
truly man.   l. 269: **Mid-numberèd**   the Son, the second Person of the
Holy Trinity.   l. 270: **Not a dooms-day dazzle**   His birth was not
trumpeted to the universe, yet it was not unheralded (by star and the
angelic hosts). (See Luke 2:8–14.)   l. 272: **the shire**   the countryside
near Bethlehem where shepherds were keeping their flocks (Luke 2:8–14).
l. 276: **roads**   offshore anchorage.   l. 277: **King**   Christ.

GOD'S GRANDEUR

*Evidence
of God
[illegible]*

The world is charged with the grandeur of God.
    It will flame out, like shining from shook foil;
    It gathers to a greatness, like the ooze of oil
Crushed. Why do men then now not reck his rod?
Generations have trod, have trod, have trod;

*One of Hopkins' peculiar uses of meter. Counterpoint
rhythm.*

And all is seared with trade; bleared, smeared with toil;
And wears man's smudge and shares man's smell: the soil
Is bare now, nor can foot feel, being shod.

And for all this, nature is never spent; *man cannot destroy it.*
    There lives the dearest freshness deep down things;   10
And though the last lights off the black West went
    Oh, morning, at the brown brink eastward, springs—
Because the Holy Ghost over the bent
    World broods with warm breast and with ah! bright wings.

1877

l. 3: **oil** perhaps, pressed olive oil.   l. 13: **Holy Ghost** often represented in the form of a dove. (See Milton, *Paradise Lost*, I, 18–21, and Gen. 1:1).

THE STARLIGHT NIGHT

Look at the stars! look, look up at the skies!
    O look at all the fire-folk sitting in the air!
    The bright boroughs, the circle-citadels there!
Down in dim woods the diamond delves! the elves'-eyes!
The grey lawns cold where gold, where quickgold lies!
    Wind-beat whitebeam! airy abeles set on a flare!
    Flake-doves sent floating forth at a farmyard scare!
Ah well! it is all a purchase, all is a prize.

Buy then! bid then!—What?—Prayer, patience, alms, vows.
Look, look: a May-mess, like on orchard boughs!   10
    Look! March-bloom, like on mealed-with-yellow sallows!
These are indeed the barn; withindoors house
The shocks. This piece-bright paling shuts the spouse
    Christ home, Christ and his mother and all his hallows.

1877

l. 6: **whitebeam** a tree with leaves showing white on the underside. l. 8: **purchase** something to be gained or won.   l. 12: **barn** Heaven. (See Matt. 13–30.)   l. 13: **piece-bright paling** a palisade shining as bright as new-minted coins.   l. 14: **hallows** holy ones, the souls of the blest.

SPRING

Nothing is so beautiful as Spring—
   When weeds, in wheels, shoot long and lovely and lush;
   Thrush's eggs look little low heavens, and thrush
Through the echoing timber does so rinse and wring
The ear, it strikes like lightnings to hear him sing;
   The glassy peartree leaves and blooms, they brush
   The descending blue; that blue is all in a rush
With richness; the racing lambs too have fair their fling.

What is all this juice and all this joy?
   A strain of the earth's sweet being in the beginning   10
In Eden garden.—Have, get, before it cloy,
   Before it cloud, Christ, lord, and sour with sinning,
Innocent mind and Mayday in girl and boy,
   Most, O maid's child, thy choice and worthy the winning.

1877

l. 2: **wheels** spiraling upward.   l. 14: **maid's** the Virgin Mary's.

THE WINDHOVER:

TO CHRIST OUR LORD

I caught this morning morning's minion, kingdom of daylight's *[points to be to god.]*
   dauphin, dapple-dawn-drawn Falcon, in his riding
  Of the rolling level underneath him steady air, and striding
High there, how he rung upon the rein of a wimpling wing
In his ecstasy! then off, off forth on swing,
   As a skate's heel sweeps smooth on a bow-bend: the hurl
     and gliding
Rebuffed the big wind. My heart in hiding   *[wished to be masterful as bird]*
Stirred for a bird,—the achieve of, the mastery of the thing!

Brute beauty and valour and act, oh, air, pride, plume, here
   Buckle! AND the fire that breaks from thee then, a billion   10
Times told lovelier, more dangerous, O my chevalier!   *[No usual reference to Christ.]*

[Enormously Attractive]

[Bird begins to remind man of Christ]

291

[handwritten: In reference to the bird? or maybe Refers back to the paradox involving the Buckle.]

No wonder of it: shéer plód makes plough down sillion
Shine, and blue-bleak embers, ah my dear,
    Fall, ~~gul~~ themselves, and gash gold-vermilion.
    [handwritten: gaul]

[handwritten right margin: most return to the simple things he m... do. This is christ like.]

1877

Title: the kestrel or European falcon, noted for its spiraling ("winding")
and hovering flight.   l. 4: **rung** circled, like a horse at the end of a
training rope.   l. 6: **bow-bend** a sharp curve, as on a frozen river.
l. 12: **sillion** furrow.

PIED BEAUTY

[handwritten: another poem of Praise]

Glory be to God for dappled things—
    For skies of couple-colour as a brinded cow;
        For rose-moles all in stipple upon trout that swim;
Fresh-firecoal chestnut-falls; finches' wings;
    Landscape plotted and pieced—fold, fallow, and plough;
        And áll trádes, their gear and tackle and trim. *[handwritten: Fishing]*

All things counter, original, spare, strange;
    Whatever is fickle, freckled (who knows how?)
        With swift, slow; sweet, sour; adazzle, dim;
He fathers-forth whose beauty is past change: 10
                Praise him.

[handwritten: all for god, a great optimism. can't fool with it]

1877

l. 8: **fickle** changeable.

DUNS SCOTUS'S OXFORD

Towery city and branchy between towers;
Cuckoo-echoing, bell-swarmèd, lark-charmèd, rook-racked,
    river-rounded;
The dapple-eared lily below thee; that country and town did
Once encounter in, here coped and poisèd powers;

Thou hast a base and brickish skirt there, sours
That neighbour-nature thy grey beauty is grounded
Best in; graceless growth, thou hast confounded
Rural rural keeping—folk, flocks, and flowers.

Yet ah! this air I gather and I release
He lived on; these weeds and waters, these walls are what   10
He haunted who of all men most sways my spirits to peace;

Of realty the rarest-veinèd unraveller; a not
Rivalled insight, be rival Italy or Greece;
Who fired France for Mary without spot.

1879

Title: Duns Scotus (1265?–1308), Scottish theologian, taught at Oxford c. 1301. In his theory of *haecceitas* ("this-ness"), which dealt with the divinely sustained identity of every particular thing and action, Hopkins found authority for his own idea of "inscape"–"instress" (set forth in "As kingfishers catch fire . . ."). l. 5: **skirt** urban growth cutting the old colleges off from the countryside. l. 12: **realty** reality, the nature of things. l. 14: **fired France** aroused opposition to those French theologians who resisted the doctrine of the Immaculate Conception. (See note to "Wreck," l. 235.)

AT THE WEDDING MARCH

God with honour hang your head,
Groom, and grace you, bride, your bed
With lissome scions, sweet scions,
Out of hallowed bodies bred.

Each be other's comfort kind:
Déep, déeper than divined,
Divine charity, dear charity,
Fast you ever, fast bind.

Then let the March tread our ears:
I to him turn with tears   10
Who to wedlock, his wonder wedlock,
Deals tríumph and immortal years.

1879

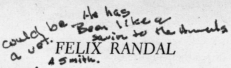

FELIX RANDAL

could be a vet. *He has Been like a savior to the Animals* *A smith.*

Felix Randal the farrier, O is he dead then? my duty all ended,
Who have watched his mould of man, big-boned and hardy-
    handsome   *Has been a very strong man, man does decay.*
Pining, pining, till time when reason rambled in it and some
Fatal four disorders, fleshed there, all contended?

He was very sick

Sickness broke him. Impatient, he cursed at first, but mended
Being anointed and all; though a heavenlier heart began some
Months earlier, since I had our sweet reprieve and ransom
Tendered to him. Ah well, God rest him all road ever he
    offended!

got broke him.   *A welsh idiom*

This seeing the sick endears them to us, us too it endears.
My tongue had taught thee comfort, touch had quenched thy
    tears,
Thy tears that touched my heart, child, Felix, poor Felix
    Randal;

A Caesura   *notice Alliteration*

Priest consoled man and the man touched the priest.

10

How far from then forethought of, all thy more boisterous
    years,
When thou at the random grim forge, powerful amidst peers,
Didst fettle for the great grey drayhorse his bright and
    battering sandal!

greatest part, Felix before he was sick

Was a very strong and powerful person.

1880

l. 6: **anointed** having received the Catholic rite of Extreme Unction
administered to persons in danger of death.   l. 7: **reprieve and ransom**
the sacraments of Confession and Holy Communion.   l. 8: **all road ever**
for all that.   l. 13: **random** built of unhewn stones.

SPRING AND FALL:

TO A YOUNG CHILD

Márgarét, are you gríeving
Over Goldengrove unleaving?
Leáves, like the things of man, you
With your fresh thoughts care for, can you?
Ah! ás the heart grows older
It will come to such sights colder

Outside it seems she grieves for the leaves, really she grieves for the mortal deaths.

294

By and by, nor spare a sigh
Though worlds of wanwood leafmeal lie;
And yet you *will* weep and know why.
Now no matter, child, the name: 10
Sórrow's spríngs áre the same.
Nor mouth had, no nor mind, expressed
What heart heard of, ghost guessed:
It is the blight man was born for,
It is Margaret you mourn for.

[handwritten margin notes: Does Margaret mourn for he loss of contact with nature,]

[handwritten margin notes: not just leaves, open for mortal life]

1880

l. 8: **wanwood**   a coined word, the prefix *wan-* meaning either *fallen* or *pale*, or both.   l. 13: **ghost**   soul or spirit.

INVERSNAID

This darksome burn, horseback brown,
His rollrock highroad roaring down,
In coop and in comb the fleece of his foam
Flutes and low to the lake falls home.

A windpuff-bonnet of fáwn-fróth
Turns and twindles over the broth
Of a pool so pitchblack, féll-frówning,
It rounds and rounds Despair to drowning.

Degged with dew, dappled with dew
Are the groins of the braes that the brook treads through,   10
Wiry heathpacks, flitches of fern,
And the beadbonny ash that sits over the burn.

What would the world be, once bereft
Of wet and of wildness? Let them be left,
O let them be left, wildness and wet;
Long live the weeds and the wilderness yet.

1881

Title: village on Loch Lomond, Scotland.   l. 1: **burn**   brook.   l. 3: **coop and comb**   trough and crest.   l. 4: **flutes**   (vb.) flows in groove-like ripples.   l. 6: **twindles**   intertwines.   l. 7: **féll-frówning**   harshly frowning—overhung by rocks (fells).   l. 9: **degged**   sprinkled.   l. 10: **groins**   creased folds.   l. 11: **heathpacks**   densely grown heather. **flitches**   clumps.   l. 12: **beadbonny**   bedecked with droplets.

"As kingfishers catch fire . . ."

As kingfishers catch fire, dragonflies dráw fláme;
As tumbled over rim in roundy wells
Stones ring; like each tucked string tells, each hung bell's
Bow swung finds tongue to fling out broad its name;

Each mortal thing does one thing and the same:
Deals out that being indoors each one dwells;
Selves—goes itself; *myself* it speaks and spells;
Crying Whát I dó is me: *for that I came.*

I say móre: the just man justices;
Kéeps gráce: thát keeps all his goings graces;   10
Acts in God's eye what in God's eye he is—
Chríst—for Christ plays in ten thousand places,
Lovely in limbs, and lovely in eyes not his
To the Father through the features of men's faces.

1881–1882?

l. 1: **catch fire** reflect sunbeams.   l. 3: **tucked** plucked.   l. 6:
indoors [which] within.   l. 7: **Selves** here, a verb; its subject, "Each
mortal thing" (l. 5).   l. 9: **justices** here, a verb.

Some of
the terrible sonnets, When he was depressed and suffering
[CARRION COMFORT] wondering whether
he is a chosen
one.

Not, I'll not, carrion comfort, Despair, not feast on thee;
Not untwist—slack they may be—these last strands of man
In me or, most weary, cry *I can no more.* I can;
Can something, hope, wish day come, not choose not to be.
But ah, but O thou terrible, why wouldst thou rude on me
Thy wring-world right foot rock? lay a lion limb against me?
  scan
With darksome devouring eyes my bruisèd bones? and fan,
O in turns of tempest, me heaped there; me frantic to avoid
  thee and flee?

  Why? That my chaff might fly; my grain lie, sheer and
    clear.
Nay in all that toil, that coil, since (seems) I kissed the rod,   10
Hand rather, my heart lo! lapped strength, stole joy, would
    laugh, chéer.

296

Cheer whom though? the hero whose heaven-handling flung
    me, fóot tród
Me? or me that fought him? O which one? is it each one?
    That night, that year
Of now done darkness I wretch lay wrestling with (my God!)
    my God.

1885?

l. 10: **rod** symbolizing spiritual obedience.   l. 14: **wrestling** as Jacob
wrestled with an angel. (See Gen. 32:24–30.)

"No worst, there is none . . ."

very low and sorrowful.

No worst, there is none. Pitched past pitch of grief,
More pangs will, schooled at forepangs, wilder wring.
Comforter, where, where is your comforting? *the Holy Spirit*
Mary, mother of us, where is your relief?
My cries heave, herds-long; huddle in a main, a chief
Woe, world-sorrow; on an áge-old anvil wince and sing—
Then lull, then leave off. Fury had shrieked 'No linger-
    ing! Let me be fell: force I must be brief'.

    O the mind, mind has mountains; cliffs of fall
Frightful, sheer, no-man-fathomed. Hold them cheap
May who ne'er hung there. Nor does long our small
Durance deal with that steep or deep. Here! creep,
Wretch, under a comfort serves in a whirlwind: all
Life death does end and each day dies with sleep.

if you ever hung there, you would not.

go asleep and comfort self.

The mind is so complex that it is dangerous. We can't deal w/ the deep.

1885

l. 3: **Comforter** the Holy Spirit.   l. 6: **sing** reverberate at a high
pitch.   l. 8: **force** perforce.

"I wake and feel the fell of dark . . ."

I wake and feel the fell of dark, not day.
What hours, O what black hoürs we have spent
This night! what sights you, heart, saw; ways you went!
And more must, in yet longer light's delay.
    With witness I speak this. But where I say

Hours I mean years, mean life. And my lament
Is cries countless, cries like dead letters sent
To dearest him that lives alas! away.

   I am gall, I am heartburn. God's most deep decree
Bitter would have me taste: my taste was me;   10
Bones built in me, flesh filled, blood brimmed the curse.
   Selfyeast of spirit a dull dough sours. I see
The lost are like this, and their scourge to be
As I am mine, their sweating selves; but worse.

1885

l. 1: **fell**   cruelty/pelt.   l. 12: **Selfyeast**   Yeast, symbolic of Christian
faith, should "raise" and sweeten the "dough" of daily life; but inflated
"self," or pride, has the opposite effect.   l. 14: **worse**   that is, without
hope; damned.

TOM'S GARLAND:

UPON THE UNEMPLOYED

Tom—garlanded with squat and surly steel
Tom; then Tom's fallowbootfellow piles pick
By him and rips out rockfire homeforth—sturdy Dick;
Tom Heart-at-ease, Tom Navvy: he is all for his meal
Sure, 's bed now. Low be it: lustily he his low lot (feel
That ne'er need hunger, Tom; Tom seldom sick,
Seldomer heartsore; that treads through, prickproof, thick
Thousands of thorns, thoughts) swings though. Commonweal
Little I reck ho! lacklevel in, if all had bread:
What! Country is honour enough in all us—lordly head,   10
With heaven's lights high hung round, or, mother-ground
That mammocks, mighty foot. But nó way sped,
Nor mind nor mainstrength; gold go garlanded
With, perilous, O nó; nor yet plod safe shod sound;
               Undenizened, beyond bound
Of earth's glory, earth's ease, all; no one, nowhere,

In wide the world's weal; rare gold, bold steel, bare
               In both; care, but share care—
This, by Despair, bred Hangdog dull; by Rage,
Manwolf, worse; and their packs infest the age.   20

1887

Title: Hopkins explained that in a just but not equalitarian common-wealth the day-laborer, "Tom," is the "foot" crowned or "garlanded" with a hobnail boot as symbol of his dignity and function. The first twelve lines describe the cheerful lot of such a workman; the remaining lines sympathize indignantly with those who "share care with the high and obscurity with the low, but wealth or comfort with neither." (Letter to Bridges, Feb. 10, 1888.)   l. 3: **rips out rockfire homeforth** with his hobnail boots strikes sparks from the paving stones as he hurries home. l. 10: **lordly head** at the other end of the social scale from Tom is the monarch, "garlanded" with gold (l. 13).   l. 12: **mammocks** crumbles or disfigures the earth ("mother-ground").   l. 13–18: **gold go . . . share care** Paraphrase: Do these laborers have the "perilous" responsi-bility of wealth and power? Far from it! Yet neither do they have safety and employment but only "care."   l. 20: **packs** of social outcasts and vandals.

THAT NATURE IS A HERACLITEAN FIRE
AND OF THE
COMFORT OF THE RESURRECTION

Cloud-puffball, torn tufts, tossed pillows | flaunt forth, then
        chevy on an air-
built thoroughfare: heaven-roysterers, in gay-gangs | they
        throng; they glitter in marches.
Down roughcast, down dazzling whitewash, | wherever an elm
        arches,
Shivelights and shadowtackle in long | lashes lace, lance, and
        pair.
Delightfully the bright wind boisterous | ropes, wrestles,
        beats earth bare
Of yestertempest's creases; | in pool and rutpeel parches
Squandering ooze to squeezed | dough, crust, dust; stanches,
        starches
Squadroned masks and manmarks | treadmire toil there
Footfretted in it. Million-fuelèd, | nature's bonfire burns on.

But quench her bonniest, dearest | to her, her clearest-selvèd
      spark   10
Man, how fast his firedint, | his mark on mind, is gone!
Both are in an unfathomable, all is in an enormous dark
Drowned. O pity and indig | nation! Manshape, that shone
Sheer off, disseveral, a star, | death blots black out; nor mark
      Is any of him at all so stark
But vastness blurs and time | beats level. Enough! the Resur-
      rection,
A heart's-clarion! Away grief's gasping, | joyless days, dejection.
      Across my foundering deck shone
A beacon, an eternal beam. | Flesh fade, and mortal trash
Fall to the residuary worm; | world's wildfire, leave but ash: 20
      In a flash, at a trumpet crash,
I am all at once what Christ is, | since he was what I am, and
This Jack, joke, poor potsherd, | patch, matchwood, immortal
      diamond,
      Is immortal diamond.

1888

Title: Heraclitus, Greek philosopher, 6th century B.C., taught that all nature, including human life, springs from and returns to the primary element of fire in a process of "flux."   l. 1: **chevy** race, scamper. l. 3: **roughcast** masonry walls.   l. 4: **Shivelights** strips of light. l. 11: **firedint** Hopkins' coinage; perhaps, man's physical individuality as well as, in the next phrase, his intellectual being.   l. 20: **wildfire** the Heraclitean fire; also, the flames of the Last Judgment.   l. 22: **What Christ is** that is, eternally with God.   l. 23: **Jack** commonest of men. **patch** worthless scrap.

"Thou art indeed just, Lord . . ."

Justus quidem tu es, Domine, si disputem tecum: verumtamen justa
loquar ad te: Quare via impiorum prosperatur? &c.

    Thou art indeed just, Lord, if I contend
    With thee; but, sir, so what I plead is just.
    Why do sinners' ways prosper? and why must
    Disappointment all I endeavour end?
        Wert thou my enemy, O thou my friend,
    How wouldst thou worse, I wonder, than thou dost
    Defeat, thwart me? Oh, the sots and thralls of lust

Do in spare hours more thrive than I that spend,
Sir, life upon thy cause. See, banks and brakes
Now, leavèd how thick! lacèd they are again   10
With fretty chervil, look, and fresh wind shakes
Them; birds build—but not I build; no, but strain,
Time's eunuch, and not breed one work that wakes.
Mine, O thou lord of life, send my roots rain.

1889

Epigraph: (See Jer. 12:1) translated in the first three lines.   l. 11:
fretty chervil   a carrot-like herb.

TO R. B.

The fine delight that fathers thought; the strong
Spur, live and lancing like the blowpipe flame,
Breathes once and, quenchèd faster than it came,
Leaves yet the mind a mother of immortal song.
Nine months she then, nay years, nine years she long
Within her wears, bears, cares and combs the same:
The widow of an insight lost she lives, with aim
Now known and hand at work now never wrong.
    Sweet fire the sire of muse, my soul needs this;
I want the one rapture of an inspiration.   10
O then if in my lagging lines you miss
The roll, the rise, the carol, the creation,
My winter world, that scarcely breathes that bliss
Now, yields you, with some sighs, our explanation.

1889

Title: To Robert Bridges (1844–1930), Hopkins' friend, correspondent,
and first editor.   l. 6: **combs**   searches through and disentangles; also,
stores up, as in a honeycomb.

ALFRED EDWARD HOUSMAN

1859–1936

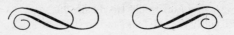

"Loveliest of trees . . ."

Loveliest of trees, the cherry now
Is hung with bloom along the bough,
And stands about the woodland ride
Wearing white for Eastertide.

Now, of my threescore years and ten,
Twenty will not come again,
And take from seventy springs a score,
It only leaves me fifty more.

And since to look at things in bloom
Fifty springs are little room,   10
About the woodlands I will go
To see the cherry hung with snow.

                                        1896

REVEILLE

Wake: the silver dusk returning
    Up the beach of darkness brims,
And the ship of sunrise burning
    Strands upon the eastern rims.

Wake: the vaulted shadow shatters,
    Trampled to the floor it spanned,
And the tent of night in tatters
    Straws the sky-pavilioned land.

Up, lad, up, 'tis late for lying:
    Hear the drums of morning play;   10
Hark, the empty highways crying
    "Who'll beyond the hills away?"

Towns and countries woo together,
    Forelands beacon, belfries call;
Never lad that trod on leather
    Lived to feast his heart with all.

Up, lad: thews that lie and cumber
    Sunlit pallets never thrive;
Morns abed and daylight slumber
    Were not meant for man alive.   20

Clay lies still, but blood's a rover;
    Breath's a ware that will not keep.
Up, lad: when the journey's over
    There'll be time enough to sleep.

                1896

MARCH

The sun at noon to higher air,
Unharnessing the silver Pair
That late before his chariot swam,
Rides on the gold wool of the Ram.

So braver notes the storm-cock sings
To start the rusted wheel of things,
And brutes in field and brutes in pen
Leap that the world goes round again.

The boys are up the woods with day
To fetch the daffodils away,   10
And home at noonday from the hills
They bring no dearth of daffodils.

Afield for palms the girls repair,
And sure enough the palms are there,
And each will find by hedge or pond
Her waving silver-tufted wand.

In farm and field through all the shire
The eye beholds the hearts desire;
Ah, let not only mine be vain,
For lovers should be loved again.   20

1896

l. 2: **Pair**   the zodiac sign *Pisces* (the Fishes) through which the sun passes just before entering *Aries* ("the Ram," l. 4) at the vernal equinox. l. 13: **palms**   not tropical palms but willows with large catkins, sometimes used to decorate English country churches on Palm Sunday.

"When I was one-and-twenty"

When I was one-and-twenty
I heard a wise man say,
"Give crowns and pounds and guineas,
    But not your heart, away;
Give pearls away and rubies,
    But keep your fancy free."
But I was one-and-twenty—
    No use to talk to me.

When I was one-and-twenty
    I heard him say again,   10
"The heart out of the bosom
    Was never given in vain;
'Tis paid with sighs a plenty
    And sold for endless rue."
And I am two-and-twenty.
    And oh, 'tis true, 'tis true.

1896

TO AN ATHLETE DYING YOUNG

The time you won your town the race
We chaired you through the market-place;
Man and boy stood cheering by,
And home we brought you shoulder-high.

Today, the road all runners come,
Shoulder-high we bring you home,
And set you at your threshold down.
Townsman of a stiller town.

Smart lad, to slip betimes away
From fields where glory does not stay,   10
And early though the laurel grows
It withers quicker than the rose.

Eyes the shady night has shut
Cannot see the record cut,
And silence sounds no worse than cheers
After earth has stopped the ears.

Now you will not swell the rout
Of lads that wore their honours out,
Runners whom renown outran
And the name died before the man.   20

So set, before its echoes fade,
The fleet foot on the sill of shade,
And hold to the low lintel up
The still-defended challenge-cup.

And round that early-laureled head
Will flock to gaze the strengthless dead,
And find unwithered on its curls
The garland briefer than a girl's.

                        1896

l. 22: **sill** threshold of a tomb.   l. 23: **low lintel** a stone set above
the doorway of a tomb.   l. 25: **early-laureled** crowned with a wreath
of laurel leaves symbolizing victory.   l. 28: **a girl's** which would be
not of leaves but of flowers.

BREDON HILL

In summertime on Bredon
  The bells they sound so clear;
Round both the shires they ring them
  In steeples far and near,
  A happy noise to hear.

Here of a Sunday morning
   My love and I would lie,
And see the coloured counties,
   And hear the larks so high
   About us in the sky.   10

The bells would ring to call her
   In valleys miles away:
"Come all to church, good people;
   Good people come and pray."
   But here my love would stay.

And I would turn and answer
   Among the springing thyme,
"Oh, peal upon our wedding,
   And we will hear the chime,
   And come to church in time."   20

But when the snows at Christmas
   On Bredon top were strown,
My love rose up so early
   And stole out unbeknown
   And went to church alone.

They tolled the one bell only,
   Groom there was none to see,
The mourners followed after,
   And so to church went she,
   And would not wait for me.   30

The bells they sound on Bredon,
   And still the steeples hum.
"Come all to church, good people,"—
   Oh, noisy bells, be dumb;
   I hear you, I will come.

                1896

"Is my team ploughing . . . ?"

   "Is my team ploughing,
      That I was used to drive
   And hear the harness jingle
      When I was man alive?"

Ay, the horses trample,
    The harness jingles now;
No change though you lie under
    The land you used to plough.

"Is football playing
    Along the river shore,   10
With lads to chase the leather,
    Now I stand up no more?"

Ay, the ball is flying,
    The lads play heart and soul;
The goal stands up, the keeper
    Stands up to keep the goal.

"Is my girl happy,
    That I thought hard to leave,
And has she tired of weeping
    As she lies down at eve?"   20

Ay, she lies down lightly,
    She lies not down to weep:
Your girl is well contented.
    Be still, my lad, and sleep.

"Is my friend hearty,
    Now I am thin and pine,
And has he found to sleep in
    A better bed than mine?"

Ay, lad, I lie easy,
    I lie as lads would choose;   30
I cheer a dead man's sweetheart.
    Never ask me whose.

              1896

THE LENT LILY

'Tis spring; come out to ramble
    The hilly brakes around,
For under thorn and bramble
    About the hollow ground
    The primroses are found.

And there's the windflower chilly
    With all the winds at play,
And there's the Lenten lily
    That has not long to stay
    And dies on Easter day.   10

And since till girls go maying
    You find the primrose still,
And find the windflower playing
    With every wind at will,
    But not the daffodil,

Bring baskets now, and sally
    Upon the spring's array,
And bear from hill and valley
    The daffodil away
    That dies on Easter day.   20

1896

"On Wenlock Edge the wood's in trouble"

On Wenlock Edge the wood's in trouble;
His forest fleece the Wrekin heaves;
The gale, it plies the saplings double,
And thick on Severn snow the leaves.

'Twould blow like this through holt and hanger
When Uricon the city stood;
'Tis the old wind in the old anger,
But then it threshed another wood.

Then, 'twas before my time, the Roman
At yonder heaving hill would stare;   10
The blood that warms an English yeoman,
The thoughts that hurt him, they were there.

There, like the wind through woods in riot,
Through him the gale of life blew high;
The tree of man was never quiet—
Then 'twas the Roman, now 'tis I.

The gale, it plies the saplings double;
It blows so hard, 'twill soon be gone.
Today the Roman and his trouble
Are ashes under Uricon.   20

1896

l. 1: **Wenlock Edge** a range of hills near Shrewsbury.   l. 2: **Wrekin**
a volcanic hill in the same region.   l. 5: **holt and hanger** wood and
thicket.   l. 6: **Uricon** ruins of an ancient Roman city in Shropshire.

"In valleys of springs of rivers"

> Clunton and Clunbury,
>   Clungunford and Clun,
> Are the quietest places
> Under the sun.

In valleys of springs of rivers,
    By Ony and Teme and Clun,
The country for easy livers,
    The quietest under the sun,

We still had sorrows to lighten,
    One could not be always glad,
And lads knew trouble at Knighton
    When I was a Knighton lad.

By bridges that Thames runs under,
    In London, the town built ill,   10
'Tis sure small matter for wonder
    If sorrow is with one still.

And if as a lad grows older
    The troubles he bears are more,
He carries his griefs on a shoulder
    That handseled them long before.

Where shall one halt to deliver
    This luggage I'd lief set down?
Not Thames, not Teme is the river,
    Nor London nor Knighton the town,   20

'Tis a long way further than Knighton,
  A quieter place than Clun,
Where doomsday may thunder and lighten
  And little 'twill matter to one.

1896

Prefatory verse: Clunton, Clunbury, etc., are little Shropshire villages.
1. 2: **Ony, Teme, Clun** Shropshire streams.   1. 7: **Knighton** a town
on the Teme.   1. 16: **handseled** first accepted.

"Far in a western brookland"

Far in a western brookland
  That bred me long ago
The poplars stand and tremble
  By pools I used to know.

There, in the windless night-time,
  The wanderer, marveling why,
Halts on the bridge to hearken
  How soft the poplars sigh.

He hears; no more remembered
  In fields where I was known,   10
Here I lie down in London
  And turn to rest alone.

There, by the starlit fences,
  The wanderer halts and hears
My soul that lingers sighing
  About the glimmering weirs.

1896

"With rue my heart is laden"

With rue my heart is laden
  For golden friends I had,
For many a rose-lipped maiden
  And many a lightfoot lad.

By brooks too broad for leaping
　　The lightfoot boys are laid;
The rose-lipped girls are sleeping
　　In fields where roses fade.

1896

" *'Terence, this is stupid stuff'* "

"Terence, this is stupid stuff:
You eat your victuals fast enough;
There can't be much amiss, 'tis clear,
To see the rate you drink your beer.
But, oh, good Lord, the verse you make,
It gives a chap the bellyache.
The cow, the old cow, she is dead;
It sleeps well, the horned head.
We poor lads, 'tis our turn now
To hear such tunes as killed the cow.　　　　10
Pretty friendship 'tis to rime
Your friends to death before their time
Moping melancholy mad.
Come, pipe a tune to dance to, lad."

Why, if 'tis dancing you would be,
There's brisker pipes than poetry.
Say, for what were hopyards meant,
Or why was Burton built on Trent?
Oh, many a peer of England brews
Livelier liquor than the Muse,　　　　20
And malt does more than Milton can
To justify God's ways to man.
Ale, man, ale's the stuff to drink
For fellows whom it hurts to think;
Look into the pewter pot
To see the world as the world's not.
And faith, 'tis pleasant till 'tis past;
The mischief is that 'twill not last.
Oh, I have been to Ludlow fair
And left my necktie God knows where,　　　　30
And carried halfway home, or near,

Pints and quarts of Ludlow beer.
Then the world seemed none so bad,
And I myself a sterling lad;
And down in lovely muck I've lain,
Happy till I woke again.
Then I saw the morning sky—
Heigho, the tale was all a lie;
The world, it was the old world yet,
I was I, my things were wet,　　　　　　　　40
And nothing now remained to do
But begin the game anew.

　　Therefore, since the world has still
Much good, but much less good than ill,
And while the sun and moon endure
Luck's a chance, but trouble's sure,
I'd face it as a wise man would,
And train for ill and not for good.
'Tis true, the stuff I bring for sale
Is not so brisk a brew as ale;　　　　　　　　50
Our of a stem that scored the hand
I wrung it in a weary land.
But take it—if the smack is sour,
The better for the embittered hour;
It should do good to heart and head
When your soul is in my soul's stead;
And I will friend you, if I may,
In the dark and cloudy day.

　　There was a king reigned in the East;
There, when kings will sit to feast,　　　　　　　　60
They get their fill before they think
With poisoned meat and poisoned drink.
He gathered all that springs to birth
From the many-venomed earth;
First a little, thence to more,
He sampled all her killing store;
And easy, smiling, seasoned sound,
Sate the king when healths went round.
They put arsenic in his meat
And stared aghast to watch him eat;　　　　　　　　70
They poured strychnine in his cup

And shook to see him drink it up.
They shook, they stared as white's their shirt;
Them it was their poison hurt.
—I tell the tale that I heard told.
Mithridates, he died old.

1896

l. 7–8: "**the cow . . . is dead**" a jeering parody of mournful lyrics.
l. 18: **Burton** Burton-upon-Trent, a brewery center on the river Trent.
l. 19: **peer** "beer-baron."   l. 29: **Ludlow** a town in Shropshire.
l. 76: **Mithridates** King of Pontus (c. 132–63 B.C.), of whom the legend
recounted in ll. 59–74 is told.

"The chestnut casts his flambeaux . . ."

The chestnut casts his flambeaux, and the flowers
　　Stream from the hawthorn on the wind away,
The doors clap to, the pane is blind with showers.
　　Pass me the can, lad; there's an end of May.

There's one spoilt spring to scant our mortal lot,
　　One season ruined of our little store.
May will be fine next year as like as not:
　　Oh ay, but then we shall be twenty-four.

We for a certainty are not the first
　　Have sat in taverns while the tempest hurled   10
Their hopeful plans to emptiness, and cursed
　　Whatever brute and blackguard made the world.

It is in truth iniquity on high
　　To cheat our sentenced souls of aught they crave,
And mar the merriment as you and I
　　Fare on our long fool's-errand to the grave.

Iniquity it is; but pass the can.
　　My lad, no pair of kings our mothers bore;
Our only portion is the estate of man:
　　We want the moon, but we shall get no more.   20

If here today the cloud of thunder lours
　　Tomorrow it will hie on far behests;

The flesh will grieve on other bones than ours
   Soon, and the soul will mourn in other breasts.

The troubles of our proud and angry dust
   Are from eternity, and shall not fail.
Bear them we can, and if we can we must.
   Shoulder the sky, my lad, and drink your ale.

1922

l. 1: **flambeaux** torch-like spires of flowers.   l. 4: **can** mug.

EIGHT O'CLOCK

He stood, and heard the steeple
   Sprinkle the quarters on the morning town.
One, two, three, four, to market-place and people
   It tossed them down.

Strapped, noosed, nighing his hour,
   He stood and counted them and cursed his luck;
And then the clock collected in the tower
   Its strength, and struck.

1922

EPITAPH ON AN ARMY OF MERCENARIES

These, in the day when heaven was falling,
   The hour when earth's foundations fled,
Followed their mercenary calling
   And took their wages and are dead.

Their shoulders held the sky suspended;
   They stood, and earth's foundations stay;
What God abandoned, these defended,
   And saved the sum of things for pay.

1922

DIFFUGERE NIVES

The snows are fled away, leaves on the shaws
    And grasses in the mead renew their birth,
The river to the river-bed withdraws,
    And altered is the fashion of the earth.

The Nymphs and Graces three put off their fear
    And unapparelled in the woodland play.
The swift hour and the brief prime of the year
    Say to the soul, *Thou wast not born for aye.*

Thaw follows frost; hard on the heel of spring
    Treads summer sure to die, for hard on hers   10
Comes autumn, with his apples scattering;
    Then back to wintertide, when nothing stirs.

But oh, whate'er the sky-led seasons mar,
    Moon upon moon rebuilds it with her beams:
Come *we* where Tullus and where Ancus are,
    And good Aeneas, we are dust and dreams.

Torquatus, if the gods in heaven shall add
    The morrow to the day, what tongue has told?
Feast then thy heart, for what thy heart has had
    The fingers of no heir will ever hold.   20

When thou descendest once the shades among,
    The stern assize and equal judgment o'er,
Not thy long lineage nor thy golden tongue,
    No, nor thy righteousness, shall friend thee more.

Night holds Hippolytus the pure of stain,
    Diana steads him nothing, he must stay;
And Theseus leaves Pirithöus in the chain
    The love of comrades cannot take away.

1936

Title: the opening phrase of Horace's Ode, iv, 7, of which this poem is a translation.   l. 15: **Tullus, Ancus** ancient kings of Rome.   l. 16: **Aeneas** the legendary founder of Rome.   l. 17: **Torquatus** ancient Roman military hero.   l. 22: **assize** trial before the judges of the underworld.   l. 25: **Hippolytus** In Euripides' *Hippolytus,* the son of Theseus and a devotee of Diana. Wrongly accused by his step-mother, Phaedra, of assaulting her, he was slain, and not even Diana could restore him to life.   l. 27: **Pirithöus** He accompanied his friend Theseus to the Underworld; Theseus escaped but Pirithöus was kept prisoner.

JOHN KEBLE

1792–1866

From *THE CHRISTIAN YEAR*

WHAT WENT YE OUT TO SEE?

(Third Sunday in Advent)

"What went ye out into the wilderness to see? A reed shaken with the wind? . . . But what went ye out for to see? A prophet? yea, I say unto you, and more than a prophet."—St. Matthew, xi, 7, 9.

What went ye out to see
    O'er the rude sandy lea,
Where stately Jordan flows by many a palm,
    Or where Gennesaret's wave
    Delights the flowers to lave,
That o'er her western slope breathe airs of balm.

All through the summer night,
    Those blossoms red and bright
Spread their soft breasts, unheeding, to the breeze,
    Like hermits watching still   10
    Around the sacred hill,
Where erst our Saviour watched upon His knees.

A Paschal moon above
    Seems like a saint to rove,
Left shining in the world with Christ alone;
    Below, the lake's still face
    Sleeps sweetly in th'embrace
Of mountains terraced high with mossy stone.

Here we may sit, and dream
Over the heavenly theme,   20
Till to our soul the former days return;
Till on the grassy bed,
Where thousands once He fed,
The world's incarnate Maker we discern.

O cross no more the main,
Wandering so wild and vain,
To count the reeds that tremble in the wind,
On listless dalliance bound,
Like children gazing round,
Who on God's works no seal of Godhead find.   30

Bask not in courtly bower,
Or sun-bright hall of power,
Pass Babel quick, and seek the holy land—
From robes of Tyrian dye
Turn with undazzled eye
To Bethlehem's glade, or Carmel's haunted strand.

Or choose thee out a cell
In Kedron's storied dell,
Beside the springs of Love, that never die;
Among the olives kneel   40
The chill night-blast to feel,
And watch the Moon that saw thy Master's agony.

Then rise at dawn of day,
And wind thy thoughtful way,
Where rested once the Temple's stately shade,
With due feet tracing round
The city's northern bound,
To th'other holy garden, where the Lord was laid.

Who thus alternate see
His death and victory,   50
Rising and falling as on angel wings,
They, while they seem to roam,
Draw daily nearer home,
Their heart untravelled still adores the King of kings.

Or, if at home they stay,
Yet are they, day by day,

In spirit journeying through the glorious land,
    Not for light Fancy's reed,
    Nor Honour's purple meed,
Nor gifted Prophet's lore, nor Science' wondrous wand.   60

    But more than Prophet, more
    Than Angels can adore
With face unveiled, is He they go to seek;
    Blessèd be God, Whose grace
    Shows Him in every place
To homeliest hearts of pilgrims pure and meek.

1827

l. 11: **sacred hill** the Mount of Olives, where Jesus prayed on the night before he was crucified. (See Luke 22:39–46.)   l. 38: **Kedron** or Kidron, a valley between Jerusalem and the Mount of Olives.   l. 39: **Springs** the Pool of Siloam, in Kidron, supposed to have healing waters. l. 48: **holy garden** the place of the sepulchre where Jesus was buried. (See John 19:38–42.)

ELIZABETH BARRETT BROWNING

1806–1861

From SONNETS FROM THE PORTUGUESE

1

I thought once how Theocritus had sung
Of the sweet years, the dear and wished-for years,
Who each one in a gracious hand appears
To bear a gift for mortals, old or young;
And, as I mused it in his antique tongue,
I saw, in gradual vision through my tears,
The sweet, sad years, the melancholy years,
Those of my own life, who by turns had flung
A shadow across me. Straightway I was 'ware,
So weeping, how a mystic Shape did move   10
Behind me, and drew me backward by the hair;
And a voice said in mastery while I strove,
"Guess now who holds thee?"—"Death!" I said.
    But there,
The silver answer rang: "Not Death, but Love."

20

Belovéd, my Belovéd, when I think
That thou wast in the world a year ago,
What time I sat alone here in the snow
And saw no footprint, heard the silence sink
No moment at thy voice, but, link by link,
Went counting all my chains as if that so
They never could fall off at any blow
Struck by thy possible hand—why, thus I drink
Of life's great cup of wonder! Wonderful,

Never to feel thee thrill the day or night   10
With personal act or speech—nor ever cull
Some prescience of thee with the blossoms white
Thou sawest growing! Atheists are as dull,
Who cannot guess God's presence out of sight.

22

When our two souls stand up erect and strong,
Face to face, silent, drawing nigh and nigher,
Until the lengthening wings break into fire
At either curvéd point,—what bitter wrong
Can the earth do to us, that we should not long
Be here contented? Think! In mounting higher,
The angels would press on us and aspire
To drop some golden orb of perfect song
Into our deep, dear silence. Let us stay
Rather on earth, Beloved,—where the unfit,   10
Contrarious moods of men recoil away
And isolate pure spirits, and permit
A place to stand and love in for a day,
With darkness and the death-hour rounding it.

43

How do I love thee? Let me count the ways.
I love thee to the depth and breadth and height
My soul can reach, when feeling out of sight
For the ends of Being and ideal Grace.
I love thee to the level of everyday's
Most quiet need, by sun and candle-light.
I love thee freely, as men strive for Right;
I love thee purely, as they turn from Praise.
I love thee with the passion put to use
In my old griefs, and with my childhood's faith.   10
I love thee with a love I seemed to lose
With my lost saints—I love thee with the breath,
Smiles, tears, of all my life!—and, if God choose,
I shall but love thee better after death.

44

Belovéd, thou hast brought me many flowers
Plucked in the garden, all the summer through
And winter, and it seemed as if they grew
In this close room, nor missed the sun and showers.
So, in the like name of that love of ours,
Take back these thoughts which here unfolded too,
And which on warm and cold days I withdrew
From my heart's ground. Indeed, those beds and bowers
Be overgrown with bitter weeds and rue,
And wait thy weeding; yet here's eglantine,   10
Here's ivy!—take them, as I used to do
Thy flowers, and keep them where they shall not pine.
Instruct thine eyes to keep their colours true,
And tell thy soul their roots are left in mine.

                                                  1850

Title: Although these sonnets were presented to Robert Browning as a
private tribute from his wife, he persuaded her to publish them thinly
veiled as "translations."   Sonnet 1. 1. 1: **Theocritus**   the Greek pastoral
poet, 3d Century B.C., in his *Idyll* xv.

From *AURORA LEIGH* (Book VI, ll. 1–149)

[Paris]

The English have a scornful insular way
Of calling the French light. The levity
Is in the judgment only, which yet stands,
For say a foolish thing but oft enough
(And here's the secret of a hundred creeds,
Men get opinions as boys learn to spell,
By reiteration chiefly), the same thing
Shall pass at last for absolutely wise,
And not with fools exclusively. And so
We say the French are light, as if we said   10
The cat mews or the milch-cow gives us milk:
Say rather, cats are milked and milch-cows mew;
For what is lightness but inconsequence,

Vague fluctuation 'twixt effect and cause
Compelled by neither? Is a bullet light,
That dashes from the gun-mouth, while the eye
Winks and the heart beats one, to flatten itself
To a wafer on the white speck on a wall
A hundred paces off? Even so direct,
So sternly undivertible of aim,   20
Is this French people.
                      All, idealists
Too absolute and earnest, with them all
The idea of a knife cuts real flesh;
And still, devouring the safe interval
Which Nature placed between the thought and act
With those too fiery and impatient souls,
They threaten conflagration to the world,
And rush with most unscrupulous logic on
Impossible practice. Set your orators
To blow upon them with loud windy mouths   30
Through watchword phrases, jest or sentiment,
Which drive our burly brutal English mobs
Like so much chaff, whichever way they blow,—
This light French people will not thus be driven.
They turn indeed,—but then they turn upon
Some central pivot of their thought and choice,
And veer out by the force of holding fast.
That's hard to understand, for Englishmen
Unused to abstract questions, and untrained
To trace the involutions, valve by valve,   40
In each orbed bulb-root of a general truth,
And mark what subtly fine integument
Divides opposed compartments. Freedom's self
Comes concrete to us, to be understood,
Fixed in a feudal form incarnately
To suit our ways of thought and reverence,
The special form, with us, being still the thing.
With us, I say, though I'm of Italy
By mother's birth and grave, by father's grave
And memory; let it be;—a poet's heart   50
Can swell to a pair of nationalities,
However ill-lodged in a woman's breast.
And so I am strong to love this noble France,

This poet of the nations, who dreams on
And wails on (while the household goes to wreck)
For ever, after some ideal good,—
Some equal poise of sex, some unvowed love
Inviolate, some spontaneous brotherhood,
Some wealth that leaves none poor and finds none tired,
Some freedom of the many that respects   60
The wisdom of the few. Heroic dreams!
Sublime, to dream so; natural, to wake:
And sad, to use such lofty scaffoldings,
Erected for the building of a church,
To build instead a brothel or a prison—
May God save France!
                And if at last she sighs
Her great soul up into a great man's face,
To flush his temples out so gloriously
That few dare carp at Caesar for being bald,
What then?—this Caesar represents, not reigns,   70
And is no despot, though twice absolute:
This Head has all the people for a heart;
This purple's lined with the democracy,—
Now let him see to it! for a rent within
Would leave irreparable rags without.

A serious riddle: find such anywhere
Except in France; and when 'tis found in France,
Be sure to read it rightly. So, I mused
Up and down, up and down, the terraced streets,
The glittering boulevards, the white colonnades   80
Of fair fantastic Paris who wears trees
Like plumes, as if man made them, spire and tower
As if they had grown by nature, tossing up
Her fountains in the sunshine of the squares,
As if in beauty's game she tossed the dice,
Or blew the silver down-balls of her dreams
To sow futurity with seeds of thought
And count the passage of her festive hours.

The city swims in verdure, beautiful
As Venice on the waters, the sea-swan.   90
What bosky gardens dropped in close-walled courts
Like plums in ladies' laps who start and laugh:

What miles of streets that run on after trees,
Still carrying all the necessary shops,
Those open caskets with the jewels seen!
And trade is art, and art's philosophy,
In Paris. There's a silk for instance, there,
As worth an artist's study for the folds,
As that bronze opposite! nay, the bronze has faults,
Art's here too artful,—conscious as a maid   100
Who leans to mark her shadow on the wall
Until she lose a 'vantage in her step.
Yet Art walks forward, and knows where to walk;
The artists also are idealists,
Too absolute for nature, logical
To austerity in the application of
The special theory,—not a soul content
To paint a crooked pollard and an ass,
As the English will because they find it so
And like it somehow.—There the old Tuileries   110
Is pulling its high cap down on its eyes,
Confounded, conscience-stricken, and amazed
By the apparition of a new fair face
In those devouring mirrors. Through the grate
Within the gardens, what a heap of babes,
Swept up like leaves beneath the chestnut-trees
From every street and alley of the town,
By ghosts perhaps that blow too bleak this way
A-looking for their heads! dear pretty babes,
I wish them luck to have their ball-play out   120
Before the next change. Here the air is thronged
With statues poised upon their columns fine
As if to stand a moment were a feat,
Against that blue! What squares,—what breathing-room
For a nation that runs fast,—aye, runs against
The dentist's teeth at the corner in pale rows,
Which grin at progress in an epigram.

I walked the day out, listening to the chink
Of the first Napoleon's dry bones in his second grave,
By victories guarded 'neath the golden dome   130
That caps all Paris like a bubble. 'Shall
These dry bones live,' thought Louis Philippe once,

And lived to know. Herein is argument
For kings and politicians, but still more
For poets, who bear buckets to the well
Of ampler draught.
           These crowds are very good
For meditation (when we are very strong),
Though love of beauty makes us timorous,
And draws us backward from the coarse town-sights
To count the daisies upon dappled fields   140
And hear the streams bleat on among the hills
In innocent and indolent repose,
While still with silken elegiac thoughts
We wind out from us the distracting world
And die into the chrysalis of a man,
And leave the best that may, to come of us,
In some brown moth. I would be bold and bear
To look into the swarthiest face of things,
For God's sake who has made them.

        .   .   .   .

1856

l. 68: **great man** Napoleon III, nephew of Napoleon Bonaparte. Elected President in 1848, he restored the Empire in 1852 and ruled until 1870.
l. 69: **his temples** his forehead, bearing a royal crown which, like Julius Caesar's laurel crown, conceals his deficiencies.   l. 126: **teeth** a garish street-sign.   l. 129: **second grave** under the dome of the *Hôtel des Invalides* in Paris; when he died in 1821 Bonaparte was buried on his island of exile, St. Helena.   l. 132: **bones** (See Ezekiel 37:1–3.)   l. 132: **Louis Philippe** the so-called Citizen King, who reigned as constitutional monarch, 1830–1848, opposed by the ardent Bonapartists who longed to restore the Empire.

EDWARD FITZGERALD

1809–1883

THE RUBÁIYÁT OF OMAR KHAYYÁM

Wake! For the Sun, who scattered into flight
The Stars before him from the Field of Night,
    Drives Night along with them from Heav'n and strikes
The Sultán's Turret with a Shaft of Light.

Before the phantom of False morning died,
Methought a Voice within the Tavern cried,   *Remember*   ← *as a majestic might enter a church*
    "When all the Temple is prepared within,
Why nods the drowsy Worshiper outside?"   *worshipper*

And, as the Cock crew, those who stood before
The Tavern shouted—"Open, then, the Door!   10
    You know how little while we have to stay,   *The tavern of the*
And, once departed, may return no more."   *world, man with one life to lead.*

Now the New Year reviving old Desires,
The thoughtful Soul to Solitude retires,
    Where the WHITE HAND of MOSES on the Bough
Puts out, and Jesus from the Ground suspires.

Iram indeed is gone with all his Rose,
And Jamshyd's Sev'n-ringed Cup where no one knows;
    But still a Ruby kindles in the Vine,
And many a Garden by the Water blows.   20

And David's lips are locked; but in divine
High-piping Pehleví, with "Wine! Wine! Wine!
    Red Wine!"—the Nightingale cries to the Rose
That sallow cheek of hers to incarnadine.

Come, fill the Cup, and in the fire of Spring

Famous

Your Winter-garment of Repentance fling;

. does one repent in the winter times?

   The Bird of Time has but a little way
To flutter—and the Bird is on the Wing.

Whether at Naishápúr or Babylon,
Whether the Cup with sweet or bitter run,   30
   The Wine of Life keeps oozing drop by drop,
The Leaves of Life keep falling one by one.

Each Morn a thousand Roses brings, you say;
Yes, but where leaves the Rose of Yesterday?
   And this first Summer month that brings the Rose
Shall take Jamshyd and Kaikobád away.

Well, let it take them! What have we to do
With Kaikobád the Great, or Kaikhosrú?
   Let Zál and Rustum bluster as they will,
Or Hátim call to Supper—heed not you.   40

With me along the strip of Herbage strown
That just divides the desert from the sown,
   Where name of Slave and Sultán is forgot—
And Peace to Mahmúd on his golden Throne!

A Book of Verses underneath the Bough,

Very Famous

A Jug of Wine, a Loaf of Bread—and Thou

This would be enough for paradise.

   Beside me singing in the Wilderness—
Oh, Wilderness were Paradise enow!

Some for the Glories of This World; and some
Sigh for the Prophet's Paradise to come;   50
   Ah, take the Cash, and let the Credit go,
Nor heed the rumble of a distant drum!

Look to the blowing Rose about us—"Lo,
Laughing," she says, "into the world I blow,
   At once the silken tassel of my Purse
Tear, and its Treasure on the Garden throw."

And those who husbanded the Golden Grain,
And those who flung it to the winds like Rain,
   Alike to no such aureate Earth are turned
As, buried once, Men want dug up again.   60

The Worldly Hope men set their Hearts upon
Turns Ashes—or it prospers; and anon,
   Like Snow upon the Desert's dusty Face,
Lighting a little hour or two—is gone.

Think, in this battered Caravanserai
Whose Portals are alternate Night and Day,
   How Sultán after Sultán with his Pomp
Abode his destined Hour, and went his way.

They say the Lion and the Lizard keep
The Courts where Jamshyd gloried and drank deep;   70
   And Bahrám, that great Hunter—the Wild Ass
Stamps o'er his Head, but cannot break his Sleep.

* I sometimes think that never blows so red   *Famous, many have*
The Rose as where some buried Caesar bled;   *preceded us to death.*
   That every Hyacinth the Garden wears   *vegitation is composed*
Dropped in her Lap from some once lovely Head.   *of them.*

And this reviving Herb whose tender Green
Fledges the River-Lip on which we lean—
   Ah, lean upon it lightly! for who knows
From what once lovely Lip it springs unseen!   80

* Ah, my Belovéd, fill the Cup that clears   *Famous*
TODAY of past Regrets and future Fears: *live so not being too*
   Tomorrow!—Why, Tomorrow I may be   *old, don't worry about*
Myself with Yesterday's Sev'n thousand Years.   *tomorrow, who knows*
   what it will bring.

For some we loved, the loveliest and the best
That from his Vintage rolling Time hath prest,
   Have drunk their Cup a Round or two before,
And one by one crept silently to rest.

And we, that now make merry in the Room
They left, and Summer dresses in new bloom,   90
   Ourselves must we beneath the Couch of Earth
Descend—ourselves to make a Couch—for whom?

* Ah, make the most of what we yet may spend,   *what may*
Before we too into the Dust descend;   *~~happy~~ happen*
   Dust into Dust, and under Dust, to lie,
Sans Wine, sans Song, sans Singer, and—sans End!   *~~tomorrow~~.*
   without, forever.

Alike for those who for TODAY prepare,
And those that after some TOMORROW stare,
    A Muezzín from the Tower of Darkness cries,
"Fools, your Reward is neither Here nor There."   100

Why, all the Saints and Sages who discussed
Of the Two Worlds so wisely—they are thrust
    Like foolish Prophets forth; their Words to Scorn
Are scattered, and their Mouths are stopped with Dust.

he did all he could to learn the truth about religion

Myself when young did eagerly frequent
Doctor and Saint, and heard great argument
    About it and about; but evermore
Came out by the same door where in I went.

With them the seed of Wisdom did I sow,
And with mine own hand wrought to make it grow;   110
    And this was all the Harvest that I reaped—
"I came like Water, and like Wind I go."

Sum total of his knowlege, we will evaporat

Into this Universe, and *W*hy not knowing
Nor *W*hence, like Water willy-nilly flowing;
    And out of it, as Wind along the Waste,
I know not *W*hither, willy-nilly blowing.

What, without asking, hither hurried *W*hence?
And, without asking, *W*hither hurried hence!
    Oh, many a Cup of this forbidden Wine
Must drown the memory of that insolence!   120

going to drown his sorrows

Up from the Earth's Centre through the Seventh Gate
I rose, and on the Throne of Saturn sate,
    And many a Knot unraveled by the Road;
But not the Master-knot of Human Fate.

There was the Door to which I found no Key;
There was the Veil through which I might not see;
    Some little talk awhile of ME and THEE
There was—and then no more of THEE and ME.

Earth could not answer; nor the Seas that mourn
In flowing Purple, of their Lord forlorn;   130
    Nor rolling Heaven, with all his Signs revealed
And hidden by the sleeve of Night and Morn.

Then of the THEE IN ME who works behind
The Veil, I lifted up my hands to find
    A lamp amid the Darkness; and I heard,
As from Without—"THE ME WITHIN THEE BLIND!"

Then to the Lip of this poor earthen Urn   pot talks
I leaned, the Secret of my Life to learn;   to him.
    And Lip to Lip it murmured—"While you live,
Drink!—for, once dead, you never shall return."   140

I think the Vessel, that with fugitive
Articulation answered, once did live,
    And drink; and Ah! the passive Lip I kissed,   somebody in
How many Kisses might it take—and give!   this little pot.

are the
Vessels
reincarnations
of men?

The earth
is made
of dead.

For I remember stopping by the way
To watch a Potter thumping his wet Clay;
    And with its all-obliterated Tongue
It murmured—"Gently, Brother, gently, pray!"

And has not such a Story from of Old
Down Man's successive generations rolled   150
    Of such a clod of saturated Earth
Cast by the Maker into Human mold?

And not a drop that from our Cups we throw
For Earth to drink of, but may steal below
    To quench the fire of Anguish in some Eye
There hidden—far beneath, and long ago.

As then the Tulip, for her morning sup
Of Heav'nly Vintage, from the soil looks up,
    Do you devoutly do the like, till Heav'n
To Earth invert you—like an empty Cup.   160

Perplexed no more with Human or Divine,
Tomorrow's tangle to the winds resign,
    And lose your fingers in the tresses of
The Cypress-slender Minister of Wine.

And if the Wine you drink, the Lip you press,
End in what All begins and ends in—Yes;
    Think that you are TODAY what YESTERDAY
You were—TOMORROW you shall not be less.

So when that Angel of the darker Drink   *don't fear*   170
At last shall find you by the river-brink,
    And offering his Cup, invite your Soul
Forth to your Lips to quaff—you shall not shrink.

Why, if the Soul can fling the Dust aside,
And naked on the Air of Heaven ride,
    Were 't not a Shame—were 't not a Shame for him
In this clay carcass crippled to abide?

'Tis but a Tent where takes his one day's rest
A Sultán to the realm of Death addrest;
    The Sultán rises, and the dark Ferrásh
Strikes, and prepares it for another Guest.   180

And fear not lest Existence closing your
Account, and mine, should know the like no more;
    The Eternal Sákí from that Bowl has poured   *we are*
Millions of Bubbles like us, and will pour.   *yeast bubbles*

When You and I behind the Veil are past,
Oh, but the long, long while the World shall last,
    Which of our Coming and Departure heeds
As the Sea's self should heed a pebble-cast.

A Moment's Halt—a momentary taste
Of BEING from the Well amid the Waste—   190
    And Lo!—the phantom Caravan has reached
The NOTHING it set out from—Oh, make haste!

Would you that spangle of Existence spend
About THE SECRET—quick about it, Friend!
    A Hair perhaps divides the False and True—
And upon what, prithee, does life depend?

A Hair perhaps divides the False and True—
Yes; and a single Alif were the clue—
    Could you but find it—to the Treasure-house,
And peradventure to THE MASTER too;   200

Whose secret Presence, through Creation's veins
Running Quicksilver-like, eludes your pains;
    Taking all shapes from Máh to Máhi; and
They change and perish all—but He remains;

A moment guessed—then back behind the Fold
Immersed of Darkness round the Drama rolled
    Which, for the Pastime of Eternity,
He doth Himself contrive, enact, behold.

But if in vain, down on the stubborn floor
Of Earth, and up to Heav'n's unopening Door,   210
    You gaze TODAY, while You are You—how then
TOMORROW, when You shall be You no more?

Waste not your Hour, nor in the vain pursuit
Of This and That endeavour and dispute;
    Better be jocund with the fruitful Grape
Than sadden after none, or bitter, Fruit.

You know, my Friends, with what a brave Carouse
I made a Second Marriage in my house;
    Divorced old barren Reason from my Bed,
And took the Daughter of the Vine to Spouse.   220

For "Is" and "Is NOT" though with Rule and Line,
And "UP-AND-DOWN" by Logic, I define,
    Of all that one should care to fathom, I
Was never deep in anything but—Wine.

Ah, but my Computations, People say,
Reduced the Year to better reckoning?—Nay,
    'Twas only striking from the Calendar
Unborn Tomorrow, and dead Yesterday.

And lately, by the Tavern Door agape,
Came shining through the Dusk an Angel Shape   230
    Bearing a Vessel on his Shoulder; and
He bid me taste of it; and 'twas—the Grape!

The Grape that can with Logic absolute
The Two-and-Seventy jarring Sects confute;
    The sovereign Alchemist that in a trice
Life's leaden metal into Gold transmute;

The mighty Mahmúd, Allah-breathing Lord,
That all the misbelieving and black Horde
    Of fears and Sorrows that infest the Soul
Scatters before him with his whirlwind Sword.   240

Why, be this Juice the growth of God, who dare
Blaspheme the twisted tendril as a Snare?
    A Blessing, we should use it, should we not?
And if a Curse—why, then, Who set it there?

Some say he drinks too much.

The issue of the nature of the diety and the reason of evil.

I must abjure the Balm of Life, I must,
Scared by some After-reckoning ta'en on trust
    Or lured with Hope of some Diviner Drink,
To fill the Cup—when crumbled into Dust!

Oh threats of Hell and Hopes of Paradise!
One thing at least is certain—*This* Life flies;   250
    One thing is certain and the rest is Lies—
The Flower that once has blown forever dies.

Strange, is it not? that of the myriads who
Before us passed the door of Darkness through,
    Not one returns to tell us of the Road,
Which to discover we must travel too.

The Revelations of Devout and Learned
Who rose before us, and as Prophets burned,
    Are all but Stories, which, awoke from Sleep,
They told their comrades, and to Sleep returned.   260

I sent my Soul through the Invisible,
Some letter of that After-life to spell;
    And by and by my Soul returned to me,
And answered, "I Myself am Heav'n and Hell"—

Heav'n but the Vision of fulfilled Desire,
And Hell the Shadow from a Soul on fire
    Cast on the Darkness into which Ourselves,
So late emerged from, shall so soon expire.

We are no other than a moving row
Of Magic Shadow-shapes that come and go   270
    Round with the Sun-illumined Lantern held
In Midnight by the Master of the Show;

But helpless Pieces of the Game He plays
Upon this Checker-board of Nights and Days;
    Hither and thither moves, and checks, and slays,
And one by one back in the Closet lays.

He puts these squares upon man do play with him.

The Ball no question makes of Ayes and Noes,
But Here or There as strikes the Player goes;
    And He that tossed you down into the Field,
He knows about it all—HE knows—HE knows!   280

Predestination

The Moving Finger writes, and, having writ,
Moves on; nor all your Piety nor Wit
    Shall lure it back to cancel half a Line,
Nor all your Tears wash out a Word of it.

And that inverted Bowl they call the Sky,
Whereunder crawling cooped we live and die,
    Lift not your hands to *It* for help—for It
As impotently moves as you or I.

With Earth's first Clay They did the Last Man knead,
And there of the Last Harvest sowed the Seed;   290
    And the first Morning of Creation wrote
What the Last Dawn of Reckoning shall read.

YESTERDAY *This* Day's Madness did prepare;
TOMORROW's Silence, Triumph, or Despair.
    Drink! for you know not whence you came, nor why;
Drink, for you know not why you go, nor where.

I tell you this—When, started from the Goal,
Over the flaming shoulders of the Foal
    Of Heav'n Parwín and Mushtarí they flung,
In my predestined Plot of Dust and Soul   300

The Vine had struck a fiber; which about
If clings my Being—let the Dervish flout;
    Of my Base metal may be filed a Key,
That shall unlock the Door he howls without.

And this I know: whether the one True Light
Kindle to Love, or Wrath—consume me quite,
    One Flash of It within the Tavern caught
Better than in the Temple lost outright.

What! out of senseless Nothing to provoke
A conscious Something to resent the yoke   310
    Of unpermitted Pleasure, under pain
Of Everlasting Penalties, if broke!

What! from his helpless Creature be repaid
Pure Gold for what he lent him dross-allayed—
    Sue for a Debt he never did contract,
And cannot answer—Oh, the sorry trade!

O Thou, who didst with pitfall and with gin
Beset the Road I was to wander in,
    Thou wilt not with Predestined Evil round
Enmesh, and then impute my Fall to Sin!

    Threw all these temptations
at me

    It is the creators fault

320

O Thou, who Man of Baser Earth didst make,
And ev'n with Paradise devise the Snake,
    For all the Sin wherewith the Face of Man
Is blackened—Man's forgiveness give—and take!

    Last undernetting part
makes the question,
god needs the
forgiveness of man.

. . . . . .

As under cover of departing Day
Slunk hunger-stricken Ramazán away,
    Once more within the Potter's house alone
I stood, surrounded by the Shapes of Clay—

    more clay,
the pots
teeth

Shapes of all Sorts and Sizes, great and small,
That stood along the floor and by the wall;
    And some loquacious Vessels were; and some
Listened perhaps, but never talked at all.

330

    began to speak.

Said one among them—"Surely not in vain
My substance of the common Earth was ta'en
    And to this Figure molded, to be broke,
Or trampled back to shapeless Earth again."

    The pots still
worry about the
same thing they
worryed about in
life. The relation
between creator
and creature

Then said a Second—"Ne'er a peevish Boy
Would break the Bowl from which he drank in joy;
    And He that with his hand the Vessel made
Will surely not in after Wrath destroy."

340

After a momentary silence spake
Some Vessel of a more ungainly Make:
    "They sneer at me for leaning all awry;
What! did the Hand, then, of the Potter shake?"

    why am I
crooked.

Whereat someone of the loquacious Lot—
I think a Súfi pipkin—waxing hot—
    "All this of Pot and Potter—Tell me then,
Who is the Potter, pray, and who the Pot?"

    a real
agnostic.

an orthodox
pot, a
gibe at
the creator

"Why," said another, "Some there are who tell   350
Of one who threatens he will toss to Hell
    The luckless Pots he marred in making—Pish!
He's a Good Fellow, and 'twill all be well."

"Well," murmured one, "Let whoso make or buy,
My Clay with long Oblivion is gone dry;   *a wine*
    But fill me with the old familiar Juice,   *pot? Ha.*
Methinks I might recover by and by."

So while the Vessels one by one were speaking
The little Moon looked in that all were seeking;
    And then they jogged each other, "Brother! Brother!
Now for the Porter's shoulder-knot a-creaking!"   360

                    .   .   .   .   .

Ah, with the Grape my fading Life provide,
And wash the Body whence the Life has died,
    And lay me, shrouded in the living Leaf,
By some not unfrequented Garden-side—

That ev'n my buried Ashes such a snare
Of Vintage shall fling up into the Air
    As not a True-believer passing by
But shall be overtaken unaware.

Indeed the Idols I have loved so long
Have done my credit in this World much wrong,   370
    Have drowned my Glory in a shallow Cup,
And sold my Reputation for a Song.

Indeed, indeed, Repentance oft before
I swore—but was I sober when I swore?
    And then and then came Spring, and Rose-in-hand
My thread-bare Penitence apieces tore.

And much as Wine has played the Infidel,
And robbed me of my Robe of Honour—Well,
    I wonder often what the Vintners buy   *what's as*
One-half so precious as the stuff they sell.   *valuable as*
                                               mine? 380

Yet Ah, that Spring should vanish with the Rose!
That Youth's sweet-scented manuscript should close!
    The Nightingale that in the branches sang,
Ah whence, and whither flown again, who knows!

Would but the Desert of the Fountain yield
One glimpse—if dimly, yet indeed, revealed,
    To which the fainting Traveler might spring,
As springs the trampled herbage of the field.

Would but some wingéd Angel ere too late
Arrest the yet unfolded Roll of Fate,   390
    And make the stern Recorder otherwise
Enregister, or quite obliterate!

Ah, Love! could you and I with Him conspire
To grasp this sorry Scheme of Things entire,
    Would not we shatter it to bits—and then
Remold it nearer to the Heart's Desire!

.   .   .   .   .

Yon rising Moon that looks for us again—
How oft hereafter will she wax and wane;
    How oft hereafter rising look for us
Through this same Garden—and for *one* in vain!   400

And when like her, O Sákí, you shall pass
Among the Guests Star-scattered on the Grass,
    And in your joyous errand reach the spot
Where I made One—turn down an empty glass!

He has taken all and enjoy all he could. But he did try to find answers.

1859: version of 1879

Title: *Rubáiyát* (a plural form) are quatrains, some 500 of which were composed by the 12th-century Persian astronomer, mathematician, and poet, Omar "The Tentmaker." FitzGerald somewhat freely adapted, selected, and arranged the quatrains into a poem distinctively his own. l. 5: **False morning** the Zodiacal Light, sometimes visible in the eastern sky before dawn.   l. 13: **New Year** in the Persian calendar, the start of spring.   ll. 15–16: **Moses; Jesus** flowers named after the revered prophets who preceded Mohammed.   l. 17: **Iram** a vanished garden. l. 18: **Jamshyd** a legendary king who owned a magical cup.   l. 21: **David** the psalmist and king of Israel.   l. 22: **Pehleví** the classical Persian language.   l. 29: **Naishapúr** where Omar was born and died. l. 36: **Kaikobád** founder of a Persian dynasty.   l. 38: **Kaikhosrú** one of Kaikobád's successors.   l. 39: **Zal; Rustum** legendary Persian heroes, father and son.   l. 40: **Hátim** according to FitzGerald, a paragon of hospitality.   l. 44: **Mahmúd** a Sultan; conqueror of India.   l. 71: **Bahrám** a king who was engulfed in a swamp while hunting a wild ass. l. 76: **once lovely Head** of Hyacinth, a youth with beautiful curls, accidentally slain by Apollo.   l. 96: **Sans** without. (See Jaques' speech,

As You Like It, II, vii, 163–166.)   l. 119: **forbidden Wine**   forbidden
to strict Moslems.   l. 122: **Saturn**   the highest planetary sphere, the
seat of wisdom.   l. 131: **Signs**   of the zodiac.   l. 153: **drop**   of
wine ceremonially poured upon the ground before drinking.   l. 164:
Minister   server.   l. 179: **Ferrásh**   servant.   l. 183: **Sákí**   wine-
bearer.   l. 198: **Alif**   first letter of the Arabic alphabet.   l. 203:
Máh to Máhi   fish to moon (low to high).   l. 226: **better reckoning**
Omar is credited with improving the calendar.   l. 237: **Mahmúd**   (See
l. 44) here, figuratively, wine as the "sovereign" who "conquers" sorrow.
l. 258: **as Prophets burned**   that is, with the "fire" of prophecy.   l. 277:
Ball   polo ball.   l. 298: **Foal**   sun.   l. 299: **Parwín and Mushtarí**
the Pleiades and Jupiter.   l. 302: **Dervish**   mystic and ascetic (who
would refuse the "base" use of wine in his search for divine illumination).
l. 317: **gin**   snare.   l. 326: **Ramazán**   (or Ramadan) a month in which
the pious Moslem fasts daily from sunrise to sunset.   l. 346: **Súfi**   mystic
(in Omar's time often fanatical).   l. 360: **Now**   with the rising of the
moon that signals the end of *Ramazán*, the wine-carrier will put the pots
back to their proper work and so stop their empty philosophizing.   l.
385: **Would but** . . .   if only the Desert would yield one glimpse of
the Fountain.

EDWARD LEAR

1812–1888

BY WAY OF PREFACE

"How pleasant to know Mr. Lear!"
    Who has written such volumes of stuff!
Some think him ill-tempered and queer,
    But a few think him pleasant enough.

His mind is concrete and fastidious,
    His nose is remarkably big;
His visage is more or less hideous,
    His beard it resembles a wig.

He has ears, and two eyes, and ten fingers,
    Leastways if you reckon two thumbs;   10
Long ago he was one of the singers,
    But now he is one of the dumbs.

He sits in a beautiful parlour,
    With hundreds of books on the wall;
He drinks a great deal of Marsala,
    But never gets tipsy at all.

He has many friends, laymen and clerical,
    Old Foss is the name of his cat:
His body is perfectly spherical,
    He weareth a runcible hat.   20

When he walks in a waterproof white,
    The children run after him so!
Calling out, "He's come out in his night-
    Gown, that crazy old Englishman, oh!"

He weeps by the side of the ocean,
    He weeps on the top of the hill;
He purchases pancakes and lotion,
    And chocolate shrimps from the mill.

He reads but he cannot speak Spanish,
    He cannot abide ginger-beer: 30
Ere the days of his pilgrimage vanish,
    How pleasant to know Mr. Lear!

                1888

THE JUMBLIES

They went to sea in a sieve, they did;
    In a sieve they went to sea;
In spite of all their friends could say,
On a winter's morn, on a stormy day,
    In a sieve they went to sea.
And when the sieve turned round and round,
And everyone cried, "You'll be drowned!"
They called aloud, "Our sieve ain't big,
But we don't care a button; we don't care a fig—
    In a sieve we'll go to sea!"   10
        Far and few, far and few,
            Are the lands where the Jumblies live.
            Their heads are green, and their hands are blue;
            And they went to sea in a sieve.

They sailed away in a sieve, they did,
    In a sieve they sailed so fast,
With only a beautiful pea-green veil
Tied with a ribbon, by way of a sail,
    To a small tobacco-pipe mast.
And everyone said who saw them go,   20
"Oh! won't they be soon upset, you know,
For the sky is dark, and the voyage is long;
And, happen what may, it's extremely wrong
    In a sieve to sail so fast."

The water it soon came in, it did;
    The water it soon came in.
So, to keep them dry, they wrapped their feet
In a pinky paper all folded neat;
    And they fastened it down with a pin.

And they passed the night in a crockery-jar;   30
And each of them said, "How wise we are!
Though the sky be dark, and the voyage be long,
Yet we never can think we were rash or wrong,
    While round in our sieve we spin."

And all night long they sailed away;
    And, when the sun went down,
They whistled and warbled a moony song
To the echoing sound of a coppery gong,
    In the shade of the mountains brown,
"O Timballoo! how happy we are   40
When we live in a sieve and a crockery-jar!
And all night long, in the moonlight pale,
We sail away with a pea-green sail
    In the shade of the mountains brown."

They sailed to the Western Sea, they did—
    To a land all covered with trees;
And they bought an owl, and a useful cart,
And a pound of rice, and a cranberry-tart,
    And a hive of silvery bees;
And they bought a pig, and some green jackdaws,   50
And a lovely monkey with lollipop paws,
And seventeen bags of edelweiss tea,
And forty bottles of ring-bo-ree,
    And no end of Stilton cheese.

And in twenty years they all came back—
    In twenty years or more;
And everyone said, "How tall they've grown!
For they've been to the Lakes, and the Torrible Zone,
    And the hills of the Chankly Bore."
And they drank their health, and gave them a feast
Of dumplings made of beautiful yeast;   60
And everyone said, "If we only live,
We, too, will go to sea in a sieve,
    To the hills of the Chankly Bore."
      Far and few, far and few,
        Are the lands where the Jumblies live.
       Their heads are green, and their hands are blue;
         And they went to sea in a sieve.

        1871

EMILY BRONTË

1818–1848

REMEMBRANCE

Cold in the earth—and the deep snow piled above thee,
Far, far removed, cold in the dreary grave!
Have I forgot, my only Love, to love thee,
Severed at last by Time's all-severing wave?

Now, when alone, do my thoughts no longer hover
Over the mountains, on that northern shore,
Resting their wings where heath and fern-leaves cover
Thy noble heart for ever, ever more?

Cold in the earth—and fifteen wild Decembers,
From those brown hills, have melted into spring;   10
Faithful, indeed, is the spirit that remembers
After such years of change and suffering!

Sweet Love of youth, forgive, if I forget thee,
While the world's tide is bearing me along;
Other desires and other hopes beset me,
Hopes which obscure, but cannot do thee wrong!

No later light has lightened up my heaven,
No second morn has ever shone for me;
All my life's bliss from thy dear life was given,
All my life's bliss is in the grave with thee.   20

But, when the days of golden dreams had perished,
And ev'n Despair was powerless to destroy,
Then did I learn how existence could be cherished,
Strengthened, and fed without the aid of joy.

Then did I check the tears of useless passion—
Weaned my young soul from yearning after thine;
Sternly denied its burning wish to hasten
Down to that tomb already more than mine.

And, even yet, I dare not let it languish,
Dare not indulge in memory's rapturous pain;　　　　30
Once drinking deep of that divinest anguish,
How could I seek the empty world again?

1846

General note: Many of Emily Brontë's poems were at first part of an elaborate romance (the "Gondal narrative") which she and her sister Anne composed for their own entertainment. But the versions published by Emily Brontë and, after her death, by her sister Charlotte, expunged direct references to the Gondal stories and are followed here. (*Cf. The Complete Poems of Emily Brontë*, ed. C. W. Hatfield, New York, 1941.)

THE PRISONER

A FRAGMENT

In the dungeon-crypts idly did I stray,
Reckless of the lives wasting there away;
"Draw the ponderous bars! open, Warder stern!"
He dared not say me nay—the hinges harshly turn.

"Our guests are darkly lodged," I whispered, gazing through
The vault, whose grated eye showed heaven more gray than blue;
(This was when glad Spring laughed in awaking pride);
"Aye, darkly lodged enough!" returned my sullen guide.

Then, God forgive my youth! forgive my careless tongue!
I scoffed, as the chill chains on the damp flagstones rung:　　　　10
"Confined in triple walls, art thou so much to fear,
That we must bind thee down and clench thy fetters here?"

The captive raised her face; it was as soft and mild
As sculptured marble saint; or slumbering unweaned child;
It was so soft and mild, it was so sweet and fair,
Pain could not trace a line, or grief a shadow there!

The captive raised her hand and pressed it to her brow;
"I have been struck," she said, "and I am suffering now;
Yet these are little worth, your bolts and irons strong;
And, were they forged in steel, they could not hold me long."   20

Hoarse laughed the jailor grim: "Shall I be won to hear;
Dost think, fond, dreaming wretch, that *I* shall grant thy prayer?
Or, better still, wilt melt my master's heart with groans?
Ah! sooner might the sun thaw down these granite stones.

"My master's voice is low, his aspect bland and kind,
But hard as hardest flint the soul that lurks behind;
And I am rough and rude, yet not more rough to see
Than is the hidden ghost that has its home in me."

About her lips there played a smile of almost scorn.
"My friend," she gently said, "you have not heard me mourn;   30
When you my kindred's lives, *my* lost life can restore,
Then may I weep and sue,—but never, friend, before!

"Still, let my tyrants know, I am not doomed to wear
Year after year in gloom, and desolate despair;
A messenger of Hope comes every night to me,
And offers for short life, eternal liberty.

"He comes with western winds, with evening's wandering airs,
With that clear dusk of heaven that brings the thickest stars,
Winds take a pensive tone, and stars a tender fire,
And visions rise, and change, that kill me with desire.   40

"Desire for nothing known in my maturer years,
When Joy grew mad with awe, at counting future tears.
When, if my spirit's sky was full of flashes warm,
I knew not whence they came, from sun or thunderstorm.

"But, first, a hush of peace—a soundless calm descends;
The struggle of distress and fierce impatience ends;
Mute music soothes my breast—unuttered harmony,
That I could never dream, till Earth was lost to me.

"Then dawns the Invisible; the Unseen its truth reveals;
My outward sense is gone, my inward essence feels: 50
Its wings are almost free—its home, its harbour found,
Measuring the gulf, it stoops—and dares the final bound.

"Oh! dreadful is the check—intense the agony—
When the ear begins to hear, and the eye begins to see;
When the pulse begins to throb, the brain to think again;
The soul to feel the flesh, and the flesh to feel the chain.

"Yet I would lose no sting, would wish no torture less;
The more that anguish racks, the earlier it will bless;
And robed in fires of hell, or bright with heavenly shine,
If it but herald death, the vision is divine!"   60

She ceased to speak, and we, unanswering, turned to go—
We had no further power to work the captive woe:
Her cheek, her gleaming eye, declared that man had given
A sentence, unapproved, and overruled by Heaven.

                                                        1846

NO COWARD SOUL IS MINE

        No coward soul is mine,
    No trembler in the world's storm-troubled sphere;
        I see Heaven's glories shine,
    And faith shines equal, arming me from fear.

        O God within my breast,
    Almighty, ever-present Deity!
        Life—that in me has rest,
    As I—undying Life—have power in Thee!

        Vain are the thousand creeds
    That move men's hearts—unutterably vain;   10
        Worthless as withered weeds,
    Or idlest froth amid the boundless main,

        To waken doubt in one
    Holding so fast by Thine infinity;
        So surely anchored on
    The steadfast rock of immortality.

        With wide-embracing love
    Thy spirit animates eternal years
        Pervades and broods above,
    Changes, sustains, dissolves, creates, and rears.   20

Though earth and man were gone,
And suns and universes ceased to be,
    And Thou were left alone,
Every existence would exist in Thee.

    There is not room for Death,
Nor atom that his might could render void;
    Thou—Thou art Being and Breath,
And what Thou art may never be destroyed.

                                    1850

PLEAD FOR ME

O thy bright eyes must answer now,
When Reason, with a scornful brow,
Is mocking at my overthrow;
O thy sweet tongue must plead for me
And tell why I have chosen thee!

Stern Reason is to judgement come
Arrayed in all her forms of gloom:
Wilt thou my advocate be dumb?
No, radiant angel, speak and say
Why I did cast the world away;   10

Why I have persevered to shun
The common paths that others run;
And on a strange road journeyed on
Heedless alike of Wealth and Power—
Of Glory's wreath and Pleasure's flower.

These once indeed seemed Beings divine,
And they perchance heard vows of mine
And saw my offerings on their shrine—
But, careless gifts are seldom prized,
And *mine* were worthily despised;   20

So with a ready heart I swore
To seek their altar-stone no more,
And gave my spirit to adore
Thee, ever present, phantom thing—
My slave, my comrade, and my King!

A slave because I rule thee still;
Incline thee to my changeful will
And make thy influence good or ill—
A comrade, for by day and night
Thou art my intimate delight—   30

My Darling Pain that wounds and sears
And wrings a blessing out from tears
By deadening me to earthly cares;
And yet, a king—though prudence well
Have taught thy subject to rebel.

And am I wrong to worship where
Faith cannot doubt nor Hope despair
Since my own soul can grant my prayer?
Speak, God of Visions, plead for me
And tell why I have chosen thee!   40

1850

COVENTRY PATMORE

1823–1893

THE AZALEA

There, where the sun shines first
Against our room,
She trained the gold azalea, whose perfume
She, spring-like, from her breathing grace dispersed.
Last night the delicate crests of saffron bloom,
For this their dainty likeness watched and nurst,
Were just at point to burst.
At dawn I dreamed, O God, that she was dead,
And groaned aloud upon my wretched bed,
And waked, ah, God, and did not waken her,   10
But lay, with eyes still closed,
Perfectly blessed in the delicious sphere
By which I knew so well that she was near,
My heart to speechless thankfulness composed.
Till 'gan to stir
A dizzy somewhat in my troubled head—
It *was* the azalea's breath, and she *was* dead!
The warm night had the lingering buds disclosed;
And I had fall'n asleep with to my breast
A chance-found letter pressed   20
In which she said,
"So, till tomorrow eve, my own, adieu!
Parting's well-paid with soon again to meet,
Soon in your arms to feel so small and sweet,
Sweet to myself that am so sweet to you!"

1877

THE TOYS

My little Son, who looked from thoughtful eyes
And moved and spoke in quiet grown-up wise,
Having my law the seventh time disobeyed,
I struck him, and dismissed
With hard words and unkissed,
His Mother, who was patient, being dead.
Then, fearing lest his grief should hinder sleep,
I visited his bed,
But found him slumbering deep,
With darkened eyelids, and their lashes yet   10
From his late sobbing wet.
And I, with moan,
Kissing away his tears, left others of my own;
For, on a table drawn beside his head,
He had put, within his reach,
A box of counters and a red-veined stone,
A piece of glass abraded by the beach,
And six or seven shells,
A bottle with bluebells,
And two French copper coins, ranged there with careful art,   20
To comfort his sad heart.
So when that night I prayed
To God, I wept, and said:
Ah, when at last we lie with trancèd breath,
Not vexing Thee in death,
And Thou rememberest of what toys
We made our joys,
How weakly understood
Thy great commanded good,
Then, fatherly not less   30
Than I whom Thou hast molded from the clay,
Thou'lt leave Thy wrath, and say,
"I will be sorry for their childishness."

1877

MAGNA EST VERITAS

Here, in this little Bay,
Full of tumultuous life and great repose,
Where, twice a day,
The purposeless, glad ocean comes and goes,
Under high cliffs, and far from the huge town,
I sit me down.
For want of me the world's course will not fail—
When all its work is done, the lie shall rot;
The truth is great, and shall prevail,
When none cares whether it prevail or not.   10

                                              1877

Title: "Great is the Truth."

Ode from *THE UNKNOWN EROS*

TO THE BODY

Creation's and Creator's crowning good;
Wall of infinitude;
Foundation of the sky,
In Heaven forecast
And long'd for from eternity,
Though laid the last;
Reverberating dome,
Of music cunningly built home
Against the void and indolent disgrace
Of unresponsive space;   10
Little, sequester'd pleasure-house
For God and for His Spouse;
Elaborately, yea, past conceiving, fair,
Since, from the graced decorum of the hair,
Ev'n to the tingling, sweet
Soles of the simple, earth-confiding feet,
And from the inmost heart
Outwards unto the thin
Silk curtains of the skin,
Every least part   20
Astonish'd hears

And sweet replies to some like region of the spheres;
Form'd for a dignity prophets but darkly name,
Lest shameless men cry "Shame!"
So rich with wealth conceal'd
That Heaven and Hell fight chiefly for this field;
Clinging to everything that pleases thee
With indefectible fidelity;
Alas, so true
To all thy friendships that no grace   30
Thee from thy sin can wholly disembrace;
Which thus 'bides with thee as the Jebusite,
That, maugre all God's promises could do,
The chosen People never conquer'd quite,
Who therefore lived with them,
And that by formal truce and as of right,
In metropolitan Jerusalem.
For which false fealty
Thou needs must, for a season, lie
In the grave's arms, foul and unshriven,   40
Albeit, in Heaven,
Thy crimson-throbbing Glow
Into its old abode aye pants to go,
And does with envy see
Enoch, Elijah, and the Lady, she
Who left the lilies in her body's lieu.
Or, if the pleasures I have known in thee
But my poor faith's poor first-fruits be,
What quintessential, keen, ethereal bliss
Then shall be his   50
Who has thy birth-time's consecrating dew
For death's sweet chrism retain'd,
Quick, tender, virginal, and unprofaned!

                                            1877

---

l. 32: **Jebusite**   since the Israelites who settled in Jerusalem could not fully
subdue the Jebusites, who were earlier inhabitants, they had to be tolerated,
albeit reluctantly. (See Jos. 15:63.)   l. 45: **Enoch, Elijah, and the Lady**
all of them supposed to have been "translated" bodily to heaven; the Lady
is the Virgin Mary, whose empty tomb was found filled with lilies.

ARBOR VITAE

With honeysuckle, over-sweet, festooned;
With bitter ivy bound;
Terraced with funguses unsound;
Deformed with many a boss
And closéd scar, o'ercushioned deep with moss;
Bunched all about with pagan mistletoe;
And thick with nests of the hoarse bird
That talks, but understands not his own word;
Stands, and so stood a thousand years ago,
A single tree.   10

Thunder has done its worst among its twigs,
Where the great crest yet blackens, never pruned,
But in its heart, alway
Ready to push new verdurous boughs, whene'er
The rotting saplings near it fall and leave it air,
Is all antiquity and no decay.
Rich, though rejected by the forest-pigs,
Its fruit, beneath whose rough, concealing rind
They that will break it find
Heart-succouring savour of each several meat,   20
And kernelled drink of brain-renewing power,
With bitter condiment and sour,
And sweet economy of sweet,
And odours that remind
Of haunts of childhood and a different day.

Beside this tree,
Praising no Gods nor blaming, sans a wish,
Sits, Tartar-like, the Time's civility,
And eats its dead-dog off a golden dish.

1877

Title: Tree of Life, probably with reference to the Catholic Church.
l. 28: **Tartar-like** stupidly, obstinately.   l. 28: **civility** perfunctory
respectability.   l. 29: **dead-dog** refuse.

CHARLES LUTWIDGE DODGSON

["Lewis Carroll"]

1832–1898

From *ALICE'S ADVENTURES IN WONDERLAND*

1

["A long and a sad tale"]

"Fury said to
a mouse, That
he met
in the
house,
'Let us
both go
to law:
I will
prosecute
you.
Come, I'll
take no
denial:
We must
have a
trial;
For
really
this
morning

```
                    I've
                  nothing
                  to do.'
               Said the
            mouse to
          the cur,
              'Such a
                 trial,
               dear sir,
            With no
          jury or
        judge,
           would be
              wasting
                 our breath.'
                  'I'll be
                 judge,
            I'll be
          jury,'
        Said
      cunning
          old Fury:
              'I'll try
           the whole
               cause,
                  and
                condemn
              you
           to
              death.' "
```

1865

2

["Important Evidence"]

"Begin at the beginning," the King said gravely, "and go on till you come to the end; then stop."

These were the verses the White Rabbit read:

"They told me you had been to her,
    And mentioned me to him:
She gave me a good character,
    But said I could not swim.

He sent them word I had not gone
    (We know it to be true):
If she should push the matter on,
    What would become of you?

I gave her one, they gave him two,
    You gave us three or more;   10
They all returned from him to you,
    Though they were mine before.

If I or she should chance to be
    Involved in this affair,
He trusts to you to set them free,
    Exactly as we were.

My notion was that you had been
    (Before she had this fit)
An obstacle that came between
    Him, and ourselves, and it.   20

Don't let him know she liked them best,
    For this must ever be
A secret, kept from all the rest,
    Between yourself and me."

                  1865

Two Songs from *THROUGH THE LOOKING-GLASS*

JABBERWOCKY

'Twas brillig, and the slithy toves
    Did gyre and gimble in the wabe;
All mimsy were the borogoves,
    And the mome raths outgrabe.

"Beware the Jabberwock, my son!
    The jaws that bite, the claws that catch!
Beware the Jubjub bird, and shun
    The frumious Bandersnatch!"

He took his vorpal sword in hand;
    Long time the manxome foe he sought—   10
So rested he by the Tumtum tree,
    And stood awhile in thought.

And, as in uffish thought he stood,
    The Jabberwock, with eyes of flame,
Came whiffling through the tulgey wood,
    And burbled as it came!

One, two! One, two! And through and through
    The vorpal blade went snicker-snack!
He left it dead, and with its head
    He went galumphing back.   20

"And hast thou slain the Jabberwock?
    Come to my arms, my beamish boy!
O frabjous day! Callooh! Callay!"
    He chortled in his joy.

'Twas brillig, and the slithy toves
    Did gyre and gimble in the wabe;
All mimsy were the borogoves,
    And the mome raths outgrabe.

1872

General note: The annotations derive from the authoritative commentary by Humpty-Dumpty in *Through the Looking-Glass*, chap. 6.   l. 1: **brillig** "means four o'clock in the afternoon—the time when you begin broiling things for dinner."   **slithy** "means 'lithe and slimy' . . . You see it's like a portmanteau—there are two meanings packed up into one word."   **toves** "are something like badgers—they're something like lizards—and they're something like corkscrews . . . also they make their nests under sun-dials—also they live on cheese."   l. 2: **gyre and gimble** "To 'gyre' is to go round and round like a gyroscope. To 'gimble' is to make holes like a gimlet."   **wabe** "the grass-plot round a sun-dial . . ."   l. 3: **mimsy** "is 'flimsy and miserable' (there's another portmanteau for you)."   **borogove** "is a thin shabby-looking bird with its feathers sticking out all round—something like a live mop."   l. 4: **mome raths** ". . . a 'rath' is a sort of green pig; but 'mome' I'm not certain about, I think it's short for 'from home' . . ."   **outgrabe** ". . . 'outgribing' is something between bellowing and whistling, with a kind of sneeze in the middle . . ."

The White Knight's Song

Haddock's Eyes or *The Aged Aged Man*
or *Ways and Means* or *A-Sitting On A Gate*

I'll tell thee everything I can;
    There's little to relate.
I saw an aged, aged man,
    A-sitting on a gate.
"Who are you, aged man?" I said.
    "And how is it you live?"
And his answer trickled through my head
    Like water through a sieve.

He said "I look for butterflies
    That sleep among the wheat;   10
I make them into mutton-pies,
    And sell them in the street.
I sell them unto men," he said,
    "Who sail on stormy seas;
And that's the way I get my bread—
    A trifle, if you please."

But I was thinking of a plan
    To dye one's whiskers green,
And always use so large a fan
    That it could not be seen.   20
So, having no reply to give
    To what the old man said,
I cried, "Come, tell me how you live!"
    And thumped him on the head.

His accents mild took up the tale;
    He said, "I go my ways,
And when I find a mountain-rill,
    I set it in a blaze;
And thence they make a stuff they call
    Rowland's Macassar Oil—   30
Yet twopence-halfpenny is all
    They give me for my toil."

But I was thinking of a way
    To feed oneself on batter,

And so go on from day to day
   Getting a little fatter.
I shook him well from side to side,
   Until his face was blue;
"Come, tell me how you live," I cried
   "And what it is you do!"   40

He said, "I hunt for haddocks' eyes
   Among the heather bright,
And work them into waistcoat-buttons
   In the silent night.
And these I do not sell for gold
   Or coin of silvery shine,
But for a copper halfpenny,
   And that will purchase nine.

"I sometimes dig for buttered rolls,
   Or set limed twigs for crabs;   50
I sometimes search the grassy knolls
   For wheels of hansom-cabs.
And that's the way" (he gave a wink)
   "By which I get my wealth—
And very gladly will I drink
   Your Honour's noble health."

I heard him then, for I had just
   Completed my design
To keep the Menai bridge from rust
   By boiling it in wine.   60
I thanked him much for telling me
   The way he got his wealth,
But chiefly for his wish that he
   Might drink my noble health.

And now, if e'er by chance I put
   My fingers into glue,
Or madly squeeze a right-hand foot
   Into a left-hand shoe,
Or if I drop upon my toe
   A very heavy weight,   70
I weep, for it reminds me so
Of that old man I used to know—
Whose look was mild, whose speech was slow,

Whose hair was whiter than the snow,
Whose face was very like a crow,
With eyes, like cinders, all aglow,
Who seemed distracted with his woe,
Who rocked his body to and fro,
And muttered mumblingly and low,
As if his mouth were full of dough,   80
Who snorted like a buffalo—
That summer evening long ago
    A-sitting on a gate.

1872

Title: in part a parody of Wordsworth's "Resolution and Independence."
l. 59: **Menai bridge** a large bridge in Wales.

RICHARD WATSON DIXON

1833–1900

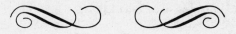

THE HOLY MOTHER AT THE CROSS

Of Mary's pains may now learn whoso will,
　　When she stood underneath the groaning tree
Round which the true Vine clung: three hours the mill
　　Of hours rolled round; she saw in visions three
The shadows walking underneath the sun,
　　And these seemed all so very faint to be,
That she could scarcely tell how each begun,
　　And went its way, minuting each degree
That it existed on the dial stone:
　　For drop by drop of wine unfalteringly,　　　　　10
Not stroke by stroke in blood, the three hours gone
　　She seemed to see.

Three hours she stood beneath the cross; it seemed
　　To be a wondrous dial stone, for while
Upon the two long arms the sunbeams teemed,
　　So was the head-piece like a centre stile;
Like to the dial where the judges sat
　　Upon the grades, and the king crowned the pile,
In Zion town, that most miraculous plat
　　On which the shadow backward did defile;　　　　20
And now towards the third hour the sun enorme
　　Dressed up all shadow to a bickering smile
I' the heat, and in its midst the form of form
　　Lay like an isle.

Because that time so heavily beat and slow
　　That fancy in each beat was come and gone;
Because that light went singing to and fro,
　　A blissful song in every beam that shone;

Because that on the flesh a little tongue
    Instantly played, and spake in lurid tone;   30
Because that saintly shapes with harp and gong
    Told the three hours, whose telling made them one;
Half hid, involved in alternating beams,
    Half mute, they held the plectrum to the zone,
Therefore, as God her senses shield, it seems
    A dial stone.

Three hours she stood beside the cross; it seemed
    A splendid flower; for red dews on the edge
Stood dropping; petals doubly four she deemed
    Shot out like steel knives from the central wedge,   40
Which quadranted their perfect circle so
    As if four anthers should a vast flower hedge
Into four parts, and in its bosom, lo,
    The form lay, as the seed-heart holding pledge
Of future flowers; yea, in the midst was borne
    The head low drooped upon the swollen ledge
Of the torn breast; there was the ring of thorn;
    This flower was fledge.

Because her woe stood all about her now,
    No longer like a stream as ran the hour;   50
Because her cleft heart parted into two,
    No more a mill-wheel spinning to time's power;
Because all motion seemed to be suspense;
    Because one ray did other rays devour;
Because the sum of things rose o'er her sense,
    She standing 'neath its dome as in a bower;
Because from one thing all things seemed to spume,
    As from one mouth the fountain's hollow shower;
Therefore it seemed His and her own heart's bloom,
    A splendid flower.   60

Now it was finished; shrivelled were the leaves
    Of that pain-flower, and wasted all its bloom,
She felt what she had felt then; as receives,
    When heaven is capable, the cloudy stroom
The edge of the white garment of the moon;
    So felt she that she had received that doom;

And as an outer circle spins in tune,
    Born of the inner on the sky's wide room,
Thinner and wider, that doom's memories,
    Broken and thin and wild, began to come   70
As soon as this: St. John unwrapt his eyes,
    And led her home.

    1861

l. 3: **Vine** Christ. (See John 15:1.)

SONG

    The feathers of the willow
    Are half of them grown yellow
      Above the swelling stream;
    And ragged are the bushes,
    And rusty now the rushes,
      And wild the clouded gleam.

    The thistle now is older,
    His stalk begins to moulder,
      His head is white as snow;
    The branches all are barer,   10
    The linnet's song is rarer,
      The robin pipeth now.

    1864

JAMES THOMSON

1834–1882

From *THE CITY OF DREADFUL NIGHT*

Proem

Lo, thus, as prostrate, "In the dust I write
   My heart's deep languor and my soul's sad tears."
Yet why evoke the spectres of black night
   To blot the sunshine of exultant years?
Why disinter dead faith from moldering hidden?
Why break the seals of mute despair unbidden,
   And wail life's discords into careless ears?

Because a cold rage seizes one at whiles
   To show the bitter old and wrinkled truth
Stripped naked of all vesture that beguiles,   10
   False dreams, false hopes, false masks and modes of youth;
Because it gives some sense of power and passion
In helpless impotence to try to fashion
   Our woe in living words howe'er uncouth.

Surely I write not for the hopeful young,
   Or those who deem their happiness of worth,
Or such as pasture and grow fat among
   The shows of life and feel nor doubt nor dearth,
Or pious spirits with a God above them
To sanctify and glorify and love them,   20
   Or sages who foresee a heaven on earth.

For none of these I write, and none of these
   Could read the writing if they deigned to try;
So may they flourish, in their due degrees,
   On our sweet earth and in their unplaced sky.

If any cares for the weak words here written,
It must be someone desolate, Fate-smitten,
    Whose faith and hope are dead, and who would die.

Yes, here and there some weary wanderer
    In that same city of tremendous night,   30
Will understand the speech, and feel a stir
    Of fellowship in all-disastrous fight;
"I suffer mute and lonely, yet another
Uplifts his voice to let me know a brother
    Travels the same wild paths though out of sight."

O sad Fraternity, do I unfold
    Your dolorous mysteries shrouded from of yore?
Nay, be assured—no secret can be told
    To any who divined it not before;
None uninitiate by many a presage   40
Will comprehend the language of the message,
    Although proclaimed aloud for evermore.

1

The City is of Night; perchance of Death,
    But certainly of Night; for never there
Can come the lucid morning's fragrant breath
    After the dewy dawning's cold gray air;
The moon and stars may shine with scorn or pity;
The sun has never visited that city,
    For it dissolveth in the daylight fair;

Dissolveth like a dream of night away,   50
    Though present in distempered gloom of thought
And deadly weariness of heart all day.
    But when a dream night after night is brought
Throughout a week, and such weeks few or many
Recur each year for several years, can any
    Discern that dream from real life in aught?

For life is but a dream whose shapes return,
    Some frequently, some seldom, some by night
And some by day, some night and day; we learn,
    The while all change and many vanish quite,   60

In their recurrence with recurrent changes
A certain seeming order; where this ranges
    We count things real; such is memory's might.

A river girds the city west and south,
    The main north channel of a broad lagoon,
Regurging with the salt tides from the mouth;
    Waste marshes shine and glister to the moon
For leagues, then moorland black, then stony ridges;
Great piers and causeways, many noble bridges,
    Connect the town and islet suburbs strewn.   70

Upon an easy slope it lies at large,
    And scarcely overlaps the long curved crest
Which swells out two leagues from the river marge.
    A trackless wilderness rolls north and west,
Savannahs, savage woods, enormous mountains,
Bleak uplands, black ravines with torrent fountains;
    And eastward rolls the shipless sea's unrest.

The city is not ruinous, although
    Great ruins of an unremembered past,
With others of a few short years ago,   80
    More sad, are found within its precincts vast.
The street-lamps always burn; but scarce a casement
In house or palace front from roof to basement
    Doth glow or gleam athwart the mirk air cast.

The street-lamps burn amidst the baleful glooms,
    Amidst the soundless solitudes immense
Of rangéd mansions dark and still as tombs.
    The silence which benumbs or strains the sense
Fulfills with awe the soul's despair unweeping;
Myriads of habitants are ever sleeping,   90
    Or dead, or fled from nameless pestilence!

Yet, as in some necropolis you find
    Perchance one mourner to a thousand dead,
So there: worn faces that look deaf and blind
    Like tragic masks of stone. With weary tread,
Each wrapped in his own doom, they wander, wander,
Or sit foredone and desolately ponder
    Through sleepless hours with heavy drooping head.

Mature men chiefly, few in age or youth,
    A woman rarely, now and then a child—   100
A child! If here the heart turns sick with ruth
    To see a little one from birth defiled,
Or lame or blind, as preordained to languish
Through youthless life, think how it bleeds with anguish
    To meet one erring in that homeless wild.

They often murmur to themselves, they speak
    To one another seldom, for their woe
Broods maddening inwardly and scorns to wreak
    Itself abroad; and if at whiles it grow
To frenzy which must rave, none heeds the clamour,   110
Unless there waits some victim of like glamour,
    To rave in turn, who lends attentive show.

The City is of Night, but not of Sleep;
    There sweet sleep is not for the weary brain;
The pitiless hours like years and ages creep,
    A night seems termless hell. This dreadful strain
Of thought and consciousness, which never ceases,
Or which some moments' stupor but increases,
    This, worse than woe, makes wretches there insane.

They leave all hope behind who enter there;   120
    One certitude while sane they cannot leave,
One anodyne for torture and despair—
    The certitude of Death, which no reprieve
Can put off long; and which, divinely tender,
But waits the outstretched hand to promptly render
    That draft whose slumber nothing can bereave.

4

He stood alone within the spacious square,
    Declaiming from the central grassy mound,
With head uncovered and with streaming hair,
    As if large multitudes were gathered round—
A stalwart shape, the gestures full of might,
The glances burning with unnatural light:

"As I came through the desert thus it was,
As I came through the desert: All was black,   210

In heaven no single star, on earth no track;
A brooding hush without a stir or note,
The air so thick it clotted in my throat;
And thus for hours; then some enormous things
Swooped past with savage cries and clanking wings.
     But I strode on austere;
     No hope could have no fear.

"As I came through the desert thus it was,
As I came through the desert: Eyes of fire
Glared at me throbbing with a starved desire;   220
The hoarse and heavy and carnivorous breath
Was hot upon me from deep jaws of death;
Sharp claws, swift talons, fleshless fingers cold
Plucked at me from the bushes, tried to hold.
     But I strode on austere;
     No hope could have no fear.

"As I came through the desert thus it was,
As I came through the desert: Lo you, there,
That hillock burning with a brazen glare;
Those myriad dusky flames with points a-glow   230
Which writhed and hissed and darted to and fro;
A Sabbath of the Serpents, heaped pell-mell
For Devil's roll-call and some fête of hell.
     Yet I strode on austere;
     No hope could have no fear.

"As I came through the desert thus it was,
As I came through the desert: Meteors ran
And crossed their javelins on the black sky-span;
The zenith opened to a gulf of flame,
The dreadful thunderbolts jarred earth's fixed frame;   240
The ground all heaved in waves of fire that surged
And weltered round me sole there unsubmerged.
     Yet I strode on austere;
     No hope could have no fear.

"As I came through the desert thus it was,
As I came through the desert: Air once more,
And I was close upon a wild seashore;
Enormous cliffs arose on either hand,
The deep tide thundered up a league-broad strand;

White foambelts seethed there, wan spray swept and flew;   250
The sky broke, moon and stars and clouds and blue.
            And I strode on austere;
            No hope could have no fear.

"As I came through the desert thus it was,
As I came through the desert: On the left
The sun arose and crowned a broad crag-cleft;
There stopped and burned out black, except a rim,
A bleeding, eyeless socket, red and dim;
Whereon the moon fell suddenly southwest,
And stood above the right-hand cliffs at rest.   260
            Still I strode on austere;
            No hope could have no fear.

"As I came through the desert thus it was,
As I came through the desert: From the right
A shape came slowly with a ruddy light;
A woman with a red lamp in her hand,
Bareheaded and barefooted on that strand;
O desolation moving with such grace!
O anguish with such beauty in thy face!
            I fell as on my bier,   270
            Hope travailed with such fear.

"As I came through the desert thus it was,
As I came through the desert: I was twain,
Two selves distinct that cannot join again;
One stood apart and knew but could not stir,
And watched the other stark in swoon and her;
And she came on, and never turned aside,
Between such sun and moon and roaring tide.
            And as she came more near
            My soul grew mad with fear.   280

"As I came through the desert thus it was,
As I came through the desert: Hell is mild
And piteous matched with that accursèd wild;
A large black sign was on her breast that bowed,
A broad black band ran down her snow-white shroud;
That lamp she held was her own burning heart,
Whose blood-drops trickled step by step apart.
            The mystery was clear;
            Mad rage had swallowed fear.

"As I came through the desert thus it was,   290
As I came through the desert: By the sea
She knelt and bent above that senseless me;
Those lamp-drops fell upon my white brow there,
She tried to cleanse them with her tears and hair;
She murmured words of pity, love, and woe,
She heeded not the level rushing flow.
     And mad with rage and fear,
     I stood stonebound so near.

"As I came through the desert thus it was,
As I came through the desert: When the tide   300
Swept up to her there kneeling by my side,
She clasped that corpse-like me, and they were borne
Away, and this vile me was left forlorn;
I know the whole sea cannot quench that heart,
Or cleanse that brow, or wash those two apart.
     They love; their doom is drear,
     Yet they nor hope nor fear;
     But I, what do I here?"

12

Our isolated units could be brought
    To act together for some common end?
For one by one, each silent with his thought,
    I marked a long loose line approach and wend
Athwart the great cathedral's cloistered square,   590
And slowly vanish from the moonlit air.

Then I would follow in among the last;
    And in the porch a shrouded figure stood,
Who challenged each one pausing ere he passed,
    With deep eyes burning through a blank white hood:
"Whence come you in the world of life and light
To this our City of Tremendous Night?"

"From pleading in a senate of rich lords
For some scant justice to our countless hordes
Who toil half-starved with scarce a human right—   600
I wake from daydreams to this real night."

"From wandering through many a solemn scene
Of opium visions, with a heart serene

And intellect miraculously bright—
I wake from daydreams to this real night."

"From making hundreds laugh and roar with glee
By my transcendent feats of mimicry,
And humour wanton as an elfish sprite—
I wake from daydreams to this real night."

"From prayer and fasting in a lonely cell,   610
Which brought an ecstasy ineffable
Of love and adoration and delight—
I wake from daydreams to this real night."

"From ruling on a splendid kingly throne
A nation which beneath my rule has grown
Year after year in wealth and arts and might—
I wake from daydreams to this real night."

"From preaching to an audience fired with faith
The Lamb who died to save our souls from death,
Whose blood hath washed our scarlet sins wool-white—   620
I wake from daydreams to this real night."

"From drinking fiery poison in a den
Crowded with tawdry girls and squalid men,
Who hoarsely laugh and curse and brawl and fight—
I wake from daydreams to this real night."

"From picturing with all beauty and all grace
First Eden and the parents of our race,
A luminous rapture unto all men's sight—
I wake from daydreams to this real night."

"From writing a great work with patient plan   630
To justify the ways of God to man,
And show how ill must fade and perish quite—
I wake from daydreams to this real night."

"From desperate fighting with a little band
Against the powerful tyrants of our land,
To free our brethren in their own despite—
I wake from daydreams to this real night."

Thus, challenged by that warder sad and stern,
    Each one responded with his countersign,

Then entered the cathedral; and in turn   640
    I entered also, having given mine,
But lingered near until I heard no more,
And marked the closing of the massive door.

14

Large glooms were gathered in the mighty fane,
    With tinted moongleams slanting here and there;
And all was hush—no swelling organ-strain,
    No chant, no voice or murmuring of prayer;
No priests came forth, no tinkling censers fumed,   690
And the high altar space was unillumed.

Around the pillars and against the walls
    Leaned men and shadows; others seemed to brood,
Bent or recumbent, in secluded stalls.
    Perchance they were not a great multitude
Save in that city of so lonely streets
Where one may count up every face he meets.

All patiently awaited the event
    Without a stir or sound, as if no less
Self-occupied, doomstricken, while attent.   700
    And then we heard a voice of solemn stress
From the dark pulpit, and our gaze there met
Two eyes which burned as never eyes burned yet—

Two steadfast and intolerable eyes
    Burning beneath a broad and rugged brow;
The head behind it of enormous size.
    And as black fir-groves in a large wind bow,
Our rooted congregation, gloom-arrayed,
By that great sad voice deep and full were swayed:

"O melancholy Brothers, dark, dark, dark!   710
O battling in black floods without an ark!
    O spectral wanderers of unholy Night!
My soul hath bled for you these sunless years,
With bitter blood-drops running down like tears;
    Oh, dark, dark, dark, withdrawn from joy and light!

"My heart is sick with anguish for your bale;
Your woe hath been my anguish; yea, I quail
   And perish in your perishing unblest.
And I have searched the heights and depths, the scope
Of all our universe, with desperate hope   720
   To find some solace for your wild unrest.

"And now at last authentic word I bring,
Witnessed by every dead and living thing;
   Good tidings of great joy for you, for all;
There is no God; no Fiend with names divine
Made us and tortures us; if we must pine,
   It is to satiate no Being's gall.

"It was the dark delusion of a dream,
That living Person conscious and supreme,
   Whom we must curse for cursing us with life;   730
Whom we must curse because the life He gave
Could not be buried in the quiet grave,
   Could not be killed by poison or by knife.

"This little life is all we must endure,
The grave's most holy peace is ever sure,
   We fall asleep and never wake again;
Nothing is of us but the moldering flesh,
Whose elements dissolve and merge afresh
   In earth, air, water, plants, and other men.

"We finish thus; and all our wretched race   740
Shall finish with its cycle, and give place
   To other beings, with their own time-doom;
Infinite æons ere our kind began;
Infinite æons after the last man
   Has joined the mammoth in earth's tomb and womb.

"We bow down to the universal laws,
Which never had for man a special clause
   Of cruelty or kindness, love or hate;
If toads and vultures are obscene to sight,
If tigers burn with beauty and with might,   750
   Is it by favour or by wrath of fate?

"All substance lives and struggles evermore
Through countless shapes continually at war,
   By countless interactions interknit;

If one is born a certain day on earth,
All times and forces tended to that birth,
  Not all the world could change or hinder it.

"I find no hint throughout the Universe
Of good or ill, of blessing or of curse;
  I find alone Necessity Supreme;   760
With infinite Mystery, abysmal, dark,
Unlighted ever by the faintest spark
  For us the flitting shadows of a dream.

"O Brothers of sad lives; they are so brief;
A few short years must bring us all relief—
  Can we not bear these years of labouring breath?
But if you would not this poor life fulfil,
Lo, you are free to end it when you will,
  Without the fear of waking after death."

The organ-like vibrations of his voice   770
  Thrilled through the vaulted aisles and died away;
The yearning of the tones which bade rejoice
  Was sad and tender as a requiem lay;
Our shadowy congregation rested still
As brooding on that "End it when you will."

20

I sat me weary on a pillar's base,
  And leaned against the shaft; for broad moonlight
O'erflowed that peacefulness of cloistered space,
  A shore of shadow slanting from the right.
The great cathedral's western front stood there,
A wave-worn rock in that calm sea of air.

Before it, opposite my place of rest,
  Two figures faced each other, large, austere;
A couchant sphinx in shadow to the breast,   1000
  An angel standing in the moonlight clear;
So mighty by magnificence of forms,
They were not dwarfed beneath that mass enorm.

Upon the cross-hilt of a naked sword
  The angel's hands, as prompt to smite, were held;
His vigilant, intense regard was poured
  Upon the creature placidly unquelled,

Whose front was set at level gaze which took
No heed of aught, a solemn trance-like look.

And as I pondered these opposéd shapes   1010
    My eyelids sank in stupor, that dull swoon
Which drugs and with a leaden mantle drapes
    The outworn to worse weariness. But soon
A sharp and clashing noise the stillness broke,
And from the evil lethargy I woke.

The angel's wings had fallen, stone on stone,
    And lay there shattered; hence the sudden sound.
A warrior leaning on his sword alone
    Now watched the sphinx with that regard profound;
The sphinx unchanged looked forthright, as aware   1020
Of nothing in the vast abyss of air.

Again I sank in that repose unsweet,
    Again a clashing noise my slumber rent;
The warrior's sword lay broken at his feet;
    An unarmed man with raised hands impotent
Now stood before the sphinx, which ever kept
Such mien as if with open eyes it slept.

My eyelids sank in spite of wonder grown;
    A louder crash upstartled me in dread—
The man had fallen forward, stone on stone,   1030
    And lay there shattered, with his trunkless head
Between the monster's large quiescent paws,
Beneath its grand front changeless as life's laws.

The moon had circled westward full and bright,
    And made the temple-front a mystic dream,
And bathed the whole enclosure with its light,
    The sworded angel's wrecks, the sphinx supreme.
I pondered long that cold majestic face
Whose vision seemed of infinite void space.

21

Anear the center of that northern crest   1040
    Stands out a level upland bleak and bare,
From which the city east and south and west
    Sinks gently in long waves; and throned there

An Image sits, stupendous, superhuman,
The bronze colossus of a wingéd Woman,
   Upon a graded granite base foursquare.

Low-seated she leans forward massively,
   With cheek on clenched left hand, the forearm's might
Erect, its elbow on her rounded knee;
   Across a clasped book in her lap the right   1050
Upholds a pair of compasses; she gazes
With full set eyes, but wandering in thick mazes
   Of somber thought beholds no outward sight.

Words cannot picture her; but all men know
   That solemn sketch the pure sad artist wrought
Three centuries and threescore years ago,
   With phantasies of his peculiar thought:
The instruments of carpentry and science
Scattered about her feet, in strange alliance
   With the keen wolf-hound sleeping undistraught;   1060

Scales, hour-glass, bell, and magic-square above;
   The grave and solid infant perched beside,
With open winglets that might bear a dove,
   Intent upon its tablets, heavy-eyed;
Her folded wings as of a mighty eagle,
But all too impotent to lift the regal
   Robustness of her earth-born strength and pride;

And with those wings, and that light wreath which seems
   To mock her grand head and the knotted frown
Of forehead charged with baleful thoughts and dreams,   1070
   The household bunch of keys, the housewife's gown
Voluminous, indented, and yet rigid
As if a shell of burnished metal frigid,
   The feet thick-shod to tread all weakness down;

The comet hanging o'er the waste dark seas,
   The massy rainbow curved in front of it.
Beyond the village with the masts and trees;
   The snaky imp, dog-headed, from the Pit,
Bearing upon its batlike leathern pinions
Her name unfolded in the sun's dominions,   1080
   The "MELENCOLIA" that transcends all wit.

Thus has the artist copied her, and thus
    Surrounded to expound her form sublime,
Her fate heroic and calamitous;
    Fronting the dreadful mysteries of Time,
Unvanquished in defeat and desolation,
Undaunted in the hopeless conflagration
    Of the day setting on her baffled prime.

Baffled and beaten back she works on still,
    Weary and sick of soul she works the more,   1090
Sustained by her indomitable will;
    The hands shall fashion and the brain shall pore,
And all her sorrow shall be turned to labour,
Till Death, the friend-foe, piercing with his saber
    That mighty heart of hearts, ends bitter war.

But as if blacker night could dawn on night,
    With tenfold gloom on moonless night unstarred,
A sense more tragic than defeat and blight,
    More desperate than strife with hope debarred,
More fatal than the adamantine Never   1100
Encompassing her passionate endeavour,
    Dawns glooming in her tenebrous regard—

The sense that every struggle brings defeat
    Because Fate holds no prize to crown success;
That all the oracles are dumb or cheat
    Because they have no secret to express;
That none can pierce the vast black veil uncertain
Because there is no light beyond the curtain;
    That all is vanity and nothingness.

Titanic from her high throne in the north,   1110
    That City's somber Patroness and Queen,
In bronze sublimity she gazes forth.
    Over her Capital of teen and threne,
Over the river with its isles and bridges,
The marsh and moorland, to the stern rock-ridges,
    Confronting them with a coëval mien.

The moving moon and stars from east to west
    Circle before her in the sea of air;

Shadows and gleams glide round her solemn rest.
   Her subjects often gaze up to her there: 1120
The strong to drink new strength of iron endurance,
The weak new terrors; all, renewed assurance
   And confirmation of the old despair.

1874

l. 120: **hope** an allusion to the inscription over the gate of Hell in Dante's *Inferno:* "Abandon all hope, ye who enter." l. 126: **draft** sleeping potion. l. 232: **Sabbath** a Satanic orgy. l. 631: **justify** Milton's purpose in *Paradise Lost.* l. 724: **great joy** the words of the angel announcing Christ's birth. (See Luke 2:10.) l. 750: **tigers burn** an allusion to William Blake's "Tiger, tiger, burning bright." l. 1055: **sketch** an engraving entitled *Melancholia* by Albrecht Dürer (1471–1528). l. 1061: **magic square** a square diagram subdivided into smaller squares, each containing a number, so arranged that the total is the same when added in any direction; sometimes worn as an amulet to ward off evil influences. l. 1078: **Pit** of Hell.

WILLIAM SCHWENK GILBERT

1836–1911

From *PATIENCE*

RECITATIVE AND SONG: BUNTHORNE

Recitative:

Am I alone,
    And unobserved? I am!
Then let me own
    I'm an aesthetic sham!
This air severe
    Is but a mere
        Veneer!
This cynic smile
    Is but a wile
        Of guile!   10
This costume chaste
    Is but good taste
        Misplaced!
    Let me confess!

A languid love for lilies does *not* blight me!
Lank limbs and haggard cheeks do *not* delight me!
   I do *not* care for dirty greens
     By any means.
   I do *not* long for all one sees
     That's Japanese.   20
   I am *not* fond of uttering platitudes
     In stained-glass attitudes.
   In short, my mediaevalism's affectation,
   Born of a morbid love of admiration!

Song:

If you're anxious for to shine in the high aesthetic line as a
   man of culture rare,
You must get up all the germs of the transcendental terms,
   and plant them everywhere.
You must lie upon the daisies, and discourse in novel phrases
   of your complicated state of mind,
(The meaning doesn't matter if it's only idle chatter of a
   transcendental kind).
             And everyone will say,
             As you walk your mystic way,
"If this young man expresses himself in terms too deep for
   me,
Why, what a very singularly deep young man this deep young
   man must be!"

Be eloquent in praise of the very dull old days which have long
   since passed away,
And convince 'em, if you can, that the reign of good Queen
   Anne was Culture's palmiest day.   10
Of course you will pooh-pooh whatever's fresh and new, and
   declare it's crude and mean,
For Art stopped short in the cultivated court of the Empress
   Josephine.
             And everyone will say,
             As you walk your mystic way,
"If that's not good enough for him which is good enough for
   me,
Why, what a very cultivated kind of youth this kind of youth
   must be!"

Then a sentimental passion of a vegetable fashion must excite
    your languid spleen,
An attachment *á la* Plato for a bashful young potato, or a not-
    too-French French bean!
Though the Philistines may jostle, you will rank as an apostle
    in the high aesthetic band,
If you walk down Piccadilly with a poppy or a lily in your
    medieval hand.   20
                        And everyone will say,
                        As you walk your flowery way,
"If he's content with a vegetable love, which would certainly
    not suit *me*,
Why, what a most particularly pure young man this pure
    young man must be!"

                                                    1881

General note: In the Gilbert and Sullivan comic opera *Patience* (1881)
Bunthorne, an aesthetical poet, is a burlesque upon the young aesthetes of
the period.   *Recitative:* ll. 15–16: **lilies . . . limbs . . . cheeks**
regarded as Pre-Raphaelite hallmarks.   l. 20: **Japanese** Japanese deco-
ration was in vogue.   *Song:* l. 10. **Anne** Queen of England, 1702–1714,
during the prevalence of neo-classical "Augustan" taste.   l. 12: **Josephine**
wife of Napoleon I.   l. 19: **Philistines** the culturally "unwashed."

THE LOST MR. BLAKE

Mr. Blake was a regular out-and-out hardened sinner,
    Who was quite out of the pale of Christianity, so to speak;
He was in the habit of smoking a long pipe and drinking a
        glass of grog on Sunday after dinner,
    And seldom thought of going to church more than twice
        (or if Good Friday or Christmas Day happened
        to come in it) three times a week.

He was quite indifferent as to the particular kinds of dresses
    That the clergyman wore at the church where he used to go
        to pray,
And whatever he did in the way of relieving a chap's distresses,
    He always did in a nasty-sneaking, under-handed, hole-and-
        corner sort of way.

I have known him indulge in profane, ungentlemanly em-
    phatics,
    When the Protestant Church has been divided on the
        subject of the width of a chasuble's hem;   10
I have even known him to sneer at albs—and as for dalmatics,
    Words can't convey an idea of the contempt he expressed
        for *them.*

He didn't believe in persons who, not being well off them-
        selves, are obliged to confine their charitable ex-
        ertions to collecting money from wealthier people,
    And looked upon individuals of the former class as ecclesi-
        astical hawks;
He used to say that he would no more think of interfering
     · with his priest's robes than with his church or his
        steeple,
    And that he did not consider his soul imperilled because
        somebody over whom he had no influence what-
        ever, chose to dress himself up like an ecclesiastical
        Guy Fawkes.

This shocking old vagabond was so unutterably shameless
    That he actually went a-courting a very respectable and
        pious middle-aged sister by the name of Biggs:
She was a rather attractive widow whose life, as such, had
        always been particularly blameless;
    Her first husband had left her a secure but moderate com-   20
        petence owing to some fortunate speculations in
        the matter of figs.

She was an excellent person in every way—and won the respect
        even of Mrs. Grundy,
    She was a good housewife, too, and wouldn't have wasted
        a penny if she had owned the Koh-i-noor;
She was just as strict as he was lax in her observance of Sunday,
    And being a good economist, and charitable besides, she
        took all the bones and cold potatoes and broken
        pie-crusts and candle-ends (when she had quite
        done with them), and made them into an excellent
        soup for the deserving poor.

I am sorry to say that she rather took to Blake—that outcast
    of society;

And when respectable brothers who were fond of her began
    to look dubious and to cough,
She would say, "Oh, my friends, it's because I hope to bring
    this poor benighted soul back to virtue and
    propriety"
(And besides, the poor benighted soul, with all his faults
    was uncommonly well off).

And when Mr. Blake's dissipated friends called his attention
    to the frown or the pout of her,
Whenever he did anything which appeared to her to savour
    of an unmentionable place,   30
He would say she would be a very decent old girl when all
    that nonsense was knocked out of her—
And his method of knocking it out of her is one that
    covered him with disgrace.

She was fond of going to church services four times every
    Sunday, and four or five times in the week, and
    never seemed to pall of them,
So he hunted out all the churches within a convenient dis-
    tance that had services at different hours, so to
    speak;
And when he had married her he positively insisted upon their
    going to all of them,
So they contrived to do about twelve churches every Sun-
    day, and, if they had luck, from twenty-two to
    twenty-three in the course of the week.

She was fond of dropping his sovereigns ostentatiously into
    the plate, and she liked to see them stand out
    rather conspicuously against the commonplace
    halfcrowns and shillings,
So he took her to all the charity sermons, and if by any
    extraordinary chance there wasn't a charity sermon
    anywhere, he would drop a couple of sovereigns
    (one for him and one for her) into the poor-box
    at the door;
And as he always deducted the sums thus given in charity
    from the housekeeping money, and the money he
    allowed her for her bonnets and frillings,

She soon began to find that even charity, if you allow it to
interfere with your personal luxuries, becomes an
intolerable bore.   40

On Sundays she was always melancholy and anything but
good society,
For that day in her household was a day of sighings and
sobbings and wringing of hands and shaking of
heads:
She wouldn't hear of a button being sewn on a glove, because
it was work neither of necessity nor of piety,
And strictly prohibited her servants from amusing them-
selves, or indeed doing anything at all except dust-
ing the drawing-rooms, cleaning the boots and
shoes, cooking the dinner, waiting generally on the
family, and making the beds.

But Blake even went farther than that, and said that, on
Sundays, people should do their own works of
necessity, and not delegate them to persons in a
menial situation,
So he wouldn't allow his servants to do so much as even
answer a bell.
Here he is making his wife carry up the water for her bath to
the second floor, much against her inclination,—
And why in the world the gentleman who illustrates these
ballads has put him into a cocked hat is more than
I can tell.

After about three months of this sort of thing, taking the
smooth with the rough of it
(Blacking her own boots and peeling her own potatoes was
not her notion of connubial bliss),   50

Mrs. Blake began to find that she had pretty nearly had
        enough of it,
    And came, in course of time, to think that Blake's own
        original line of conduct wasn't so much amiss.

And now that wicked person—that detestable sinner ("Belial
        Blake" his friends and well-wishers call him for his
        atrocities),
    And his poor deluded victim whom all her Christian
        brothers dislike and pity so,
Go to the parish church only on Sunday morning and after-
        noon and occasionally on a week-day, and spend
        their evenings in connubial fondlings and affec-
        tionate reciprocities,
    And I should like to know where in the world (or rather,
        out of it) they expect to go.

1873

l. 10: **Chasuble's hem** alluding to the controversy in the Church of
England over the reintroduction of "ornaments" and vestments, such as
chasubles, albs, and dalmatics (l. 11) regarded by "Low" and "Broad"
churchmen as too "High" or "Popish."   l. 14: **hawks** street-vendors,
perhaps with a glance at the Salvation Army.   l. 18: **sister** a "Low-
Church" word for fellow-member.   l. 21: **Mrs. Grundy** fictitious em-
bodiment of an undue concern for respectable appearances.   l. 24:
economist housekeeper.   l. 26: **brothers** (See note to l. 18.)   l.
30: **place** Hell, a word politely avoided by the conspicuously pious.
l. 38: **charity sermons** preached to solicit contributions to worthy causes.
l. 43: **work** except as mentioned, sternly prohibited by strict observers of
the Sabbath.   l. 53: **Belial** one of the fallen angels, a "devil."

WALTER HORATIO PATER

1839–1894

MONA LISA

She is older than the rocks among which she sits;
Like the Vampire,
She has been dead many times,
And learned the secrets of the grave;
And has been a diver in deep seas,
And keeps their fallen day about her;
And trafficked for strange webs with Eastern merchants;
And, as Leda,
Was the mother of Helen of Troy,
And, as St. Anne,   10
Was the mother of Mary;
And all this has been to her but as the sound of lyres and flutes,
And lives
Only in the delicacy
With which it has moulded the changing lineaments,
And tinged the eyelids and the hands.

1869

Title: These lines from Pater's essay, *Leonardo da Vinci* (1869), were arranged as verse by W. B. Yeats in his *Oxford Book of Modern Verse* (1937).

HENRY AUSTIN DOBSON

1840–1921

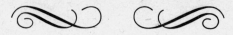

ARS VICTRIX

Yes; when the ways oppose—
    When the hard means rebel,
Fairer the work outgrows,—
    More potent far the spell.

O POET, then, forbear
    The loosely-sandalled verse,
Choose rather thou to wear
    The buskin—straight and terse;

Leave to the tiro's hand
    The limp and shapeless style,   10
See that thy form demand
    The labour of the file.

SCULPTOR, do thou discard
    The yielding clay,—consign
To Paros marble hard
    The beauty of thy line;—

Model thy Satyr's face
    In bronze of Syracuse;
In the veined agate trace
    The profile of thy Muse.   20

PAINTER, that still must mix
    But transient tints anew,
Thou in the furnace fix
    The firm enamel's hue;

Let the smooth tile receive
    Thy dove-drawn Erycine;
Thy Sirens blue at eve
    Coiled in a wash of wine.

All passes. ART alone
    Enduring stays to us;   30
The Bust outlasts the throne,—
    The Coin, Tiberius;

Even the gods must go;
    Only the lofty Rhyme
Not countless years o'erthrow,—
    Not long array of time.

Paint, chisel, then, or write;
    But, that the work surpass,
With the hard fashion fight,—
    With the resisting mass.   40

1876

Title: "Art Victorious"; a partial translation of a poem by Théophile Gautier (1811–1872).   l. 6: **loosely-sandalled** easy-going.   l. 9: **tiro** rank beginner.   l. 12: **file** exacting revision.   l. 15: **Paros** Greek island noted anciently for its fine white marble.   l. 18: **Syracuse** Sicilian city noted for its bronzes.   l. 32: **Tiberius** Roman emperor (42 B.C.–37 A.D.) whose profile appeared on his coins.

ROBERT SEYMOUR BRIDGES

1844–1930

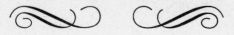

From *THE GROWTH OF LOVE*

All earthly beauty hath one cause and proof,
To lead the pilgrim soul to beauty above;
Yet lieth the greater bliss so far aloof,
That few there be are weaned from earthly love.
Joy's ladder it is, reaching from home to home,
The best of all the work that all was good;
Whereof 'twas writ the angels aye upclomb,
Down sped, and at the top the Lord God stood.
But I my time abuse, my eyes by day
Centered on thee, by night my heart on fire—   10
Letting my numbered moments run away—
Nor e'en 'twixt night and day to heaven aspire—
So true it is that what the eye seeth not
But slow is loved, and loved is soon forgot.

1889

l. 5: **Joy's ladder**   with an allusion to the ladder which Jacob saw reaching
from earth to heaven. (See Gen. 28:10–12.)

NIGHTINGALES

Beautiful must be the mountains whence ye come,
And bright in the fruitful valleys the streams wherefrom
            Ye learn your song:
Where are those starry woods? O might I wander there,
    Among the flowers, which in that heavenly air
            Bloom the year long!

Nay, barren are those mountains and spent the streams:
Our song is the voice of desire, that haunts our dreams,
   A throe of the heart,
Whose pining visions dim, forbidden hopes profound,   10
  No dying cadence nor long sigh can sound,
   For all our art.

Alone, aloud in the raptured ear of men
We pour our dark nocturnal secret; and then,
   As night is withdrawn
From these sweet-springing meads and bursting boughs of May,
  Dream, while the innumerable choir of day
   Welcome the dawn.

           1893

MY DELIGHT AND THY DELIGHT

  My delight and thy delight
  Walking, like two angels white,
  In the gardens of the night;

  My desire and thy desire
  Twining to a tongue of fire,
  Leaping live, and laughing higher;
  Through the everlasting strife
  In the mystery of life.

  Love, from whom the world begun,
  Hath the secret of the sun.   10

  Love can tell, and love alone,
  Whence the million stars were strewn,
  Why each atom knows its own,
  How, in spite of woe and death,
  Gay is life, and sweet is breath;

  This he taught us, this we knew,
  Happy in his science true,
  Hand in hand as we stood
  'Neath the shadows of the wood,
  Heart to heart as we lay   20
  In the dawning of the day.

        1899

PATER FILIO

Sense with keenest edge unuséd,
   Yet unsteeled by scathing fire;
Lovely feet as yet unbruiséd
   On the ways of dark desire;
Sweetest hopes that lookest smiling
O'er the wilderness defiling!

Why such beauty, to be blighted
   By the swarm of foul destruction?
Why such innocence delighted,
   When sin stalks to thy seduction?   10
All the litanies e'er chaunted
Shall not keep thy faith undaunted.

I have prayed the sainted Morning
   To unclasp her hands to hold thee;
From resignful Eve's adorning
   Stolen a robe of peace to enfold thee;
With all charms of man's contriving
Armed thee for thy lonely striving.

Me too once unthinking Nature
   —Whence Love's timeless mockery took me—   20
Fashioned so divine a creature,
   Yea, and like a beast forsook me.
I forgave, but tell the measure
Of her crime in thee, my treasure.

                               1899

Title: "Father to Son."

EROS

Why hast thou nothing in thy face?
Thou idol of the human race,
Thou tyrant of the human heart,
The flower of lovely youth that art;
Yea, and that standest in thy youth
An image of eternal Truth,
With thy exuberant flesh so fair,

That only Pheidias might compare,
Ere from his chaste marmoreal form
Time has decayed the colours warm;   10
Like to his gods in thy proud dress,
Thy starry sheen of nakedness.

Surely thy body is thy mind,
For in thy face is nought to find,
Only thy soft unchristen'd smile,
That shadows neither love nor guile,
But shameless will and power immense,
In secret sensuous innocence.

O king of joy, what is thy thought?
I dream thou knowest it is nought,   20
And wouldst in darkness come, but thou
Makest the light where'er thou go.
Ah yet no victim of thy grace,
None who e'er long'd for thy embrace,
Hath cared to look upon thy face.

1899

ll. 8–10: **Pheidias . . . warm** Greek classical statues, such as those of
Pheidias (or Phidias), 5th century B.C., were originally painted in lifelike
colors.

WILLIAM ERNEST HENLEY

1849–1903

From *IN HOSPITAL*

BEFORE

Behold me waiting—waiting for the knife.
A little while, and at a leap I storm
The thick, sweet mystery of chloroform,
The drunken dark, the little death-in-life.
The gods are good to me—I have no wife,
No innocent child, to think of as I near
The fateful minute; nothing all-too dear
Unmans me for my bout of passive strife.
Yet I am tremulous and a trifle sick,
And, face to face with chance, I shrink a little;   10
My hopes are strong, my will is something weak.
Here comes the basket? Thank you. I am ready.
But, gentlemen my porters, life is brittle;
You carry Cæsar and his fortunes—steady!

OPERATION

You are carried in a basket,
Liike a carcass from the shambles.
To the theatre, a cockpit
Where they stretch you on a table.

Then they bid you close your eyelids,
And they mask you with a napkin,
And the anæsthetic reaches
Hot and subtle through your being.

And you gasp and reel and shudder
In a rushing, swaying rapture,   10
While the voices at your elbow
Fade—receding—fainter—farther.

Lights about you shower and tumble,
And your blood seems crystallizing—
Edged and vibrant, yet within you
Racked and hurried back and forward.

Then the lights grow fast and furious,
And you hear a noise of waters,
And you wrestle, blind and dizzy,
In an agony of effort,   20

Till a sudden lull accepts you,
And you sound an utter darkness . . .
And awaken . . . with a struggle . . .
On a hushed, attentive audience.

                                                        1888

l. 1: **basket** a kind of stretcher.   l. 3: **theatre, cockpit** an operating
room, or "theater," with tiers of seats for observers.

I. M.
MARGARITAE SORORIS

A late lark twitters from the quiet skies;
And from the west,
Where the sun, his day's work ended,
Lingers as in content,
There falls on the old, gray city
An influence luminous and serene,
A shining peace.

The smoke ascends
In a rosy-and-golden haze. The spires
Shine, and are changed. In the valley   10
Shadows rise. The lark sings on. The sun,
Closing his benediction,
Sinks, and the darkening air

Thrills with a sense of the triumphing night—
Night with her train of stars
And her great gift of sleep.

So be my passing!
My task accomplished and the long day done,
My wages taken, and in my heart
Some late lark singing, 20
Let me be gathered to the quiet west,
The sundown splendid and serene,
Death.

1888

Title: In memory of Henley's sister Margaret.

From *LONDON VOLUNTARIES*

ALLEGRO MAËSTOSO

Spring winds that blow
As over leagues of myrtle-blooms and may;
Bevies of spring clouds trooping slow,
Like matrons heavy bosomed and aglow
With the mild and placid price of increase! Nay,
What makes this insolent and comely stream
Of appetence, this freshet of desire
(Milk from the wild breasts of the willful Day!),
Down Piccadilly dance and murmur and gleam
In genial wave on wave and gyre on gyre? 10
Why does that nymph unparalleled splash and churn
The wealth of her enchanted urn
Till, over-billowing all between
Her cheerful margents, gray and living green,
It floats and wanders, glittering and fleeing,
An estuary of the joy of being?
Why should the lovely leafage of the Park
Touch to an ecstasy the act of seeing?
—Sure, sure my paramour, my Bride of Brides,
Lingering and flushed, mysteriously abides 20
In some dim, eye-proof angle of odourous dark,

Some smiling nook of green-and-golden shade,
In the divine conviction robed and crowned
The globe fulfills his immemorial round
But as the marrying-place of all things made!

There is no man, this deifying day,
But feels the primal blessing in his blood.
There is no woman but disdains—
The sacred impulse of the May
Brightening like sex made sunshine through her veins—   30
To vail the ensigns of her womanhood.
None but, rejoicing, flaunts them as she goes,
Bounteous in looks of her delicious best,
On her inviolable quest;
These with their hopes, with their sweet secrets those,
But all desirable and frankly fair,
As each were keeping some most prosperous tryst,
And in the knowledge went imparadised!
For look! a magical influence everywhere,
Look how the liberal and transfiguring air   40
Washes this inn of memorable meetings,
This centre of ravishments and gracious greetings,
Till, through its jocund loveliness of length
A tidal-race of lust from shore to shore,
A brimming reach of beauty met with strength,
It shines and sounds like some miraculous dream,
Some vision multitudinous and agleam,
Of happiness as it shall be evermore!

Praise God for giving
Through this His messenger among the days   50
His word the life He gave is thrice-worth living!
For Pan, the bountiful, imperious Pan—
Not dead, not dead, as impotent dreamers feigned,
But the gay genius of a million Mays
Renewing his beneficent endeavour!—
Still reigns and triumphs, as he hath triumphed and reigned
Since in the dim blue dawn of time
The universal ebb-and-flow began,
To sound his ancient music, and prevails,
By the persuasion of his mighty rime,   60
Here in this radiant and immortal street

Lavishly and omnipotently as ever
In the open hills, the undissembling dales,
The laughing-places of the juvenile earth.
For lo! the wills of man and woman meet,
Meet and are moved, each unto each endeared,
As once in Eden's prodigal bowers befell,
To share his shameless, elemental mirth
In one great act of faith; while deep and strong,
Incomparably nerved and cheered,   70
The enormous heart of London joys to beat
To the measures of his rough, majestic song;
The lewd, perennial, overmastering spell
That keeps the rolling universe ensphered,
And life, and all for which life lives to long,
Wanton and wondrous and forever well.

                                                    1892

Title: A voluntary is a freely extemporized musical performance, as on an organ.   **Subtitle:** *Allegro maëstoso*   quickly but majestically.   l. 27: **blessing** "Be fruitful; multiply." (See Gen. 1:27–28.)   l. 67: **as once** (See Gen. 2:21–25.)   **prodigal** luxuriant.

WHERE FORLORN SUNSETS
FLARE AND FADE

Where forlorn sunsets flare and fade
  On desolate sea and lonely sand,
Out of the silence and the shade
  What is the voice of strange command
Calling you still, as friend calls friend
  With love that cannot brook delay,
To rise and follow the ways that wend
  Over the hills and far away?

Hark to the city, street on street
  A roaring reach of death and life,   10
Of vortices that clash and fleet
  And ruin in appointed strife,
Hark to it calling, calling clear,
  Calling until you cannot stay

From dearer things than your own most dear
   Over the hills and far away.

Out of the sound of the ebb-and-flow,
   Out of the sight of lamp and star,
It calls you where the good winds blow,
   And the unchanging meadows are—   20
From faded hopes and hopes agleam,
   It calls you, calls you night and day
Beyond the dark into the dream
   Over the hills and far away.

                    1892

OSCAR WILDE

1856–1900

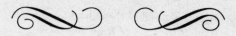

HÉLAS!

To drift with every passion till my soul
Is a stringed lute on which all winds can play,
Is it for this that I have given away
Mine ancient wisdom, and austere control?
Methinks my life is a twice-written scroll
Scrawled over on some boyish holiday
With idle songs for pipe and virelay,
Which do but mar the secret of the whole.
Surely there was a time I might have trod
The sunlit heights, and from life's dissonance
Struck one clear chord to reach the ears of God:
Is that time dead? lo! with a little rod
I did but touch the honey of romance—
And must I lose a soul's inheritance?

1881

Title: Alas!

IMPRESSION DU MATIN

The Thames nocturne of blue and gold
   Changed to a Harmony in grey:
     A barge with ochre-coloured hay
Dropt from the wharf: and chill and cold

The yellow fog came creeping down
   The bridges, till the houses' walls
     Seemed changed to shadows and St. Paul's
Loomed like a bubble o'er the town.

Then suddenly arose the clang
    Of waking life; the streets were stirred   10
    With country waggons: and a bird
Flew to the glistening roofs and sang.

But one pale woman all alone,
    The daylight kissing her wan hair,
    Loitered beneath the gas lamps' flare,
With lips of flame and heart of stone.

                    1881

Title: an impressionistic sketch of a morning scene.

THE HARLOT'S HOUSE

We caught the tread of dancing feet,
We loitered down the moonlit street,
And stopped beneath the harlot's house.

Inside, above the din and fray,
We heard the loud musicians play
The "Treues Liebes Herz" of Strauss.

Like strange mechanical grotesques,
Making fantastic arabesques,
The shadows raced across the blind.

We watched the ghostly dancers spin   10
To sound of horn and violin,
Like black leaves wheeling in the wind.

Like wire-pulled automatons,
Slim silhouetted skeletons
Went sidling through the slow quadrille.

They took each other by the hand,
And danced a stately saraband;
Their laughter echoed thin and shrill.

Sometimes a clockwork puppet pressed
A phantom lover to her breast,   20
Sometimes they seemed to try to sing.

Sometimes a horrible marionette
Came out, and smoked its cigarette
Upon the steps like a live thing.

Then, turning to my love, I said,
"The dead are dancing with the dead,
The dust is whirling with the dust."

But she—she heard the violin,
And left my side, and entered in:
Love passed into the house of lust.   30

Then suddenly the tune went false,
The dancers wearied of the waltz,
The shadows ceased to wheel and whirl.

And down the long and silent street,
The dawn, with silver-sandalled feet,
Crept like a frightened girl.

1885

l. 6: **"Treues Liebes Herz"**   "My True Love's Heart."

SYMPHONY IN YELLOW

An omnibus across the bridge
    Crawls like a yellow butterfly,
    And, here and there, a passer-by
Shows like a little restless midge.

Big barges full of yellow hay
    Are moored against the shadowy wharf,
    And, like a yellow silken scarf,
The thick fog hangs along the quay.

The yellow leaves begin to fade
    And flutter from the Temple elms,   10
    And at my feet the pale green Thames
Lies like a rod of rippled jade.

1885

l. 10: **Temple**   The Inns of Court, ancient law buildings.

FRANCIS THOMPSON

1859–1907

THE HOUND OF HEAVEN

I fled Him, down the nights and down the days;
  I fled Him, down the arches of the years;
I fled Him, down the labyrinthine ways
  Of my own mind; and in the mist of tears
I hid from Him, and under running laughter.
         Up vistaed hopes I sped;
         And shot, precipitated,
Adown Titanic glooms of chasméd fears,
  From those strong Feet that followed, followed after.
        But with unhurrying chase,   10
        And unperturbéd pace,
    Deliberate speed, majestic instancy,
      They beat—and a Voice beat
      More instant than the Feet—
    "All things betray thee, who betrayest Me."

        I pleaded, outlaw-wise,
By many a hearted casement, curtained red,
  Trellised with intertwining charities
(For, though I knew His love Who followed,
        Yet was I sore adread   20
Lest, having Him, I must have naught beside);
But, if one little casement parted wide,
  The gust of His approach would clash it to.
  Fear wist not to evade, as Love wist to pursue.
Across the margent of the world I fled,
  And troubled the gold gateways of the stars,
  Smiting for shelter on their clangéd bars;
        Fretted to dulcet jars

And silvern chatter the pale ports o' the moon.
I said to dawn, Be sudden; to eve, Be soon;   30
   With thy young skyey blossoms heap me over
        From this tremendous Lover!
Float thy vague veil about me, lest He see!
   I tempted all His servitors, but to find
My own betrayal in their constancy,
In faith to Him their fickleness to me,
   Their traitorous trueness, and their loyal deceit.
To all swift things for swiftness did I sue;
   Clung to the whistling mane of every wind.
        But whether they swept, smoothly fleet,   40
      The long savannahs of the blue;
          Or whether, Thunder-driven,
        They clanged his chariot 'thwart a heaven
Plashy with flying lightnings round the spurn o' their feet—
   Fear wist not to evade as Love wist to pursue.
        Still with unhurrying chase,
        And unperturbéd pace,
      Deliberate speed, majestic instancy,
        Came on the following Feet,
        And a Voice above their beat—   50
      "Naught shelters thee, who wilt not shelter Me."

I sought no more that after which I strayed
        In face of man or maid;
But still within the little children's eyes
      Seems something, something that replies;
They at least are for me, surely for me!
I turned me to them very wistfully;
But, just as their young eyes grew sudden fair
      With dawning answers there,
Their angel plucked them from me by the hair.   60
"Come then, ye other children, Nature's—share
With me" (said I) "your delicate fellowship;
      Let me greet you lip to lip,
      Let me twine with you caresses,
        Wantoning
      With our Lady-Mother's vagrant tresses,
        Banqueting
      With her in her wind-walled palace,

Underneath her azured daïs,
Quaffing, as your taintless way is, 70
From a chalice
Lucent-weeping out of the dayspring."
So it was done;
I in their delicate fellowship was one—
Drew the bolt of Nature's secrecies.
I knew all the swift importings
On the willful face of skies;
I knew how the clouds arise
Spuméd of the wild sea-snortings;
All that's born or dies 80
Rose and drooped with—made them shapers
Of mine own moods, or wailful or divine—
With them joyed and was bereaven.
I was heavy with the even,
When she lit her glimmering tapers
Round the day's dead sanctities.
I laughed in the morning's eyes.
I triumphed and I saddened with all weather,
Heaven and I wept together,
And its sweet tears were salt with mortal mine; 90
Against the red throb of its sunset-heart
I laid my own to beat,
And share commingling heat;
But not by that, by that, was eased my human smart.
In vain my tears were wet on Heaven's gray cheek.
For ah! we know not what each other says,
These things and I; in sound *I* speak—
Their sound is but their stir, they speak by silences.
Nature, poor stepdame, cannot slake my drouth;
Let her, if she would owe me, 100
Drop yon blue bosom-veil of sky, and show me
The breasts o' her tenderness;
Never did any milk of hers once bless
My thirsting mouth.
Nigh and nigh draws the chase,
With unperturbéd pace,
Deliberate speed, majestic instancy;
And past those noiséd Feet
A voice comes yet more fleet—

"Lo naught contents thee, who content'st not Me."   110

Naked I wait Thy love's uplifted stroke!
My harness piece by piece Thou hast hewn from me,
                    And smitten me to my knee;
          I am defenseless utterly.
          I slept, me thinks, and woke,
And, slowly gazing, find me stripped in sleep.
In the rash lustihead of my young powers,
          I shook the pillaring hours
And pulled my life upon me; grimed with smears,
I stand amid the dust o' the mounded years—   120
My mangled youth lies dead beneath the heap.
My days have crackled and gone up in smoke,
Have puffed and burst as sun-starts on a stream.
          Yea, faileth now even dream
The dreamer, and the lute the lutanist;
Even the linked fantasies, in whose blossomy twist
I swung the earth a trinket at my wrist,
Are yielding; cords of all too weak account
For earth with heavy griefs so overplussed.
          Ah! is Thy love indeed   130
A weed, albeit an amaranthine weed,
Suffering no flowers except its own to mount?
          Ah! must—
          Designer infinite!—
Ah, must Thou char the wood ere Thou canst limn with it?
My freshness spent its wavering shower i' the dust;
And now my heart is as a broken fount,
Wherein tear-drippings stagnate, spilt down ever
          From the dank thoughts that shiver
Upon the sightful branches of my mind.   140
          Such is; what is to be?
The pulp so bitter, how shall taste the rind?
I dimly guess what Time in mists confounds;
Yet ever and anon a trumpet sounds
From the hid battlements of Eternity;
Those shaken mists a space unsettle, then
Round the half-glimpséd turrets slowly wash again.
          But not ere him who summoneth
          I first have seen, enwound

With glooming robes purpureal, cypress-crowned;   150
His name I know, and what his trumpet saith.
Whether man's heart or life it be which yields
            Thee harvest, must Thy harvest fields
            Be dunged with rotten death?

            Now of that long pursuit
            Comes on at hand the bruit;
            That Voice is round me like a bursting sea:
                "And is thy earth so marred,
                Shattered in shard on shard?
            Lo, all things fly thee, for thou fliest Me!   160
            Strange, piteous, futile thing,
Wherefore should any set thee love apart?
Seeing none, but I makes much of naught"
                (He said)
"And human love needs human meriting,
            How hast thou merited—
Of all man's clotted clay the dingiest clot?
            Alack, thou knowest not
How little worthy of any love thou art!
Whom wilt thou find to love ignoble thee
            Save Me, save only Me?   170
All which I took from thee I did but take,
            Not for thy harms,
But just that thou might'st seek it in My arms.
            All which thy child's mistake
Fancies as lost, I have stored for thee at home;
            Rise, c'asp My hand, and come!"

    Halts by me that footfall;
    Is my gloom, after all,
Shade of His hand, outstretched caressingly?
    "Ah, fondest, blindest, weakest,   180
    I am He Whom thou seekest!
Thou dravest love from thee, who dravest Me."

                                    1893

l. 66: **Lady-Mother's** the earth's.   l. 119: **pulled my life** an allusion
to Samson's pulling down on himself the pillars of a pagan temple. (See
Judges 16:28–31.)

THE KINGDOM OF GOD

'In no Strange Land'

O world invisible, we view thee,
O world intangible, we touch thee,
O world unknowable, we know thee,
Inapprehensible, we clutch thee!

Does the fish soar to find the ocean,
The eagle plunge to find the air—
That we ask of the stars in motion
If they have rumour of thee there?

Not where the wheeling systems darken,
And our benumbed conceiving soars!—   10
The drift of pinions, would we hearken,
Beats at our own clay-shuttered doors.

The angels keep their ancient places;—
Turn but a stone and start a wing!
'Tis ye, 'tis your estrangèd faces,
That miss the many-splendoured thing.

But when so sad thou canst not sadder
Cry;—and upon thy so sore loss
Shall shine the traffic of Jacob's ladder
Pitched betwixt Heaven and Charing Cross.   20

Yea, in the night, my Soul, my daughter,
Cry,—clinging Heaven by the hems;
And lo, Christ walking on the water
Not of Gennesareth, but Thames!

1913

Epigraph: **strange land** any place far from the Holy Land. (See Psalm 137:4.) l. 9: **systems** galaxies. l. 11: **pinions** wings (of angels). l. 19: **ladder** Jacob's vision of angels ascending and descending a ladder reaching from heaven to earth. (See Gen. 28:12.) l. 20: **Charing Cross** a heavily traveled section of central London. l. 24: **Gennesareth** the Sea of Galilee. (See Matt. 14:22–33.)

RUDYARD KIPLING

1865–1936

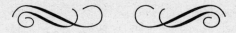

THE LADIES

I've taken my fun where I've found it;
  I've rogued and I've ranged in my time;
I've 'ad my pickin' o' sweethearts,
  An' four o' the lot was prime.
One was an 'arf-caste widow,
  One was a woman at Prome,
One was the wife of a *jemadar-sais*
  An' one is a girl at 'ome.

Now I aren't no 'and with the ladies,
  For, takin' 'em all along,   10
You never can say till you've tried 'em,
  An' then you are like to be wrong.
There's times when you'll think that you might'nt,
  There's times when you'll know that you might;
But the things you will learn from the Yellow an' Brown,
  They'll 'elp you a lot with the White!

I was a young un at 'Oogli,
  Shy as a girl to begin;
Aggie de Castrer she made me,
  An' Aggie was clever as sin;   20
Older than me, but my first un—
  More like a mother she were—
Showed me the way to promotion an' pay,
  An' I learned about women from 'er!

Then I was ordered to Burma,
  Actin' in charge o' Bazar,
An' I got me a tiddy live 'eathen
  Through buyin' supplies off 'er pa.
Funny an' yellow an' faithful—
  Doll in a teacup she were—   30

407

But we lived on the square, like a true-married pair,
    An' I learned about women from 'er!

Then we was shifted to Neemuch
    (Or I might ha' been keepin' 'er now),
An' I took with a shiny she-devil,
    The wife of a nigger at Mhow;
'Taught me the gipsy-folks' *bolee*;
    Kind o' volcano she were,
For she knifed me one night 'cause I wished she was white,
    An' I learned about women from 'er!   40

Then I come 'ome in a trooper,
    'Long of a kid o' sixteen—
'Girl from a convent at Meerut,
    The straightest I ever 'ave seen.
Love at first sight was 'er trouble,
    She didn't know what it were;
An' I wouldn't do such, 'cause I like 'er too much,
    But—I learned about women from 'er!

I've taken my fun where I've found it,
    An' now I must pay for my fun,   50
For the more you 'ave known o' the others
    The less will you settle to one;
An' the end of its sittin' and thinkin',
    An' dreamin' Hell-fires to see;
So be warned by my lot (which I know you will not),
    An' learn about women from me!

What did the Colonel's Lady think?
    Nobody never knew.
Somebody asked the Sergeant's Wife,
    An' she told 'em true!   60
When you get to a man in the case,
    They're like as a row of pins—
For the Colonel's Lady an' Judy O'Grady
    Are sisters under their skins!

                            1892

---

l. 6: **Prome** in Burma.   l. 7: **jemadar-sais** head-groom. (Kipling's
note.)   l. 17: **'Oogli** Hoogli or Hugli, near Calcutta.   l. 33:
Neemuch Nimach (Central India).   l. 36: **Mhow** South of Nimach.
l. 37: **bolee** slang. (Kipling's note.)   l. 43: **Meerut** near Delhi.

PAN IN VERMONT

About the 15th of this month you may expect
our Mr. ———, with the usual Spring Seed, etc.,
Catalogues.

——FLORIST'S ANNOUNCEMENT

It's forty in the shade to-day, the spouting eaves declare;
The boulders nose above the drift, the southern slopes are bare;
Hub-deep in slush Apollo's car swings north along the Zod-
iac. Good lack, the Spring is back, and Pan is on the road!

His house is Gee & Tellus' Sons,—so goes his jest with men—
He sold us Zeus knows what last year; he'll take us in again.
Disguised behind the livery-team, fur-coated, rubber-shod—
Yet Apis from the bull-pen lows—he knows his brother God!

Now down the lines of tasselled pines the yearning whispers
     wake—
Pithys of old thy love behold! Come in for Hermes' sake!   10
How long since that so-Boston boot with reeling Mænads ran?
Numen adest! Let be the rest. Pipe and we pay, O Pan.

(What though his phlox and hollyhocks ere half a month
     demised?
What though his ampelopsis clambered not as advertised?
Though every seed was guaranteed and every standard true—
Forget, forgive they did not live! Believe, and buy anew!)

Now o'er a careless knee he flings the painted page abroad—
Such bloom hath never eye beheld this side the Eden Sword;
Such fruit Pomona marks her own, yea, Liber oversees,
That we may reach (one dollar each) the Lost Hesperides!   20

Serene, assenting, unabashed, he writes our orders down:—
Blue Asphodel on all our paths—a few true bays for crown—
Uncankered bud, immortal flower, and leaves that never fall—
Apples of Gold, of Youth, of Health—and—thank you, Pan,
     that's all. . . .

1893

l. 5: **house** the company he represents.   **Gee & Tullus** the Greek
and Roman names, respectively, for Earth.   l. 7: **livery-team** horses
hired from the local livery-stable.   l. 8: **Apis** in ancient Egypt a sacred

bull-god. l. 10: **Pithys** a maiden loved by Pan and transformed into a pine tree. l. 12: **Numen adest!** The god is here! l. 18: **Sword** the flaming sword which barred mankind's return to Eden. (See Gen. 3:24.) l. 19: **Pomona** goddess of fruit. **Liber** god of the vine and fertile fields. l. 20: **Lost Hesperides** the islands where apples of gold were said to grow, guarded by a dragon. A variety of apple is named "Hesperides." *Read this one.*

RECESSIONAL

God of our fathers, known of old—
    Lord of our far-flung battle-line—
Beneath whose awful Hand we hold
    Dominion over palm and pine—
Lord God of Hosts, be with us yet,
Lest we forget—lest we forget!

The tumult and the shouting dies—
    The Captains and the Kings depart—
Still stands Thine ancient Sacrifice,
    An humble and a contrite heart.   10
Lord God of Hosts, be with us yet,
Lest we forget—lest we forget!

Far-called our navies melt away—
    On dune and headland sinks the fire—
Lo, all our pomp of yesterday
    Is one with Nineveh and Tyre!
Judge of the Nations, spare us yet,
Lest we forget—lest we forget!

If, drunk with sight of power, we loose
    Wild tongues that have not Thee in awe—   20
Such boasting as the Gentiles use
    Or lesser breeds without the Law—
Lord God of Hosts, be with us yet,
Lest we forget—lest we forget!

For heathen heart that puts her trust
    In reeking tube and iron shard—
All valiant dust that builds on dust,
    And guarding calls not Thee to guard—

For frantic boast and foolish word,
Thy mercy on Thy People, Lord!   30

1897

Title: written in 1887, the "Diamond Jubilee" year of Queen Victoria's
reign.   1. 10: **heart** (See Psalm 51:17.)   1. 21: **Gentiles** people
who have not had to assume the burdens of colonial administration. (See
Romans 2:12–21.)   1. 26: **tube . . . shard** cannon; high explosive
shells.   *also this one.*

THE WHITE MAN'S BURDEN

THE UNITED STATES AND THE PHILIPPINE ISLANDS

urging U.S.
to deal with
the Phil. the
way England
was.

Take up the White Man's burden—
  Send forth the best ye breed—
Go bind your sons to exile
  To serve your captives' need;
To wait in heavy harness,
  On fluttered folk and wild—
Your new-caught, sullen peoples,
  Half-devil and half-child.

Take up the White Man's burden—
  In patience to abide,   10
To veil the threat of terror
  And check the show of pride;
By open speech and simple,
  An hundred times made plain,
To seek another's profit,
  And work another's gain.

Take up the White Man's burden—
  The savage wars of peace—
Fill full the mouth of Famine
  And bid the sickness cease;   20
And when your goal is nearest
  The end for others sought,
Watch Sloth and heathen Folly
  Bring all your hope to nought.

Take up the White Man's burden—
  No tawdry rule of kings,
But toil of serf and sweeper—
  The tale of common things.
The ports ye shall not enter,
  The roads ye shall not tread,   30
Go make them with your living,
  And mark them with your dead.

Take up the White Man's burden—
  And reap his old reward:
The blame of those ye better,
  The hate of those ye guard—
The cry of hosts ye humour
  (Ah, slowly!) toward the light:—
"Why brought ye us from bondage,
  Our loved Egyptian night?"   40

Take up the White Man's burden—
  Ye dare not stoop to less—
Nor call too loud on Freedom
  To cloak your weariness;
By all ye cry or whisper,
  By all ye leave or do,
The silent, sullen peoples
  Shall weigh your Gods and you.

[handwritten: They will judge you for what you do.]

Take up the White Man's burden—
  Have done with childish days—   50
The lightly proffered laurel,
  The easy, ungrudged praise.
Comes now, to search your manhood
  Through all the thankless years,
Cold-edged with dear-bought wisdom,
  The judgment of your peers!

                   1899

Title: an admonition to the United States which had just acquired, by the Spanish-American War, the Philippines and other former Spanish colonial possessions.   l. 39: **Why brought ye us** the complaint of the people of Israel to Moses. (See Exod. 16:2–3.)

GIFFEN'S DEBT

Imprimis he was "broke." Thereafter left
His Regiment and, later, took to drink;
Then, having lost the balance of his friends,
"Went Fantee"—joined the people of the land,
Turned three parts Mussulman and one Hindu,
And lived among the Gauri villagers,
Who gave him shelter and a wife or twain,
And boasted that a thorough, full-blood *sahib*
Had come among them. Thus he spent his time,
Deeply indebted to the village *shroff*   10
(Who never asked for payment), always drunk,
Unclean, abominable, out-at-heels;
Forgetting that he was an Englishman.
You know they dammed the Gauri with a dam,
And all the good contractors scamped their work
And all the bad material at hand
Was used to dam the Gauri—which was cheap,
And, therefore, proper. Then the Gauri burst,
And several hundred thousand cubic tons
Of water dropped into the valley, *flop*,   20
And drowned some five-and-twenty villagers,
And did a lakh or two of detriment
To crops and cattle. When the flood went down
We found him dead, beneath an old dead horse
Full six miles down the valley. So we said
He was a victim to the Demon Drink,
And moralised upon him for a week,
And then forgot him. Which was natural.

But, in the valley of the Gauri, men
Beneath the shadow of the big new dam,   30
Relate a foolish legend of the flood,
Accounting for the little loss of life
(Only those five-and-twenty villagers)
In this wise:—On the evening of the flood,
They heard the groaning of the rotten dam,
And voices of the Mountain Devils. Then
An incarnation of the local God,
Mounted upon a monster-neighing horse,
And flourishing a flail-like whip, came down,

Breathing ambrosia, to the villages,   40
And fell upon the simple villagers
With yells beyond the power of mortal throat,
And blows beyond the power of mortal hand,
And smote them with his flail-like whip, and drove
Them clamourous with terror up the hill,
And scattered, with the monster-neighing steed,
Their crazy cottages about their ears,
And generally cleared those villages.
Then came the water, and the local God,
Breathing ambrosia, flourishing his whip,   50
And mounted on his monster-neighing steed,
Went down the valley with the flying trees
And residue of homesteads, while they watched
Safe on the mountain-side these wondrous things,
And knew that they were much beloved of Heaven.

Wherefore, and when the dam was newly built,
They raised a temple to the local God,
And burnt all manner of unsavoury things
Upon his altar, and created priests,
And blew into a conch and banged a bell,   60
And told the story of the Gauri flood
With circumstance and much embroidery. . . .
So he, the whiskified Objectionable,
Unclean, abominable, out-at-heels,
Became the Tutelary Deity
Of all the Gauri valley villages,
And may in time become a Solar Myth.

                                                      1899

l. 10: **shroff** money-lender (Kipling's note). l. 22: **lakh** 100,000
rupees.   l. 67: **Solar Myth** Some nineteenth-century anthropologists
attempted to explain folk-myths as remnants of sun-worship.

A DEATH-BED, 1918

        "This is the State above the Law.
          The State exists for the State alone."
        [*This is a gland at the back of the jaw,
          And an answering lump by the collar-bone.*]

Some die shouting in gas or fire;
   Some die silent, by shell and shot.
Some die desperate, caught on the wire;
   Some die suddenly. This will not.

"Regis suprema voluntas Lex"
   [*It will follow the regular course of—throats.*]   10
Some die pinned by the broken decks,
   Some die sobbing between the boats.

Some die eloquent, pressed to death
   By the sliding trench, as their friends can hear.
Some die wholly in half a breath.
   Some—give trouble for half a year.

"There is neither Evil nor Good in life
   Except as the needs of the State ordain."
[*Since it is rather too late for the knife,*
   All we can do is to mask the pain.]   20

Some die saintly in faith and hope—
   One died thus in a prison-yard—
Some die broken by rape or the rope;
   Some die easily. This dies hard.

"I will dash to pieces who bar my way.
   Woe to the traitor! Woe to the weak!"
[*Let him write what he wishes to say.*
   It tires him out if he tries to speak.]

"The war was forced on me by my foes.
   All that I sought was the right to live."   30
[*Don't be afraid of a triple dose;*
   The pain will neutralize half we give.

Here are the needles. See that he dies
   While the effects of the drug endure. . . .
What is the question he asks with his eyes?—
   Yes, All-Highest, to God, be sure.]

1919

Title: Based on the widely-published, though false, report that ex-Kaiser
Wilhelm II, who was widely blamed for World War I, had an "incurable"
ailment of the ear or jaw.   1. 5: **gas** poison gas used in World War I.
1. 7: **wire** barbed-wire fencing of entrenchments. 1. 36: **All-Highest**
one of the Kaiser's titles of honor.

ARTHUR SYMONS

1865–1945

JAVANESE DANCERS

Twitched strings, the clang of metal, beaten drums,
Dull, shrill, continuous, disquieting;
And now the stealthy dancer comes
Undulantly with cat-like steps that cling;

Smiling between her painted lids a smile,
Motionless, unintelligible, she twines
Her fingers into mazy lines,
The scarves across her fingers twine the while.

One, two, three, four glide forth, and, to and fro,
Delicately and imperceptibly,   10
Now swaying gently in a row,
Now interthreading slow and rhythmically,

Still, with fixed eyes, monotonously still,
Mysteriously, with smiles inanimate,
With lingering feet that undulate,
With sinuous fingers, spectral hands that thrill

In measure while the gnats of music whirr,
The little amber-coloured dancers move,
Like painted idols seen to stir
By the idolaters in a magic grove.   20

1892

EMMY

Emmy's exquisite youth and her virginal air,
Eyes and teeth in the flash of a musical smile,
Come to me out of the past, and I see her there
As I saw her once for a while.

Emmy's laughter rings in my ears, as bright,
Fresh and sweet as the voice of a mountain brook,
And still I hear her telling us tales that night,
Out of Boccaccio's book.

There, in the midst of the villainous dancing-hall,
Leaning across the table, over the beer,   10
While the music maddened the whirling skirts of the ball,
As the midnight hour drew near,

There with the women, haggard, painted and old,
One fresh bud in a garland withered and stale,
She, with her innocent voice and her clear eyes, told
Tale after shameless tale.

                                                        1892

HÉRODIADE

HÉRODIADE.
To mine own self I am a wilderness.
You know it, amethyst gardens numberless
Enfolded in the flaming, subtle deep,
Strange gold, that through the red earth's heavy sleep
Has cherished ancient brightness like a dream,
Stones whence mine eyes, pure jewels, have their gleam
Of icy and melodious radiance, you,
Metals, which into my young tresses drew
A fatal splendour and their manifold grace!
Thou, woman, born into these evil days   10
Disastrous to the cavern sibylline,
Who speakest, prophesying not of one divine,
But of a mortal, if from that close sheath,
My robes, rustle the wild enchanted breath
In the white quiver of my nakedness,

If the warm air of summer, O prophetess,
(And woman's body obeys that ancient claim)
Behold me in my shivering starry shame,
I die!
The horror of my virginity   20
Delights me, and I would envelop me
In the terror of my tresses, that, by night,
Inviolate reptile, I might feel the white
And glimmering radiance of thy frozen fire,
Thou that art chaste and diest of desire,
White night of ice and of the cruel snow!
Eternal sister, my lone sister, lo
My dreams uplifted before thee! now, apart,
So rare a crystal is my dreaming heart,
I live in a monotonous land alone,   30
And all about me lives but in mine own
Image, the idolatrous mirror of my pride,
Mirroring this Hérodiade diamond-eyed.
I am indeed alone, O charm and curse!

NURSE.
O lady, would you die then?

HÉRODIADE.
No, poor nurse;
Be calm, and leave me; prithee, pardon me,
But, ere thou go, close-to the casement; see
How the seraphical blue in the dim glass smiles,
But I abhor the blue of the sky!   40
Yet miles
On miles of rocking waves! Know'st not a land
Where, in the pestilent sky, men see the hand
Of Venus, and her shadow in dark leaves?
Thither I go.
Light thou the wax that grieves
In the swift flame, and sheds an alien tear
Over the vain gold; wilt not say in mere
Childishness?

NURSE.
Now?   50

HÉRODIADE.
Farewell. You lie, O flower
Of these chill lips!
I wait the unknown hour,
Or, deaf to your crying and that hour supreme,
Utter the lamentation of the dream
Of childhood seeing fall apart in sighs
The icy chaplet of its reveries.

                                                              1896

Title: Hérodiade is presumably that daughter of Herod Philip and Herodias
who danced before Herod in order to persuade him into beheading John
the Baptist. She is also known as Salome. (See Mark 6:22.) A translation
from Mallarmé.

HASCHISCH

Behind the door, beyond the light,
Who is it waits there in the night?
When he has entered he will stand,
Imposing with his silent hand
Some silent thing upon the night.

Behold the image of my fear:
O rise not, move not, come not near!
That moment, when you turned your face,
A demon seemed to leap through space;
His gesture strangled me with fear.   10

And yet I am the lord of all,
And this brave world magnifical,
Veiled in so variable a mist
It may be rose or amethyst,
Demands me for the lord of all!

Who said the world is but a mood
In the eternal thought of God?
I know it, real though it seem,
The phantom of a haschisch dream
In that insomnia which is God.   20

                                                              1899

BY THE POOL AT THE THIRD ROSSES

I heard the sighing of the reeds
In the grey pool in the green land,
The sea-wind in the long reeds sighing
Between the green hill and the sand.

I heard the sighing of the reeds
Day after day, night after night;
I heard the whirring wild ducks flying,
I saw the sea-gulls' wheeling flight.

I heard the sighing of the reeds
Night after night, day after day,   10
And I forgot old age, and dying,
And youth that loves, and love's decay.

I heard the sighing of the reeds
At noontide and at evening,
And some old dream I had forgotten
I seemed to be remembering.

I heard the sighing of the reeds:
Is it in vain, is it in vain
That some old peace I had forgotten
Is crying to come back again?   20

1900

Title: This poem and the next derive from Symons' visit to the "Yeats country," in western Ireland.

IN THE WOOD OF FINVARA

I have grown tired of sorrow and human tears;
Life is a dream in the night, a fear among fears,
A naked runner lost in a storm of spears.

I have grown tired of rapture and love's desire;
Love is a flaming heart, and its flames aspire
Till they cloud the soul in the smoke of a windy fire.

I would wash the dust of the world in a soft green flood:
Here, between sea and sea, in the fairy wood,
I have found a delicate, wave-green solitude.

Here, in the fairy wood, between sea and sea, 10
I have heard the song of a fairy bird in a tree,
And the peace that is not in the world has flown to me.

1900

THE ART OF POETRY

Music first and foremost of all!
Choose your measure of odd not even,
Let it melt in the air of heaven,
Pose not, poise not, but rise and fall.

Choose your words, but think not whether
Each to other of old belong:
What so dear as the dim grey song
Where clear and vague are joined together?

'Tis veils of beauty for beautiful eyes,
'Tis the trembling light of the naked noon, 10
'Tis a medley of blue and gold, the moon
And stars in the cool of autumn skies.

Let every shape of its shade be born;
Colour, away! come to me, shade!
Only of shade can the marriage be made
Of dream with dream and of flute with horn.

Shun the Point, lest death with it come,
Unholy laughter and cruel wit
(For the eyes of the angels weep at it)
And all the garbage of scullery-scum. 20

Take Eloquence, and wring the neck of him!
You had better, by force, from time to time,
Put a little sense in the head of Rhyme:
If you watch him not, you will be at the beck of him.

O, who shall tell us the wrongs of Rhyme?
What witless savage or what deaf boy
Has made for us this twopenny toy
Whose bells ring hollow and out of time?

Music always and music still!
Let your verse be the wandering thing   30
That flutters in flight from a soul on the wing
Towards other skies at a new whim's will.

Let your verse be the luck of the lure
Afloat on the winds that at morning hint
Of the odours of thyme and the savour of mint . . .
And all the rest is literature.

1913

Title: a translation of Paul Verlaine's "Art Poëtique," (1884).   l. 17:
Point exact and factual definition.   l. 21: **Eloquence** impressive but
empty rhetoric.   l. 36: **literature** (used contemptuously).

ERNEST DOWSON

1867–1900

THE PASSING OF TENNYSON

As his own Arthur fared across the mere,
With the grave Queen, past knowledge of the throng,
Serene and calm, rebuking grief and tear,
Departs this prince of song.

Whom the gods love Death doth not cleave nor smite,
But like an angel, with soft trailing wing,
He gathers them upon the hush of night,
With voice and beckoning.

The moonlight falling on that august head
Smoothed out the mark of time's defiling hand,   10
And hushed the voice of mourning round his bed—
'He goes to his own land'.

Beyond the ramparts of the world where stray
The laureled few o'er fields Elysian,
He joins his elders of the lyre and bay,
Led by the Mantuan.

We mourn him not, but sigh with Bedivere,
Not perished be the sword he bore so long,
Excalibur, whom none is left to wear—
His magic brand of song.   20

1892

Title: On the occasion of Tennyson's death, 1892; with an allusion to
Tennyson's "The Passing of Arthur," (also known as "Morte d'Arthur"),
the final episode of *Idylls of the King*. Deeply wounded, and tended only
by Bedivere (l. 17) the last of the knights of the Round Table, Arthur has
his sword (or "brand," *Excalibur*, ll. 19–20) flung into the sea, and he is
then carried away in a magical barge.   l. 9: **moonlight** over Tennyson's
death-bed.   l. 16: **Mantuan** Virgil, a native of Mantua, Italy.

EXTREME UNCTION

Upon the eyes, the lips, the feet,
    On all the passages of sense,
The atoning oil is spread with sweet
    Renewal of lost innocence.

The feet, that lately ran so fast
    To meet desire, are soothly sealed;
The eyes, that were so often cast
    On vanity, are touched and healed.

From troublous sights and sounds set free;
    In such a twilight hour of breath,   10
Shall one retrace his life, or see,
    Through shadows, the true face of death?

Vials of mercy! Sacring oils!
    I know not where nor when I come,
Nor through what wanderings and toils,
    To crave of you Viaticum.

Yet, when the walls of flesh grow weak,
    In such an hour, it well may be,
Through mist and darkness, light will break,
    And each anointed sense will see.   20

1894

Title: the Catholic rite of anointing with oil persons in danger of death.
l. 20. **Viaticum** literally, provision for a journey; the Eucharist received
by someone near death.

BENEDICTIO DOMINI

Without, the sullen noises of the street!
    The voice of London, inarticulate,
Hoarse and blaspheming, surges in to meet
    The silent blessing of the Immaculate.

Dark is the church, and dim the worshippers,
    Hushed with bowed heads as though by some old spell,
While through the incense-laden air there stirs
    The admonition of a silver bell.

Dark is the church, save where the altar stands,
  Dressed like a bride, illustrious with light,   10
Where one old priest exalts with tremulous hands
  The one true solace of man's fallen plight.

Strange silence here: without, the sounding street
  Heralds the world's swift passage to the fire:
O Benediction, perfect and complete!
  When shall men cease to suffer and desire?

1896

Title: The Lord's Benediction: a Catholic service in which the conse-
crated host (or wafer) is displayed and the people are blessed with it.
l. 4: **Immaculate** the spotlessly pure host.   l. 8: **bell** requiring
reverent silence.   l. 12: **solace** the host, Christ's sacramental body.

VITAE SUMMA BREVIS SPEM NOS VETAT INCOHARE LONGAM

They are not long, the weeping and the laughter,
  Love and desire and hate:
I think they have no portion in us after
  We pass the gate.

They are not long, the days of wine and roses:
  Out of a misty dream
Our path emerges for a while, then closes
  Within a dream.

1896

Title: from Horace, Odes, I, 4: "The brief sum of life permits no pro-
longation of hope."

NON SUM QUALIS ERAM BONAE SUB REGNO CYNARAE

Last night, ah, yesternight, betwixt her lips and mine
There fell thy shadow, Cynara! thy breath was shed
Upon my soul between the kisses and the wine;

And I was desolate and sick of an old passion,
    Yea, I was desolate and bowed my head:
I have been faithful to thee, Cynara! in my fashion.

All night upon mine heart I felt her warm heart beat,
Night-long within mine arms in love and sleep she lay;
Surely the kisses of her bought red mouth were sweet;
But I was desolate and sick of an old passion,   10
    When I awoke and found the dawn was gray:
I have been faithful to thee, Cynara! in my fashion.

I have forgot much, Cynara! gone with the wind,
Flung roses, roses riotously with the throng,
Dancing, to put thy pale, lost lilies out of mind;
But I was desolate and sick of an old passion,
    Yea, all the time, because the dance was long:
I have been faithful to thee, Cynara! in my fashion.

I cried for madder music and for stronger wine,
But when the feast is finished and the lamps expire,   20
Then falls thy shadow, Cynara! the night is thine;
And I am desolate and sick of an old passion,
    Yea, hungry for the lips of my desire:
I have been faithful to thee, Cynara! in my fashion.

                            1896

Title: from Horace, Odes, IV, 1: "I am not as once I was in the times of Cynara the good." (The connection with Horace's poem is remote.)

AFTER PAUL VERLAINE, I

    Tears fall within mine heart,
    As rain upon the town:
    Whence does this languor start,
    Possessing all mine heart?

    O sweet fall of the rain
    Upon the earth and roofs!
    Unto an heart in pain,
    O music of the rain!

Tears that have no reason
Fall in my sorry heart: 10
What! there was no treason?
This grief hath no reason.

Nay! the more desolate,
Because, I know not why,
(Neither for love nor hate)
Mine heart is desolate.

1899

Translated from Paul Verlaine (1844–1896), *Romances sans Paroles*, 1874.

AFTER PAUL VERLAINE, IV

The sky is up above the roof
    So blue, so soft!
A tree there, up above the roof,
    Swayeth aloft.

A bell within that sky we see,
    Chimes low and faint:
A bird upon that tree we see,
    Maketh complaint.

Dear God! is not the life up there,
    Simple and sweet?   10
How peacefully are borne up there
    Sounds of the street!

What hast thou done, who comest here,
    To weep alway?
Where hast thou laid, who comest here,
    Thy youth away?

1899

Translated from Paul Verlaine (1844–1896), *Sagesse*, 1881.

LIONEL JOHNSON

1867–1902

BY *THE STATUE OF KING CHARLES AT CHARING CROSS*

Somber and rich, the skies;
Great glooms, and starry plains.
Gently the night wind sighs;
Else a vast silence reigns.

The splendid silence clings
Around me; and around
The saddest of all kings
Crowned, and again discrowned.

Comely and calm, he rides
Hard by his own Whitehall.   10
Only the night wind glides;
No crowds, nor rebels, brawl.

Gone too, his Court; and yet,
The stars his courtiers are—
Stars in their stations set,
And every wandering star.

Alone he rides, alone,
The fair and fatal king;
Dark night is all his own,
That strange and solemn thing.   20

Which are more full of fate—
The stars, or those sad eyes?
Which are more still and great—
Those brows, or the dark skies?

Although his whole heart yearn
In passionate tragedy,
Never was face so stern
With sweet austerity.

Vanquished in life, his death
By beauty made amends;   30
The passing of his breath
Won his defeated ends.

Brief life, and hapless? Nay;
Through death, life grew sublime.
Speak after sentence? Yea—
And to the end of time.

Armoured he rides, his head
Bare to the stars of doom;
He triumphs now, the dead,
Beholding London's gloom.   40

Our wearier spirit faints,
Vexed in the world's employ;
His soul was of the saints,
And art to him was joy.

King, tried in fires of woe!
Men hunger for thy grace;
And through the night I go,
Loving thy mournful face.

Yet, when the city sleeps,
When all the cries are still,   50
The stars and heavenly deeps
Work out a perfect will.

1895

Title: Charles I of England was beheaded in 1649. After the Restoration of the Stuart monarchy in 1660, the day of his death, Jan. 30, was observed in the Church of England as the anniversary of "the martyrdom of the Blessed King Charles I."   l. 35: **sentence** His supporters were outraged that after being sentenced to death Charles was not permitted to address the court.

THE DARK ANGEL

Dark Angel, with thine aching lust
To rid the world of penitence:
Malicious Angel, who still dost
My soul such subtile violence!

Because of thee, no thought, no thing
Abides for me undesecrate:
Dark Angel, ever on the wing,
Who never reachest me too late!

When music sounds, then changest thou
Its silvery to a sultry fire: 10
Nor will thine envious heart allow
Delight untortured by desire.

Through thee, the gracious Muses turn
To Furies, O mine Enemy!
And all the things of beauty burn
With flames of evil ecstasy.

Because of thee, the land of dreams
Becomes a gathering-place of fears:
Until tormented slumber seems
One vehemence of useless tears.   20

When sunlight glows upon the flowers,
Or ripples down the dancing sea:
Thou, with thy troop of passionate powers,
Beleaguerest, bewilderest me.

Within the breath of autumn woods,
Within the winter silences:
Thy venomous spirit stirs and broods,
O master of impieties!

The ardour of red flame is thine,
And thine the steely soul of ice: 30
Thou poisonest the fair design
Of nature, with unfair device.

Apples of ashes, golden bright;
Waters of bitterness, how sweet!
O banquet of a foul delight,
Prepared by thee, dark Paraclete.

Thou art the whisper in the gloom,
The hinting tone, the haunting laugh:
Thou art the adorner of my tomb,
The minstrel of mine epitaph.   40

I fight thee, in the Holy Name!
Yet, what thou dost, is what God saith:
Tempter! should I escape thy flame,
Thou wilt have helped my soul from Death:

The second Death, that never dies,
That cannot die, when time is dead:
Live Death, wherein the lost soul cries,
Eternally uncomforted.

Dark Angel, with thine aching lust!
Of two defeats, of two despairs: 50
Less dread, a change to drifting dust,
Than thine eternity of cares.

Do what thou wilt, thou shalt not so,
Dark Angel! triumph over me:
Lonely, unto the Lone I go;
Divine, to the Divinity.

1895

l. 36: **Paraclete** The Holy Spirit or Comforter; here, the opposite.
l. 45: **Second Death** eternal damnation.

BIOGRAPHICAL NOTES

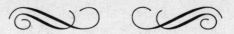

ARTHUR HUGH CLOUGH (1819–1861)

He was born in Liverpool but spent his childhood in Charleston, South Carolina. Between 1829 and 1837 he attended Rugby, where he was the ideal pupil of Matthew Arnold's father, Dr. Thomas Arnold, a muscularly affirmative "Broad Churchman." At Balliol College, Oxford, and as Fellow of Oriel College from 1842 to 1848, he formed the friendship with Matthew Arnold that is commemorated in Arnold's "Thyrsis." Buffeted by the controversies of the Oxford Movement, then at its climax, and by the forces of theological liberalism and the "Higher Criticism" of the Bible, he resigned his fellowship in 1848, at least partly because he could no longer assent to the dogmas of religious orthodoxy. In 1852 he visited Boston and Cambridge and was warmly received by his friend Charles Eliot Norton and by Emerson, Lowell, and Longfellow. Upon returning to England he became an examiner in the Education Office. He married in 1854. In search of relief from consumption, he traveled in 1861 to Florence, Italy, where he died and was buried.

The Bothie of Tober-na-Vuolich, 1848; *Ambarvalia*, 1849; *Amours de Voyage* (in *The Atlantic Monthly*, 1858), 1862; *Dipsychus*, 1862; *Songs in Absence*, 1862; *Mari Magno*, 1862; *Poems and Prose Remains*, ed. by B. S. Clough (2 vols.), 1869.

The Poems, ed. by H. F. Lowry, A. L. P. Norrington, and F. L. Mulhauser, 1951.

GEORGE MEREDITH (1828–1909)

Son of a naval outfitter at Portsmouth, he received a part of his education in Germany, briefly studied law in London, then turned to journalism and literature. In 1849 he married the daughter of the elder satiric novelist and critic, Thomas Love Peacock. In 1858 he was separated from his wife, who died three years later—their estrangement supplying the theme of *Modern Love*. In 1860 he began his long association, as reader and literary adviser, with the publishing firm of Chapman and Hall. For a short time he lived in

Chelsea with Swinburne and D. G. Rossetti. In 1864 he married Marie Vulliamy and moved to Flint Cottage in the scenic neighborhood of Box Hill, Surrey. During 1867–1868 he edited the *Fortnightly Review*, and in 1877 delivered his lecture on *The Idea of Comedy*. During the 1880's he achieved long overdue recognition as a novelist (notably, for *The Ordeal of Richard Feverel*, 1859; followed by *Evan Harrington*, 1861; *Emilia in England*, 1864; *Rhoda Fleming*, 1865; *Vittoria*, 1867; *The Adventures of Harry Richmond*, 1871; *Beauchamp's Career*, 1876; *The Egoist*, 1879; *Diana of the Crossways*, 1885; and *The Amazing Marriage*, 1895). In his latter years he was much depressed by the death of his wife, in 1885, and by a crippling illness that curtailed his athletic enjoyment of nature. He was awarded the Order of Merit in 1905. Upon his death he was denied burial in Westminster Abbey (on account of his unorthodoxy) even though permission was sought by very eminent persons.

Poems, 1851; *Modern Love, and Poems of the English Roadside*, 1862; *Poems and Lyrics of the Joy of Earth*, 1883; *Ballads and Poems of Tragic Life*, 1887; *A Reading of Earth*, 1888; *Poems*, 1892; *Odes in Contribution to the Song of French History*, 1898; *A Reading of Life, with Other Poems*, 1901; *Last Poems*, 1909.

Poetical Works, with some notes by G. M. Trevelyan, 1912. *Modern Love*, with intro., by C. Day Lewis, 1948.

DANTE GABRIEL ROSSETTI (1828–1882)

As son of Gabriele Rossetti, an Italian exile, liberal patriot, and man of letters, he was educated privately, with his sister Christina and his brother William Michael, in the unconventional and cosmopolitan atmosphere of the Rossetti household. He studied painting briefly at the Royal Academy but rebelled against academicism, and with William Michael Rossetti, the sculptor Thomas Woolner, the painters Holman Hunt, John Everett Millais, and others, he founded in 1848 the "Pre-Raphaelite Brotherhood," a loosely organized club of artists and poet-artists who cultivated in their work a scrupulous realism of detail mingled with romantic feeling and medieval symbolism. In 1850 he edited *The Germ* (meaning *the seed*), a short-lived but influential magazine of the "P.R.B.," whose work was soon championed by the critic, John Ruskin. In 1860 he married Elizabeth Siddal, who was (like Jane Burden, later Mrs. William Morris) an example of the Pre-Raphaelite ideal of languorous aesthetic-erotic beauty. After her somewhat mysterious death in 1862, he suffered increasingly from physical and nervous disorders that, despite the generous nursing of the Morrises, gradually sapped his creative energy. In 1871 his work was harshly attacked by Robert Buchanan in "The Fleshly School of Poetry," to which he retorted in "The Stealthy School of Criticism." His last years were much overcast by illness.

The Early Italian Poets (later entitled *Dante and his Circle*), 1861; *Poems* (many from a manuscript enclosed for years in his wife's grave), 1870; revised and enlarged, 1881; *Ballads and Sonnets* (including the completed sonnet sequence, *The House of Life*), 1881.

Complete Poetical Works, ed. by W. M. Rossetti, 1903; *Poems, Ballads, and Sonnets*, ed. by P. F. Baum, 1937; *The House of Life*, with intro. and notes by P. F. Baum, 1928.

CHRISTINA GEORGINA ROSSETTI (1830–1894)

Sister of Dante Gabriel and William Michael Rossetti, she was reared with them in the same somewhat hectic, yet devout and cultured, family circle. She contributed verses to *The Germ* and gave sympathetic support to the Pre-Raphaelites, but—being a "High" Anglican—kept aloof from the bohemian exploits of the group. Twice she refused, on grounds of delicate religious scruple, to marry men to whom she was strongly drawn. After the onset, in 1871, of a slowly debilitating illness, she led an increasingly secluded and meditative life.

Goblin Market and Other Poems, 1862; *The Prince's Progress and Other Poems*, 1866; *Sing-Song, A Nursery Rhyme Book*, 1872; *A Pageant and Other Poems*, 1881; *Verses*, 1893; *New Poems*, ed. by W. M. Rossetti, 1896.

Poetical Works, with memoir and notes by W. M. Rossetti, 1904.

WILLIAM MORRIS (1834–1896)

Full of enthusiasm for the Middle Ages and Gothic architecture, he entered Exeter College, Oxford, in 1853 with the intention of becoming an Anglican priest. Under the influence of the painter, Burne-Jones, and other Pre-Raphaelites, and of Ruskin's *Stones of Venice*, he turned his energies from theology to poetry, architecture and painting. In 1856 he founded and financially supported the

Oxford and Cambridge Magazine as an organ of the continuing "P.R.B." In 1859 he married Jane Burden, who—like Mrs. D. G. Rossetti—became a Pre-Raphaelite "type." He built the famous "Red House" at Bexley and for many years tried to counteract the shoddy ugliness of Victorian manufacture by making by hand, and teaching others to make by hand, well-designed textiles, wallpaper, church furnishings, and domestic furniture (including the "Morris chair"). During the 1880s he strenuously supported, as a socialist, various working-class movements. In 1890 he established the Kelmscott Press, dedicated to fine printing, and in 1896 issued the "Kelmscott Chaucer."

The Defence of Guenevere, and Other Poems, 1858; *The Life and Death of Jason*, 1867; *The Earthly Paradise*, 1868–1870; *Love is Enough*, 1872; *The Æneids of Virgil*, 1875; *The Story of Sigurd the Volsung and the Fall of the Niblungs*, 1876; *Hopes and Fears for Art*, 1882; *The Odyssey of Homer*, 1887; *A Dream of John Ball*, 1888; *Signs of Change*, 1888; *A Tale of the House of the Wolfings*, 1889; *News from Nowhere*, 1890; *Poems by the Way*, 1891; *Gothic Architecture*, 1893; *The Well at the World's End*, 1896; *Old French Romances*, 1896; *The Sundering Flood*, 1897; *Architecture, Industry and Wealth*, 1902.

Poetical Works (11 vols.), 1896–1898; *Collected Works* (24 vols.), ed. by May Morris, 1910–1915.

A. C. SWINBURNE (1837–1909)

Like Arnold, Clough, and Hopkins, he was educated at Balliol College, Oxford, where he was particularly brilliant in classics, though he left without taking a degree. In London, under the tutelage of D. G. Rossetti, Meredith, and Morris, he mastered the Pre-Raphaelite manner, cultivated a taste for French poetry, and wrote *Poems and Ballads*, which created a furor. After a remarkable course of dissipation he was persuaded to devote his energies to extolling the Italian struggle for liberty. Following a physical breakdown in 1879, he remained under the watchful care of his friend, the poet and critic, Theodore Watts-Dunton, who safeguarded him from self-indulgence and directed his still considerable literary powers into rather placid enterprises.

The Queen Mother and Rosamond, 1860; *Atalanta in Calydon*, 1865; *Chastelard*, 1865; *Poems and Ballads*, 1866; *A Song of Italy*, 1867; *Songs before Sunrise*, 1871; *Bothwell*, 1874; *Songs of Two*

Nations, 1875; *Erectheus*, 1876; *Poems and Ballads: Second Series*, 1878; *Song of the Springtides*, 1880; *The Heptalogia* (parodies), 1880; *Tristram of Lyonesse and Other Poems*, 1882; *A Century of Roundels*, 1883; *A Midsummer Holiday and Other Poems*, 1884; *Marino Faliero*, 1885; *Locrine*, 1887; *Poems and Ballads: Third Series*, 1889; *Astrophel and Other Poems*, 1894; *The Tale of Balen*, 1896; *Rosamund, Queen of the Lombards*, 1899; *A Channel Passage and Other Poems*, 1904; *The Duke of Gandia*, 1908; *Posthumous Poems*, ed. by Edmund Gosse and T. J. Wise, 1918.

Complete Works (20 vols.), ed. by Edmund Gosse and T. J. Wise, 1925–1927.

THOMAS HARDY (1840–1928)

Most of his life was spent in the county of his birth, Dorset, in the heart of the ancient kingdom of Wessex. At sixteen, he was apprenticed to a local architect, and after 1862 continued his architectural studies in London where he also acquired a literary education at the University of London. He devoted himself increasingly to poetry but met with no encouragement from publishers. In an effort to support himself by literature, he turned to prose fiction and produced a series of successful novels (*Desperate Remedies*, 1871; *Under the Greenwood Tree*, 1872; *A Pair of Blue Eyes*, 1873; *Far from the Madding Crowd*, 1874; *The Hand of Ethelberta*, 1876; *The Return of the Native*, 1878; *The Trumpet-Major*, 1880; *A Laodicean*, 1881; *Two on a Tower*, 1882; *The Mayor of Casterbridge*, 1886; *The Woodlanders*, 1887; *Tess of the D'Urbervilles*, 1891; *The Well-Beloved*, 1892; *Jude the Obscure*, 1895). Under embittered attack because of his candid treatment of sex, he renounced fiction and thereafter published only poetry, including *The Dynasts*, a massive lyrical drama of the Napoleonic era. In his last years honors were showered upon him, but he lived quietly at Max Gate and continued to write poetry. His ashes are interred in Westminster Abbey but his heart rests in the grave of his first wife, in Stinsford, Dorset.

Wessex Poems and Other Verses, 1898; *Poems of the Past and the Present*, 1902; *The Dynasts* (in three parts), 1903–1908; *Time's Laughingstocks and Other Verses*, 1909; *Satires of Circumstance*, 1911–1914; *Moments of Vision*, 1917; *Late Lyrics and Earlier*, 1922; *Human Shows*, 1925; *Yuletide in a Younger World*, 1927; *Winter Words*, 1928.

Collected Poems, 1925.

GERARD MANLEY HOPKINS (1844–1889)

One of a talented family, he was early encouraged to develop his gifts for verse and for drawing, and at Highgate School won the poetry prize. At Balliol College, Oxford, from 1863 to 1867, he was tutored by Walter Pater, wrote poetry in the Pre-Raphaelite vein, and won first-class honors in classics. He abandoned his intention of taking holy orders in the Church of England, and in 1866 was received into the Roman Catholic Church by Dr. John Henry Newman (whose influence at Oxford had been revived by his controversy with Charles Kingsley and the publication of *Apologia Pro Vita Sua* in 1864). In 1868 he entered the Society of Jesus and wrote no more poetry until 1875, when the drowning of five nuns aboard the *Deutschland* provided the occasion of a major poem. In 1877 he was ordained priest and thereafter served in Liverpool, Oxford, London, and elsewhere. For several years he carried on a remarkable correspondence with Coventry Patmore, Richard Watson Dixon, and Robert Bridges, his old friend and later his editor. In 1884 he was appointed Professor of Classics in University College, Dublin, where he remained until his death. During his lifetime he did not permit his poems to be published.

Poems, ed. with notes by Robert Bridges, 1918; *Poems* (fourth edition, revised and enlarged), ed. by W. H. Gardner and N. H. MacKenzie, 1970.

ALFRED EDWARD HOUSMAN (1859–1936)

Born in Worcestershire, he was educated at a private school in Worcester and at St. John's College, Oxford. Being disappointed in his academic prospects, he toiled for ten years as a clerk in the British Patent Office. In 1892 he became Professor of Latin at University College, London. In 1895 he wrote, under "continuous excitement," most of the lyrics of *A Shropshire Lad*, which became extraordinarily popular. In 1911 he was appointed Fellow of Trinity College and Professor of Latin at Cambridge University, where he lived in semi-seclusion and edited the works of the Latin poets Manilius and Juvenal.

A Shropshire Lad, 1896; *Last Poems*, 1911; *More Poems* (published after his death), 1936.
Collected Poems, 1940.

INDEX OF TITLES AND FIRST LINES

Rinehart Editions